JOURNAL FOR THE STUDY OF THE OLD TESTAMENT
SUPPLEMENT SERIES

Editors
David J A Clines
Philip R Davies

Department of Biblical Studies
The University of Sheffield
Sheffield S10 2TN
England

# CLASSICAL HEBREW POETRY

## A Guide to its Techniques

## WILFRED G.E. WATSON

Journal for the Study of the Old Testament
Supplement Series 26

Published by
JSOT Press
Department of Biblical Studies
The University of Sheffield
Sheffield S10 2TN
England

Printed in Great Britain
by Redwood Burn Ltd.,
Trowbridge, Wiltshire.


*British Library Cataloguing in Publication Data*

Watson, Wilfred G.E.
    Classical Hebrew poetry.—(Journal for the
    study of the Old Testament supplement series,
    ISSN 0264-64; 98; v.26)
    1. Hebrew poetry—History and criticism
    I. Title            II. Series
    892.4'              PJ5022

    ISBN 0-905774-57-4

# CONTENTS

# FOREWORD

The origins of the present work lie in my unpublished doctoral dissertation (1973, on Isa 1-66) of which a considerable section dealt with poetic devices and, in part, with poetic technique. My interest in poetry since led to extensive reading in literary criticism, particularly studies with a linguistic approach. The impetus for actually writing a book came from Dr John Gibson while I was at the Institute for Advanced Studies in the Humanities, Edinburgh.

Whether consciously or not the model I have followed in my presentation has been Geoffrey Leech's *A linguistic guide to English poetry*, an invaluable beginner's textbook. This is apparent from the term 'Guide' common to both works and is even more evident from my basic layout. Like Leech I use worked examples throughout, aim at providing clear explanations of technical points, list passages for private study and give individual bibliographies for each topic. Of course I do not agree with Leech on every point, notably on hyperbole, but in the main his *Guide* has been mine, too.

This book is intended principally for readers with a good working knowledge of classical Hebrew. Some acquaintance at least with either Ugaritic or Akkadian (or both, of course) is preferable but not expected. To a certain extent, also, the book can be used by someone conversant with none of these languages since translations are always provided.

My main aim has been to provide a working tool for lecturers and students who need a reference book in a rapidly expanding field. Since I began serious groundwork for this book several lengthy books on Hebrew poetry have appeared (by O'Connor, Kugel, Collins, Stuart, van der Lugt) not to mention dissertations (Cooper, Sappan) and even an anthology (Carmi). Far from obviating the need for yet another book on the same subject, it is clear, instead, that there is a great deal of confusion over aspects of terminology, analysis and, particularly, theory. While not claiming to solve all the problems involved—and here metre stands out as more intractable than any—I have tried to clarify and explain what scholars are in the main agreed on. I hope, at least, to have set out the difficulties of classical Hebrew poetry in as clear a way as present knowledge permits.

My inclusion of Ugaritic and Akkadian verse in a study of Hebrew poetry is not without reason. It has precedents, and here I am thinking chiefly of T. Donald's unpublished thesis *Parallelism in Akkadian, Hebrew and Ugaritic* which I read several years ago. More to the point, it is important to present ancient Hebrew verse, so removed from us in time, place and language, in as near its own setting as possible. Apart from the books of the Hebrew bible practically no classical Hebrew literature has survived. In the absence of such literature, second best is comparison with the verse-making traditions of Ugaritic and Akkadian poetry as attempted here.

Financial assistance for the making of this book came from a Visiting Research Fellowship to the Institute of Advanced Studies, Edinburgh and a seventeen-month research grant from the Alexander von Humboldt Stiftung, Bonn—Bad Godesberg. I am grateful to Professor Oswald Loretz for providing research facilities at Ugarit-Forschung, Münster (Westphalia). Through all the preparatory stages Dr John Gibson of New College, Edinburgh, gave me encouragement spiced with the right amount of critical comment. The editors of *JSOT* courageously accepted the typescript in as yet incomplete form and patiently experimented with advanced methods of typesetting it. And now my wife and daughter, to whom I dedicate the present work, can take brief respite until the next book is begun.

# ABBREVIATIONS

| | |
|---|---|
| *AAASH* | Acta Antiqua Academiae Scientiae Hungaricae (Magyar Tudomanyos Akadémia), Budapest. |
| *AANLR* | Atti della Accademia Nazionale dei Lincei. Rendiconti (della) Classe di Scienze morali, storiche a filologiche, Rome. |
| *AB* | Anchor Bible, Garden City. |
| *AbrN* | Abr-Nahrain, University of Melbourne, Parkville, Victoria. |
| *AcOr* | Acta orientalia. Copenhagen. |
| *AfO* | Archiv für Orientforschung, Graz. |
| *AHw* | Soden, W. von, *Akkadisches Handwörterbuch.* |
| *AION* | Annali dell'Istituto orientale di Napoli (sezione linguistica), Naples. |
| *AJBA* | Australian Journal of Biblical Archaeology, Sydney. |
| *AJBI* | Annual of the Japanese Biblical Institute, Tokyo. |
| *AJP* | American Journal of Philology, Baltimore. |
| *AJSL* | American Journal of Semitic Languages and Literatures, Chicago. |
| *AL* | Archivum Linguisticum, London. |
| *ALLCB* | Association for Literary and Linguistic Computing: Bulletin, London. |
| *AMOLAD* | Margalit, B., *A Matter of Life and Death.* |
| *AnBib* | Analecta Biblica, Rome. |
| *ANET* | Pritchard, J.B. (ed.), *Ancient Near Eastern Texts.* |
| *Anglia* | Anglia. Zeitschrift für englische Philologie, Tübingen. |
| *AnOr* | Analecta Orientalia, Rome. |
| *AnSt* | Anatolian Studies, London. |
| *AOAT(S)* | Alter Orient und Altes Testament (Sonderreihe), Kevelaer-Neukirchen/Vluyn. |
| *AOS* | American Oriental Series, New Haven. |
| *ARM* | Archives Royales de Mari. |
| *ArOr* | Archiv orientalni, Prague. |
| *ASTI* | Annual of the Swedish Theological Institute, Leiden. |
| *Atr* | Lambert, W.G.—Millard, A.R., *Atrahasis.* |
| *BA* | Biblical Archaeologist, New Haven. |
| *BASOR* | Bulletin of the American Schools of Oriental Research, New Haven. |
| *BASP* | Bulletin of the American Society of Papyrologists, New Haven. |

| | |
|---|---|
| *BDB* | Brown, F., Driver, S.R. and Briggs, C.A., *Hebrew and English Lexicon of the Old Testament*. |
| *BH* | Kittel, R. (ed.), *Biblia Hebraica* (3rd edition). |
| *BHS* | Elliger, K., Rudolph, W. et al. (edd.), *Biblia Hebraica Stuttgartensia*. |
| *Bib* | Biblica, Rome. |
| *BJRL* | Bulletin of the John Rylands Library, Manchester. |
| *BN* | *Biblische Notizen*, Bamberg. |
| *BO* | Bibliotheca Orientalis, Leiden. |
| *BS* | Biblische Studien, Neukirchen. |
| *BSOAS* | Bulletin of the School of Oriental and African Studies, London. |
| *BWL* | Lambert, W.G., *Babylonian Wisdom Literature*. (Oxford 1960) |
| *BZ* | Biblische Zeitschrift, Paderborn. |
| *BZAW* | Beiheft zur *ZAW*. |
| *CAD* | *The Assyrian Dictionary of the Oriental Institute of Chicago* (vols. A, B, D, E, G, H, I/J, K, L, M, N, Ṣ, Z). |
| *CBQ* | Catholic Biblical Quarterly, Washington, D.C. |
| *CE* | College English, Chicago. |
| *CML* | Gibson, J.C.L., *Canaanite Myths and Legends*. (Edinburgh 1978) |
| *CompL* | Comparative Literature, Eugene, Oregon. |
| *CompHum* | Computers and the Humanities, New York/Oxford. |
| *ClassQ* | Classical Quarterly, London/Oxford. |
| *CRAIBL* | Comptes Rendus de l'Académie des Inscriptions et Belles-Lettres, Paris. |
| *CT* | Cuneiform Texts from Babylonian Tablets in the British Museum. |
| *CTA* | Herdner, A., *Corpus des tablettes en cunéiformes alphabétiques découvertes à Ras Shamra-Ugarit de 1929 à 1939*. (Paris 1963) |
| *CTJ* | Calvin Theological Journal, Grand Rapids, Michigan. |
| *CuthLeg* | 'The Cuthaean Legend of Naram-Sin', edition by Gurney, O.R. in *AnSt* 5 (1955) 93-113. |
| *CV* | Communio viatorum, Prague. |
| *CW* | Classical World, Pittsburgh. |
| *DissAbsInt* | Dissertation Abstracts International, Ann Arbor. |
| *DT* | Daily Telegraph (= tablet signature, British Museum). |
| *EA* | El-Amarna (tablet). |
| *Ee* | Enuma eliš. |
| *ErIs* | Eretz-Israel, Archaeological, Historical and Geographical Studies, Jerusalem. |
| *Erra* | Cagni, L., *L'Epopea di Erra*. |

| | |
|---|---|
| *Etana* | Etana Myth. |
| *ExpT* | Expository Times, Edinburgh. |
| *FFC* | Folklore Fellows Communications, Helsinki. |
| *FL* | Foundations of Language. International Journal of language and philosophy, Dordrecht. |
| *GAG* | Soden, W. von, *Grundriss der akkadischen Grammatik.* |
| *Gilg* | Epic of Gilgamesh. |
| *GL* | General Linguistics, University Park, Pennsylvania. |
| *Glotta* | Glotta. Zeitschrift für griechische und lateinische Sprache, Göttingen. |
| *HAL* | Baumgärtner, W. et al., *Hebräisches und aramäisches Lexikon zum Alten Testament.* |
| *HCSP* | Harvard Studies in Classical Philology, Harvard. |
| *Hel* | Helicon, Budapest/Leipzig. |
| *Henoch* | Henoch, Turin. |
| *Herm* | Hermathena. A Dublin University Review, Dublin. |
| *HTR* | Harvard Theological Review, Cambridge, Mass. |
| *HUCA* | Hebrew Union College Annual, Cincinnati. |
| *ICC* | International Critical Commentary, Edinburgh. |
| *IDB(S)* | Interpreter's Dictionary of the Bible (Supplement), New York/Nashville. |
| *IEJ* | Israel Exploration Journal, Jerusalem. |
| *IOS* | Israel Oriental Studies, Tel Aviv. |
| *Iraq* | Iraq, London. |
| *JA* | Journal asiatique, Paris. |
| *JAF* | Journal of American folklore, Austin, Texas. |
| *JANES* | Journal of the Ancient Near Eastern Society of Columbia University, New York. |
| *JAOS* | Journal of the American Oriental Society, New Haven. |
| *JBL* | Journal of Biblical Literature, Philadelphia. |
| *JCS* | Journal of Cuneiform Studies, New Haven. |
| *JEOL* | Jaarbericht . . . ex oriente lux, Leiden. |
| *JETS* | Journal of the Evangelical Theological Society, Wheaton, Ill. |
| *JJS* | Journal of Jewish Studies, London. |
| *JL* | Journal of Linguistics, Cambridge. |
| *JNES* | Journal of Near Eastern Studies, Chicago. |
| *JNSL* | Journal of Northwest Semitic Languages, Leiden/Pretoria. |
| *JPOS* | Journal of the Palestine Oriental Society, Jerusalem. |
| *JQR* | Jewish Quarterly Review, Philadelphia. |
| *JR* | Journal of Religion, Chicago. |
| *JRAS* | Journal of the Royal Asiatic Society of Great Britain and Ireland, London. |
| *JSOT* | Journal for the Study of the Old Testament, Sheffield. |
| *JSS* | Journal of Semitic Studies, Manchester. |

| | |
|---|---|
| *JThC* | Journal for Theology and the Church, New York. |
| *JTS* | Journal of Theological Studies, Oxford. |
| *K* | Kouyunjik (= tablet signature, British Museum). |
| *Kadmos* | Kadmos. Zeitschrift für vor- und frühgriechische Epigraphik, Berlin/New York. |
| *KAI* | Donner, H.—Röllig, W., *Kanaanäische und aramäische Inschriften*. |
| *KTU* | Dietrich, M.—Loretz, O.—Sanmartin, J., *Keilalphabetische Texte aus Ugarit*. |
| *Lang* | Language. Journal of the Linguistic Society of America, Baltimore. |
| *LeS* | Lingua e Stile, Bologna. |
| *Lesh* | Leshonenu, Jerusalem. |
| *Ling* | Linguistics, The Hague. |
| *LS* | Language and Style. An International Journal, New York. |
| *LXX* | Septuagint. |
| *MAARAV* | Maarav. A Journal for the Study of the Northwest Semitic Language and Literatures, Santa Monica. |
| *Maqlu* | Meier, G. *Maqlu*. |
| *MDOG* | Mitteilungen der Deutschen Orient-Gesellschaft, Berlin. |
| *MIO* | Mitteilungen des Instituts für Orientforschung, Berlin. |
| *MLN* | Modern Language Notes, Baltimore. |
| *MT* | Masoretic Text. |
| *MUSJ* | Mélanges de l'Université Saint-Joseph, Beirut. |
| *MVAG* | Mitteilungen der Vorderasiatisch-Ägyptischen Gesellschaft, Leipzig. |
| *NCB* | New Century Bible, London. |
| *NEB* | New English Bible, London. |
| *NTT* | Norsk Teologisk Tidsskrift, Wageningen. |
| *NUgSt* | Newsletter for Ugaritic Studies, Calgary. |
| *OrAnt* | Oriens Antiquus, Rome. |
| *OLP* | Orientalia Lovaniensia Periodica, Louvain. |
| *OLZ* | Orientalische Literaturzeitung, Leipzig. |
| *Or* | Orientalia, Rome. |
| *OTL* | Old Testament Library, London/Philadelphia. |
| *OTS* | Oudtestamentische Studien, Leiden. |
| *OTWSA* | Die Ou Testamentiese Werkgemeenskap in Suid-Afrika. |
| *PAPS* | Proceedings of the American Philosophical Society, Philadelphia. |
| *PEPP* | Preminger, A. et al., *Princeton Encyclopedia of Poetry and Poetics*, London. |
| *PEQ* | Palestine Exploration Quarterly, London. |
| *PIBA* | Proceedings of the Irish Biblical Association, Dublin. |

| | |
|---|---|
| *PMLA* | Proceedings of the Modern Language Association of America, New York. |
| *Poetica* | Poetica, Zeitschrift für Sprach- und Literaturwissenschaft, Munich. |
| *Poétique* | Poétique. Revue de théorie et d'analyse littéraires, Paris. |
| *PRU* | Nougayrol, J., *Le Palais Royal d'Ugarit.* |
| *QS* | Quaderni di semitistica, Florence. |
| *RA* | Revue d'assyriologie et d'archéologie orientale, Paris. |
| *RB* | Revue Biblique, Paris. |
| *RBI* | Rivista Biblica Italiana, Brescia. |
| *REI* | Revue des études italiennes, Paris. |
| *RES* | Revue des études sémitiques, Paris. |
| *RHPR* | Revue d'Histoire et de Philosophie Religieuses, Strasbourg. |
| *RlA* | Reallexikon der Assyrologie, Berlin. |
| *RevQ* | Revue de Qumran, Paris. |
| *ResQ* | Restoration Quarterly. |
| *RS* | Ras Shamra (= tablet signature). |
| *RSF* | Rivista di studi fenici, Rome. |
| *RSO* | Rivista degli studi orientali, Rome. |
| *RSP* | Fisher, L. (ed.), *Ras Shamra Parallels*, I-II; Rummel, S. (ed.), *Ras Shamra Parallels* III. |
| *RSV* | Revised Standard Version. |
| *SBL* | Society of Biblical Literature. |
| *ScrH* | Scripta Hierosolymitana, Jerusalem. |
| *SEÅ* | Svensk Exegetisk Årsbok, Uppsala. |
| *Sef* | Sefarad, Madrid. |
| *Sem* | Semitica, Paris. |
| *Semeia* | Semeia, Missoula. |
| *Semitics* | Semitics, Pretoria. |
| *SJT* | Scottish Journal of Theology, Edinburgh. |
| *Surpu* | Reiner, E., Šurpu. |
| *StPohl* | Studia Pohl, Rome. |
| *Syr* | Syria. Revue d'art oriental et d'archéologie, Paris. |
| *TAPA* | Transactions and Proceedings of the American Philological Association, Cleveland. |
| *Tarb* | Tarbiz, Jerusalem. |
| *Tel-Aviv* | Tel-Aviv, Journal of the Tel Aviv University Institute of Archaeology, Tel Aviv. |
| *THAT* | Theologisches Handwörterbuch zum Alten Testament, Munich (etc.) |
| *ThR* | Theologische Rundschau, Munich. |
| *ThZ* | Theologische Zeitschrift, Basel. |
| *TLS* | Times Literary Supplement, London. |

| | |
|---|---|
| *TO* | Caquot, A.—Sznycer, M.—Herdner, A., *Textes ougaritiques, tome I: Mythes et légendes.* |
| *TS* | Theological Studies, New York. |
| *TSLL* | Texas Studies in Language and Literature. A Journal of the Humanities, Austin, Texas. |
| *TTQ* | Tübinger Theologischer Quartalschrift, Tübingen. |
| *TynB* | Tyndale House Bulletin, Cambridge. |
| *UAJb* | Ural-Altaische Jahrbücher, Wiesbaden. |
| *Ugar 5* | Ugaritica V, Paris. |
| *UF* | Ugarit-Forschungen, Kevelaer-Neukirchen/Vluyn. |
| *VD* | Verbum Domini, Rome. |
| *VT(S)* | Vetus Testamentum (Supplements), Leiden. |
| *WA* | World Archaeology, London. |
| *WMANT* | Wissenschaftliche Monographien zum Alten und Neuen Testament, Neukirchen. |
| *WO* | Welt des Orients, Göttingen. |
| *Word* | Word. Journal of the International Linguistic Association, New York. |
| *WUS* | Aistleitner, J., *Wörterbuch der ugaritische Sprache.* |
| *YCS* | Yale Classical Studies, New Haven. |
| *YOS* | Yale Oriental Series, Babylonian Texts. |
| *ZA* | Zeitschrift für Assyriologie und Vorderasiatische Archäologie, Berlin. |
| *ZDMG* | Zeitschrift der deutschen morgenländische Gesellschaft, Wiesbaden. |
| *ZSem* | Zeitschrift für Semitistik und verwandte Gebiete, Leipzig. |

*OT books*

Gen Ex Lev Nb Dt Jos Jgs 1,2 Sm 1,2 Kgs Isa Jer Ez Hos Joel Am Obd Jonah
Mic Nah Hab Zeph Hag Zech Mal Ps(s) Job Prov Ruth Song Qoh Lam Est
Dan 1,2 Chr Sir Bar

# SHORT TITLES OF FREQUENTLY MENTIONED WORKS

Alonso Schökel, *Estudios* — *Estudios de poética hebrea.*

Andersen-Freedman, *Hosea* — *Hosea (AB 24).*

Bühlmann-Scherer, *Stilfiguren* — *Stilfiguren der Bibel.*

Cassuto, *Anath* — *The Goddess Anath.*

Collins, *Line-forms* — *Line-Forms in Hebrew Poetry.*

Culler, *Poetics* — *Structuralist Poetics.*

Culley, *Oral-Formulaic* — *Oral Formulaic Language in the Biblical Psalms.*

Dahood, *Psalms I, II, III* — *Psalms I-III (AB 16-17a).*

Driver, *Writing* — *Semitic Writing.*

Dubois, *Dictionnaire* — *Dictionnaire de Linguistique.*

Elkhadem, *Dictionary* — *York Dictionary of Literary Terms.*

Fowler, *Essays* — *Essays on Style and Language.*

Geller, *Parallelism* — *Parallelism in Early Hebrew Poetry.*

Gevirtz, *Patterns* — *Patterns in the Early Poetry of Israel.*

Gray, *Forms* — *The Forms of Hebrew Poetry (1972 ed.).*

Gray, *Legacy* — *The Legacy of Canaan (1965 ed.).*

Häublein, *Stanza* — *The Stanza.*

Hecker, *Epik* — *Untersuchungen zur akkadischen Epik.*

Irwin, *Isaiah 28-33* — *Isaiah 28-33. Translation with philological notes.*

Kugel, *Idea* — *The Idea of Biblical Poetry. Parallelism and Its History.*

Leech, *Guide* — *A linguistic guide to English poetry.*

Loretz, *Psalmen II* — *Die Psalmen. Teil II.*

Lugt, *Strofische structuren* — *Strofische structuren in de bijbels-hebreeuwse poëzie.*

Nowottny, *Language* — *The Language Poets Use.*

O'Connor, *Structure* — *Hebrew Verse Structure.*

Pope, *Job* — *Job (AB 15).*

Pope, *Song* — *Song of Songs (AB 7).*

Riffaterre, *Semiotics* — *The Semiotics of Poetry.*

Sebeok, *Style* — *Style in Language (Symposium).*

Seux, *Hymnes* — *Hymnes et prières aux dieux de Babylonie et d'Assyrie*

Smith, *Closure* — *Poetic Closure. A Study of How Poems End.*

Speiser, *Genesis* — *Genesis (AB 1).*

xvii

Ullmann, *Semantics*  *Principles of Semantics.*

Ullmann, *Language*  *Language and Style.*

Watson, 'Chiastic Patterns'  'Chiastic Patterns in Biblical Hebrew Poetry' in Welch, *Chiasmus*, 118-168.

Watson, 'Gender Parallelism'  'Gender-Matched Synonymous Parallelism in the OT', *JBL* 99 (1980) 321-341.

Watson, 'Pivot Pattern'  'The Pivot Pattern in Hebrew, Ugaritic and Akkadian Poetry', *ZAW* 88 (1976) 239-253.

Watters, *Formula*  *Formula Criticism and the Poetry of the OT.*

Welch, *Chiasmus*  *Chiasmus in Antiquity.*

Wimsatt, *Versification*  *Versification: Major Language Types.*

# FESTSCHRIFTEN

Albright (1961)
  Wright, G.E. (ed.)
  *The Bible and the Ancient Near East: Essays in Honor of William Foxwell Albright* (London, 1961).
Albright (1971)
  Goedicke, H. (ed.)
  *Near Eastern Studies in Honor of W.F. Albright* (Baltimore/London, 1971).
Bagatti
  *Studia Hierosolymitana in onore di P. Bellarmino Bagatti. II Studi esegetici* (Jerusalem, 1976).
Cameron
  Orlin, L.L. et al. (edd.)
  *Michigan Oriental Studies in Honor of George G. Cameron* (Ann Arbor, 1976).
Driver
  Thomas, D.W.—McHardy, W.D. (edd.)
  *Hebrew and Semitic Studies presented to G.R. Driver* (Oxford, 1963).
Dupont-Sommer
  *Hommages à André Dupont-Sommer* (Paris, 1971).
Gaster (1973)
  Hoffner, H.A. jr. (ed.)
  *Orient and Occident. Essays presented to Cyrus H. Gordon* (Neukirchen-Vluyn, 1973).
Gordon (1973)
  Hoffner, H.A. jr. (ed.)
  *Orient and Occident. Essays presented to Cyrus H. Gordon . . . Sixty-fifth Birthday* (Neukirchen-Vluyn, 1973).
Gordon (1980)
  Rendsburg, G. et al. (edd.)
  *The Bible World: essays in honor of Cyrus H. Gordon* (New York, 1980).
Hooke
  Bruce, F.F. (ed.)
  *Promise and Fulfilment. Essays . . . Hooke* (Edinburgh, 1963).
Irwin
  Hobbs, E.C. (ed.)
  *A Stubborn Faith. Papers on Old Testament and Related Subjects Presented to Honor William A. Irwin* (Dallas, 1956).

Kramer
  Eichler, B.L. et al. (edd.)
  *Studies in Honor of Samuel Noah Kramer* (*AOAT 25*; Kevelaer/
  Neukirchen-Vluyn, 1976).
Loewenstamm
  Avishur, Y.—Blau, J. (edd.)
  *Studies in Bible and the Ancient Near East Presented to Samuel E.
  Loewenstamm on His Seventieth Birthday* (Jerusalem, 1978).
Myers
  Bream, H.N. et al. (edd.)
  *A Light unto My Faith: Old Testament Studies in Honor of Jacob M.
  Myers* (Gettysburg Theological Studies 4; Philadelphia, 1974).
Neuman
  Ben-Horin, M. et al. (edd.)
  *Studies and Essays in honor of Abraham A. Neuman* (Leiden, 1962).
Nida
  Black, M.—Smalley, W.A. (edd.)
  *On Languages, Culture and Religion: in honor of Eugene A. Nida*
  (Approaches to semiotics 54; The Hague, 1974).
Prado
  Alvarez Verdes, L.—Alonso Hernandez, E.J. (edd.)
  *Homenaje a Juan Prado. Miscelanea de estudios biblicos y hebraicos*
  (Madrid, 1975).
Rowley
  Noth, M.—Thomas, D.W. (edd.)
  *Wisdom in Israel and in the Ancient Near East, presented to H.H.
  Rowley* (*VTS* 3; Leiden, 1955).
Schaeffer
  *UF* 11 (1979).
Selms
  Eybers, I.M. et al. (edd.)
  *De fructu oris sui. Essays in honour of Adrianus van Selms* (Pretoria
  Oriental Series 9; Leiden, 1971).
Widengren
  Bergman, J.—Drynjeff, K. (edd.)
  *Ex Orbe Religionum. Studia Geo Widengren Oblata* (Leiden, 1972).
Ziegler
  Schreiner, J. (ed.)
  *Wort, Lied und Gottesspruch. Festschrift für Joseph Ziegler. II: Beiträge
  zu Psalmen und Propheten* (*Forschungen zur Bibel* 2; Würzburg, 1972).

# 1

## INTRODUCTION

### 1.1 Scope and Aims

A textbook or manual of poetry should be the end-product of close and detailed analysis of the poetry in question. Implied, therefore, is a long period of study. A further requisite is the assertion of an overall theory which will account for the findings and provide a framework within which they can be presented in a coherent way.

Turning to classical Hebrew poetry, it would appear than analytical studies are by no means lacking. Also, these investigations have been carried out for hundreds of years.[1] All that is missing, it seems, is a systematic presentation of the findings, based on established theory. However, things are not so simple. In spite of many centuries' study, detailed analysis of all the poetic texts has not yet been completed. This is in part due to the same set of texts being chosen for study (Gen 49; Ex 15; Jgs 5; Isa 1-12; particular Psalms) to the exclusion of others.[2] Another reason is that the main interest of commentators is exegesis, so that remarks on poetic technique are more or less of a random nature.[3] The principal reason, though, is of a different order: it is only since the discovery of poetic texts in Ugaritic and Akkadian that certain techniques of poetry could be recognised in Hebrew. This knowledge is still expanding: at the same

---

1. The present book does not provide surveys of a historical nature. For the history of research see D. Broadribb, 'A Historical Review of Studies of Hebrew Poetry', *AbrN* 13 (1972-73) 66-87, and the somewhat narrower survey, A. Baker, 'Parallelism: England's Contribution', *CBQ* 35 (1973) 429-440. Also, Kugel, *Idea*, 96-170, and A.S. Cooper, Biblical Poetics: A Linguistic Approach (Yale thesis, 1976).

2. However, see Irwin, *Isaiah 28-33*, although his presentation of poetic elements is by no means systematic.

3. Exceptions are L. Krinetzki, *Das Hohe Lied* (Düsseldorf, 1964), R. Gordis, *The Song of Songs and Lamentations* (New York, 1954) and the Appendix to Dahood, *Psalms III*.

time as these techniques are becoming better understood, their presence is being determined in Hebrew.[4]

The purpose of this GUIDE is twofold: to give an account of the methods and results of current scholarship, and to provide both lecturers and students with guidelines for further study. With particular reference to the student, questions of the following kind will be answered: How begin analysing a poetic passage? How are the beginning and end of a poetic section determined? What is the point of using a chiastic pattern in this particular passage? Which structural devices were available to the poet and how did he (or she) use them? How much has Hebrew poetry in common with Ugaritic and Akkadian poetry and in what way does it differ? And so on.[5]

The methods and approaches outlined here make no claim to be either definitive or exhaustive; there is still a large amount of room for further research and investigation. Only when a complete examination of each poetic device with respect to occurrence, types, functions, relationship to other poetic devices and to the various literary forms is available will a full description of classical Hebrew poetry be possible. Rather than delay until all such research is complete, it seems preferable to present the results so far achieved in order to indicate the present state of the art and the areas still requiring examination.

The book will comprise both general theory and worked examples. Throughout, clear examples are used to illustrate the various techniques and devices described. Such excerpts, though, will of necessity be context-free. To offset any possible distortion, therefore, some longer specimen texts will be provided within the body of the book and also as a kind of appendix, in chapter 13: WORKED EXAMPLES.

A problem that almost defies solution is how the various topics should be arranged.[6] Should 'parallelism' come under the heading of 'verse patterns', for instance, or is it a topic in its own right? The intricate nature of Hebrew poetic technique is resistant to neat

4. No account of this extending knowledge is provided by Alonso-Schökel's *Estudios*. Since the bulk of my book was completed, several extensive works on Hebrew poetry have been published: Collins, *Line-forms*; Kugel, *Idea*; Lugt, *Strofische Structuren*; and O'Connor, *Structure*. Some account of these works has been taken in the final draft of this GUIDE.

5. Much of the material presented here has been used in lectures and seminars. The detailed analysis of Prov 23,29-35 was discussed at a joint seminar (Trinity College, Dublin and University College, Dublin).

6. An arrangement under six general headings is provided by Bühlmann-Scherer, *Stilfiguren*, 5.

classification; there is too much overlap. For the sake of presentation, however, a framework has been adopted; others, of course, are equally possible.[7]

## Stylistics and Hebrew Poetry

The study of style in Hebrew poetry has been sporadic rather than systematic.[8] The present work is an attempt to remedy such a piecemeal approach, without making any claims to be definitive.

One of the best introductions to the problems involved is Widdowson's *Stylistics and the Teaching of Literature*.[9] He points out that there are two *disciplines*:[10] these are literary criticism and linguistics. This is because the critic looks at a poem in one way (as literary communication) while the linguist perceives literature as text.

> The linguist ... directs his attention primarily to how a piece of language exemplifies the language system. We will say that he treats literature as *text*.
> The literary critic searches for underlying significance, for the essential artistic vision that the poem embodies and we will say that he treats literary works as *messages*.[11]

The discipline of stylistics lies between linguistics and literary criticism: it treats literature as *discourse*:

> Between these two is an approach to literature which attempts to show specifically how elements of a linguistic text combine to create messages, how, in other words, pieces of literary writing function as a form of communication.[12]

Accordingly, the two related disciplines of linguistics and literary criticism will be brought to bear on Hebrew poetic texts—but the chief interest of the following chapters will be the style of Hebrew verse.

---

7. Where applicable, each section will be structured in the same way. After a definition of the particular topic, examples will be given in Hebrew, Ugaritic and Akkadian. Next will come sub-classification (with Hebrew examples) and notes on function. Text references for further study are then given, followed by cross-references and an extensive bibliography.

8. For example, Blenkinsopp, *Bib* 42 (1961) 61-76.

9. H.G. Widdowson, *Stylistics and the Teaching of Literature* (London, 1975).

10. For the distinction between discipline and subject cf. Widdowson: 1975, 1-5.

11. Widdowson: 1975, 6.

12. Widdowson: 1975, 6. See, too, E.C. Traugott—M.L. Pratt, *Linguistics for Students of Literature* (New York, 1980).

# 2

## OTHER SEMITIC LANGUAGES

### 2.1 *Introduction*

For a fuller understanding of the poetic techniques used in classical Hebrew poetry some comparison will be made, in this book, with poetic texts in Ugaritic and Akkadian. This comparison will take the form of text citation along the following lines. Normally, for each topic two examples will be given, one from Ugaritic and one from Akkadian. Where occasion warrants further examples will be quoted either from these two languages, or, rarely, from other languages, though discussion of such non-Hebrew texts will be kept to an absolute minimum as will any bibliography.

Several considerations have led to the inclusion of such extensive reference to Ugaritic and Akkadian verse. The principal reason is that there are no other comparable bodies of poetic literature in ancient Semitic languages. Rather than quote scrappily from a variety of traditions it seems preferable to use just these two in which most of the poetic techniques to be discussed are actually attested. It will also make for uniformity of presentation. In spite of many obscurities we have now progressed to the stage where translation from both these languages is very reliable and poetic analysis is therefore possible. Finally, the existence of identical or similar techniques and formal poetic devices in Hebrew and in both Ugaritic and Akkadian (with allowance being made for the individual traditions in each language) acts as a control and reduces subjectivity in reconstruction or emendation.

Apart from reasons of available time and space, poetic texts in other Semitic traditions (besides Ugaritic and Akkadian) are not considered largely because they do not present the same range. Texts in Aramaic,[1] Phoenician,[2] Punic[3] and Ammonite[4] are generally short. Gleanings from the Amarna[5] and Mari letters,[6] interesting as they are for comparative purposes, have not been included; they are much too brief. On the other hand, post-biblical Hebrew texts have been taken into account since they belong to the tradition of classical Hebrew poetry and are a continuation of it. Texts in non-Semitic languages such as Egyptian, Sumerian and Hittite are well outside the frame of reference posited here.

## 2.2 *Ugaritic Poetry*

To provide a general background to the non-Hebrew literatures that will be quoted, some mention of their date, literary types, general poetic technique and value for comparative purposes will now be made. Each section will have a short, relevant bibliography.

There is no need to repeat here how the Ugaritic tablets were discovered at Ras Shamra, how they were deciphered and so on; such accounts are easily available.[7] They are particularly significant for Hebrew poetry because Ugaritic is a closely related language, much closer than, say, Akkadian.[8]

1. Exceptions are the proverbs in the Aḥiqar Tale (which derives in part from Mesopotamian tradition), the poetic sections of Daniel, parts of Tobit as represented in Qumran Cave 4; 11Qtg Job; 1QapGen 20,2-7 and 4QpsDanᶜ; for this list cf. J.A. Fitzmyer, *A Wandering Aramean. Collected Aramaic Essays* (SBL Monograph Series 25; Missoula, 1979) 16-17. Cf. C.C. Torrey, 'A Specimen of Old Aramaic Verse', *JAOS* 46 (1926) 24-25; J.C. Greenfield, 'Early Aramaic Verse', *JANES* 11 (1981) 45-51; Towner, *CBQ* 31 (1969) 317-326; etc. The Assyrian-Aramaic inscription on the statue from Tell Fekheriyeh is a dramatic addition to the corpus; see *BA* 45 (1982) 135-141 [with bibliography].
2. See Avishur, *UF* 7 (1975) 13-47; *UF* 8 (1976) 1-22; T. Collins, 'The Kilamuwa Inscription—A Phoenician Poem', *WO* 6 (1971) 183-188—with the dissent of O'Connor, *BASOR* 226 (1977) 15-29. Also, J.C. Greenfield, 'Scripture and Inscription: The Literary and Rhetorical Elements in Some Early Phoenician Inscriptions', *Albright FS* (1971) 253-268. Also, J.C.L. Gibson, *Textboook of Syrian Semitic Inscriptions, Vol. 3. Phoenician Inscriptions* (Oxford, 1982) 80-81. 105 and esp. 33.
3. C.R. Krahmalkov, 'Two Neo-Punic Poems in Rhymed Verse', *RSF* 3 (1975) 169-205.
4. Baldacci, *VT* 31 (1981) 363-368.
5. See S. Gevirtz, 'On Canaanite Rhetoric. The Evidence of the Amarna Letters from Tyre', *Or* 42 (1973) 162-177; also *JNES* 32 (1973) 99-104.
6. Weinfeld, *VT* 27 (1977) 178-195; A. Marzal, *Gleanings from the Wisdom of Mari* (StPohl 11; Rome, 1976) (the second work to be used with circumspection).
7. For example, Gibson, *CML*, 1-2.
8. The affinity or non-affinity of Ugaritic and Hebrew is a matter of dispute, but it is undeniable they are cognate languages.

The Ugaritic tablets were actually found in levels which archae-
ologists date between 1600 and 1200 BC (the second date being
determined by the invasion of the Sea Peoples, who sacked the city)
and the indications are that the literary texts were written down in
approximately 1400-1350 BC.[9] The main poetic material comprises
the Baal Cycle (a series of episodes recounting Baal's 'adventures');
the legends[10] of Keret and Aqhat (both human heroes); the Story of
'Dawn', 'Dusk' and the Fair gods, and the Nuptials of Nikkal. In all
they comprise some 4,000 or so lines of verse (many of which are
verbatim repetitions of the same stock lines). Although dating in
written form to about the fourteenth century BC, the compositions
themselves are very probably much earlier. Not only that: it is fairly
safe to assume that they first circulated in *oral* form (and therefore in
various different versions), to be ultimately 'frozen' by being committed to writing. It is in this final form that we know Ugaritic
poetry.

In the main, then, the literature of Ugarit comprises myths, tales
and legends, or, less specifically, narrative cast in poetic form. There
are one or two prayers,[11] at least one incantation,[12] and perhaps a
hymn,[13] but as Ugaritic poetry is chiefly narrative in character it
cannot be directly compared with Hebrew poetic texts. Even so,
there is a large overlap between the two sets of literature since they
share a common poetic technique and in many respects would appear
to belong to the same tradition of versification.

The translations offered here for the examples are very largely my
own, though I have kept an eye on the principal translations that
have been made. Problems of a textual and philological kind have
been ignored, except where clarification was essential.

9.   As shown by the colophons; see Gibson, *CML*, 1.
10.   The term 'legend' is used very loosely here; the exact genre of these narrative
poems has not yet been determined. On this aspect cf. Parker, *Maarav* 2/1 (1979-80)
7-41.
11.   A prayer to Anath has been identified by de Moor; cf. *UF* 11 (1979) 648-649.
Another prayer is *KTU* 1.119, set out in 13.2, WORKED EXAMPLES.
12.   *Ugar* 5, 7. For an incantation from Ras Ibn Hani cf. de Moor, *UF* 12 (1980)
429-432. Note, too, J.C. de Moor, 'An Incantation Against Infertility (*KTU* 1.13)', *UF*
12 (1980) 305-310.
13.   *CTA* 6 vi 40-52 (end of tablet), though not all scholars agree that this is a
hymn; see, most recently, Dietrich—Loretz, *UF* 12 (1980) 399-400.

## BIBLIOGRAPHY

(a) *Text and translation*
*KTU* is the most comprehensive collection of texts (in transcription only). It should be supplemented by reference to *CTA*, *Ugar* 5 and more recently published texts.

Gibson, *CML*, is the most useful translation to consult not only because it has a comprehensive glossary but principally because it provides the Ugaritic text (in transcription), making comparison with Hebrew poetry possible at the level of language. For an extensive critical review cf. Pardee, *BO* 37 (1980) 269-291.

Most recently G. Del Olmo Lete's *Mitos y leyendas de Canaan segun la tradicion de Ugarit* (Madrid, 1981) provides full text, translation, notes and glossary for the Ugaritic literary texts.

(b) *Studies in Ugaritic poetry*
Cross, F.M. 'Prose and poetry in the mythic and epic texts from Ugarit', *HTR* 67 (1974) 1-15.
Margalit, B. 'Introduction to Ugaritic Prosody', *UF* 7 (1975) 289-313.
Pardee, D. 'A Philological and Prosodic Analysis of the Ugaritic Serpent Incantation UT 607', *JANES* 10 (1978) 73-108.
Parker, S.B. 'Parallelism and prosody in Ugaritic narrative verse', *UF* 6 (1974) 283-294.
Segert, S. 'Die Form des ugaritischen Verses', *ArOr* 28 (1960) 666.
—'Ugaritic Poetry and Poetics: Some Preliminary Observations', *UF* 11 (1979) 729-738.
Watson, W.G.E. 'Quasi-acrostics in Ugaritic Poetry', *UF* 12 (1980) 445-447.
—'An Example of Multiple Wordplay in Ugaritic', *UF* 12 (1980) 443-444.
—'Gender-Matched Parallelism in Ugaritic Poetry', *UF* 13 (1981) 181-187.
—'Lineation (Stichometry) in Ugaritic Verse', *UF* 14 (1982) forthcoming.
Welch, J.W. 'Chiasmus in Ugaritic', *UF* 6 (1974) 421-436 = Welch, *Chiasmus*, 36-49.
Wilson, G.H. 'Ugaritic word order and sentence structure in the *Krt* text', *JSS* 27 (1982) 17-32.

(c) *Comparison between Ugaritic and Hebrew poetry*
There are too many studies to be listed here; cf. *CML*, xix-xx, for bibliography; also *NUgSt*, *RSP* I-III and works listed in the bibliographies to each section.

### 2.3 *Akkadian (Assyro-Babylonian) Poetic Material*

The term *Akkadian* denotes the poetic literature of ancient Meso-potamia, written in Semitic (as opposed to Sumerian, say, or Elamite). Akkadian is, in fact, the designation used by native speakers for their tongue 'after the Akkadians who had established the first great Semitic empire in the middle of the third millennium

BC, under their renowned leader Sargon (I) of Akkad'.[14] The Semitic languages involved (or dialects of the same language; scholars are divided over this) comprise Old Akkadian; Old, Middle and New Assyrian; Old, Middle and New Babylonian.[15]

Since the poetic material in Akkadian ranges from the Epic of Gilgamesh to popular sayings, the corresponding *dates* cover a long span of time and are, in any case, difficult to determine with certainty.[16] One reason for this is that many tablets unearthed in excavation are later copies of much earlier works which have not yet been discovered (or are lost forever) for which dates of composition can only be surmised. Further, some types of literature, such as hymns or proverbs, are essentially timeless. Also, even though we may know the date of a particular dialect in which a poetic text is cast (for example, New Babylonian), this can only give an approximate indication of date and is rather unreliable. Lambert has drawn up a very useful time chart for Akkadian literature which the reader can consult for a general overview.[17] In practice each composition has to be studied individually for its date of composition to be determined or guessed at. Examples are the Erra Epic, dating possibly to the eighth century BC (von Soden suggests 765 BC, which may be optimistic in terms of precision), and the Atraḥasis Epic, written around 1000 BC.

Many of the patterns and devices found in Hebrew poetry also belong to *poetic technique* in Akkadian: parallelism in all its forms, chiasmus, enjambment, acrostics and so on. An exception is staircase parallelism, which hardly occurs, if at all (there are some dubious examples),[18] perhaps because it is peculiar to Canaanite poetic traditions. Another rarity is the tricolon, though it is by no means unknown. Metre is a problem in its own right, more language-specific than other features. To balance these common characteristics with Hebrew verse-making it is important to remember that Akkadian poetry was influenced, to a certain extent, by Sumerian tradition. Peculiar to such poetry is the stock repetitive quatrain comprising

---

14. Gelb in the Introduction to *CAD* A/1, vii.
15. See *GAG*, 2-4 (= §1).
16. W. von Soden, 'Das Problem der zeitlichen Einordnung akkadischer Literaturwerke', *MDOG* 85 (1953) 14-26.
17. Lambert, *BWL*, xx.
18. See Watson, *UF* 7 (1975) 492 n. 54. Also, Watson, 'A Note on Staircase Parallelism', *VT* [in press].

two almost identical couplets, the second making implicit what is only implicit in the first. For example:

> My king, toothed pickaxe that uproots the evil land,
> arrow that breaks up the rebellious land;
> Lord Ninurta, toothed pickaxe that uproots the evil land,
> arrow that breaks up the rebellious land.[19]

Since the main thrust of the present work is a description of Hebrew poetry, only a restricted selection of texts from Assyro-Babylonian verse has been included. For a broader and more exact picture the student is referred to the specialist works in the bibliography, especially Hecker, *Epik*.[20]

### BIBLIOGRAPHY

(a) *Introductions to Mesopotamian literature*
Jacobsen, T. *The Treasures of Darkness. A History of Mesopotamian Religion* (New Haven/London, 1976) 165-219.
Lambert, *BWL*, 1-20.
Oppenheim, A.L. *Ancient Mesopotamia* (Chicago, 1964.1972) 250-275.
Saggs, H.W.F. *The Greatness that was Babylon* (London, 1962) 390-444.

(b) *Akkadian poetry with accompanying translation*
Cagni, *Erra*.
Farber, W. *Beschwörungsrituale an Ištar und Dumuzi* (Wiesbaden, 1977) esp. 64-73.99.140-155.188-197.212-213.236-245.
Lambert, *BWL*.
Lambert, W.G. 'The Fifth Tablet of the Era Epic', *Iraq* 24 (1962) 119-125.
Lambert—Millard, *Atr.* (for an extensive bibliography cf. Oden, *ZAW* 93 [1981] 197-216, esp. 197 n. 4).
Landsberger, B.—Kinnier-Wilson, J.V. 'The fifth tablet of Enuma eliš', *JNES* 20 (1961) 154ff.
Other editions are scattered in various specialist journals; a good selection is to hand in *JNES* 33 (1974).

(c) *Studies of Akkadian poetry*
Groneberg, B. Untersuchungen zum hymnisch-epischen Dialekt der altbaby-lonischen literarischen Texte (dissertation, Münster, 1971) esp. 129ff.

---

19.  Hymn to Ninurta, *ANET*, 577; another example, *ANET*, 578. The Hymn to Ishtar also uses this type of quatrain several times. See Hecker, *Epik*, 146-151.
20.  Published papers comparing Hebrew and Akkadian poetic traditions are too many to be listed here. Among the more recent can be mentioned Westhuizen: 1980; J.S. Kselman, 'rb//kbd: a new Hebrew-Akkadian formulaic pair', *VT* 29 (1979) 110-114; Barré, *VT* 29 (1979) 107-110 and *Or* 50 (1981) 241-245.

Hecker, *Epik* (the most important study to date).

Mayer, W. *Untersuchungen zur Formensprache der babylonischen 'Gebetsbeschwörungen'* (*StPohl: Series Maior* 5; Rome, 1976).

Smith, R.F. 'Chiasm in Sumero-Akkadian', in Welch, *Chiasmus*, 17-35.

Tigay, J.H. *The Evolution of the Gilgamesh Epic* (Philadelphia, 1982).

Westermann, C. *The Praise of God in the Psalms* (London, 1967) esp. 36-51.

Westhuizen, J.P. van der 'Assonance in Biblical and Babylonian Hymns of Praise', *Semitics* 7 (1980) 81-101.

# 3

## ANALYSING HEBREW POETRY: NOTES ON METHOD

### 3.1 *Terminology*

Clear terminology is basic to this book, so the terms used will be defined and kept to, as far as is possible without the danger of monotonous repetition. (So, the 'bicolon' will generally be called a bicolon, but for the sake of variety, other terms such as couplet will be used. However, where there is any possibility of ambiguity or misunderstanding, the strictly defined terms will be employed.)

Different scholars or writers use different names for the same components, which can lead to a great deal of confusion, even though a particular writer may use such terms consistently. What for some is a 'colon' is referred to by others as 'stichos' or even 'hemistich'; even worse, 'stanza' and 'strophe' are used almost interchangeably. In order to avoid ambiguity of this kind, I will define my terms as clearly as possible, and then stick to them. It is not just a matter of nomenclature, though; in defining my terms I imply an underlying theory concerning structure in poetic texts, which can be sketched as follows. The larger units such as poems or stanzas are composed of strophes, and the strophes in their turn are made up of one or more cola. The cola consist of even smaller units. Accordingly, a poem can be considered as a set of components forming larger and larger complexes which ultimately combine to form a single unified structure: the poem.

In accordance with the method of analysis outlined above, the definitions will proceed from the smallest units to the largest. Correct analysis can only begin once such terms have been defined with precision.[1]

---

1.  This approach is implied in de Moor's studies, e.g. *UF* 10 (1978) 187-217. Terms relating to metre, 'stress', 'accent', 'word', 'syllable', etc., are dealt with in the chapter

## HEMISTICH

A subdivision of the colon, generally equal to half the length of the colon. So, the phrase מהר ענני, 'Quickly, answer me', is approximately half the colon-length in Ps 69,18:

כי צר לי מהר ענני    Because it is hard on me/*quickly, answer me*

—and is a metrico-structural unit since it recurs, unchanged in Pss 102,3 ביום אקרא מהר ענני, 'On the day I call, *quickly, answer me*', and 143,7 מהר ענני יהוה, '*Quickly, answer me*, Yahweh'.[2]

## COLON

A single line of poetry, either as a semi-independent unit (= monocolon), or as part of a larger strophe (bicolon, tricolon, quatrain, etc.). So

מה אעשה לך יהודה    What shall I do to you, Judah? (Hos 6,4)

is a single verse-line, or a colon. Other designations include 'stichos', 'stich' and even 'hemistich'.

## MONOCOLON

A colon standing on its own as a strophe, within a stanza or poem. It can be defined as a single colon which does not cohere closely with another colon, although in a wide sense no element of a poem stands in total isolation.[3]

## BICOLON

A couplet or line-pair[4] made up of two lines or cola, generally (but by no means always) in parallel. The two-colon unit can almost be taken as standard in Hebrew poetry, for example:

קשרם על אצבעתיך    Bind them on your fingers,
כתבם על לוח לבך    write them on the tablet of your mind. (Prov 7,3)

---

on METRE. For other attempts at a unified terminology see Lotz, *Hel* 4 (1948) 132; Fowler, *Anglia* 86 (1968) 285-297; PEPP generally, and Leech, *Guide*. For Hebrew see Boadt, *CBQ* 35 (1973) 24, n. 14; Holladay, *JBL* 85 (1966) 403; Kugel, *Idea*, 2, no. 4, and Watson, 'Chiastic Patterns', 119-121.

2. See Culley, *Oral-Formulaic*, 45, who notes 'formal divisions smaller than the colon are occasionally apparent so that a colon may be viewed as being composed of two units about half a colon long'.

3. See Jakobson, *Lang* 42 (1966) 429.

4. O'Connor, *Structure*, 52.

Note that bicola can be extremely brief:

עלי עילם    Elam: Attack!
צורי מדי    Medes: Besiege! (Isa 21,2b)

—or so long that often further subdivision seems required:

יהוה מלך ירגזו עמים    Yahweh is king, let peoples tremble;
ישב כרובים תנוט הארץ    is throned on the cherubim, may earth totter.
                                     (Ps 99,1)

## TRICOLON

A set of three cola forming a single whole, or strophe, as

זרעם נכון    Their line is stable,
לפניהם עמם    their fathers are with them,
וצאצאיהם לעיניהם    and their offspring are in front of their eyes. (Job 21,8[5])

Also called a 'triplet' or 'tercet', but rarely.

## TETRACOLON, PENTACOLON, etc.

Groups of *four* cola are termed tetracola or quatrains (e.g. Jer 2,13), of *five* cola: pentastich or even quintet; of *six* cola: hexacola and so on.

## STROPHE

A strophe is a verse-unit of one or more cola, considered as part of the higher unit termed the stanza. The monocolon, bicolon, tricolon and so on are all strophes. Confusingly, many authors call such a verse-unit 'stanza', but this is only valid when a stanza consists of a single strophe.

## STANZA

A sub-section of a poem: the poem is made up of stanzas, and each stanza consists of one or more strophes. So, for instance, the poem 2 Sm 1,19-27 consists of 5 stanzas:

|     |        |
| --- | ------ |
| I   | 19-20  |
| II  | 21-22a |
| III | 22b-23 |
| IV  | 24-25  |
| V   | 26-27a |

and, as is sometimes the case, the stanzas are marked off by refrains.[6]

---

5. For translation, cf. Dahood, *Bib* 47 (1966) 411.
6. In 2 Sm 1, the refrain occurs at the end of stanzas II, IV and V, and at the beginning of stanza I.

POEM

An independent unit of poetry such as a psalm, a prophetic oracle (Jer 9,17-21), a speech (Job 25), a wisdom poem (Prov 3,19-20) or an acrostic (Prov 31,10-31). Several poems can be collected to form a book so that quite often it is difficult to determine where each begins and ends.[7]

The accompanying *table* will clarify the definitions given.[8]

| | |
|---|---|
| HEMISTICH | |
| COLON | hemistich hemistich |
| BICOLON | colon<br>colon |
| TRICOLON | colon<br>colon<br>colon |
| TETRACOLON or<br>QUATRAIN (etc.) | colon<br>colon<br>colon<br>colon |
| STROPHE | monocolon/bicolon/tricolon (etc.) |
| STANZA | strophe 1<br>strophe 2<br>strophe 3 (etc.) |
| POEM | stanza I<br>stanza II<br>stanza III<br>stanza IV (etc.) |

A significant term related to the analysis of verse is STICHOMETRY or, as some prefer, 'lineation'.[9] This denotes the segmenting of a text into verse-lines. A guide to marking off lines in Hebrew is the occurrence of pausal forms, as in Job 3,26:

---

7. Particularly in the prophetic books where individual poems have often been run together into larger units. It would be an interesting exercise to incorporate terms such as 'canto' and 'cycle' into this scheme.

8. A preliminary form of this table appears in Watson, 'Chiastic Patterns', 121.

9. So O'Connor, *Structure*, 30.

לא שלותי ולא שקטתי ולא נחתי  I have neither peace, nor quiet, nor rest,
ויבא רגז  but turmoil comes.

Here, the only pausal form is נחתי which indicates line-end.[10]

STICHOGRAPHY is the setting out of an ancient text (clay tablet, stela, prepared goatskin, etc.) into lines of poetry by either punctuation or spacing (or both). The ancients were by no means consistent so that though ideally scribal practice (stichography) and modern analysis (stichometry) should coincide, in actual fact they commonly do not.[11]

### 3.2 Method

#### 1. *Analysis in literary criticism*
Some idea of the method and approach to be adopted in analysing Hebrew poetry can be gained from considering how the literary critic proceeds when dealing with either a single poem or a collection of poems. A clear example for the anlysis of one poem is provided by Sinclair.[12] His method is, first to examine the poem for particular features, such as sentence and clause structure, line and stanza boundaries, and then to tabulate his findings. The procedure is completed by showing how all the features isolated (by analysis) interrelate to make up the complete poem (synthesis). By contrast, Austerlitz adopts a more mathematical approach in his metrico-strophic analysis of folk poetry.[13] His method entails segmentation of the text into its constituent units (or: analysis into strophe and stanza), description and classification of the segments, description of the inner structure of each segment and finally, the application of quantitative criteria. As will be seen, though, such methods can provide only approximate models for the study of ancient Hebrew poetry largely because the tradition and language in which they were composed can now only be reconstructed in part.

---

10. See Revell, *VT* 31 (1981) 186-199, esp. 191.
11. For the term 'stichography' see Kugel, *Idea*, 119-120, 121-123, 126-127, and 193-194. For Ugaritic texts cf. W.G.E. Watson, 'Lineation (Stichometry) in Ugaritic Verse', *UF* 14 (1982) [in press].
12. J.M. Sinclair, 'Taking a Poem to Pieces', in D.C. Freeman, *Linguistics and Literary Style* (New York, 1970) 129-142 (= Fowler, *Essays*, 68-81).
13. R. Austerlitz, *Ob-Ugric metrics* (Helsinki, 1958).

### 2. *Analysis of Hebrew poetry: General outline*

By adapting what can be learned from literary criticism, singling out the best from existing discussions of Hebrew poems[14] and from experience, a general outline for analysis would include the following:[15]

    (h)    delimitation
    (i)    segmentation
    (j)    inner-strophic analysis
    (k)    isolation of poetic devices
    (l)    tabulation
    (m)   synthesis
    (n)    comparison with other literature.

Delimitation means isolating the stretch of poetic text or poem to be analysed. After division into strophes and stanzas—segmentation or stichometry—each strophe is examined in detail. The presence of various poetic devices both structural and non-structural is established and the results can be tabulated. Finally, the relationship of the components to the whole are determined.

An outline such as the one just described must remain to a certain extent theoretical. No single, uniform method of analysis applicable to every poem can, in fact, be proposed. It is more realistic to describe a variety of approaches which can be used either singly or in combination. Ultimately, of course, the poem is an individual entity which cannot be fitted into the straightjacket of rigid classification. (No poem worthy of the name 'follows the rules'.) One's choice of analytical procedure, therefore, must take all this into account.

### 3. *Some preliminaries*

Before tackling a poem it is advisable to do some preparatory work; a possible approach is outlined here.

    a. *Selection.* For a beginner it is probably easiest to choose a passage that is short and at the same time self-contained, for example, one of the briefer psalms. Choosing a short piece provides the opportunity for seeing the whole poem almost at a glance (and, incidentally, reduces the amount of time required). With practice longer poems can be tackled. Further, if a psalm is selected, then there is no problem about determining where it begins and where it

---

14. Analysis of ancient Near Eastern poetry is also helpful here. For the determination of metrical patterns cf. 5.3 METRE.

15. The bracketed letters refer to the paragraphs set out below.

ends, as would be the case in, say, a passage from the prophets. The fewer such problems to resolve the better.

b. *Commentaries*. It is always difficult to decide whether to study a passage without looking at what others have said about it, or whether to read the commentaries first. To come to a poem with fresh eyes is certainly very valuable and better than having someone else tell you how to read it. On the other hand, to consult commentaries and the like can save a great deal of work, especially as far as philology is concerned. Perhaps the best way is to read the chosen section of verse once or twice slowly, and only after personal reflection to look at the opinions of other scholars. The worked examples in the appendix of this book should be approached in much the same way.

c. *Translation*. At this point it is advisable to make a translation (although stylistic analysis has always to be based on the Hebrew text); textual and philological difficulties will come to light, which can either be solved now or may be held over until the poem is better understood. Often, such difficulties cannot be resolved without a close look at poetic structure; at the same time, this analysis is itself dependent on correct understanding of the Hebrew. The vicious circle can sometimes be broken by comparison with extra-biblical texts (in Ugaritic, Akkadian, etc.).

d. *Levels in* MT. The next obstacle to overcome is deciding at which level of the Masoretic text to operate. In many cases an 'original' layer of text has been overlaid by re-interpretations made at later stages, not to mention the various editorial hands which have been at work. Similar problems, it is worth remembering, exist for Ugaritic and Akkadian texts.[16] Should you try and reconstruct the basic or original text before stylistic analysis? The trouble here is that there is always the danger of working in a circle, for example, by cutting out what does not seem to fit and then arguing from the regularity of the resulting pattern. If, on the other hand, you take the text exactly as it is, there is the danger of considering later glosses or insertions as belonging to the poem. It is a matter of balance, though as a general rule it is better to leave the text alone and not begin emending.[17]

e. *Reading the poem through*. Once the poem has been selected for study it is a good idea to read it through a few times—aloud if possible—in order to get to know it and acquire the feel of it. In

---

16. Even though the clay tablets unearthed on excavation sites are originals, in many cases the text is a copy of a previous text.

17. See 3.7 on TEXTUAL CRITICISM.

practice this means how it sounds, where the repetitions lie, the general movement of thought and so on. Each time, the text must be read through *completely*. The poem must always be considered as a whole, even in the process of detailed analysis, since this acts as a check against excess (it is all too easy to pick out a structural pattern, for instance, but rather more difficult to fit it into the rest of the poem). Reading through is also a guide for selecting the most suitable approach (see g, below).

f. *Practicalities*. It is very useful to have to hand coloured pens or pencils,[18] squared paper, a stack of index cards and a ruler. They can be very time-saving, and can make keywords or gender-patterns evident at a glance, or speed up the compilation of a poem's vocabulary. Needless to add that besides commentaries, a good Hebrew dictionary and a concordance are essential items.

g. *Approaches*. The method of analysis already outlined (and set out in more detail below) is a general, all-purpose approach which has to be adapted for each poem. Some experimentation is required to determine the most suitable approach. Quite obviously, for example, a stretch of text where no words are repeated rules out the need to tabulate keywords. This is why a preliminary reading of the poem is of paramount importance and more than one read-through may be needed before the correct approach becomes evident.

4. *Analysis of Hebrew poetry: notes on method*
The brief synopsis given in section (2) will be expanded here and illustrated with examples.

h. *Delimitation*. The first stage, once the preliminaries are over, is to determine the beginning and end of the poem. While relatively easy when a poem is set in a prose context (for example, 1 Sm 2,1-10, the 'Song of Hannah', or Jer 30,5-7) delimitation is much more difficult when the bulk of a book is in verse. This is particularly true of the prophetical books where it is so often hard to tell where one oracle ends and another begins. Even in Job, where each speaker has his own stretch of text, there are problems. Fortunately, the individual Psalms[19] can be considered as independent poems—and at the other end of the scale, proverbial sayings (as preserved in Proverbs) are mini-poems, again with independent status. As will be seen, there are

18. Advocated by Margalit (Margulis), *UF* 7 (1975) 311, and Holladay, *JBL* 85 (1966) 412.
19. With exceptions such as Pss 42-43 or 9-10.

certain indications of opening and closure (e.g. an initial tricolon; a
final refrain), but an element of judgment cannot always be excluded.[20]

i. *Segmentation.* The next step is to divide the poem into its
components. Segmentation means strophic analysis (marking off the
couplets, tricola and so on) in combination with correct stichometry
(determining the limits of each colon).[21] Here, the principal guide is
*parallelism.* For example, Isa 29,14 runs:

לכן הנני יוסף להפליא את העם הזה הפלא ופלא

Therefore, see I am the one who is going to shock this people,
adding shock to shock.

It can be segmented as follows:

| | |
|---:|:---|
| לכן הנני | 14a |
| יוסף להפליא | 14b |
| את העם הזה | 14c |
| הפלא ופלא | 14d |

where 14a is an introductory monocolon, and 14bcd comprises an
ABA′ (chiastic) tricolon—which closes the stanza 29,13-14.

j. *Inner-strophic analysis.* Once the limits of each strophe are
known, then each strophe can be analysed into its components: type
of parallelism, sound-patterns, chiastic structure and the like. Note
that in the worked examples inner-strophic analysis has been set out
stanza by stanza, as it is then easier to follow.

k. *Isolation of poetic devices.* Both the poem as a whole and its
separate units should be looked at with an eye to structural and non-
structural devices (such as word-pairs, enjambment, metaphor, the
break-up of stereotype phrases). At this point it may be possible to
find out whether a particular device stands out more than the others
(for example, the dominant device in Ps 100 is ellipsis).

l. *Tabulation.* To achieve objectivity and in the interests of
accuracy it is occasionally helpful to draw up tables of repeated
words, structural patterns, alliterating consonants, word-pairs,
repeated words in parallelism (e.g. 'not//not' in Ps 131,1), formulae,
vocabulary peculiar to a poem, etc. If not already recognised,

---

20. A case in point is the collection of ten discourses in Prov 1-9, the exact allocation
of verses being a matter of dispute; see, conveniently, R.N. Whybray, *Wisdom in
Proverbs* (London, 1965).

21. E.J. Revell, 'Pausal Forms and the Structure of Biblical Poetry', *VT* 31 (1981)
186-199, argues that line-ends are marked by *pausal* forms or, conversely, that
'contextual forms are not used at the end of stichs'.

repeated elements such as the refrain or the envelope figure may become apparent at this stage. (Some of the worked examples show the use of tabulation.)

m. *Synthesis: functional analysis.* Having extracted as much data as possible from the chosen text, it remains to determine how the various poetic devices interact within the poem. Look for a dominant poetic device within each strophe or for the whole poem, and determine its function. Assess what particular purpose a refrain, say, has in the poem under analysis. Establish the relationship of sound-patterns to keywords; and so on.

n. *Comparison.* Although not always possible it is very helpful when a similar poem—whether within the Hebrew tradition or outside it—can be looked at for comparative purposes. It is more useful (though again, not always possible) to compare poems of similar literary form; for example a Hebrew lament with a Sumerian lament.

### Prov 23,29-35—Hangovers are Horrible

In this example both the preliminary steps and the methodical analysis will be followed. A final paragraph will deal with closure.

### Preliminaries

a. I *chose* this particular poem because at first glance it looked to be slightly out of the ordinary. It is not too long, but long enough to offer a challenge as regards interpretation.

b. The *commentaries* I looked at—after going over the poem several times first—included McKane and Scott, as well as Dahood's brief monograph.[22] Of these, McKane's was the most detailed and Scott's much shorter, but less hidebound by tradition. None paid any attention to structure; in fact, McKane obscured the series of repetitions in v. 29 by translating: 'Who has sorrow and care?' etc. Ultimately, my own analysis is independent of previous attempts.

c. As far as the *text* is concerned there are few problems—the kethibh/qere at 29c (מדינים for מדונים) and at 31c (כוס for כיס). The 'corrections' suggested in the apparatus of BH are simply attempts at making the text intelligible and can be ignored. I have set out the

---

22. W. McKane, *Proverbs. A New Approach* (OTL, 1970) 393-396; R.B.Y. Scott, *Proverbs and Ecclesiastes* (AB 18; Garden City, 1965); M.J. Dahood, *Proverbs and Northwest Semitic Philology* (Rome, 1963).

Hebrew text in anticipation of the structural analysis;[23] this is simply for reasons of space.

| | | |
|---:|:---:|:---:|
| למי אוי | 29a | I |
| למי אבוי | b | |
| למי מדינים | c | |
| למי שיח | d | |
| למי פצעים חנם | e | |
| למי חכללות עינים | f | |
| למאחרים על היין | 30a | |
| לבאים לחהקור ממסך | b | |
| אל תרא יין | 31a | II |
| כי יתאדם | b | |
| כי יתן בכוס עינו | c | |
| יתהלך במישרים | d | |
| אחריתו כנחש ישך | 32a | |
| כצפעני יפרש | b | |
| עיניך יראו זרות | 33a | |
| ולבך ידבר תהפכות | b | |
| והיית כשכב בלב ימוך | 34a | |
| (כ)שכב בראש חבל | b | |
| הכוני בל חליתי | 35a | |
| הלמוני בל ידעתי | b | |
| מתי אקיץ | c | |
| אוסיף אבקשנו עוד | d | |

Because of their rarity some of the words are obscure so that the *translation* is not perfectly straightforward. Problems are discussed in a separate section at the end. The style of my rendering is somewhat colloquial to match the content.

| | | |
|:---:|:---:|:---|
| I | 29a | Who gets the groans? |
| | b | Who gets the moans? |
| | c | Who gets (into) quarrels? |
| | d | Who gets (into) trouble? |
| | e | Who gets bruises for no reason? |
| | f | Who gets shadowy eyes? |

23. For the distinction between 'l'analyse. structurale' (of deep structures) and 'l'analyse structurelle' (of surface structure) cf. Vogels, *Bib* 60 (1979) 411. If anything, my approach belongs to the second category.

30a   People who stay up late over wine.
  b   People on the lookout for mixed drink.

II   31a   Don't look at wine
  b   if it looks like blood,
  c   if it sparkles in the goblet,
  d   (if) it sloshes up and down with bubbles.

32a   In the end it will bite like a snake,
  b   sting like a serpent.

33a   Your eyes will see weird things,
  b   your mind will talk nonsense;

34a   and you'll be like a person with a sinking stomach,
  b   like a person lying with a splitting head.

35a   'They bashed me: I felt no pain.
  b   They hit me: I did not realise (it).

  c   When I wake up
  d   I'll go searching for it again.'

d. Although the poet has undeniably expanded an eight-line poem to make it of full acrostic length, the pre-MT *level* will not be considered here, but the completed stage of the poem.

e. I *read through* the text several times and was struck, naturally, by the repetition, but also by a certain element of end-rhyme (though it was hard at this stage to tell whether it was intended) and by a feeling that many of the words had double meanings or contained hidden allusions. I realised, too, that there were problems in sticho-metry about halfway through (31) and right at the end. It also occurred to me that the overall pattern might be chiastic since certain words (keywords?) came more than once. Another striking feature was the double change of speaker and mood:

| | |
|---|---|
| 29-30 | interrogative + statement |
| 31-34 | imperative (prohibitive) |
| 35 | quotation of first person speaker |

f. Which *approach* (or combination of approaches) to use? As there were several unusual words, a lot of repetition and a suspected chiastic pattern, *tabulation* is required. No other patterns looked probable (except, of course, the obvious acrostic-type repetition in the first eight lines) so that ordinary step-by-step analysis seems suitable enough.

## Methodological analysis

g. The *limits* of the poem are clear enough: the immediate context at both ends (23,26-28 and 24,1ff.) deals with completely different topics. Whether 23,29-35 itself can be broken up into smaller units remains to be discussed.

h. *Segmentation* into verse-lines or cola presents no real problems, the first eight lines evidently each beginning with ל. They are probably to be grouped as couplets. The only quatrain is 31, perhaps with the structure 1 + 3. Finally, though 35cd could be a single, long line, it is more probably a bicolon (with enjambment), as the poem would then number 22 lines (couplet, couplet, couplet, couplet, quatrain, couplet, couplet, couplet, couplet, couplet). Two *stanzas* make up the poem (29-30 and 31-35), each to be subdivided as follows:

|     |     |     |     |
| --- | --- | --- | --- |
| I   | (a) 29abcdef | II  | (a) 31abcd-32ab |
|     | (b) 30ab |     | (b) 33ab-34ab |
|     |     |     | (c) 35abcd |

The stanza division is indicated by a combination of mood change (interrogative to imperative) and break in the sequence of lines beginning with the same letter.

i. *Inner-strophic analysis*: 29ab, cd and ef comprise a list formed of three parallel couplets, every line having two stresses except for 29ef which has 3+3. 30ab is another parallel couplet, and though the lines are quite long the stress pattern is again 2+2. The next stanza opens with a quatrain comprising one line (31a) plus three lines in parallel (31bcd). Then come an abc//b'c' couplet (32ab), three more couplets (33-35ab) and the final strophe, a structurally 'parallel' couplet (35cd).

j. Slightly inverting the recommended sequence, isolation of poetic devices will come after *tabulation*. The first table is of repeated words showing how they are distributed over the twenty-two lines.

| | | | | | | | |
|---|---|---|---|---|---|---|---|
| 29a | | | | | | מי ל | |
| b | | | | | | מי ל | |
| c | | | | | | מי ל | |
| d | | | | | | מי ל | |
| e | | | | | | מי ל | |
| f | | | | עין | | מי ל | |
| 30a | | | יין אחר | | | ל | |
| b | | | | | | ל | (חקר) |
| 31a | | | ראה יין | | | | |
| b | | | | כי | | | |
| c | | | עין | ב כי | | | |
| d | | | | ב | | | |
| 32a | | | אחר | כ | | | |
| b | | | | כ | | | |
| 33a | | | ראה | עין | | | |
| b | | לב | | | | | |
| 34a | | שכב לב כ ב | | | | | |
| b | | שכב   כ ב | | | | | |
| 35a | בל | | | | | | (בקש) |
| b | בל | | | | | | |
| c | | | | | | | |
| d | | | | | | | |

The only three repeated words (or roots) used throughout the whole poem are אחר, יין and עין. Note that a word for 'to search for' occurs in the final line of both stanzas (30b: חקר, 35b: בקש).

The second table lists rare or unique lexical items:

| | |
|---|---|
| אבוי | '(interjection)'; only here; cf. Akk. *aba*, 'what'. |
| אדם | 'to look like blood' or 'to appear red'; hitp. only here. |
| חבל | obscure: 'painful'(?), 'mast' (? if correct, only here) or 'mountain' (? metathetic form only here). |
| חכללות | 'dullness'; also Gen 49,12. |
| ממסך | 'mixed wine' or 'mixing bowl'; cf. Isa 65,11 and Ug. *mmskn*; obscure (see philological notes). |
| עין | 'bubble' (if so, only here); cf. Akk. *īnu*, 'bubble' and Ug. *yn 'n*, 'sparkling wine' (*CTA* 6 iv 42).[24] |
| פרש | 'to sting, pierce' (? only here). |
| צפעני | '(serpent)'; rare: Isa 11,8; 59,5 (cf. 14,29) and Jer 8,17. |
| מישרים | 'bubbles' (?) if related to Akk. *šāru*, 'wind, bubble'. |

---

24. For a somewhat different view cf. Driver, *JSS* 9 (1964) 348-349.

k. The following *poetic devices* are used in the poem: (for ease of evaluation they will be grouped into 'structural' and 'non-structural').

The first structural feature is *repetition*, as set out in table 1, and also of line-initial ל (eight times; seven times in the form למ־) in stanza I (*acrostic* pattern).[25] *Alliteration* occurs in 31bcd and 33b-35 (see below); also as initial—א in 35cd. In 31a and 31c the Ug. expression *yn 'n* 'bubbly wine' is *broken up*; similarly, the phrase נחשים צפענים 'viper-snakes' (Jer 8,17) is split up in 32ab. Table 1 indicates that there is *no* chiasmus, but the overall pattern of the poem seems to be:

| | |
|---|---|
| A | HEADACHE ('groans, moans', 29ab) |
| B | BRUISES ('bruises', 29e) |
| C | SEARCH FOR WINE (30b) |

[central section, perhaps chiastic:

| | |
|---|---|
| D | SEE WINE (31) |
| E | WINE 'STINGS' (32) |
| D' | SEE STRANGE THINGS (33)] |

| | |
|---|---|
| A' | HEADACHE (34a) |
| B' | BEATING (35ab) |
| C' | SEARCH FOR WINE (35cd). |

Of the non-structural components, the most striking is the *riddle* (posed in 29) set as a series of questions, in combination with *delayed explicitation* (as the answer is postponed to 30). Table 2 lists the *rare words* which form a sharp contrast to the almost infantile nature of the other lexical items used. Sound patterns (apart from alliteration) include *assonance* (35ab), *end-rhyme* (29ab: *'oy*, *ᵃboy*; 33ab *zarot*, *tahpukot*; cf. 35ab) and *onomatopoeia* (32 and perhaps 35cd). There are two sets of *paired similes* (32; 34), two examples of *wordplay* (29e פצעים and 32b צפעני = rootplay; עין = 'eye' in 29f and 33a, but by metaphorical extension, 'bubble' in 31c), and one case of *enjambment* (35cd: 'When I wake up I'll go searching for it again'). It is noteworthy that in almost the whole of the second stanza (that is, apart from 31a), the word 'wine' is never mentioned: this is *allusion* at its best. (For allusions to other Hebrew and Ugaritic texts, see below.)

Finally, the *imagery* requires comment: there is the general

---

25. Note the very similar pattern in the Kilamuwa Inscription, lines 10-12.13.15.

portrayal of a drunk which forms the basis of the poem. This is supplemented not only by the detailed observation (the intoxicated man who picks fights, has hallucinations, talks drivel, feels very sick and still craves drink on waking) but also by apt similes and an evocative description of wine.

1. The *functions* of the poetic features described can be evaluated in terms of the relationship between poet and audience, in terms of structure and in terms of other effects.

The opening riddle immediately engages the audience's attention: they feel invited to solve it. The clues, in the form of questions, are vague at first but become more and more specific, so that by the time the answer is given (30), it simply confirms what most of the listeners must have guessed already.[26]

To keep the audience interested, the poet breaks his steady sequence of *lamedh*-initial lines and changes to direct admonition ('Do not look at wine', 31a) going on to describe how enticing the beverage is. Similes help sustain interest, and their originality commands respect. In 35a the change to the first person ('I felt no pain . . . ') prepares for the close, but more importantly, makes the listeners identify with the unfortunate drinker. Finally comes the punch-line: the habitual imbiber is hard to cure.

At the macro-structural level, the poem is defined by its quasi-acrostic form (= 22 lines). The ABC,DED'A'B'C'-pattern identified serves to depict the inevitability of the cyclic sequence: craving for drink—imbibing—bad effects of alcohol—recovery and craving for drink.

At a lower level, alliteration serves to bond together certain groups of lines:[27]

| | | |
|---|---|---|
| 31b | *kî YIT'addām* | |
| c | *kî YITTēn bakkōs* . . . | |
| d | *YIThallēk bᵉ* . . . | |
| | | |
| 33b | *wLBk* | |
| 34a | *BLB* | |
| b | *ḥBL* | |
| 35a | *BL* | |
| b | *BL* | |

26. Comparable are the photograph quizzes where a small portion of an object is depicted (perhaps viewed from a peculiar angle) and contestants have to guess what it is; as more and more of the object is revealed, it becomes progressively easier to determine what it is.

27. In the second group there is alliterative rootplay, evidently.

and to bond the pseudo-couplet 35cd. The same bonding effect is achieved by the word-pairs in 31a.c, 32ab and by rhyme (29ab, 33ab, 35ab) which also indicates where these particular lines end (stichometry).

A variety of devices also adds to the aesthetic effect of the poem. Onomatopoeia in 32 evokes the well-known hissing of snakes:

> *k<sup>e</sup>nāḥāš yiššāk*
> *k<sup>e</sup>ṣip'onî yapriš*

while the hiccough-line sequences in 35 bring to mind the noise of vomiting. The final enjambment (35cd) helps round off the poem by creating a strong contrast with the chopped up phrases right at the beginning (29). The use of repressed reference in most of the second stanza, where the significant word 'wine' is hardly mentioned, complements the riddle-sequence in the first stanza.

Reverting to the relationship between poet and audience, two further points can be made. The poet has included quite a few rare words and forms (see table 2) to enhance his authority since, ultimately, his poem is an admonition against excessive drinking. The same applies to his many inner-Hebrew allusions (to Song, to Gen 49, Isa 5,11, to the style of the Instructions in Prov 1-9) which mark him as a man of traditional learning and therefore worthy of respect.[28]

m. Although no other poem of exactly this type is known, the second half can be *compared* with other wisdom-compositions such as RS 22.439 i 21-25.[29] The theme of excessive drinking is commonplace and is found not only in such texts as Prov 20,1; 23,20; Qoh 2,24; 7,2 and Sir 31,25-30[30] but in the composition just cited (line 17: 'Son, do not go into the house of drinking') as well.

If 35b of our poem (הלמוני בל ידעתי) is an allusion to the expression *wdlyd'nn ylmn* of *Ugar.* 5, 1 obv. 8, then the poem may mock the orgy-like wakes of Ugaritic tradition.[31] Other links with the same tradition include the simile 'bite like a serpent' and the phrase 'which bubbles in the cup', as well as the word-pair 'heart//head'.

---

28. Another function of such allusions is economy of expression.

29. See Smith, *RSP* II, 233-234; according to him the structure of stanza II, which he treats as an independent poem, is I: Admonition (31); II: Motivation—(a) wisdom sentence (32), (b) conditional result (33-35).

30. Texts (except Sir) cited by Khanijan, *RSP* II, 376-377.

31. See, too, Ludlul II, 49-109 (*BWL*, 40-45); it is significant that Egyptian parallels are lacking.

It seems apposite to end this analysis of poetic technique in Prov 23,29-35 by commenting on how the poem achieves closure (see CLOSURE). By closure is meant not merely the way the poem ends (though this is a fundamental aspect of closure) but how it effects completeness. Our text appears to be complete since it uses a twenty-two line frame which corresponds to the completeness of the alphabet. Yet, it begins halfway through the standard run of letters (at *lamedh*), and ends with an *aleph*-line (reinforced by *aleph*-initial alliteration). The inescapable implication, therefore, is that the poem is describing a continuous cycle, the 'ending' (with the drunkard preparing for another bout) being only a return to the 'beginning'. The poem, in fact, starts after proceedings have already begun and the real opening line is at the beginning of stanza II. If the cycle can be stopped here ('Do not look at wine . . . ') then all is well and the poet has drawn attention to his hidden opening line by using an initial *aleph* (אל תרא יין) in v. 31a.[32]

### Philological notes

Here I will only comment on obscurities of meaning, without repeating what was set out in table 2 (rare words). The first difficulty is חכללות (29f.). It is in no way related to Akkadian *ekêlu*, 'to be dark', as Byington once suggested,[33] and probably means 'shadowy' or perhaps 'lustreless'.[34] A variant (it would seem) or the same word occurs in Gen 49,12 where the colour in question is compared to wine and contrasted with dazzling white teeth:

| | |
|---|---|
| חכלילי עינים מיין | Darker(?) are his eyes than wine, |
| ולבן שנים מחלב | whiter his teeth than milk.[35] |

Disputed, too, is ממסך (30b); Joüon's proposal of the rendering 'bowl'

---

32. For such cyclic non-closing poems see Smith, *Closure*, 66-67. Le Groupe μ, *Rhétorique de la poésie* (Paris, 1977), 151-152, point out that such cyclic sequences have the effect of neutralising time, as in James Joyce's *Finnegan's Wake*, the closing sentence of which is completed by the opening words of the whole book. Such timelessness is a recognised feature of proverbial material.

33. Byington, *JBL* 66 (1945) 351, who considered the expression to mean 'black eyes from fighting'.

34. 'The reference is perhaps to lustreless eyes rather than to dark rings under the eyes' (McKane: 1970, 393).

35. For this couplet see most recently C.H. Gordon, 'The Wine-Dark Sea', *JNES* 37 (1978) 51-52.

would appear to be bolstered by Ugaritic *mmskn*, 'mixing-bowl',[36] but not all scholars accept this view.[37] Although יתאדם in 31b is normally translated 'looks red' (hitp. of אדם, 'to be red'), the metaphorical expression דם עצים, 'blood of trees',[38] indicates 'looks like blood' to be preferable. The verb would then be a denominative from אדם, 'blood' (a by-form of commoner דם).[39] Since עין in 31c must mean 'bubble'[40] it can be argued that מישרים (31d) may be related to Akkadian *šāru*, 'wind, bubble',[41] and so I translate 'it sloshes (lit. goes) up and down with bubbles'.[42] Less likely cognates are Ugaritic *mšr*, 'to go', and Akkadian *šarāru*, 'to tip'.[43] The real crux of these few lines, though, is 34 with its twin similes. The first simile is generally translated 'like a man on the high seas'[44] and is understood as a reference to the agonising sea-sickness of a landlubber in mid-ocean. Accordingly, all commentators attempt to force a nautical meaning on 34b as well since it is evidently parallel to 34a. For example, NEB has 'like one who clings to the top of the rigging', while Scott, emending the text, suggested 'like one who rolls drunkenly like the top of the mast'.[45] As it stands the Hebrew can be rendered 'like one who is lying on the masthead'—although חבל, 'mast', occurs only here—and both similes could then be interpreted as describing a drunken man tossing about like a ship at sea. Such imagery is attractive, but unfortunately explanations remain unsatisfactory.

36. The Ugaritic evidence is adduced by Dahood: 1963, 49, who refers to Joüon, *MUSJ* 4 (1911) 3.

37. For example, McKane: 1970, 393 accepts the meaning for Isa 65,11 but not for our passage.

38. Gen 49,11 and Dt 32,14—corresponding to Ug. *dm 'ṣm*, 'blood of trees' (*CTA* 4 iii 44); cf. דם ענב, 'grape blood', in Sir 39,26.

39. The by-form may also occur in Isa 63,2, 'Why is there blood (אדם) on your clothing?' Kevin Cathcart reminded me of Akk. *adāmu*, 'blood' and *adamatu*, 'black blood' (*CAD* A/1, 94 and 95).

40. Cf. Akk. *īnu*, 'bubble' (*CAD* I/J, 157b) and the Ug. phrase *yn 'n* 'sparkling wine' (*CTA* 6 iv 42). For a good discussion of the existence of effervescent wines in ancient times cf. J.C. de Moor, *The Seasonal Pattern in the Ugaritic Myth of Ba'lu* (*AOAT* 16; Neukirchen/ Vluyn, 1971) 223-224. For another view cf. Margalit, *AMOLAD*, 172, who translates the Ug. expression 'I'll cast an eye', reading *šdyn* as a single word.

41. *AHw*, 1192-1193.

42. In Akk., too, the Gt of *alāku* ('to go') refers to the motion of liquids; texts in *CAD* A/1, 326, meaning 6c.

43. The Ug. verb would require the Heb. to be repointed with *s*. For the Akk. verb cf. *AHw*, 1185-1186.

44. NEB, 'Like a man tossing out at sea'.

45. Scott: 1970, 142 and n.g.

The clue to understanding the similes correctly is provided by the final lines of a difficult Ugaritic text where the cure for a hangover is set out.[46] The wording is

| | |
|---|---|
| *dyšt llṣbh ḫš* | What the troubled one should put on his forehead, |
| *ʿrk lb [w]riš* | settling heart (and) head: |
| *pqq wšrh yšt* | the knot of a vine-shoot and its centre should he put, |
| *aḥdh dm zt ḥrpnt* | together with autumnal olive-juice. |

The topic is similar to that of Prov 23, but the most relevant feature of this prescription is the phrase *lb [w]riš*, 'heart (and) head', indicating that the equivalent Hebrew terms should be understood literally as referring to parts of the body. The couplet in v. 34 can then be translated:

> And you will be like one lying down with a heart that sinks,
> (like) one lying down with a headache.

This involves a minor textual change: the first two letters of line *b* (וכ־) are to be read at the end of line *a*, to give *bᵉlêb yâmûk*. The verb here is either מוד or מכך, both meaning 'to be low, to sink'.[47] In line *b*, the comparative particle is either to be understood (cf. כשכב in line *a*) or is to be read after the sequence ימוד (perhaps omitted by haplography).[48]

### 3.2 *Function in Poetry*

In spite of its brevity, this paragraph is one of the most important in the whole book. The principle of function, in fact, pervades all that is said about poetic devices and is fully illustrated in the worked examples.

It is not enough merely to single out, identify and label a whole range of poetic devices in a poem or set of poems. Of course (as

46. *Ugar* 5 1: rev. 4-6 = *KTU* 1.114, 29-31. For the translation cf. K.J. Cathcart—W.G.E. Watson, 'Weathering a Wake: A Cure for a Carousal. A Revised Translation of *Ugaritica* V text 1', *PIBA* 4 (1980) 35-58.

47. Note the kindred usage of Ug. *m(w)k* or *mkk*, 'to sink down', in *CTA* 2 iv 17-18: 'Strong was Yammu: he did not sink down (*lymk*); his vertebrae did not quiver; his frame did not quake'—a passage specially significant since it describes what happens (or rather, does not happen) after Yammu had been struck (*ylm*) on the chest by Baal's axe (lines 15-17a). (Note, too, that both this passage and the verses from Prov use a list of body-parts.) For the verb cf. de Moor: 1971 (cited, note 40), 136 and compare the noun *mk*, 'low place, hollow pit' (*CTA* 4 viii 12).

48. A third possibility is a shared consonant at word-boundary. Margalit, *AMOLAD*, 73, n. 2 suggests instead 'with a "swollen" head'.

spelled out above in detail) analysis of this kind is essential, but it is only a beginning and unless continued, leads nowhere.[49] For instance, it is not immediately apparent that the paired nouns in each of the following two lines are matched in gender:

| | |
|---|---|
| כסה שמים הודו | His GLORY (m.) covered the HEAVENS (m.), |
| ותהלתו מלאה הארץ | and the EARTH (f.) was full of his PRAISE (f.) |
| | (Hab 3,3) |

Once the pattern has been noticed by analysis, the poetic device 'gender-matched synonymous parallelism' can be recognised. The next essential step, then, is to find out *why* this poetic device has been used here. Closer inspection suggests it functions as *merismus* (meaning that certain representative components of a larger object are mentioned instead of the whole). Another look at the couplet shows the polar word-pair 'heavens//earth' to be present, and, more significantly, the verb מלא, 'to be full'. All these elements—gender-matched synonyms, the verb, and the word-pair and the verb ארץ—שמים combine to convey the idea of *completeness* which fits in with the meaning of the couplet. In other words, *the main function* of the poetic features identified is *to express merismus*.[50]

After identifying a poetic device, therefore, its function has to be determined. Note that evaluation of function can take place at various levels: with respect to strophe, stanza or poem; with respect to audience and poet; or with respect to style and aesthetic effect. (See presently.) When more than one poetic feature is present (as is usually the case), they interrelate, within the context of the whole poem.

---

49. See especially Leech, *Guide*, 4. For the concept of rhetorical function in Hebrew and in Hebrew poetry see F.I. Andersen, *The Sentence in Biblical Hebrew* (The Hague, 1974) 121-124; Ceresko, *CBQ* 40 (1978) 1-10 and Watson, 'Chiastic Patterns', 145-149. The functions of proverbs are discussed by J.M. Thompson, *The Form and Function of Proverbs in Ancient Israel* (The Hague/Paris, 1974). According to him, poetic devices are used to make proverbs ring true and to give them popular appeal; the function of proverbs themselves is mainly to provide philosophical insight with sub-functions such as entertainment, instruction and embodiment of legal usage. G.M. Green, 'Some Wherefores of English Inversions', *Lang* 56 (1980) 582-601, discusses the connective, introductory, emphatic, pragmatic and rhetorical functions of inversion, pointing out that there is no one-to-one correspondence between function and form.

50. Chiasmus is also present ('glory heavens—earth praise') which may function as merismus (in line with the other devices), add an element of tension, or combine both these functions.

Note, also, that a particular poetic device need not always have the same function every time it is used; chiasmus, for example, can serve to link the components of a poem (as in Nah 1,2) or can express emphatic negation (Ps 89,34); merismus is not the only idea gender-matched synonymous parallelism can convey: it can also express abundance (Isa 54,2), antithesis (Mic 7,6) or it may simply be used for the sake of parallelism (Gen 49,11). Accordingly, care is required to establish which particular function is operative in the poem to hand.

*Functions and sub-functions.* A particular poetic device generally has only one characteristic function; onomatopoeia, for example, serves to convey the meaning of a word by sound. Other devices may have one dominant function and several subordinate ones; chiasmus, say, is basically a structural device, but it can also heighten antithesis, depict reversal, connote identity and so on. Again, certain poetic features have two equally important functions; a case in point is the refrain which marks off the segments of a poem and at the same time acts as a link throughout the succession of stanzas. Finally, where several poetic devices are present together, they may either combine to achieve one single effect (in Hab 3,3—cited above—this would be merismus), or they may each have their own function.[51]

*Classifying functions.* In general, functions can be classified in at least three ways, with a certain degree of overlap. First of all they can be related to the interplay between poet and audience (performance); then, they can belong to the way a poem is built up (structure); lastly, come non-structural functions (stylistic-aesthetic). A table will illustrate these groupings:

| 1. | functions in respect of performance | *poet*: to help him produce verse |
| | | *audience*: to sustain their interest |
| 2. | functions in respect of structure | of *whole poem* |
| | | of *stanza* |
| | | of *strophe* |
| 3. | stylistic-aesthetic functions | i.e. non-structural functions |

---

51. Such overlap, where it exists, is very useful as a *control* in determining function.

1. *Functions related to performance*
Evidently many poetic devices and techniques relate to oral improvisation in front of an audience. They can be divided into those required by the poet for spontaneous and continuous composition, and those intended to promote fuller audience participation.[52] The division, of course, is not so clear-cut in practice since the two sets overlap.

POET: The chief function of a repertoire of poetic devices is to facilitate smooth, imaginative verse composition and so maintain the attention of a potentially critical audience. By using the technique of adding style, a set of traditional patterns and a measure of economy, the trained poet is able to keep up the flow. The more versatile performer can display his skill in a variety of ways. Accordingly, *performer-related functions* can be set out as follows:

> —*adding-style*: here can be grouped such devices as parataxis, word-pairs, traditional formulae, formulaic phrases, expletives (= ballast variants), parallelism (also phrase break-up; certain structural patterns). Generally speaking, these are the ready-made components of a poem. Also, lists.
> —*structure*: though related to the foregoing, they are not part of the adding-style technique. Instead they form a framework into which the poet can fit his improvised lines. Such a framework can be an acrostic, a chiastic pattern, a graded numerical sequence or a series of motifs. (Related are repetition and parallelism.)
> —*thrift* dictates the use of devices such as allusion, hyperbole and merismus.
> —*skill*: to display his skill the poet can use allusion, gender-matched parallelism, lists and tours, wordplay and parody.

AUDIENCE: The factors already mentioned are operative here, but form a different aspect. The listening audience needs aids to attention, and assistance in following the movement of the poem especially when long or difficult. It must also be charmed by the familiar, yet aroused and captivated by the unexpected. *Audience-related functions* are, therefore, set out under the following heads:

> —*Sequence or continuity* is indicated by such devices as repetition (in all its forms, e.g. terrace-pattern), numerical word-pairs, three synonym cola, simile.

---

52. See Green, *Lang* 56 (1980) 585, for a brief discussion of audience-related and speaker-related functions.

—*Aids to attention* can take two forms: either devices which slow down the onward movement of the poem, allowing time for the listeners to absorb its content (these are repetition, parallelism, word-pairs), or devices intended to jar interest (such as various kinds of symmetry breakers, defeated expectancy, staircase parallelism).

—*Other functions* include assisting the forward movement of a poem (devices which create suspense or surprise); increasing dramatic tension (enjambment, delayed identification, staircase parallelism); highlighting certain elements (by sound patterns); replacing overworked adjectives (e.g. hyperbole) and so on.

## 2. *Functions related to structure*

A whole variety of devices are structural in function, used to build up a strophe, stanza or poem, as well as to emphasise or demarcate certain structural features. They can be divided into three classes:

—*Metrical.* Certain devices are demanded by the metre and the appropriate ones are selected by the poet to create or maintain the metrical pattern of his lines, for example, archaic words, expletives and the broken construct chain.

—*Segmental.* Other devices mark off the divisions of a poem or provide it and its components with a structural pattern. The envelope figure and the refrain mark off larger segments of a poem; overall chiastic patterns provide a framework for stanzas and groups of stanzas, suggest the relationship between parts of poems and mark off their limits. Other structural-segmental devices are keywords, the acrostic pattern, changes in metre or strophic pattern and so on.

—*Cohesive.* The function of binding together components of strophe, stanza or poem is filled by quite a spectrum of devices. The exploitation of sound (by assonance, alliteration, etc.) can link otherwise separate elements or even provide a sound-pattern for a whole poem. Cohesion can also be achieved by repetition, occasionally by similes, by word-pairs (and parallelism in general), and by verse patterns such as the terrace, staircase parallelism, tours and lists.

## 3. *Stylistic-aesthetic functions*

Under this rather general heading are included largely non-structural devices. The following functions can be listed:

—to provide a particular effect, for example the staccato (two-stress) style to indicate battle or flight; onomatopoeia to evoke a definite sound (of a bird, say);

—to convey a certain idea: of completeness by using an acrostic,[53]
or of vagueness and mystery by repressed reference and allusion;
—for ornamentation (simile) or rhetorical effect (repetition);
—to provide a pleasing sound by assonance, rhyme, alliteration
either together or separately;
—to heighten antithesis or express reversal of events by using
chiasmus, reversed gender-matching or reversed word-pairs;

and the list could be extended.

To conclude the section on function, it must be evident by now
how important it is in interpreting poetry. The classification set out
above is intended only as a guideline—and it is clear that there is a
great deal of overlap as well as a certain degree of omission. However,
the section is only in the nature of a general statement; in the chapter
on individual poetic devices the functions to be assigned each device
are set out in finer detail. The worked examples, particularly Prov
23,29-35, show how poetic devices and function are related within
individual poems.[54]

### 3.4 *Archaisms*

A distinction has to be made between *archaic usage*, when ancient
forms are used with consistent correctness in recent writings, and
*archaising*, when there is mixed (incorrect with correct) use of
ancient words and forms.[55] Because any language is in a state of
continual change, it will contain a mixture of archaic speech, new
coinages and a main body of what can be termed 'neutral' language.
In any given community older and younger people share a common
language, yet represent the extremes of that language. The older part
of the community, resistant to change, will preserve archaic usage,
while their younger counterparts will tend to innovate and accept if
not invent new forms of speech. As the older generation dies out, the
younger people in their turn will take over as preservers of the older
speech, while *their* children become the innovators. The change is
gradual so that at any one time[56] there is the mixture of older,

---

53. Also by gender-matched synonymous parallelism, merismus, three-synonym
cola, the list and by tours (= lists of synonyms).

54. For the importance of providing an explanation to data collected from a poem
see H.G. Widdowson, *Stylistics and the Teaching of Literature* (London, 1975), 23, and
the worked example, 7-14 ('Leda and the Swan').

55. On archaisms in Hebrew poetry see the bibliography for this section and under
DATING, below. See, in general, Ullmann, *Language*, 167-172.

56. That is to say, synchronically as opposed to diachronically.

established and more recent levels of language. Other factors besides the generation or grandparent-parent-child cycle are operative, too. For instance, speech in provincial and isolated areas will change at a slower rate than in a busy city; the differing levels of education and class play their part, and there is always the influence of foreign language to be reckoned with, particularly in trade-centres or in frontier settlements.

Traditional poetic diction follows much the same pattern of change as does ordinary language,[57] though slightly different factors are at work. The rate of change will be very much slower, chiefly because there is a whole range of advantages for the composing poet who retains archaisms. They are metrically useful and in any case traditional formulae, word-pairs, rare vocabulary and the like forged by previous poets are too handy to be easily abandoned, forming as they do the stock-in-trade of the professional.[58]

In Hebrew, archaisms were preserved in traditional poetry, particularly folk-songs and proverbs, and in liturgical compositions such as the psalms. Unfortunately, we can only guess at the extent of archaisms and archaic forms in Hebrew poetry for a variety of reasons. Identification of outmoded usage depends on 1. the time between the original composition of a text and contemporary language; on 2. our knowledge of the linguistic background to a text (which implies dating); and 3. on the context.[59] Taking these indicators one by one we arrive at the following picture for Hebrew. It can be safely assumed that the prophets used the language of their time, so that theoretically at least it should be possible to detect archaisms; with regard to liturgical and wisdom poems, tradition tended to live on, so that a timeless element has to be reckoned with. In the case of wisdom literature, though, modern usage must inevitably have crept in—resulting in a mixture. Hypothetically, therefore, we should be in a position to determine archaic elements in certain kinds of poetry. What is sketchy, though, is our knowledge of the linguistic background to the various stages in the Hebrew language. Archaeological discovery and scholarly research are gradually extending the limits of this knowledge, but we are far from being able to put together anything like a complete picture.[60] Finally, detection of archaisms

57. Parry, *HSCP* 43 (1932) 9-12.
58. See Leech, *Guide*, 13-16.52.
59. For these theoretical principles see Ullmann, *Language*, 161-172.
60. Particularly useful in this regard is the Hebrew inscriptional material from the

varies from context to context. The Books of Chronicles, to take a prose example, purport to have been written in pre-exilic times, but are in fact the product of the post-exilic period. To mask his modernity the author[61] has used a sprinkling of archaisms (strictly speaking: archaising), and these can be picked out.[62]

In addition, there is a whole range of complicating factors which needs to be taken into account. There is obviously the problem of older material which may have been taken over unchanged from ancient sources. And these ancient sources may have been part of Hebrew tradition, or they may have been, let us say, Canaanite. Here again, the source-material will probably have been tampered with (pagan components could not be used in Hebrew tradition), making the recognition of archaic elements even more difficult.[63] The presence of 'Ugaritisms' such as the meaning 'from' for the preposition ל (to take only one out of hundreds of examples) is by no means a clear indication of archaic usage. Another complicating factor is dialect: diphthongs were contracted in Northern Hebrew (as in Ugaritic), but not in Southern Hebrew.[64] There is, too, the problem of so-called prosaic elements such as the relative אשׁר, the definite article (-הַ), the object-marker את and colon-initial ו which, it would seem, were absent from early poetry.[65] Also, obsolete terms could be revived and become part of current language.[66] In view of such a welter of imbricating components, it is not surprising that the identification of archaisms has yielded few results. Some idea of what is involved can be gained from the accompanying table.

Leech distinguishes between *archaism*, 'the survival of the language of the past into the language of the present', and what he terms *linguistic anachronism* or 'the conscious and calculated resurrection of language belonging to a bygone age'[67] which brings us to the

---

Levant; see, conveniently, J.C.L. Gibson, *Textbook of Syrian Semitic Inscriptions*, vol. I (Oxford, 1971).

61. Or authors; cf. S. Japhet, 'The Supposed Common Authorship of Chronicles Considered Anew', *VT* 18 (1968) 330-371.

62. See Watson: 1972.

63. A possible example of a Canaanite poem which has been absorbed into Hebrew tradition is Ps 29, though many scholars (e.g. Craigie) dispute this.

64. An oversimplification; see, further, Z.S. Harris, *Development of the Canaanite Dialects* (*AOS* 16; New Haven, 1939); G. Garbini, *Le lingue semitiche* (Naples, 1972), and the survey in Watson: 1969, 11-43.

65. See Watson: 1969, 48-52.

66. Ullmann, *Language*, 171.

67. Leech, *Guide*, 52.

problem of *dating* poetry (discussed more fully in 3.5). All language contains archaisms; poetic language merely tends to use more archaisms than normal, a difference of degree which has to be taken into account in determining dates. The presence of obsolete language in Ruth, for example, does not show it to be an ancient book *tout court*, since closer inspection reveals that the outmoded turns of phrase have been put into the mouths of older people. The question that has to be put, therefore, is not whether archaisms are present, but *why* they are used and *how*. Only by correctly answering such questions can any progress in assigning dates to particular compositions be made.

Accordingly, the next topic is the variety of reasons for using archaisms. As already indicated, poets were heavily dependent on traditional material in composing and improvising: it was what they had been trained with and what they best knew. For practical reasons, then, they incorporated old-fashioned elements of all kinds (word-pairs, expressions, grammatical usage, etc.) into their works. Archaisms were also used deliberately in order to convey an antiquated flavour to poetry, making it seem more venerable and authentic and so more acceptable. Archaisms could also help convey the personality of a character,[68] be used to humorous effect or provide a touch of local colour.

| prosaic/more recent elements | dialect components | archaic words (or forms) preserved | Ugaritic material |
|---|---|---|---|
| את | contraction or not of | dem. pron. | $b$ = 'from' |
| אשר | diphthongs | remnants of nominal cases[69] | $l$ as vocative enclitic *mem* |
| ה־ | colloquialisms [68a] | | vocabulary[70] |

TABLE showing a few of the complexities involved
in determining whether archaisms are present.

68.  In the Book of Ruth, for example, 'Boaz and Naomi talk like older people. Their speeches contain archaic morphology and syntax' (E. Campbell, *Ruth* [AB 7; Garden City, 1975] 17)—confirmed by Ruth 2,21 where young Ruth uses archaic language when quoting Boaz.

68a.  Cf. G. Abrahamson, 'Colloquialisms in the OT', *Semitics* 2 (1971-72) 1-16.

69.  An example in poetry is the disguised accusative ending in Isa 30,1, recognised by Dahood, *Bib* 50 (1969) 57-58.

70.  See Dahood's series of contributions on Ugaritic-Hebrew lexicography in *Bib*.

BIBLIOGRAPHY

Albright, W.F. 'Archaic Survivals in the Text of Canticles', *Driver FS*, 1963, 1-7.
Freedman, D.N. 'Archaic Forms in Early Hebrew Poetry', *ZAW* 31 (1960) 101-106.
Watson, D.G. *Text-Restoration Methods in Contemporary U.S.A. Biblical Scholarship* (Naples, 1969) 45-136, with bibliography.
Watson, W.G.E. 'Archaic Elements in the Language of Chronicles', *Bib* 53 (1972) 191-207, esp. 205-206.

## 3.5 *Dating*

*Overview*

The only work specifically on the problem of dating Hebrew poetry is Robertson: 1972, and he deals with 'early' poems—twelfth to ninth centuries BC. Here the problem of assigning dates to poems or the application of criteria for dating can be dealt with only marginally, for two reasons. One is lack of space; the other is that the present work is a diachronic rather than a synchronic study. It is concerned with the poetry of all periods. All that can be done here is to outline criteria for dating and then set out the generally accepted dates for the various blocks of Hebrew poetry as a working guide.

*Criteria*

Broadly speaking, criteria for dating can be assigned to one of two classes: grammatical and stylistic. More work has been carried out on grammatical criteria since 'measurement' can be more rigorous; little has been effected for criteria of style, though claims in this area are often stated boldly. *Grammatical criteria* include such aspects as spelling (the older the text the fewer the vowel letters, for example),[71] the use of *yqtl* as a past tense (cf. Ugaritic), the use of ה as a relative pronoun and so on. The most detailed study is, again, Robertson: 1972.

*Stylistic criteria* would embrace *yqtl-qtl* and *qtl-yqtl* parallel sequences,[72] the use of the terrace pattern or staircase parallelism[73] and other poetic devices. In this category, too, belongs comparison with datable poetry: if it can be shown that a certain poem is similar in style to early poetry (e.g. Ugaritic verse) or a poem such as Ps 137,

---

71. Full discussion in Watson: 1969, 45-136.
72. Held, *Neuman FS*, 281-290.
73. Loewenstamm, *JSS* 14 (1969) 176-196.

then that particular poem may be of the same date. To be reckoned with here, of course, is the possible presence of archaisms, which tend to confuse the issue.

*Chronological table*

The problems associated with assigning dates to poems or even to complete books in classical Hebrew are very complex. However, as a working hypothesis and for the sake of convenience, a table is provided here for the books of the OT and for some of the more important poems.[74]

```
1150—Ex 15* Jgs 5* Ps 29
1000—Dt 32* Hab 3* Job* Ps 18*
 950—Song
 900—Ps 78* Dt 33* Gen 49 Nb 23-24
 850—
 800—
 750—Am
 740—Isa I
 730—Hos
 700—Isa 28-33, 36-39
 650—Zeph
 625—Jer
 615—Nah
 600—Hab
 580—Ez
 550—Isa II
 520—Hag, Zech
 500—
 450—Mal Obd
 400—Joel
 350—
 300—Qoh
 250—
 200—
 150—Dan
 100—
```

74.  Those marked * have been dated by Robertson: 1972, 155. Most commentators would assign Job to about the 6th century. A.D.H. Mayes, *Deuteronomy* (London, 1979), 382, dates Dt 32 to the same period, following Fohrer.

BIBLIOGRAPHY

The only work directly on this topic is a 1966 doctoral thesis:
Robertson, D.A. *Linguistic Evidence in Dating Early Hebrew Poetry* (SBL Dissertation Series 3, Missoula, 1972).
For a different approach see:
Watson, W.G.E. 'Trends in the Development of Classical Hebrew Poetry: A Comparative Study', *UF* 14 (1982) [in press].
Also: Becking, B. 'Bee's Dating Formula and the Book of Nahum', *JSOT* 18 (1980) 100-104.
Bee, R.E. 'Dating the Book of Nahum: A Response to the Article by Bob Becking', *JSOT* 18 (1980) 104.
—'An Empirical Dating Procedure for OT Prophecy', *JSOT* 11 (1972) 23-35 ('texts produced after 440 B.C. were accurately scanned by the Masoretes').
Fensham, F.C. 'The use of the Suffix Conjugation and the Prefix Conjugation in a few old Hebrew Poems', *JNSL* 6 (1978) 9-18 (on Pss 29; 82 and 93).
Hurvitz, A. 'The Chronological Significance of "Aramaisms" in Biblical Hebrew', *IEJ* 18 (1968) 234-40.
—'The Date of the Prose-tale of Job Linguistically Reconsidered', *HTR* 67 (1974) 17-34.
Watson, D.G. *Text-restoration Methods in Contemporary U.S.A. Biblical Scholarship* (Naples, 1969).

For the history of Hebrew language, especially in relation to extra-biblical inscriptions:
Gibson, J.C.L. *Syrian Semitic Inscriptions, vol. 1. Hebrew and Moabite Inscriptions.* (Oxford, 1971).
Lémaire, A. 'L'épigraphie paléo-hébraïque et la bible', *VTS* 29 (1978) 165-176.
Millard, A.R. 'The Canaanite Linear Alphabet and its Passage to the Greeks', *Kadmos* 15 (1976) 130-144, esp. the table, 142-143.
Moran, W.L. 'The Hebrew Language and its Northwest Semitic Background', *Albright FS*, 1961, 54-72.
See also under ARCHAISMS.

## 3.6 *Textual Criticism*

'The ideal of textual criticism is to present the text which the author intended.'[75] Textual criticism aims at establishing that the text in existence now is identical with the text as it left the hands of the author, or at reconstructing that text if only part of it exists now. However, such a description remains an ideal. Aside from the obvious difficulties inherent in the transmission of any text over time

---

75. Thorpe: 1972, 50 and 79.

and space—due to omissions, copyists' errors, loss or destruction of text, later editing and the like—the very concept of 'one author one manuscript' is inexact. Even with the invention of printing and where modern books are concerned the published work does not always coincide with the original manuscript. And conditions in the ancient Near East hardly compare with a modern publishing house. In any case, for the people of Mesopotamia and Syria 'author' was almost meaningless. Most writers stayed anonymous (the classical prophets of the Hebrew tradition are exceptional, but can we say who wrote each psalm?) and many literary works are the result of compilation. The picture is complicated even more: often several versions of the same work were in circulation at the same time. This was the case with the Epic of Gilgamesh, available in Sumerian, Akkadian and Hittite, and it was certainly true for the Hebrew text of what we call the Old Testament. Is the search for the correct Hebrew text doomed from the start, then?

In practice the normative edition of the Hebrew text is the Masoretic text.[76] Criticism of this text reached absurd proportions in the last century, when obscure words and expressions were emended away or changes were made for the sake of metre. A turning-point was the finding of the scrolls from Qumran and the Judean Desert, which agree substantially with the oldest known codices prior to their discovery. (Of course, however, the picture is much more complex than that.) At the same time, our knowledge of Hebrew is now much deeper, due to the discovery and decipherment of languages such as Akkadian, Ugaritic and Phoenician.

Here is not the place to go into any further detail; textbooks are available. What has to be pointed out is that textual criticism is basic to establishing the text we use for analysis—but at the same time, literary criticism can contribute to determining the correct text.

Correct identification of poetic features does have implications for textual criticism. Without in any way being exhaustive, a few examples will show this.

Since *repetition* is an acknowledged factor in Hebrew poetry, there is no need to alter the second occurrence of the same word to a synonym,[77] or delete it. So, in Ps 77,1 both lines of the couplet begin

---

76. With the exception of such works as Ben Sirach and the works from Qumran.
77. For the relationship between repetition and textual criticism see Muilenburg, *VTS* 1 (1953), 99; Dahood, *RSP* I, 79-80 [he cites Isa 11,5 'girdle//girdle' and Ps 106,10b 'hand//hand'].

קוֹלִי, 'with my voice'—and BH³ unnecessarily suggested the deletion of the second occurrence.

If it can be established that *chiasmus* is present in a passage, then it can be better understood at the philological level, which in turn may obviate textual emendation. Since chiasmus operates at a different level, there is no danger of circular reasoning. For example, the abc // c'b'a' pattern in Isa 32,1 (ignoring the initial anacrusis) shows the ל at the beginning of the second line to be emphatic:

| הן | See: |
| לצדק ימלך מלך | justly will the king reign, |
| ולשרים למשפט ישרו | *yes*, rulers will rule uprightly. |

There is no need, then, to delete the ל[78] since its function has been determined by recognition of the chiastic pattern. There are many other examples.[79]

Similarly, once a passage is seen to be *patterned* on the *genders* of the nouns used, textual problems can be solved. Once חָצִיר, 'grass' (m.), is corrected to חָצֵר, 'habitat' (f.), in Isa 34,13 (as demanded by both context and LXX) the gender-pattern is immediately obvious:

| והיתה נוה תנים | It will be a haunt (m.) of jackals (m.), |
| חצר לבנות יענה | *a habitat* (f.) for ostriches (f.). |

The nouns in the first lines are both masculine, while those in the second are now both feminine.

Another example is Isa 11,4:

| והכה ארץ בשבט פיו | He will strike the *land* (f.) with the rod (m.) of his mouth (m.), |
| וברוח שפתיו ימית רשע | with the breath (f.) of his lips (f.) he will kill the wicked (m.). |

Here the chiastic structure:

| victim | weapon |
| weapon | victim |

---

78. As in BH and NEB; see Watson, *Bib* 59 (1978) 133.

79. See J.S. Kselman, 'A Note on Isaiah II 2', *VT* 25 (1975) 225-227; Isa 32,6—Cresko, *CBQ* 38 (1976) 306; Jer 4,14-16—Dahood, *Bib* 57 (1976) 108; Ps 10,11-12—Dahood, *Psalms I*, 64; Ps 138,1—*Psalms III*, 276. Note particularly M.J. Dahood, 'Chiasmus in Job: A Text-Critical and Philological Criterion', *Myers FS*, 119-130, where he discusses Job 6,15; 8,5; 11,14; 12,10; 13,12; 15,18; 17,7; 19,14; 21,8-9; 26,5; 28,2; 31,16; 32,14; 34,6; 36,3.12; 37,3; 39,6.8; and 41,7.

combines with the mismatch of gender in each line (f. + m. // f. + m.) to depict the *inversion*[80] of existing fortunes. Altering ארץ, 'land' (f.), to עריץ, 'ruthless' (m.), would break the gender-pattern.[81]

Other poetic features that have been discussed are word-pairs,[82] interchangeable components in word-pairs[83] and doublets in LXX caused by non-recognition of 'staircase parallelism'.[84] In Prov 10,7 רקב, 'to rot', was chosen for its alliteration with ברכה, 'blessing', so correction to יוקב is pointless. On the other hand, van Dijk is right in altering MT בם דברי to במדבר in Ps 105,27 since it results in a perfect cross-match of genders:

שמו במדבר אתותיו   They (= Moses and Aaron) produced his signs (f.) in the desert (m.)

ומפתים בארץ חם   and his portents (m.) in the torrid land (f.).[85]

## BIBLIOGRAPHY

(a) *General*
Luck, G. 'Textual Criticism Today', *AJP* 102 (1981) 164-194.
Thorpe, J.P. *Principles of Textual Criticism* (San Marino, Ca., 1972).

(b) *Hebrew*
Barr, J. *Comparative Philology and the Text of the Old Testament* (Oxford, 1968).
Talmon, S. 'Synonymous Readings in the Textual Traditions of the Old Testament', *ScrH* 8 (1961) 335-383.

### 3.7 *Prose or Poetry?*

*Introduction*

Everybody knows, or rather thinks he knows, the difference between prose and poetry. And even modern readers of ancient Hebrew can appreciate the difference between these two ways of composition. The problem for us is to establish criteria: *how* can we tell whether a

80. Discussed in section on INVERSION; see, briefly, Talmon: 1961, 360.

81. Contrast NEB and BH. See also Isa 5,29 (kethibh preferable).

82. Dahood, *RSP* I, 78-79, on Isa 51,17.22; Ps 89,34; Job 36,28; Prov 23,10 and Jer 51,35.

83. Talmon: 1961, 338ff.

84. I.e. Jgs 5,12—cf. Tov, *VT* 28 (1978) 230-231; and Ps 29,1—cf. Van Uchelen, *NTT* 24 (1970) 173.

85. Van Dijk, *VT* 18 (1968) 28—who failed to notice the gender parallelism. See further, Boadt, *CBQ* 35 (1973) 34; Gerleman, *VT* 1 (1951) 168-180; and Muilenburg, *JBL* 60 (1940) 344. Also, P. Hanson, *The Dawn of Apocalyptic* (Philadelphia, 1975), 46-49.

particular passage is poetry or not? What sort of *quantifiers* can we resort to in making judgments of this order? Is there an in-between zone of poetic prose or prosaic poetry? And what about free or blank verse in Hebrew (or Ugaritic or Akkadian)?

It has been noted for some time that our notion of what is poetry (in our native language as well as in Hebrew, etc.) depends to a large extent on how the material is presented to us. In other words, if a passage is printed out as prose we automatically assume it to be prose. To an extent, then, we classify the Hebrew text on the basis of Kittel's editions, and in accordance with the lay-out of the standard versions. Once we are aware of these external criteria, we can ignore them and try to focus on the texts themselves in an attempt at determining their true character: are they poetry or prose?

## Recognition or reconstruction?

It is very important to distinguish the process of recognising poetry from that of its reconstruction. *Recognition* implies that a text previously classified as prose must now be considered poetry; no tampering with the text is involved. An example is Ez 26,20.[86] On the other hand, *reconstruction* means that an extant prose text has been 'corrected' and its presumed original poetic form restored; an instance is Gen 1,16 where deletion of ואת הכוכבים results in a balanced tricolon.[87] The assumption is that prosaic elements have been inserted into the poetic text, so obscuring its true character. (For the view that a poetic epic lay behind the prose text of large portions of Hebrew narrative see section on EPIC.) It would seem safer and more objective to look at the text as it stands and determine which sections are in fact poetry. This procedure would provide guidelines in the possible reconstruction of poetic texts from prosaic passages. The other side of the coin must not be ignored, though: some passages unanimously deemed poetry may not be so, in fact. Ps 23 is a case in point, as is Ps 1.

---

86. Dahood, *RSP* I, 213.
87. Kselman, *JBL* 97 (1978) 165. He would read:

| | |
|---|---|
| ויעש אלהים שני המארת הגרלים | God made the two great luminaries, |
| את המאור הגרל לממשלת היום | the larger luminary to rule Day, |
| ואת המאור הקטן לממשלת הלילה | the lesser luminary to rule Night. |

[My translation.]

*The characteristics of poetry*

'The difference between verse and prose or speech is not that verse
has rhythm and prose and speech have not, but that in verse a
rhythmical unit, the line, is superimposed upon the grammatical unit
of all discourse, the sentence.'[88] This statement applies to Hebrew
poetry, of course, but it cannot be used as a test because the
oral/aural element is lacking: there are no native speakers who can
supply the relevant information. We are, therefore, forced to turn to
external criteria such as parallelism, structural patterning, the presence
of archaic vocabulary and the like in order to assess the nature of a
text. For convenience, a summary table of these criteria has been set
out, and in the pages that follow these indicators will be discussed
more at length, with illustrations from Hebrew texts.

*Prose or poetry: table of indicators*

|  | *indicator* | *examples* (so-called prose = poetry) |
|---|---|---|
| *A: Broad* | | |
| 1 | presence of established line-forms | Gen 37,8; Ez 26,13-14; Jer 12,6. |
| 2 | ellipsis, especially verb-gapping | Ez 16,11.12. |
| 3 | unusual vocabulary | Ez 27,12-24. |
| 4 | conciseness | Ez 16,8. |
| 5 | unusual word-order | Jer 45,4. |
| 6 | archaisms | Ez 38,7. |
| 7 | use of metre and rhythm | 1 Sm 10,12; 1 Kgs 20,22; Jer 49,13b. |
| 8 | regularity and symmetry | Qoh 3,1-9. |
| *B: Structural* | | |
| 9 | parallelism in various forms | 1 Sm 26,12; Ez 26,20; Gen 37,8.24b.33; 39,6; Hag 2,21-22; Esth 3,2; 7,5; 9,12. staircase: Jgs 4,18. number: 1 Kgs 5,29. pivot: Jon 1,16. |
| 10 | word-pairs | Gen 1,20; 5,1-2; Ex 16,12; Ez 13,6-9. |

88. G.S. Fraser, *Metre, Rhyme and Free Verse* (London, 1970) 1-2. For other
comments see P. Valéry, *The Art of Poetry* (New York, 1958) 52-99; Leech, *Guide*, 5-
6.25-33. S.R. Levin, *Linguistic Structures in Poetry* (The Hague, 1962) 30, n. 1.
According to E. Stankiewicz, 'Poetic and Non-poetic Language in their Interrelation',
*Poetics I* (Warsaw, 1961) 11-23, there is no sharp dividing line between prose and
poetry but two poles, one unmarked and the other marked. 'Poetic language is the
message oriented towards itself, the message is an autonomous structure' (14).

| | | |
|---|---|---|
| 11 | chiastic patterns | Gen 1,5; 12,1-3; Ex 20,23; Lev 19,32; Jgs 9,8-15; Nb 12,6-8; 1 Sm 2,25; 2 Sm 5,20; Ez 21,12; 29,11; 12,27; Mal 3,19; Hag 1,6.10; Job 3,1; Jer 11,21. |
| 12 | envelope figure | Ez 16,4 (cf. Nb 12,6-8). |
| 13 | break-up of stereotyped phrases | Isa 22; 4,3-6; 7,1-6.10-17; 8,1-4; 14,1-3; 19,16-20. |
| 14 | repetition in various forms | refrain: Esth 9,12; 14,12-20; (Hag 1,6). terrace: Ez 22,2. triple: 1 Sm 26,12. |
| 15 | gender-matched parallelism | Gen 1,2; 2 Sm 3,29; (Gen 31,52); Ex 21,23-25; Dt 4,18; 28,13; Jon 1,8; Ez 7,15-19a; 12,27; 14,21. |
| 16 | tricolon | Gen 5,1-2; 35,11; 37,33; 1 Sm 8,3; Ez 26,3a.14; Jer 14,3d; 1 Sm 26,12. |

*C: Other*

| | | |
|---|---|---|
| 17 | rhyme | Esth 4,3; 8,6.16(=17). |
| 18 | other sound patterns | Gen 30,43b. |

*D: Negative*

| | | |
|---|---|---|
| 19 | absence/rarity of prose elements | Nb 12,6-8. |

## Indicators of poetry and prose

The indicators of criteria have been grouped into four sets: general or broad (syntax, metre, vocabulary, style); structural (parallelism, chiasmus, etc.); devices concerned with sound (wordplay and rhyme); and lastly, negative criteria: the absence of components associated with prose. They will be considered in turn.[89]

## A. *Broad indicators*

1. *Line-forms.* 'If a text contains established line-forms then it is verse' is the principle formulated by Collins.[90] It is, in fact, a basic criterion, as will be seen. His clearest example is Jer 12,6 which is to be analysed as follows:

| | | |
|---|---|---|
| כי גם אחיך ובית אביך גם המה בגדו בך | $NP_1$ V M | = I B:i)1 |
| גם המה קראו אחריך מלא | $NP_1$ V M $NP_2$ | = I D:i)2 |
| אל תאמן בם | V M | = IV B/D:ii)1 |
| כי ידברו אליך טובות | V M $NP_2$ | |

---

89. See the table in Wimsatt, *PMLA* 65 (1950) 10.

90. Collins, *Line-forms*, 276.

> For even your brothers, your very own kin, even they have
>    betrayed you;
> even they are in full cry behind you;
> do not trust them,
> even though they address you as friends.

Collins comments: 'The unusual feature here is the extended $NP_1$ in the first line, but there are other instances of the same kind of thing, particularly in [line-form] I A. Both BH and BHS print these lines as prose, but they seem to me to be an essential part of the poem of which they are the opening lines.'[91]

Collins also discusses Isa 24,4-5; Ez 37,24; Jer 14,3; Isa 19,13-15 and Ez 26,3-14.

2. *Ellipsis*. While ellipsis in general is particularly frequent in poetry, there is one form of ellipsis which is characteristic of verse. This is *verb gapping*. Gapping is the omission of a word in a second clause when it is identical to a word used in the first. For example, Am 5,12:

| | |
|---|---|
| כי ידעתי רבים פשעיכם | For *I know* your many sins |
| ועצמים חטאתיכם | your powerful crimes,[92] |

which can be analysed as

$$V \quad NP_2$$
$$\emptyset \quad NP_2$$

—the ø representing the expected verb 'I know'. O'Connor, in fact, asserts that in Hebrew 'verb gapping only occurs in poetry'.[93] If proved to be correct, this is a powerful test and would outweigh any other criterion listed in the table. An example would be Ez 16,11:

| | |
|---|---|
| ואתנה צמידים על ידיך | I put bracelets on your arms |
| ורביד על גרונך | and a chain on your neck |

with gapping of the verb 'I put'. Similarly Ez 16,12 where there is gapping of 'I put' in clause two and clause three.

91. Collins, *Line-forms*, 275. J. Bright, *Jeremiah* (AB 21; Garden City, 1965) 83-84, whose rendering is followed here, already recognised the poetic element though he considered the strophe to close Jer 12,1-6. Greenstein, *UF* 9 (1977) 83, states that 'nominal clauses are common in biblical prose but uncommon in poetry', but his assertion is belied by the findings of Collins, *Line-forms*, 215-219.

92. Or 'For I know how many are your sins . . .'.

93. O'Connor, *Structure*, 124; also 122-127, etc., and *BASOR* 226 (1977) 18. However, Kugel, *Idea*, 321-322, lists prose texts such as Gen 28,20; Lev 26,19 and 1 Kgs 8,50 which also exhibit verb-gapping.

3. *Unusual vocabulary.* Of itself arcane and rare vocabulary is not indicative of verse; one only has to think of the many technical terms used in Leviticus, most of which is undoubtedly written in prose. In conjunction with other factors, though, the use of rare lexical items can point to the presence of poetry—as in Ez 27,12-24. This would appear to be confirmed by Job and Song which have an unusually high percentage of strange words and hapaxlegomena.

4. *Conciseness.* More an impressionistic criterion than a measurable gauge, it is undeniable that good poetry is written with economy. As with criterion 3, this test is corroborative rather than absolute, but nevertheless deserves mention.[94]

5. *Unusual word order.* Ancient Hebrew is a V(erb), S(ubject), O(bject) language—unlike modern Hebrew which tends to be SVO.[95] In poetry, this sequence is not always followed, e.g. Isa 22,6a which is SVO:

ועילם נשא אשפה    Elam lifted a quiver.

The sequence OSV used twice in Jer 45,4 suggests the couplet[96] is verse:

הנה    See,
אשר בניתי אני הרס    what I have built, I shall demolish;
ואת אשר נטעתי אני נתש    and what I have planted, I shall uproot.

Clearly there is a good deal of overlap with criterion 11: chiastic word order.

6. *Archaisms.* Under the heading archaisms come not lexical items so much (see already criterion 3, unusual vocabulary) as grammatical elements. These would include enclitic *mem*, vocative *lamedh*, emphatic *waw* and like, but particularly, use of *yiqtol* for the past tense. Since the topic of archaisms has already been dealt with (section 3.4) and the individual elements are discussed throughout the book, there is little need to go into further detail. Of course the presence of archaisms of this order is not sufficient as a criterion; further factors are density (an unusual number of archaisms in a short text) and more positive indicators such as parallelism.

---

94. See Holladay: 1966, 402.

95. For discussion see O'Connor, *Structure*, 117f. 125f. Also, R.A. Berman, 'The Case of an (S)VO Language: Subjectless Constructions in Modern Hebrew', *Lang* 56 (1980) 759-776.

96. The last line, 'So will it be with the whole earth', does not form part of the couplet.

7. *Use of metre.* Lines which are metrical are verse, almost by definition. Judgment in this area is not always easy; is Jer 49,13b written in metre?

כי לשׁמׄה לחרפׄה ולקללה תהׄיה בצרׄה
וכל־ערׄיה תהיׄינה לחרבות עולם

Truly shall Bozrah become a horror, a shame and a curse-word,
and all her cities shall become perpetual wastes.[97]

The 5 + 3 stress beat is punched home by the assonance:

-ậ  -ậ  -ậ  ...  -ậ
o-ê-â  -ê-â   -o---ô  -ô-ậ

8. *Regularity and symmetry.* The classic example is Qoh 3,1-9, with its regular (sonnet-like) repetitive pattern 'A time for . . . '.[98]

B. *Structural indicators*

9. *Parallelism.* Of itself, of course, parallelism is not indicative of poetry since prose, too, uses parallelism. Persistent parallelism, however, is strong enough to warrant re-classifying as poetry what might have been considered prose. A short example of parallelism within a prose passage is 1 Sm 26,12:

| | |
|---|---|
| ואין ראה | No one saw; |
| ואין יודע | no one noticed; |
| ואין מקיץ | no one woke— |
| כי כלם ישׁנים | for they were all sleeping; |
| כי תרדמת יהוה נפלה עליהם | for a dead sleep[99] had fallen on them. |

And again, in 2 Sm 5,2:

| | |
|---|---|
| אתה תרעה את עמי את ישראל | You shall shepherd my people, Israel; |
| ואתה תהיה לנגיד על־ישראל | and you shall become leader over Israel. |

Since these are a direct quotation of Yahweh's words they are probably poetry embedded in a section of narrative prose. Further examples of special types of parallelism also occur in prose contexts: Jgs 4,18 (= staircase parallelism); Gen 1,2 etc. (= gender-matched

---

97. Omitting לחרב, 'a waste', with LXX; its origin is by dittography. Note that the prevailing gender is f. and חרב would jar as it is m.

98. See Loader, *ZAW* 81 (1969) 240-242. On regularity and symmetry cf. T.H. Robinson, *The Poetry of the Old Testament* (London, 1947) 11-19.

99. Lit. 'sleep of Yahweh'; possibly the divine name here is used simply as a superlative.

parallelism: see indicator 15); also word-pairs and chiastic parallelism can be found (see next two indicators).

10. *Word-pairs.* Kselman has collected several short texts in prose settings which use word-pairs and are very probably poetic fragments;[100] for example, Ex 16,12:

בין הערבים תאכלו בשר — Between the evenings you shall eat meat,
ובבקר תשבעו־לחם — and in the morning you shall be sated with bread.

The word-pairs used are אכל//שבע (cf. Ps 81,17); לחם//בשר (Isa 58,7) and ערב//בקר (Gen 49,27; Isa 17,14; Zeph 3,3; Pss 30,6; 90,5; Qoh 11,6) as well as the inverted ballasted prepositional pair בין//ב־. Other examples include:

| Gen 1,5 | word-pairs | אור//חשך | 'light//dark' |
| | | יום//לילה | 'day//night' |
| Gen 28,17 | word-pair | בית//שער | 'house//gate' |
| Ex 14,8 | word-pair | ארץ//מדבר | 'land//desert' |

For other examples see bibliography.[101]

11. *Chiastic patterns.* Chiasmus, whether strophic or within a stanza, does suggest that lines previously considered prose should be re-classified as verse. In 1 Sm 3,17 two clauses recur with almost identical wording ('the word which he spoke to you' and 'you conceal from me'); these clauses, marked A, A' and B, B' below, frame a central clause which also uses repetitive elements (C and C'). The resulting combination is a chiastic pattern with 'God' (marked D) as the central component:

| מה הדבר אשר דבר אליך | A | What was it he said to you? |
| אל־נא תכחד ממני | B | Now, don't you conceal (it) from me. |
| כה יעשה־לך | C | This will befall you |
| אלהים | D | (from) God, |
| וכה יוסיף | C' | and this besides |
| אם־תכחד ממני דבר | B' | if you conceal from me |
| מכל־הדבר אשר־דבר אליך | A' | any of the words he spoke to you. |

Here verse is used to emphasise a curse. Other examples include 1 Sm 2,25; Jer 11,21 and Job 3,1. Particularly instructive is Jgs 9,8-15

100. Kselman: 1978, 169-170.
101. Kselman: 1973, 492, exaggerates, perhaps, in stating: 'The distinguishing mark of Hebrew poetry, however, is not single words or phrases; it is rather the formulaic pairs that make up the repertoire of the oral poet, and out of which he composes his verse'; cf. also Kselman: 1978, 163.

(Jotham's Fable) where a chiastic gender pattern is used over the four stanzas:

| | | | | |
|---|---|---|---|---|
| I (vv. 8b-9) | : | Olive-tree | זית | : masc. |
| II (10-11) | : | Fig-tree | תאנה | : fem. |
| III (12-13) | : | Vine | גפן | : fem. |
| IV (14-15) | : | Boxthorn | אטד | : masc. |

resulting in the sequence: KING—QUEEN—QUEEN—KING. See also Esth 5,3.6.8; 7,2.3; 8,5.[102]

12. *Envelope figure.* The envelope figure (or inclusio) is not only indicative of poetry (though it can occur in prose), it also marks off a particular segment as verse. In the example just quoted (Jgs 9,8-15) the expression 'to anoint a king' occurs both in the preamble (v. 8a) and in the final stanza (v. 15). Another example is Ez 16,4:

| | |
|---|---|
| ביום הולדת אתך | On the day you were born |
| | ... [8 or 9 lines of poetry] ... |
| ביום הולדת אתך | On the day you were born. |

13. *Break-up of stereotype phrases.* This topic is related to indicator 10, 'word-pairs', but merits a separate section. In prose, significant words occur in juxtaposition, as in Jgs 13,3:

| | |
|---|---|
| והרית וילדת בן | You shall *conceive* and *bear* a son; |

(similarly Gen 29,34). The same sets are split up in poetry, forming parallel couplets of the type:

| | |
|---|---|
| תהרו חשש | You *conceive* chaff, |
| ותלדו קש | you *bring forth* stubble. (Isa 33,11; cf. Job 3,3) |

Using this criterion it is possible to determine whether a passage is prose or not; a convenient example is Isa 22. Watters has shown[103] that there is high percentage of parallel word-pairs, particularly in vv. 8b-11 and 15-25. Other non-prose texts include Isa 4,3-6; 7,1-6.10-17; 8,1-4; 14,1-3; 19,16-20. Conversely, Job 1,1–2,13 is in fact prose.[104]

14. *Repetition in various forms.* Repetition pure and simple is

---

102. Porten, in Welch, *Chiasmus*, 178-180.

103. So Watters, *Formula Criticism*, 117-126. The same criterion had already been proposed by W. Whallon, *Formula, Character and Context* (Cambridge, Mass., 1969) 148-150.

104. Following Watters, *Formula Criticism*, 120-122. By the same token Watters shows Ruth to be prose, not poetry.

frequent enough in prose texts, witness Jer 7,4, היכל יהוה היכל יהוה היכל
יהוה המה, 'It is: Yahweh's temple; Yahweh's temple; Yahweh's
temple',[105] and the triple repetition in Ez 7,1-2. More significant are
repetitions in the form of the envelope figure (see indicator 12,
above), refrain (see presently) and the like, i.e. structured or patterned
repetition.

15. *Gender-matched parallelism*. This particular type of parallelism
is used in prose (examples are Ex 2,1-10; Lev 5,6; Jos 11,6; Ruth 1,8-9;
2,21-22) but is very much commoner in poetry. Its presence can
corroborate that passages singled out as verse have been correctly
identified. The two nouns in the first colon of Lev 26,19 (considered
verse by some scholars)[106] are both masculine. Instead, a feminine
noun is paired with a noun of the same gender in the second colon:

| | |
|---|---|
| ונתתי את שמיכם כברזל | I shall make your heavens (m.) like iron (m.) |
| ואת ארצכם כנחשה | and your land (f.) like brass (f.). |

In Dt 28,23 (also verse in a prose context) the pattern has been
altered slightly (to m. + f. // f. + m., perhaps to underline the reversal
effect) but can still be recognised. Similarly, Gen 1,2—considered
verse on the strength of its many word-pairs[107]—has the gender-
pattern f. + m. // m. + f. // f. + m. Another example is Gen 1,10.[107]
In all these passages gender-matched parallelism is present, showing
them to be verse, as posited.

16. *Tricolon*. The well-knit, carefully structured tricolon is only
found in true verse so that its presence is an almost unequivocal
pointer to poetry. After an introductory monocolon ('His sons did not
follow in their father's footsteps'), 1 Sm 8,3 continues:

| | |
|---|---|
| ויטו אחרי הבצע | They were intent on profit; |
| ויקחו־שחד | they took bribes; |
| ויטו משפט | they perverted justice. |

Perhaps this example is open to question; it was chosen to show the
issue is not always clear-cut. Better are Gen 28,17; 5,1; etc. (see
table). See, too, 1 Kgs 5,11; Ez 16,4.

Under the heading 'Other' come sound-related components such
as *rhyme* (17)—chiefly end-rhyme, and *other sound patterns* (18)

---

105. The plural pronoun refers to the temple complex; cf. Watson, *Bib* 53 (1972)
204.
106. See D.R. Hillers, *Treaty-Curses and the Old Testament Prophets* (*BibOr* 16;
Rome, 1964) 38-42.
107. Kselman: 1978, 163-164.

including paronomasia, assonance, alliteration and the like. Such elements occur in prose, too, but once again it is a question of high density.

Finally, the table of indicators lists negative pointers to poetry: where prosaic elements are missing there is at least the likelihood of verse.

19. *Absence or rarity of prose elements.* The prose elements in question are the relative pronoun, the definite article and the object-marker. Also to be included in this section is consecutive *waw*. Studies have been carried out which show that, statistically, the more such particles are used in a text the less that text should be classified as poetry.[108] To illustrate rather than prove this assertion we can look at Nb 12,6-8 which Kselman has already shown to be poetry on other grounds.[109]

| | |
|---|---|
| אם־יהיה נביאכם | If there be a prophet among you, |
| במראה אליו אתודע | I make myself known to him in a vision; |
| בחלום אדבר־בו | in a dream I speak with him. |
| לא־כן עבדי משה | Not so (with) my servant Moses; |
| בכל־ביתי נאמן הוא | in all my household he (alone) is faithful. |
| פה אל־פה אדבר־בו | Mouth to mouth I speak with him, |
| ומראה ולא בחידת | in clarity and not in riddles; |
| ותמנת יהוה יביט | the form of Yahweh he beholds. |

Neither the relative particle nor the object-marker occurs even once while the presence of the definite article is indicated only by the vowels (which are secondary);[110] there is no consecutive *waw*. These findings corroborate the arguments of Cross and Kselman showing that this pointer (absence of prosaic elements) is a valuable guide to assessing how 'poetic' a passage might be.[111]

---

108. See D.N. Freedman, 'Pottery, Poetry and Prophecy: An Essay on Biblical Poetry', *JBL* 96 (1977) 5-26, esp. 5-8. He concludes: 'Statistically the results establish beyond cavil that the occurrence of these particles is a valid discriminant, and the difference in distribution reflects an intrinsic distinction between prose and poetry' (7).

109. F.M. Cross, *Canaanite Myth and Hebrew Epic* (Cambridge, Mass., 1973) 203-204; J.S. Kselman, 'A Note on Numbers XII 6-8', *VT* 26 (1976) 500-505. Kselman argues from chiastic patterning (BCDD'C'B'A', following Cross), and from assonance, word-pairs, wordplay and comparison with older poetic material.

110. Similarly, Kugel, *Idea*, 90: 'In its elided form the definite article is not represented in the consonantal text'.

111. Kugel, *Idea*, 89-90 and 89, n. 55.

*Some additional comments*

It must be emphasised that the indicators spelled out above are not the only pointers to poetry; there are many others such as the use of figurative language (simile, metaphor) or imagery generally, and the whole range of non-structural devices (irony, allusion, hyperbole and so on). Further, the mere presence of one or even of several of these indicators proves very little. Ultimately, the decision owes a great deal to mature reflection which will consider content as well as form, with an eye on traditions both in Classical Hebrew and in ancient Near Eastern literature generally. For example, content is significant since we know that very few laws (not to mention contracts, letters and the like) are in poetry. Similarly, very little narrative—even 'heroic narrative'—is cast in poetic form (see §4.6 on EPIC). One expects a prophecy to be verse, but this is by no means always the case. With these provisos in mind, then, we can look at a difficult example and apply the indicators set out above and determine whether the passage is poetry or prose.

EXAMPLE: Ez 23,2-4

This passage, generally considered prose, has been chosen to illustrate how the indicators described above can be used to test whether a text is poetry or not. Not all the components of the table are present, of course, but enough to provide a working model. The passage will first be set out and translated; then will come the discussion, followed by conclusions.

|  |  | *line-form analysis* |
|---|---|---|
| 2d | שתים נשים בנות אם־אחת היו | NP$_1$ M V |
| 3a | ותזינה במצרים | V M |
| b | בנעוריהן זנו | M V |
| c | שמה מעכו שדיהן | M V NP$_2$ |
| d | ושם עשו דדי בתוליהן | M V NP$_2$ |
| 4a | ושמותן אהלה הגדולה | nom. |
| b | ואהליבה אחותה | nom. |
| c | ותהיינה לי | V M |
| d | ותלדנה בנים ובנות | V NP$_2$ |
| e | ושמותן שמרון אהלה | nom. |
| f | וירשלם אהליבה | nom. |

2d Once there were two women, daughters of a single mother.

3a They fornicated in Egypt;
  b in their youth they fornicated.

c There, others fondled their breasts,
d and there others pressed their virginal bosoms.

4a And their names: Oholah, the elder;
b and Oholibah, her sister.

c They became mine;
d they bore sons and daughters.

e And their names: Oholah is Samaria,
f and Oholibah, Jerusalem.

The established line-forms (#1) used are: IIB ii)2 in 3ab; IID ii)29[112] in 3cd; IV B/C ii[113] in 4cd. This last form is extremely rare (cf. Isa 47,6). The other lines (4ab and 4ef) are nominalised forms.

The only instance of *ellipsis* (#2) is in 4b (equivalently, 4f), and even there it is weak. *Unusual vocabulary* (#3) comprises מעך, 'to press, squeeze' (only here in Ez; elsewhere Lev 22,4; 1 Sm 26,7); עשה also 'to press, squeeze'—cf. v. 8.[114] Also rare: דד, 'breast';[115] בתולים (f.), 'tokens of virginity',[116] found in v. 8 and five times in Dt 22, twice in Jgs 11 and once in Lev.[117] The opening line (v. 2) has *unusual word order* (#5) but there appear to be no *archaisms* (#6). The *metre* (#7) of v. 3 is 2 + 2 followed by 3 + 3; elsewhere it is irregular.

As for structural indicators of verse, here, *parallelism* (#9) is present in vv. 3ab, 3cd, 4ab and 4ef; the matching line-forms in 3cd (M V NP$_2$ // M V NP$_2$) are particularly evident. The *word-pair* (#10) דד//שד (v. 3b) recurs only in Ez 23,21. The pair מעך//עשה (v. 3cd) is found only here.[118] *Chiasmus* (#11) appears once: 3ab (see the line-form analysis V M // M V). There is neither *envelope figure* (#12) nor *phrasal break-up* (#13). *Repetition* (#14): 4ef is a variant of 4ab. Absent are *gender-parallelism* (#15) and the *tricolon* (#16).

Other indicators are thin on the ground: *end-rhyme* in 3cd (-êhēn) and 4ab.ef (-ā) (= #17).[119]

112. Collins, *Line-forms*, 121.
113. Collins, *Line-forms*, 171; in general, though, IV ii lines are common in Ez, see 176.
114. See also Isa 28,15; it may be that the homonyms 'to make, do' and 'to press, squeeze' belong to the same, single root, in view of Ug. 'šy.
115. Or 'teat, nipple': Ez 23,3.8.21; Prov 5,19 (perhaps 7,18).
116. For this term cf. Wenham, *VT* 22 (1972) 331ff.
117. Lev 21,13; Dt 22,14.15.17.20; Jgs 11,37.
118. Unless מעך is read in v. 21.
119. Note, too, the rare *inversion* of numbers in 2d: 'two . . . one', occurring elsewhere, perhaps, only in Ugaritic: *atm bštm wan šnt*, 'You in two years, but I in one' (*CTA* 3D iv 77, as translated by Dahood, *Bib* 62 [1981] 276).

The negative indicator *absence of prose elements* (#19) strongly favours construing these lines as verse since neither את nor אשר occurs.

## Discussion and evaluation

The mere listing of several mechanical and structural poetic elements in these lines is not conclusive proof that they are poetry. Such a judgment can only come after several careful readings and long reflection. The poetic elements mentioned are *pointers* of a positive kind and so, cumulatively, indicate that Ez 23,2-4 is verse.

Corroboration comes from two quarters. First, from *content* (since mere form, unmatched to content, means nothing). Ezekiel is using the metaphor of Israel as whore, which already places the passage outside the realm of pure history. We are dealing with rhetoric. Secondly, the poet gives this metaphor a new depth, an unusual twist. To appreciate this it is necessary to remember two things. The metaphor of whoring means to make an alliance with other gods (with foreign powers, if you like) rather than with Yahweh. Further, the expression 'to seize or press the breast' is idiomatic for 'to contract a covenant' since the contracting parties would ceremonially face each other and touch each other's chests to seal the treaty.[120] Evidence for this comes from Isa 28,15:[121]

| | |
|---|---|
| כי אמרתם | For you said: |
| כרתנו ברית את־מות | 'We have "cut a covenant" with Death, |
| ועם־שאול עשינו חזה | and with Sheol we have "pressed breasts"'. |

Accordingly, just as 'to fornicate' both here and elsewhere simply means 'to break covenant with Yahweh'—in figurative language—so does 3cd ('There, others fondled their breasts, and there others pressed their virginal bosoms') imply the more heinous act of actually making treaties with foreigners.

Finally, though no insistence can be placed on this, the line-count of vv. 2b-4 is eleven, a stock number for a stanza in poetry.

## Reconstructing poetry in its 'original form'

As pointed out already, there is a vast difference between recognising poetry and reconstruction. To bring home this distinction it is worth

---

120. See *CAD* Ṣ, 165-166.
121. Corroborated by v. 18; see Watson, *JBL* 99 (1980) 330-331; *Bib* 59 (1978) 132-133.

looking at a concrete example. Recognition implies that a text
previously classified as prose must now be considered verse and that
no tampering with the text is involved. So, in Esth 9,12, the Persian
king says to Queen Esther:

> In Susa, the capital, the Jews have slain five hundred men and also
> the ten sons of Haman. What, then, have they done in the rest of
> the king's provinces? Now what is your petition? It shall be granted
> to you. And what further is your request? It shall be fulfilled.

Closer inspection shows that the last four sentences are really poetry:
there is both parallelism and repetition, and the couplet

ומה־שאלתך וינתן לך

ומה־בקשתך עוד ותעש

comprises a variant refrain (cf. 7,2 etc.). Reconstruction, instead, *does*
involve alteration of the text. There are three different levels of
reconstruction:

### a. *re-vocalisation*

By this is meant restoring what is considered to be the original
vocalisation of the presumed poetic passage, on the basis of MT.

Without going into detail[122] some idea of the implications can be
gained from the following example (Ex 15,12):

| | |
|---|---|
| *naṭīta yamīnka* | You stretched out your hand |
| *tibla'emō 'ārṣ* | the netherworld swallowed them.[123] |

### b. *pruning of prose particles*

In an attempt at obtaining the most primitive form of a (poetic)
text, all prose elements (ו, ה־, את, אשר) are deleted. This method is
generally used in combination with (a).[124] See, for example, Isa
10,33:

| | |
|---|---|
| (ו)רמי (ה)קומה גדועים | The great in height are hewed down, |
| ו(ה)גבהים ישפלו | the lofty are brought low, |

where the omitted elements are the copula (twice) and the definite
article (once).[125]

---

122. See Freedman, *Myers FS*, 173-175 and elsewhere. Note J.C.L. Gibson, 'The
Massoretes as Linguists', *OTS* 19 (1974) 86-96, for an opposing view based on
linguistic principles.
123. So Freedman, *Myers FS*, 172.
124. Chiefly by Cross, Freedman and their students; see bibliography.
125. Christensen, *VT* 26 (1976) 385-399.

## c. *Emendation*

The term 'emendation' is used rather loosely to denote the excision of all (presumed) glosses, editorial inserts, scribal repetitions, woodenly repeated formulae (נאם יהוה, etc.). An example among many is Ez 11,14-20 of which only the first two verses need be quoted here. Bracketed words are to be omitted—so Brownlee[126]—as extraneous to the original poem:

| | |
|---|---|
| (ויהי דבר־יהוה אלי לאמר) | (The word of Yahweh came to me saying:) |
| בן־אדם אחיך אחיך | O man, your brothers, your brothers, |
| אנשי גאלתך | the men of your redemption, |
| (וכל בית ישראל כלה) | (namely, the whole house of Israel, all of it) |
| אשר אמרו להם | are those to whom have said |
| ישבי ירושלם | the inhabitants of Jerusalem: |
| רחקו מעל יהוה | 'Get you afar from Yahweh; |
| לנו היא | this is ours' |
| (נתנה הארץ למורשה) | (the land is given us for possession). |

Such procedures are valid, but must be used with some caution. They will not be discussed further here since this book is principally concerned with establishing norms for poetic technique. Once these have been assured, then poetry can be redeemed from its prose embedding. For studies of this kind see the bibliography.

### The value of recognising poetry in 'prose'

Apart from the obvious effect of extending the corpus of poetic texts,[127] certain benefits accrue from the correct identification of so-called prose as poetry. Evidently, the true form and character of the words are revealed. Further, richness of style can be demonstrated, as in Jer 16,1-9.[128] We are enabled to penetrate the power of the words used[129] and these words can be aligned with other authentic material in disputed books such as Jeremiah and Ezekiel.[130] Finally, we may learn something of ancient epic in Israel (see on EPIC),

---

126. Brownlee, *JBL* 89 (1970) 396-399. The brackets round the first line are mine.

127. For an exciting example of this in Neo-Punic, cf. C.F. Krahmalkov, 'Two Neo-Punic Poems in Rhymed Verse', *RSF* 3 (1975) 169-205.

128. Holladay: 1966, 421.

129. Holladay: 1966, 435.

130. For example, Jer 16,1-9 is 'worthy to be placed alongside the call in 1,4-10 as a central testimony by the prophet of his own self-understanding' (Holladay: 1966, 420). Again, all authentic Ezekiel material can be shown as speaking of doom (so Brownlee: 1970, 393-404).

though it seems more likely that, traditionally, prose narrative used poetic fragments as a stylistic device (i.e. they are not relics of a once poetic epic now turned into prose).

*Prose or poetry in Ugaritic and Akkadian*
With regard to the *Ugaritic* texts there is very little difficulty in distinguishing prose texts from those written in verse. The deciding factor is *content*:

> prose:  letters, treaties, economic documents, etc.
> poetry: religious and mythological texts

Form cannot be totally neglected as a criterion, as the above table shows, but 'stories' such as the Legend of Keret, the Tale of Aqhat, the Baal-Cycle set and a few incantations, prayers and other fragments are verse; the rest is prose. What is more, there appears to be a difference in language[131] reinforcing the distinction made on the basis of content.[132]

As for *Akkadian*, similar factors are operative. Prayers, hymns, epics and the like are in verse. Historical documents, treaties, business letters and so on are prose. However there are borderline cases; examples are the prologue and epilogue to the Code of Hammurapi (though the style could probably be described as high-flown prose); Sargon's eighth campaign.

Poetic elements are present, too, in incantation series such as Šurpu and Maqlû. Since the problem has not been discussed very much by scholars it is premature to present the topic as more than a matter for deeper investigation.[133]

BIBLIOGRAPHY

(a) *General*
Lotman, Y. *Analysis of the poetic text* (Ann Arbor, 1974).
Tarlinskaja, M.G.—Teterina, L.M. 'Verse-Prose-Metre', *Linguistics* 129 (1974) 63-86.
Žirmunsky, V. *Introduction to Metrics. The Theory of Verse* (London, 1966).
(b) *Semitic*
Cassuto, U. *A Commentary on the Book of Genesis* (Jerusalem, 1961).

---

131. See M. Liverani, 'Elementi innovativi nell'ugaritico non letterario', *AANLR* 8,19 (1964) 173-191.
132. See the classification adopted in *KTU*.
133. Buccellati, *JAOS* 101 (1981) 35-47, discusses this aspect briefly.

Cross, F.M. 'Prose and Poetry in the Mythic and Epic Texts from Ugarit', *HTR* 67 (1974) 1-15.

Cross, F.M.—Freedman, D.N. 'Some Observations on Early Hebrew', *Bib* 53 (1972) 413-420.

—*Studies in Ancient Yahwistic Poetry* (Missoula, 1975).

Horst, F. 'Die Kennzeichen der hebräischen Poesie', *ThRund* 21 (1953) 97-121.

König, E. 'Poesie und Prosa in der althebräischen Literatur abgegrenzt', *ZAW* 37 (1917-18) 145-187; 245-250.

Kugel, *Idea*, 59-95.

Radday, Y.T.—Shore, H. 'The Definite Article: A Type- and/or Author-specifying Discriminant in the Hebrew Bible', *ALLCBull* 4 (1976) 23-31.

Watters, *Formula*, 118-126.

Whallon, W. *Formula, Character and Context* (C mbridge, Mass., 1969) 148-150.

(c) *Particular Studies*

Albright, W.F. '"And God Saw Ki Tob" in Genesis', *Robert FS*, 22-26.

Althann, R. 'Jeremiah iv 11-12: stichometry, parallelism and translation', *VT* 28 (1978) 385-391.

Brownlee, W.H. 'Exorcising the Souls from Ezekiel 13:17-23', *JBL* 69 (1950) 367-373.

—'Ezekiel's Poetic Indictment of the Shepherds', *HTR* 51 (1958) 191-203.

—'The Aftermath of the Fall of Judah According to Ezekiel', *JBL* 89 (1970) 393-404.

—'Ezekiel's parable of the watchman and the editing of Ezekiel', *VT* 28 (1978) 392-408.

Bruno, D.A. *Jeremia. Eine rhythmische Untersuchung* (Stockholm, 1954).

Campbell, E.F. *Ruth* (*AB* 7; Garden City, 1975).

Ceresko, A.R. 'The A:B::B:A Word Pattern in Hebrew and Northwest Semitic, with Special Reference to the Book of Job', *UF* 7 (1975) 73-88.

—'The Chiastic Word Pattern in Hebrew' *CBQ* 38 (1976) 303-311.

Frank, R.M. 'A Note on 3 Kings 19,10.14', *CBQ* 25 (1963) 410-414.

Gordon, R. 'Qoheleth and Qumran—A Study in Style', *Bib* 41 (1960) 402ff.

Hanson, P.D. 'The Song of Heshbon and David's NIR', *HTR* 61 (1968) 297-320.

Holladay, W.L. 'The Recovery of Poetic Passages of Jeremiah', *JBL* 85 (1966) 401-435.

—*The Architecture of Jeremiah 1-20* (Lewisburg, 1975).

Hölscher, G. *Hesekiel - der Dichter und das Buch* (*BZAW* 39, 1924).

Irwin, W.A. *The Problem of Ezekiel, an Inductive Study* (Chicago, 1943).

Kikawada, I. 'The Shape of Genesis 11:1-9', *Muilenburg FS*, 18-32.

Kselman, J.S. 'A Note on Gen. 7:11', *CBQ* 35 (1973) 491-493.

—'The Recovery of Poetic Fragments from the Pentateuchal Priestly Source', *JBL* 97 (1978) 161-173.

Lipiński, E. 'Prose ou poésie en Jér. xxxiv 1-7', *VT* 14 (1964) 112-113.

Long, B.O. 'Recent Field Studies in Oral Literature and their Bearing on OT Criticism', *VT* 26 (1976) 187-198.

Loretz, O. 'Vergleich und Kommentar in Amos 3,12',*BZ* 20 (1976) 121-125.

—'Psalmenstudien', *UF* 3 (1971) 101-115; 5 (1973) 213-218; 6 (1974) 175-210; 211-240.

Porten, B.—Rappaport, U. 'Poetic Structure in Genesis IX 7', *VT* 21 (1971) 363-369.

Roche, M. de, 'Is Jeremiah 25:15-29 a Piece of Reworked Jeremianic Poetry?', *JSOT* 10 (1978) 58-67.

Sarna, N.M. 'Epic Substratum in the Book of Job', *JBL* 76 (1957) 13-25.

## 3.8 *Closure: Notes on Theory*

The term *closure* implies both the way in which a poem comes to an end, and the status of a poem as an autonomous entity, the two aspects overlapping to a certain extent. The second aspect (the poem as a unit) is wider and so will be considered first; then after looking at endings to poems some specific examples will be set out.

### 1. *The poem as 'closed'*
Stated baldly, the principle of closure maintains that the reader of a poem should not feel obliged to refer to texts outside the poem in order to understand it. In other words, the poem is a self-contained

unit, intelligible in its own terms and needing no other text for its correct interpretation. The basis for such a claim is that a poem is a scaled down model of the universe, expressing the relationship between Man and the Cosmos. We are in the realm of pure theory, however, and in practice, matters are rather different. The reasons are clear, and have been set out by Barbara Smith:

> First of all, a poem cannot be regarded as totally independent of the poet's and reader's extrinsic experiences—not if we recognize that our experiences include *language* itself, and that it is upon our past linguistic experiences that poetry depends for its most characteristic effects. Moreover, a poem does not, like the propositional systems of mathematical logic, make its own rules; it adopts and adapts the rules (i.e., the conventions of nonliterary discourse), so that the principles which generate and conclude the one are conspicuously reflected in those of the other.[134]

No poem is totally self-contained and autonomous in absolute terms; if it were, it would be completely unintelligible. In reality there is a certain degree of tension between the independence of a poem and its relation to the 'extraneous' world. Often a poem can only be understood with reference to other poems by the same author or in the same tradition, and sometimes texts beyond even these confines act as keys unlocking a poem's mysteries.[135]

## 2. *Ending a poem*

Though not utterly irrelevant, the aspect of closure as autonomy is not the main issue here. Of more concern is the way in which poems come to a close, or, to look at it from the author's viewpoint, the way in which poets bring their creations to a conclusion. Only two critics have examined the topic: Barbara Smith, at length, in the book already mentioned[136] and, all too briefly, I.A. Richards in a rather slight contribution to a symposium.[137] Distinguishing between the form of a poem and its content (simply for convenience) Smith considers closure to be either *structural* or *thematic*. A poem can terminate with a particular pattern—a parallel couplet say, or a

---

134. Smith, *Closure*, 97.
135. This embodies the concept of *intertextuality*, namely, reference to another text for complete intelligibility. See Riffaterre, *Semiotics*, 81ff.
136. See note 134; also, Häublein, *Stanza*.
137. Richards: 1963; he is more concerned with the psychological aspect of the creative process. For him, a poem ends by solving the problem posed at its beginning.

variant refrain; this is *structural* or *formal closure*. It can also come to
an end by referring to finality in some guise (sleep, death, tranquillity)
using thematic closure. In addition, of course, there can be overlapping mixtures of formal and thematic closure which serve to
reinforce the closural effect. Rather than catalogue the different
kinds of closure, it seems preferable to look at some points of theory.
It is first necessary to elaborate the concept of *retroactive reading*, as
the semioticians term it,[138] a concept already envisaged by Smith in
the guise of 'retrospective patterning'.[139] In the process of linear
reading[140] of a poem, when one is reading it through from beginning
to end (or listening to it read/performed), patterns of expectancy are
continually being set up and then corrected. So the first word or line
of a poem implies that the next word (or line) will correspond to it in
some way. As each successive line is read, its pattern as experienced
serves to alter what the reader tends to expect, and he (or she) then
makes what has already been read conform to the pattern actually
present. Or, to put it more concretely, let us suppose that line 1 has
been read: it has a certain metre, a specific content and length. Line 2
is expected to conform to the characteristics of line 1. Of course, it
may or it may not. After line 2, line 1 is rapidly re-scanned by the
reader (= retroactive reading) and a further pattern, based on both
these lines, is envisaged for line 3. Once line 3 has been read, the
previous two lines are examined again, and a corresponding pattern
is imagined for line 4—and so on. The poem may be so regular that
practically no retrospective patterning is required—and one could
argue that such a poem would be extremely boring. At the other
extreme, a poem might be so quirky that mental feedback of this kind
is needed all the way through. It is a matter of degree. Riffaterre
comments that 'the maximal effect of retroactive reading, the climax
of its function as a generator of significance, naturally comes at the
end of the poem'.[141]

### 3. *Structural closure*

As will be noted (especially in the section on structural poetic
devices) certain patterns can determine the end of a poem. An
obvious example is the acrostic where the final letter of the alphabetic

138. Riffaterre, *Semiotics*, 6.
139. Smith, *Closure*, 10-14, with clear explanation.
140. See Le Groupe μ, *Rhétorique de la poésie* (Paris, 1977), 161-188 and 123.
141. Riffaterre, *Semiotics*, 6.

sequence marks the end of the poem. Other examples include the tricolon (e.g. Ps 27,14—contrast Ps 31,25), the closing monocolon (Isa 33,24), envelope figure (Ps 135) and refrain (Pss 24; 42-43; 46; 67) and enumeration in number parallelism (Prov 30,15ff). A simile, too, can mark closure (Jer 9,21; 23,14; 23,29; 49,22; 51,40), as can gender-matched synonyms (Jer 48,46).

## 4. *Thematic closure*
Reference of some kind to finality is often used as an indicator of closure. Examples include reference to death (Isa 22,13; Ps 137; Job 7; 8; 32) to destruction (Nah 2,14; Isa 28,22; Jer 51,58) to eternity (Pss 133; 139; 145; 146; etc.) or simply to finality (Jer 5,31d). The allusion need not necessarily be negative; it can describe a change of state, deliverance, for instance (Jer 15,21) or joy (Pss 53, 65) or generally to the future (Pss 22; 31-32; 51; 52) and so on.

## 5. *Closure in Ugaritic and Akkadian*
In *CTA* 24, for example, the envelope figure closes the section lines 40-50; *CTA* 16 vi 54-58 comprises a final curse on Yassubu; the final lines of the Baal Cycle (*CTA* 6 vi 42-52) comprise a closing hymn. In the Babylonian Theodicy, the final line of the last stanza is a monocolon (*BWL*, 88-89), while the Epic of Atrahasis closes with a solution to the problem of overpopulation with which the poem began.[142]

### BIBLIOGRAPHY

(a) *General*
Richards, I.A. 'How Does a Poem Know When It Is Finished?', *Parts and Wholes. The Hayden Colloquium on Scientific Method and Concept* (ed. Lerner, D.; New York/London, 1963), 163-174.
Smith, *Closure*.

(b) *Semitic*
Mirsky, A. 'Stylistic Devices for Conclusion in Hebrew', *Semitics* 5 (1977) 9-23.Cf. O'Connor, *Structure*, 424-425.

142. 'It is in this ending, I would insist, that we find the key to understanding the whole': Kilmer, *Or* 41 (1972) 171; cf. 173. For closure as a solution to a problem, see note 137 above.

# 4

## THE HEBREW POET IN ACTION

### 4.1 *Oral Poetry*

*What is oral poetry?*

True oral poetry is composed and performed before an audience[1] and belongs to a stage in the history of a culture prior to the widespread use of writing. The basic components of such poetry are improvisation, the complete absence of writing in any form, and an audience. These components will be considered in detail later. Unfortunately, as a moment's thought will indicate, no direct record of such poetry from ancient times is available to us: we can only surmise and extrapolate from written documents. Further, oral poetry for a particular culture developed over a number of years, to be radically changed by the advent of writing. However, certain characteristics mark oral poetry and these can be recognised even in such written records as survive from the past.

*The new approach*

The modern approach to the study of ancient poetry, which assesses to what degree it is oral in origin, was initiated by Parry in his research on Homeric verse.[2] 'His contributions to Homeric scholarship are twofold: he saw the relevance of the modern oral poetry of Yugoslavia and succeeded in recording a great deal of it; and he demonstrated beyond doubt that Homer was an oral poet, depending on a gradually evolved traditional store of fixed phrases which covered most common ideas and situations.'[3] In other words, he showed that such poetry was formulaic.[4] Parry's work, especially on

---

1. 'Live' in modern parlance.
2. See Parry: 1971.
3. Kirk: 1962, 59.
4. For a full account see Parry: 1971.

the subject of 'theme',[5] was continued by his student and co-worker, Lord, who is still in the process of publishing the Serbo-Croatian material they recorded together.

### Limitations of the Parry-Lord approach

Study of the Serbo-Croatian singers and their poetry has provided us with a very good idea of how such poets were trained, how they composed their poetry and the way they performed in public (see 2.1 below). It is now beyond doubt that even very long compositions could be created (and transmitted) without the aid of writing; that literacy, in fact, marks the end of true oral poetry.

However, the application of such findings to Greek epic poetry requires some caution.[6] The same care should be exercised when drawing conclusions concerning ancient Semitic oral poetry from a consideration of Yugoslav poetry and its poets. For, not only are there great differences in culture and language between the Serbo-Croatian material and Semitic poetry; caution is required mainly because (by the very nature of the subject matter) we are working in the realm of conjecture. We can have no record of ancient Semitic *oral* poetry, so that extrapolations from Yugoslavian songs and song-making[7] remain hypothetical, no matter how well based they may seem.[8]

### 4.2 Oral Poetry: Theory

The theory of oral poetry, now rather evolved since Parry's day, embraces the oral poet or bard, the relationship between non-written and written verse, the tension between creativity and tradition, the parts played by the audience and musical instruments and, finally, the factor of transmission.

### The bard

'The true oral poet ... is one who transmits and composes poetry without the aid of writing, who absorbs songs easily from others and elaborates them extempore without the help of trial versions jotted down in notebooks, and who reproduces them on demand with the

---

5. Lord: 1960; for 'theme' see 3.2 below.
6. See especially Kirk: 1962, 88ff.
7. And, of course, from Greek epic poetry.
8. See below.

aid of a fixed vocabulary and a powerful and highly trained memory.'[9]

The poet was, in the first instance, *a performer* who sang in front of an audience. This meant that he had to satisfy his listeners with regard to speech (he could not hesitate over his choice of words), to topics and to use of language, and with regard to development of theme. He had to treat traditional subjects in a traditional manner yet at the same time maintain the interest of his audience by innovating. By maintaining a strict balance between the well-worn which was familiar and the new which was strange, he avoided boring or alienating his audience. Accordingly, in order to perform live and inventively to a critical auditorium the poet required a *special technique* of composition.

It would appear that in order to acquire this technique, the oral poet first served a term of *apprenticeship*. Lord distinguishes three stages in training. First, simply listening while others performed and so absorbing themes, formulas and rhythms. Then, a period of practice in singing the basic rhythmic pattern and 'fitting his thoughts and their expression into this fairly rigid form'. With the ability to sing one song well, the apprentice bard could move on to the final stage: learning further songs and improvising his own. By this process the oral poet acquired a 'special grammar within the grammar of the language necessitated by the versification. The formulas [were] the phrases and clauses and sentences of this specialized poetic grammar'.[10] He enlarged, too, his repertoire of formulas and themes—the poet of real ability and worth going on, then, to create his own formulaic material.

*Oral poetry and written poetry*
If the introduction of writing can be imagined as having taken place at a single point in time, then the relationship between pre-literate (or oral) and post-literate poetry can be represented by a chart:

9. Kirk: 1962, 55.
10. Lord: 1960, 36.

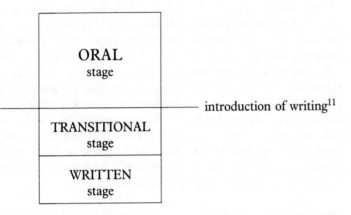

introduction of writing[11]

At the *completely oral stage* poets were able to compose even very long stretches of verse and these compositions could be passed on for generations.[12] Of such literature we have no direct record.

With the *introduction of writing* there came a revolutionary change. Although writing was probably first used for commercial purposes, it must gradually have been adopted even by oral poets who were now no longer totally dependent on memory and could, at the very least, jot down some written reminders for their compositions. However, whether they did or not, and if so, to what extent, are also matters for conjecture. At this *transitional stage* true oral poetry was starting to decline while literate poets were beginning to find their feet.

The final stage was that of *written poetry*, embracing both the written record of oral poetry and poetry composed purely in writing. The documents we possess of any civilisation belong to this final stage and it is the task of scholars to determine which elements belong to oral tradition and which do not. There is no clear-cut division between the two, however, as is generally recognised.[13]

11. For a more detailed chart see 2.3. Note that graphic representation (art) can overlap the whole set of three stages; cf. P. Garelli (ed.), *Gilgameš et sa légende* (Paris, 1960) 179.

12. As has been demonstrated by the field studies of Parry and Lord.

13. 'A written poetry based on the cultural assumptions of its parent oral poetry would long preserve the traditional metre and methods of the improvising art, before cultural change brought about new literary expectations and different means of composing poetry' (Lawrence: 1966, 176).

Two other problems remain to be considered, namely *how* purely oral poetry was committed to writing, and *why*. With regard to the methods of recording oral poetry, it might seem obvious that dictation was the simplest way.[14] Lord has shown, however, by actual experiment, that this can lead to distortion in a text. Other possibilities are that the poet himself wrote down his orally composed text, or that such a text was memorised (either by the poet or by a listener) and written down later from memory. Once again we can only speculate. As to the reasons for preserving such orally composed texts in writing, the main one must have been to prevent them being lost for ever. Secondarily, other poets may have wanted such poems as sources for their own compositions.[15]

*Spontaneity and tradition*

Two basic but not unrelated questions are involved in the contrasting of spontaneity with tradition. The first, concerned with the influence of writing on the creativity of oral poets, has already been discussed.[16] The other asks how cliche-ridden traditional poetry can be considered either spontaneous or creative.[17]

The solution can be stated fairly concisely: Traditional poetic diction was almost a secondary language, learnt (as has been seen) largely through apprenticeship; and it was in this acquired 'language' that the oral poets composed. Their originality 'did not lie in the choice of specially appropriate epithets or phrases, but on the one hand in the whole conception and scale of the poem, and on the other in the consistently fluid and adept handling of traditional phraseology'.[18]

As for the *origins* of this tradition: it evolved gradually over the lifetimes of several poets. 'A single man or even a whole group of men who set out in the most careful way could not make even a beginning at such an oral diction. When one singer . . . has hit upon a phrase

14. Hillers-McCall: 1976.
15. On this point see B. Alster, *Dumuzi's Dream* (Mesopotamia 1; Copenhagen, 1972) 22.27.132.
16. See above and the 'life-cycle' set out below.
17. Or: How poets, bound slavishly to stereotyped formulas and set poetic diction can never produce original and spontaneous verse. See Nagler: 1974.
18. Kirk: 1962, 82 on Homer. 'The good singer wins his fame by his ease and versatility in handling a tradition which he knows more thoroughly than anyone else and of which his talent shows him the highest use, but his poetry remains throughout the sum of longer and shorter passages which he has heard' (Parry: 1932, 15).

which is pleasing and easily used other singers will hear it, and then, when faced at the same point in the line with the need of expressing the same idea, they will recall it and use it.'[19] The analogy with natural language is powerful: both are acquired from an early age over a number of years by the 'direct method'; both are largely made up of traditional vocabulary and expressions; and both gradually shed archaisms as new words and phrases are invented in their stead.[20]

Returning to the question touched on in the previous section and repeated at the beginning of this, to wit the effect of writing on oral poetry, it has been shown by Lord and Parry that it tends to destroy spontaneity.[21] Four stages, in fact, can be posited within the development of an oral tradition:[22]

*The life-cycle of an oral tradition* (after Kirk)

(1) ORIGINATIVE STAGE

The beginnings of narrative poetry with short, relatively simple songs; no information is available for this stage.

(2) CREATIVE STAGE

'The range of narrative songs is greatly extended and the technique of memory and improvisation is refined from generation to genera- tion . . . singers learn an initial repertoire from older men, but in the course of time considerably extend this repertoire by their own inventions and improvisations.'

(3) REPRODUCTIVE STAGE

'The established oral techniques are still used by unlettered bards both for memorization and to facilitate the transposition, often though not always intentional, of language or minor episodes from one acquired song to another.' *Writing* is introduced.

(4) PERIOD OF DECLINE

The use of writing, introduced at some time in the previous stage, is now widespread and 'the reproductive poet now begins to lose control of his inherited oral techniques'.

19. Parry: 1932, 7.
20. 'Every creative oral poet extends, in some degree at least, the range of the traditional vocabulary and the inherited thematic material' (Kirk: 1962, 82). See also Notopoulos: 1962, 366.
21. See now Nagler: 1974.
22. Following Kirk: 1962, 95-98; all quotations are from these pages. On the decline of such poetry see, too, C.M. Bowra, *Heroic Poetry* (London, 1952) 537-567.

This, of course, is a schematic representation, but it is helpful in clarifying the issues involved.

### Oral poetry and communication theory

By using a simple model for communication theory (based on Jakobson's schematic representation)[23] it is possible to show the interaction of the various elements comprising oral poetry. At the two poles are the sender or oral poet (addresser/bard) and the receiver (addressee/audience). What is sent and received is the message, in this case a poem. The poem is recited in the context of a live performance. Accordingly, there is contact between sender and receiver(s), a contact maintained by singing (the bard's contribution) and by the reaction of the audience (stony indifference, applause, traditional responses, etc.). Both bard and audience share a common code, i.e. the traditional language of oral poetry, with its conventions and its peculiar vocabulary. The only element in this interchange which survives for us to examine is, of course, the poem (the message).

The basic elements are:

| SENDER | MESSAGE | RECEIVER |
|---|---|---|
| (author, | (text, | (reader, |
| poet, | poem, | audience, |
| bard, etc.) | 'song') | etc.) |

These elements can be set out in a table, as follows:

SENDER

BARD
*themes*
—action
—time
—place

*principle of thrift*

*formulas*
—word-pairs
—expressions

*technique*
—adding style
—repetitions
—verse-patterns
  (and music)

23. Jakobson in Sebeok, *Style*, 353 and 357.

MESSAGE                    POETRY
                           (poet and audience interact)

                           *feedback*
                           —choruses
                           —responses
                           —applause
                           —questions

RECEIVER                   LIVE AUDIENCE

Table applying communication theory (left) to oral poetic technique (right).

## Audience participation

'The members of the audience remain the most important figures in any study of tradition both in the restrictions which they place upon the poet and in the advantage their special type of knowledge offers to the poet.'[24] In an oral poetic tradition the audience—for whose benefit the poet recited—fulfilled a dual function, being at the same time catalysts for creativity, yet staunch preservers of tradition. The poet's role was to entertain; this he did by being spontaneous, creative and inventive, but always without going too far beyond the confines of tradition. He had to keep his listeners amused, but could not afford to estrange them by introducing too much novelty. Part of his skill, therefore, lay in reacting correctly to the audience, and they, in their turn, acted as a stabilising influence on his performance. Naturally, the audience participated by joining in choruses and refrains, by clapping or stamping their feet, and even perhaps by asking direct questions.

## Music

Our knowledge of the extent to which musical accompaniment was a feature of ancient oral poetry is derived by inference from the field studies already mentioned[25] and from indications in Greek poetry. Yugoslav poets sing to the sound of the *gusle* (a one-stringed violin); in ancient Greece the *kitharis* (a harp) was used. Such instruments were used (a) to mark the accentual stresses in a line of verse; (b) to

---

24. Scott: 1974, 188.
25. See, too, J.R. Smart, 'A Bedouin Song from the Egyptian Western Desert', *JSS* 12 (1967) 245-267. For the relationship between music and poetry cf. M.C. Beardsley, 'Verse and Music', in Wimsatt, *Versification*, 238-252.

fill out the line, especially at the beginning or end; (c) to provide emphasis at important points, and (d) to hide the poet's hesitation as he improvised, allowing him time to think.[26]

## Transmission

This topic has already been considered.[27] The elements of an oral tradition most likely to persist were the technically more perfect. Accordingly, crisp formulas, lines exhibiting assonance or rhyme, chiastically patterned verses and the like were all preserved because they represented the best results of creative endeavour. Re-working by true oral poets and verbatim recitation by their lesser fellows, in combination with some form of written record, were together effective in maintaining the poetic tradition.[28]

### 4.3 *Techniques and Characteristics of Oral Poetry*

#### The formula

The formula is a ready-made phrase taken from traditional diction (or invented by a poet and eventually becoming part of traditional poetic diction) which fits the metrical slots characteristic of a particular verse-form.[29]

---

26. In the final stage of an oral tradition the reciting poets (or rhapsodes) used a long staff instead of a *kitharis*, which 'was in fact a traveller's staff in origin, and is often shown with a crook'—it was used by the vagrant reciter (as perhaps by some of his creative predecessors) in his journeys from town to town and village to village. It became especially associated with the rhapsode, I suggest, because from the beginning it was used during his performance to give emphasis to his words' (Kirk: 1962, 315; also 91 and plate 7b). For ancient Near Eastern traditions cf. M. Duchesne-Guillemin, 'Music in Ancient Mesopotamia and Egypt', *WA* 12, 3 (Feb. 1981) 287-297, and in fact the whole of this issue of *WA*. Also, W.G. Lambert, 'The Converse Tablet: A Litany with Musical Instructions', *Albright FS* (1971) 336-353; A.D. Kilmer, 'The Discovery of an Ancient Mesopotamian Theory of Music', *PAPS* 115 (1971) 131-149; and A. Shaffer, 'A New Musical Term in Ancient Mesopotamian Music', *Iraq* 43 (1981) 79-83 [*sihpum* = 'inversion'].

27. See above; for Homeric poetry cf. Kirk: 1962, 301-315.

28. As noted above, poetic material was written down for fear that otherwise it would be lost. Exactly the same process is happening today when the songs and sagas of non-literate peoples are being recorded before the memory of them dies out. Electronic equipment makes the task easier and perhaps more objective results are achieved, but the purpose remains identical. This would suggest that in ancient times the writing down of texts took place at a time when oral tradition was on the wane and writing well established.

29. Parry defined the formula as 'a group of words which is regularly employed under the same metrical conditions to express a given essential idea', but the metrical aspect need not be so strong; Culley, *Oral Formulaic*, 10, in fact prefers 'a repeated

*Theme*
The theme is 'a group of ideas regularly used in telling a tale in the formulaic style' (Parry), or 'a recurrent element of narration or description in traditional oral poetry'.[30] Examples of themes are: the description of a hero's weapon; exhortation by a leader; assembly of troops. The oral poet had to hand a stock of ready-made scenes and descriptions on which he drew to flesh out the bare bones of his narrative verse.[31]

*Adding style*
Since improvising poetry to an audience is by necessity a continuous process, its demands are most easily met by composing one line after another.[32] Known as adding style, this procedure results in poetry which reflects the technique used. For instance, end-stopping is preferred so that enjambment (or run-on lines) rarely occurs. See also next paragraph.

*Characteristics*
Because poetry of this kind is created by the use of formula and theme in an agglomerative style it exhibits certain characteristics. There is a high density of *archaisms* due to the restraints imposed by the technique. Both formula and theme preserve obsolete components of language that would otherwise have fallen into disuse. *Sound-patterns* such as alliteration, onomatopoeia, assonance and rhyme are all fully exploited and within the formulas there is manipulation in order to achieve particular effects. *Repetition* in all its forms is, of course, a pervasive feature. It is true that most, if not all, of the above

---

group of words the length of which corresponds to one of the divisions in the poetic structure'.

30. Another definition: 'a repeated narrative element together with its verbal expression, that portion of a poem, an aggregate of specific verses, that tells a certain repeated part of the narrative, measurable in terms of lines and even words and word combinations' (Lord, in Duggan: 1975, 20).

31. 'In a sense almost nothing really unexpected happens in the Iliad. This is the result of oral composition which depends on the use of standard language and to a large extent on fixed and traditional themes. It also gives a poem an important part of its effect of authenticity and concentration' (Kirk: 1962, 77).

32. This is not so evident as it sounds. A poet, for example, could think up five-line stanzas and deliver each stanza as a unit, but it would entail longish intervals of silence between the stanzas during which an audience would tend to grow restless. Cf. also J.A. Notopoulos, 'Parataxis in Homer: A New Approach to Literary Criticism', *TAPA* 80 (1949) 1-23.

characteristics are to be found in non-oral poetry. However, oral poetry is distinctive in other ways, a real hallmark being *contradiction*. In the course of improvising, an oral bard will perhaps apply a simile or a formula in a mechanical fashion, even where it quite obviously does not suit, though most probably neither he nor the audience will notice. Evidently, too, oral poetry will make no use of such features as the acrostic which belong exclusively to written verse. The same applies to certain forms of wordplay. Finally, *variants* of the same poem are more likely to co-exist within a non-writing tradition where there is less tendency to uniformity.

### 4.4 *Ancient Hebrew Oral Poetry*

*Introductory*

In addition to the cautions voiced in 1.3[33] further circumspection needs to be exercised when applying theories derived from such comparisons to Hebrew literature. In a recent survey, Long concludes that due to sheer lack of evidence, especially at the sociological level, much of the surmise concerning oral elements in ancient Hebrew poetry must remain conjecture.[34] We know very little about the performer (for instance, questions about his identity, training, pay, special literary forms preferred all remain unanswerable) or about his social position, the behaviour of the audience, where and when the performances took place and so on.[35] Without subscribing totally to Long's rather negative views, the following paragraphs have to be read with his provisos in mind.

Little or no account has been taken here of researches into the oral-formulaic character of either Ugaritic or Akkadian poetry since they too can only be largely speculative. They are important, in spite of this, and cannot be ignored by the interested student.[36]

---

33. With regard to comparisons made between the Serbo-Croatian material collected by Parry and Lord, and ancient Greek verse.

34. B.O. Long, 'Recent Field Studies in Oral Literature and their Bearing on OT Criticism', *VT* 26 (1976) 187-198.

35. 'Another area demanding re-examination has to do with attempts at reconstructing the wording of oral compositions or Vorlage on the basis of written texts. In the light of newer field studies, such attempts seem highly dubious.' 'Attempts at reconstruction have usually viewed style as mostly a matter of words, completely ignoring or denying what is most characteristic of oral literature, namely, the living, variegated, shifting social context in which performance takes place' (Long: 1976, 195).

36. See Afanasjeva: 1974-75; Hillers-McCall: 1976; and Whitaker's thesis.

*The bard*

'We must assume that there was in Israel . . . a class of professional story-tellers. These popular story-tellers, familiar with old songs and legends, wandered about the country and were probably to be found regularly at popular festivals.'[37] Gunkel's assumption now seems even more likely in view of the field work by Parry and Lord (discussed at length already). Building on this assumption, Campbell argues that 'a good, if speculative case can be made that stories such as Ruth . . . were transmitted orally . . . in the elevated prose style which we have attested in the end product, and indeed were probably originally composed in that style. Differences of style between one story and another would be due to the individual creativity of the story-tellers, each of whom could probably recite a number of tales from memory. They were told and retold, and were passed down from one generation to the next within the guild.'[38]

Campbell suggests that such tales were told in the villages and towns of the countryside rather than in the main capitals, most probably in the village square or to folk gathered round a well or spring, in the evening. His suggestion is certainly plausible. As to the identity of these itinerant bards, he considers them to have been the country levites and the wise women. The *country levites* had the task of going round the country[39] teaching and explaining the law to unlettered people; they were also skilled singers.[40] The *wise women* feature in stories such as 2 Sm 14,1-20 and 20,16-22 as having a way with words. Further, women singers are well-attested in Israel, notably Miriam (Ex 15,21), Deborah (Jgs 5,12) and Jephthah's daughter (Jgs 11,34.40).[41] Sennacherib exacted tribute from King Hezekiah and it included both male and female singers,[42] while the 'woman with tambourine'-figurines have been found in Palestinian sites from the eleventh to the eighth centuries BC.[43] The *prophets* were masters, too, in varying degrees, of oral improvised poetry.

---

37. H. Gunkel, *Genesis* (Göttingen, 1910) XXXI.
38. E.J. Campbell, *Ruth* (*AB* 7A; Garden City, 1975) 19. Cf. Bar 3,23.
39. Is the root of 'levite' cognate perhaps with Akk. *lamû, lawû*, 'to go round'?
40. See Dt 33,10; 2 Chr 17,7-9; 35,3; Neh 8,7-9, and H.-J. Kraus, *Worship in Israel* (ET: Oxford, 1966) 94-99.
41. Also Jer 9,16-21; 31,13 and the Ug. *ktrt*, 'skilly ones'.
42. *ANET*, 228.
43. Lapp, *BASOR* 173 (1964) 39-40; *BA* 30 (1967) 24-25.

*Oral or written poetry*

The fact remains that our only testimony to the poetic traditions of Israel, whether they were oral or written or both, is a written testimony. It is possible to share Long's pessimism that reconstructions based on a written text, our 'first, and only objective datum', are 'fundamentally and inherently misleading simply because too many of the necessary data are unavailable'.[44] It seems though, that by looking at neighbouring civilisations (notably Ugarit and Mesopotamia), by examining the Hebrew text very carefully and by general inference from analogy with the folk-poetry of elsewhere it is extremely likely that *Hebrew poetry, too, was oral*, at least in origin.

The invention of writing for Northwest Semitic[45] languages (not to mention the origin of writing itself) predates the known beginnings of Israel by a thousand years. The ancient inscriptions from Ebla (Tell Mardikh), the tablets of Ugarit and the Amarna Letters all attest as much. It is more than likely that scribal schools were set up in Israel[46] and existing oral compositions must have been written down for practice and as a way of recording a vanishing heritage for posterity. Such schools probably produced a new breed of writing poets whose compositions betray a preoccupation with the written rather than the spoken word.[47]

*The audience*

In general it can be assumed that the audience were not mere passive spectators, but joined in actively, perhaps even by a certain amount of their own improvisation. Of such activities we can gain a few hints. *Refrains* and *questions* show that the people listening were not mute; for example: 'Who is the Glorious King?' (Ps 24,8.10); 'Sorely have they afflicted me from my youth—Let Israel now say: "Sorely have

44. It must be remembered, of course, that most Hebrew poetry is *non-narrative*, so that conclusions derived from the field studies already mentioned cannot be applied automatically. See Long, *VT* 26 (1976) 198.

45. Or 'Syrian Semitic' in Gibson's terminology.

46. See J.P.J. Olivier, 'Schools and Wisdom Literature', *JNSL* 4 (1975) 49-60; Ahlström, *HTR* 59 (1966) 69-81; and 2 Sm 12,25; 1 Kgs 12,8; 2 Kgs 10,1.5; 1 Chr 27,32.

47. On the wordplay in Job 39,13, for instance, Guillaume, *Hooke FS*, 125, comments: 'This verse is of extraordinary interest because it indicates that the poetry of Job is a literary composition. Had it been recited, or, like the poetry of the prophets, been proclaimed in the ears of the people, the homonyms would have vanished into thin air. The author must have written this book for a highly cultured and sophisticated society.'

they afflicted me from my youth"' (Ps 129,1-2); 'Truly his steadfast love endures for ever' repeated after each of the 25 verses in Ps 136. Possibly the repeated question: 'Watchman! What is left of the night?' (Isa 21,11 NEB) was chanted by the audience. Note, too, the explicit rubric in 2 Chr 20,21: 'Jehoshaphat appointed singers for Yahweh, who in holy attire were to go out ahead of the troops praising (him) with: "Praise Yahweh/Truly his lovingkindness is eternal"'.[48]

## Social settings

A few words are in order here to give some idea of the occasions[49] at which poetry was sung or recited. Broadly speaking, two main classes of occasion can be posited: family affairs, such as birth, marriage or death, and inter-tribal occasions such as the big yearly feasts and liturgical festivals.[50] Before and at birth there were oracles (Gen 25,23; cf. Isa 11,1-9) and explanations of names given. Coming of age was marked by a blessing (Gen 27,27-29.40) and marriage was an excuse for a feast at which songs were sung and riddle-contests held (Jgs 14,12-18).[51] At death a final blessing could be in poetic form (Gen 49) and there were, of course, funeral chants.[52] Songs were also sung at work: while digging a well (Nb 21,17-18), harvesting (Isa 16,10) or guarding the city (Isa 21,11-12).

The yearly festivals included the Feast of Passover and Unleavened Bread, the Feast of Weeks, the Feast of Ingathering and the Feast of Atonement—largely following the annual cycle of spring to winter. In addition there was the monthly 'New Moon celebration', when trading was suspended—and, of course, the weekly observation of the Sabbath. Other annual feasts were Hanukkah and Purim (Esth 9,19). The people, streaming to these gatherings, would sing traditional songs[53] and there must have been plenty of opportunity for professional entertainers (the wandering bards) to perform in public.

---

48. Campbell: 1975, 14 (and 19), speculates that 'the audience participated in crafting these delightful *inclusios* [in Ruth] during the period of the oral transmission of the story, aiding the story-teller in his craft'.
49. 'Social setting' is my version of over-used 'Sitz im Leben'.
50. For the former see chiefly O. Eissfeldt, *The Old Testament. An Introduction* (ET: Oxford, 1965) 64-127; for the feasts: H.-J. Kraus, *Worship in Israel* (ET: Oxford, 1966) 26-91.
51. As well as the number-riddles in Proverbs, e.g. 30,15.
52. Jer 22,18-19; etc.
53. Such as the pilgrim songs alluded to in Pss 132; 84; etc.

Somewhere between these two categories come the tribal celebrations, when tribal law was laid down (Gen 9,6), or victory chants sung by women[54] during triumphal marches and at victory banquets. Popular proverbs were passed on from one country to the next by travelling merchants while at the other end of the scale, the classics of the ancient world were re-copied and translated by schoolboys in the temple schools.

## Music

In common with her neighbours Israel had a strong musical tradition, as is attested by the large variety of technical terms associated with music-making and by the archaeological evidence.[55] Although there is no direct testimony that bards improvised to the strains of music[56] it cannot be doubted that, at the various gatherings already mentioned, besides the well-known songs, singers created new ones. At such occasions music was provided by the bards who perhaps strummed as they sang, by the audience and by professional musicians.[57]

### 4.5 *Techniques and Characteristics of Oral Poetry in Hebrew*

The techniques and characteristics of oral poetry are to be found in classical Hebrew poetry, indicating that it, too, is oral in origin.[58]

---

54. Ex 15,20; Jgs 5; 11,34; 16,23-24; 1 Sm 18,6-7; Ps 68.

55. See the entries 'Music' and 'Musical Instruments' (both by E. Werner) in *IDB* (K-Q) 457-469 and 469-476; also 'Music' (by A.D. Kilmer) in *IDBS* 610-612—all with extensive bibliography.

56. Werner (*IDB* [K-Q] 463) notes that the levites were professional musicians who (according to Josephus Antiq. XX ix 6) were permitted to learn new hymns. 'What these new hymns were, we do not know; but that a change in the musical repertoire was nothing unheard of, is proved by the repeated exhortation "Sing to the Lord a new song".' For bardic songs see Gen 4,23-24 (cited by Werner).

57. The ancient Hurrian cult song (found at Ras Shamra) discussed by Kilmer (see note 55) is now available in reconstructed form on a record entitled 'Sounds from Silence. Recent Discoveries in Ancient Near Eastern Music'—by A.D. Kilmer, R.L. Crocker and R.R. Brown (Berkeley, Bit Enki Publications, 1977). For an evaluation of recent opinion on Canaanite music cf. O'Connor, *Structure*, 40-41. Relevant bibliography includes M. Duchesne-Guillemin, 'Les problèmes de la notation hourrite', *RA* 69 (1975) 159-173; H.G. Güterbock, 'Musical Notation in Ugarit', *RA* 64 (1970) 45-52; A.D. Kilmer, 'The Cult Song with Music from Ancient Ugarit. Another Interpretation', *RA* 68 (1974) 69-82; and D. Wulstan, 'The Earliest Musical Notation', *Music and Letters* 52 (1971) 365-382; 'Music from Ancient Ugarit', *RA* 68 (1974) 125-128.

58. No attempt at rigorous proof is made in paragraph 5 (which follows the sequence of paragraph 3) since the nature of the evidence is only indicative.

*Formula*
Formulas and formulaic expressions account for a certain amount of Hebrew poetry. For example:

שירו ליהוה שיר חדש    Sing to Yahweh a new song

is a stock formula used four times in quite separate poems: Isa 42,10; Pss 96,1; 98,1; 149,1[59]—and such examples could be multiplied. Further instances are given in 4.6, on Hebrew epic. The stereotyped *word-pair* is also formulaic, indicative of the improvising activity of the poets; this topic is dealt with fully in the section on word-pairs (6.3).

*Theme*
Theme, which is 'an intermediate structural device between the line and the poem itself',[60] really concerns content or subject-matter, for example, a stock scene or a stereotyped description. A typical theme in oral poetry is the mustering of an army, a theme developed in a poem such as Jgs 5.[61] Related to the theme, as Culley has pointed out, is the *motif* which is, in fact, a smaller component than the theme. An example is the manner in which enemies are described in individual complaint psalms.[62] It must be admitted, though, that so far very little work has been done in the area of theme in Hebrew poetry.[63]

*Adding style*
Perhaps one of the strongest indications that ancient Hebrew poetry was composed orally is *parataxis*, 'the placing side by side of words, images, clauses, or scenes without connectives that directly and immediately coordinate the parts with one another'.[64] To this can be added the pervasive presence of both extension and parallelism. *Extension*, in the form of lists, cumulative similes, metaphors and similes in series, numerical sets and the like, is so significant that it is reviewed in a separate section (12.2); there is no need to repeat the

---

59. Culley, *Oral Formulaic*, provides these and other examples.
60. Culley, *Oral Formulaic*, 100; see 17-19.
61. Also Joel 4,9-12; the same theme occurs in Ugaritic; cf. Watson, *Or* 43 (1979) 112-117.
62. Details in Culley, *Oral Formulaic*, 101.
63. Cf. Clines, *CBQ* 38 (1976) 483-507 and Culley, *Semeia* 3 (1975) 3-13.
64. So A.J. Hauser, 'Judges 5: Parataxis in Hebrew Poetry', *JBL* 99 (1980) 23-41 (esp. 26). See also Gerleman, *VT* 1 (1951) 168-180. Another example is Ps 19,3-4.

material here. *Parallelism*, too, has its own chapter (Chapter 6). It is clear that by the use of these techniques which amount to the adding style of oral poetry, a bard could produce quantities of verse with little effort.

## Characteristics

Most of the characteristics of oral poetry are present in Hebrew: *archaisms* (see 3.4), exploitation of *sound patterns* (see Chapter 9), *repetition* in all its forms (11.2) and *expletives* or ballast variants (see 11.3). Here can be mentioned the *variant forms* of a given poem (for example, 2 Sm 22 and Ps 18)[65] and *contradictions* due to misapplied similes or the mechanical use of stock word-pairs[66] common in oral poetry. As in this kind of poetry, too, Hebrew verse uses *enjambment* (11.3) only rarely.

### BIBLIOGRAPHY

(a) *General*

*Haymes Bibliography of the Oral Theory* (Publications of the Milman Parry Collection, Cambridge, Mass., 1973); a supplement is in preparation.

Duggan, J.J. (ed.) *Oral Literature: Seven Essays* (Edinburgh, 1975).

Kirk, G.S. *The Songs of Homer* (Cambridge, 1962).

Lawrence, R.F. 'The Formulaic Theory and its Application to English Alliterative Poetry' in Fowler, *Essays* (1966) 166-183.

Lord, A.B. *The Singer of Tales* (Harvard Studies in Comparative Literature 24, Cambridge, Mass., 1960).

Nagler, M.N. *Spontaneity and Tradition: A Study in the Oral Art of Homer* (Berkeley, 1974).

Notopoulos, J.A.'The Homeric Hymns as Oral Poetry. A Study of the Post-Homeric Oral Tradition', *AJP* 83 (1962) 337-368.

Parry, M. 'Studies in the Epic Technique of Oral Verse-Making II. "The Homeric Language" as the Language of Oral Poetry', *HSCP* 43 (1932) 1-50.

65.  Also Gen 49 and Dt 33; 1 Chr 16,8-36 = Pss 105,1-15; 96,1-13 and 106,1.47-48; Ps 31,2-4b = Ps 71,1-3; Ps 60,7-14 = Ps 108,8-14.

66.  'No clear examples of contradictions due to oral formulaic composition [in the Psalms] can be cited. This is not surprising. The examples of this phenomenon from other oral poetry . . . concerned inappropriate adjectives in noun-adjective combinations. Since this combination is not nearly as common in Hebrew as in some other languages, no stock epithets have developed in Hebrew poetry which could be used inappropriately' (Culley, *Oral Formulaic*, 97). However, see Ps 84,9, adduced by Boling, *JSS* 14 (1969) 121. Note, additionally, that the *anonymity* of most Hebrew (and ancient Near Eastern) poetry also points to oral composition; see C.M. Bowra, *Heroic Poetry* (London, 1952) 404-405.

—*The Making of Homeric Verse: the collected papers of Milman Parry*. Edited by A. Parry (Oxford, 1971).

Scott, W.C. *The Oral Nature of the Homeric Simile* (Supplements to Mnemosyne XXVIII; Leiden, 1974).

(b) *Semitic*

Afanasjeva, V. 'Mündlich überlieferte Dichtung (oral poetry) und schriftlich Literatur in Mesopotamien', *AAASH* 22 (1974) 121-135; 23 (1975) 41-63.65-76.

Gitay, Y. 'Deutero-Isaiah: Oral or Written?', *JBL* 99 (1980) 185-197.

Hillers, D.R.—McCall, M.H. Jr 'Homeric Dictated Texts: A Reexamination of Some Near Eastern Evidence', *HCSP* 80 (1976) 19-23.

Niditch, S. 'The Composition of Isaiah 1', *Bib* 61 (1980) 509-529.

Parunak, H. Van Dyke 'Oral Typesetting: Some Uses of Biblical Structure', *Bib* 62 (1981) 153-168.

Whitaker, R.E. *A Formulaic Analysis of Ugaritic Poetry* (Harvard, 1969). He examines traditional usage of epithets, line patterns, formulae and clusters of formulae associated with specific themes and shows Ugaritic verse to have the characteristics of oral poetry; cf. summary, *HTR* 63 (1970) 523-524.

—'Ugaritic Formulae', *RSP* III, 207-219.

Zwettler, M.J. 'Classical Arabic Poetry between Folk and Oral Tradition', *JAOS* 96 (1976) 198-212.

## 4.6 *Epic Poetry in Hebrew?*

*Epic in general*

Before turning to consider whether the classification 'epic' can be applied to classical Hebrew poetry, at least in part, it is of course necessary to look at what the term means.[67] From one aspect, the mode of recitation determines the class to which sets of words belong.[68] If, instead, epic is accepted as a concrete literary type, then epic, narrowly defined, can be either traditional or literary. *Traditional* epic is a narrative poem which has evolved through the process of oral composition; *literary* epic, on the other hand, is the work of an

---

67. Much of what follows derives from Conroy's excellent survey.

68. In tabular form:

| *when words are* | *we have* |
|---|---|
| (a) ACTED | DRAMA |
| (b) READ | FICTION |
| (c) SUNG | LYRIC |
| (d) SPOKEN | EPIC |

following N. Frye, *Anatomy of Criticism. Four Essays* (Princeton, 1957) 246-248. The distinctions are notional. For other modes of classification see Conroy: 1980, 16-18.

individual writing poet. The primary characteristic of traditional epic poetry is that it is heroic.[69]

According to *the mode of composition*, then, epic is either

| | |
|---|---|
| (i) TRADITIONAL | —if composed by traditional *oral* techniques; |
| (ii) LITERARY | —if composed in *writing* (by an individual author). |

As to *content* it is generally agreed that this must be 'heroic' (which also refers to the kind of society this kind of epic reflects). 'The first concern of heroic poetry is to tell of action'—'(the hero) must pass through an ordeal to prove his worth and this is almost necessarily some kind of violent action'—and it implies the belief 'that human beings are in themselves sufficient objects of interest and that their chief claim is the pursuit of honour through risk'.[70]

As to *form*, again there is general agreement that an epic must be lengthy: 'a long poem of a heroic age'[71] is a sample definition. Evidently 'long' and 'lengthy' are comparative terms and cannot be quantified absolutely.[72]

Summarising, then, an epic is poetry which is spoken, rather than acted, sung or read silently.[73] It is a long narrative poem, composed orally, and is concerned chiefly with heroic deeds of an edifying kind.

### Epic poetry in the ancient Near East

Since terms such as 'epic', 'myth', 'legend' and so on are used very loosely by scholars dealing with literature of the ancient Near East (chiefly of Mesopotamia and Syria), these labels cannot be accepted without question. The term 'epic', as defined above, can be applied to the Gilgamesh Cycle, perhaps to the Story of Atraḥasis. In its secondary sense (literary epic), the same designation can, perhaps, be applied to the Poem of Erra—though there the 'hero' is a god.[74]

---

69. 'It is clear that the term "heroic" is crucial to a definition of primary epic as understood in contemporary general literary studies' (Conroy: 1980, 19).

70. C.M. Bowra, *Heroic Poetry* (London, 1952) 48 and 4-5.

71. *Concise Oxford Dictionary of English Literature* (Oxford, 1970) 176, cited by Conroy.

72. C.M. Bowra, *Heroic Poetry* (London, 1952) 330-367, discusses this aspect.

73. Evidently this classification cannot be rigid. An oral poet would mime some of the actions, sing snatches of song and use a form of recitative in the course of a long narrative poem. On mime cf Gibson, *CML*, 116 n. 3.

74. See the discussion by L. Cagni, *The Poem of Erra* (Malibu, 1977) 6-13.

As for Ugaritic literature, the Aqhat Tale and the Story of King Keret can be classed as epic. Both have a king as the main protagonist (or hero);[75] both draw from a stock of traditional narrative patterns and motifs; both can be compared with Homeric epic.[76] They are, therefore, heroic narrative poetry, and 'in their final form at least they are the product of a courtly setting and were sung no doubt by professional minstrels'.[77] The Baal Cycle, on the other hand, does not belong to the same category.

*Epic poetry in classical Hebrew*
There has been much debate on whether the Pentateuch in its original form was poetry, and if so, whether it could be classed as epic. Aside from the partially hypothetical nature of this point of view (since it can only be based on a reconstructed text) it must be rejected on the grounds of content alone. The pentateuchal material (in particular the J-E sources) does not deal with heroes and so cannot be classed as epic.[78] However, the debate is rather wider than scholars such as Conroy and Talmon suppose.

While it is true, as Talmon argues, that 'the ancient Hebrew writers purposefully nurtured and developed prose narration to take the place of the epic genre which by its content was intimately bound up with the world of paganism and appears to have had a special standing in the polytheistic cults',[79] this is not the whole story. Traces of epic remain, even in a book as late as Job.[80] There are strong elements of the heroic epic in Jgs 13-16 and the editors of Genesis did not manage to expurgate every trace of epic poetry. The Song of Deborah, too, has been compared with ancient Near Eastern epic.[81]

---

75. However the dissent of J.C.L. Gibson, 'Myth, Legend and Folklore in the Ugaritic Keret and Aqhat Texts', *VTS* 28 (1975) 60-68 must be registered here.

76. Cf. C.H. Gordon, *Introduction to Old Testament Times* (Ventnor, 1953) 89-99.

77. Conroy: 1980, 24.

78. As Conroy: 1980, 27, concludes.

79. Talmon: 1978, 354. The converse is also true, namely, that in contradistinction to their ancient Near Eastern counterparts (notably at Mari), the Hebrew prophets used verse modelled on popular Canaanite poetry.

80. N.M. Sarna, 'Epic Substratum in the Book of Job', *JBL* 76 (1957) 13-25.

81. Talmon's cautionary words are worth repeating here, however: 'The combined evidence marshalled by scholars from their survey of biblical literature cannot provide a sound basis for positing the existence of full-fledged Hebrew epics in the biblical period . . . There can be no doubt that in the historiographies, the narratives, Psalms

BIBLIOGRAPHY

(a) *Epic in general*
Ker, W.P. *Epic and Romance. Essays on Medieval Literature* (London, 1908; repr. New York, 1957).
Merchant, P. *The Epic* (The Critical Idiom 17; London, 1971).

(b) *Ancient Near Eastern epic (including Hebrew)*
Conroy, C. 'Hebrew Epic: Historical Notes and Critical Reflections', *Bib* 61 (1980) 1-30 (with ample references).
Talmon, S. 'The "Comparative Method" in Biblical Interpretation—Principles and Problems', *VTS* 19 (1978) 320-356, esp. 351-356.
—'Did There Exist a Biblical National Epic?', *Proceedings 7th World Congress of Jewish Studies, 1977* (Jerusalem, 1981) 41-62.

---

and even in the prophetic books we do encounter features which are characteristic of the epic genre: poetic rhythm, parallelistic structure and formulaic language. However, these features are found also in literature to which the designation "epic" cannot be applied' (Talmon: 1978, 354).

# 5

## METRE

### 5.1 *What is Metre?*

*Rhythm*

Since it is generally agreed that metre is a form of rhythm,[1] then our first consideration must be to understand what is meant by rhythm. Without repeating technical definitions,[2] rhythm can be described as *a recurring pattern of sounds*, banal examples being tum-ti-ti—tum-ti-ti; bara-boom—bara-boom. Note that the listener tends to group sounds together in patterned bundles, even when no pattern is in evidence. The sequence dum dum dum dum dum will be heard (or read) as, say, *dum*-dum *dum*-dum, etc., or even *dum*-dum-dum, *dum*-dum-dum and so on. In other words, the mind insists on grouping and highlighting what would otherwise be the repetition of identical sounds.[3] The listener is *predisposed* for rhythmic sequences, especially when listening to poetry.

Rhythm can be marked by stress (a strong accent on a word), by loudness, by pitch (a syllable pronounced in a tone higher or lower than the norm) and by length (drawing out a syllable). Metre, then, is the measured use of such prominences, grouping them regularly over segments of time.

*Metre*

Metre cannot be scientifically measured by the use of oscilloscopes and the like (e.g. sound spectrography)—it has to be determined

---

1. Cf. Chatman: 1965, 18.
2. See E.A. Sonnenschein, *What is Rhythm?* (Oxford, 1925); P. Fraisse, *Les structures rhythmiques; étude psychologique* (Louvain, 1956) 3-4; Chatman: 1965, 18-29.
3. Chatman: 1965, 25.

linguistically.[4] It belongs to the surface structure of language rather than to its deep structure.[5]

Metre is a 'sequential pattern of abstract entities' (Halle, 1970), in other words, the moulding of a line (of verse) to fit a preconceived shape made up of recurring sets. The classic metre in English verse is iambic, an alternation of unstressed and stressed syllables, as in

> Than all my army to Damascus' walls
> o  /  o  /  o /  o /  o   /   (Marlowe, *Tamburlaine* V i)

The abstract metrical pattern is the regular recurrence of *unstress + stress* (o /). Points to notice are, firstly, that each such set of o / is a 'foot'; secondly, that metre can cut across word-boundary (as in 'my army to'), and thirdly, that in general the stress-patterns are those of ordinary speech.

In the discussion to follow little importance will be attached to different types of foot (iamb, trochee, etc.). Instead, more crucial problems will be the focus of attention. First, there is some disagreement as to whether we can even speak of metre in connection with ancient languages. Granted even that they are metrical, it is then necessary to determine which kind of metre is being used: is it accentual or stress metre? Is it syllabic or perhaps a combination of syllable and stress (with both accents and syllables being counted)? Or, finally, is the metre quantitative, with feet made up of long and short syllables? In view of the lack of consensus among scholars regarding metre in English poetry, it is not surprising that no agreement has yet been reached concerning ancient Semitic verse on the same topic. Even so, some attempt must be made to describe metre, at least for classical Hebrew, and the pages which follow will summarise current thinking on these matters.

*Glossary*

For convenience, some of the terms used in discussions of metrical theory are set out here with brief definitions and examples. Fuller

---

4. 'Neither the event feature, the syllable, nor the prominence feature, the ictus, can be totally accounted for by acoustic traces. For such traces are continuous and the metrical features are discrete ... We need to turn again to the study of sounds in their linguistic function to interpret the raw acoustic profiles gathered from the machines', Chatman: 1965, 94.

5. Fowler: 1968, 284.

discussion of some items can be found in the body of the chapter. The sequence is alphabetical.

*Accent*—see *stress* and *ictus*.

*Caesura*—'the natural sense- and breath-pause in a line';[6] 'a perceptible break in the performance of a line, properly described as an interlinear terminal juncture',[7] a metrical break in the rhythm of a line. For example, Ps 78,13:

בקע ים ויעבירם    He split the sea. / He brought them over.

*Enjambment*—a verse-line running over into the next line (see section 11.15 on enjambment), hence the alternative 'run-on line'.

*End-stopping*—when caesura coincides with syntactic boundary, chiefly at the end of a verse-line.

*Flick*—a sonant of weak word-classes such as the article, conjunctions, affixes. These can be ignored in metrical analysis.

*Foot*—a basic unit in measuring metre. It is 'a measurable, patterned unit of poetic rhythm'[8] and a line of poetry contains a certain number of feet. Theoretically, feet are of equal duration (they are isochronous, meaning that each foot can be recited in identical segments of time). In practice, though, the duration tends to vary.

*Ictus*—metrical prominence marked either by stress or by syllable-length. Note that languages can have either syllable-timed rhythm or stress-timed rhythm, never both.[9]

*Prosody* (or prosodic analysis)—another term for metrical analysis. Unfortunately, the same expression denotes intonation in patterns of language and this can lead to confusion. The word is avoided here.

*Rhythm*—a difficult concept to grasp or describe. It can be defined as the way in which stessed and unstressed syllables succeed each other.[10] Put simply, it is the general flow of speech, and it should not be forgotten that verse is based on the rhythm of everyday speech. The difference is that verse uses regular rhythmical units or lines of verse, whereas normal speech is far less regular.

6. Fraser: 1970, 6.
7. Chatman: 1965, 167.
8. *PEPP*, 285-286.
9. Abercrombie: 1967, 36.96-98.
10. Abercrombie: 1967, 36.

*Stichometry*—segmenting a text into *verse-lines*.[11] Sense, stichometry and metre are interrelated.

*Stress*—a suprasegmental feature of utterance: a stressed syllable is pronounced more energetically, often with a rise in pitch or increase of loudness.[12] Stress functions to emphasise or contrast one word, or to indicate syntactic relationships.

*Syllable*—difficult to define without mixing of levels; there is no agreed phonetic definition. It is perhaps best described from the speaker's point of view as the element of maximum intensity in a chain of speech sounds. Whether or not the syllable is relevant to metrics is a matter of debate.

*Tone*—pitch fluctuation (or speech melody) which alters the meaning of a word within a tone language, for instance, Chinese.[13]

*Verse-line*—'a line of verse . . . is a rhythmical unit, which can be analysed in some way, and which sets up an expectation that it will be followed by a number of similar rhythmical units'.[14]

*Word*—linguists cannot agree on the definition of this term, for which some prefer the expression 'lexical item'. Note that *word* is at a level different to syllable, stress, etc.

For further definitions of relevant terms, consult the standard handbooks on metre. Particularly useful is Fowler: 1968, who distinguishes between verse type, verse design, metrical set and verse instance.

### BIBLIOGRAPHY

(a) *General and linguistic.*
Chatman, S. *A Theory of Metre* (The Hague, 1965).
Fowler, R. 'What is metrical analysis?', *Anglia* 86 (1968) 280-320.
Fraser, G.S. *Metre, Rhyme and Free Verse* (The Critical Idiom 8; London, 1970).
Nijhoff, M. *Metrical Myths: An Experimental-Phonetic Investigation into the Production and Perception of Metrical Speech* (Boston/The Hague, 1980).

11. Unlike much Akkadian poetry, texts in Ugaritic and Hebrew verse, as transmitted to us, do not separate the individual verse-lines but tend to be written continuously.
12. Ladefoged: 1975, 97-103.222ff.
13. Abercrombie: 1967, 104-110.
14. Fraser: 1970, 3.

Žirmunsky, V.M. *Introduction to Metrics* (The Hague, 1966).

(b) *Hebrew metre*
Cobb, W.H. *A Criticism of Systems of Hebrew Metre. An Elementary Treatise* (Oxford, 1905).
Kuryłowicz, J. *Studies in Semitic Grammar and Metrics* (Warsaw, 1972).
Longman, T. 'A Critique of Two Recent Metrical Systems', *Bib* 63 (1982) 230-254.
Wansbrough, J. 'Hebrew verse: scansion and parallax', *BSOAS* 45 (1982) 5-13.

(c) *Phonetics and phonology*
Abercrombie, D. *Elements of General Phonetics* (Edinburgh, 1967).
Ladefoged, P. *A Course in Phonetics* (New York, 1975).


## 5.2 Metre in Ancient Semitic Languages

*Can ancient semitic metre be known?*
Before considering the problem of metre in various ancient Semitic languages (meaning, chiefly, Ugaritic, Hebrew and Akkadian) it is worthwhile setting out the following quotations which throw considerable doubt on the possibility of its reconstruction.

> Perhaps the most important fact to bear in mind is that the poets of the ancient Near East . . . did not know of exact meter.[15]

> Only in modern, westernized thinking concepts like the mean number of words, syllables or even consonants became measuring-rods to restore 'order' and to recover the 'proper' versification.[16]

> As far as meter is concerned, there is no way for modern scholarship to reconstruct the rhythm of ancient poems, if indeed they were written with conscious metrical considerations in mind.[17]

In the face of such informed scepticism it might seem presumptuous to continue. Nor is this all: such metricists who have taken up the problem fail to come to an agreement. Add the very poor tradition available to us concerning Hebrew metre[18] and the total lack of any such tradition for both Ugaritic and Akkadian, and

15. Gordon, *UT*, 131 n.2.
16. Dijkstra—De Moor, *UF* 7 (1975) 178.
17. Willis, *CBQ* 25 (1973) 141 n.12. In similar vein: Segert, *MIO* 15 (1969) 313-314; Young, *JNES* 9 (1950) 124-133. For Kugel's and O'Connor's views see below.
18. Surveyed briefly by Gray, *Forms*, 9-33.

reconstructing ancient Semitic metre would appear a lost cause at the very outset.[19]

There is no need for such a pessimistic view, however. We can proceed from certain linguistic principles and from our knowledge of the various languages concerned and propose solutions which are reasonably acceptable, at least as working hypotheses.

The two questions to be faced, then, are first, is ancient Semitic poetry really metrical? And, secondly, if so, is it possible for us to reconstruct the metre peculiar to each poetic tradition? The answer to the first question is definitely in the affirmative, as will be shown presently. Confusion arises because scholars fail to distinguish between metre as actually present in verse, and *regular* metre. There is metre, yes, but not regular metre, since metrical patterns are never maintained for more than a few verses at a stretch, if even that.

As to our ability to determine the various kinds of metre, a certain amount of progress can be charted over the many years during which Hebrew, and now Akkadian and Ugaritic, poetry have been studied[20] and there is a degree of consensus among informed experts. While we may never be totally sure of the metre in which languages now dead were composed (in particular, Ugaritic) we have enough material to work with.

It is important to note that metre is not monolithic and inflexible in character. Alongside (or even instead of) stress and non-stress there may have been subsidiary stresses of differing force[21] or even of varying tone. Also, the metre of a poem could change once it was sung to a melody.[22] Finally, there is no reason why metre should not have evolved over the very long periods involved, just as the pronunciation did.[23]

---

19. A further complication, of course, is the question of pronunciation.
20. Here is not the place to provide a historical survey.
21. Compare the studies of Trager—Smith for English poetry.
22. It is fairly safe to assume that most, if not all ancient poetry was recited or composed to the accompaniment of a musical instrument (see ORAL POETRY). Further, although for the most part such music was largely in the nature of rhythmic accompaniment, many compositions must have been sung to definite melodies (as is shown by the titles to many of the Hebrew psalms). Language when sung may have differed from ordinary spoken language, which in turn may have affected the traditions of metre.
23. For many of these points see von Soden: 1976.

*Metre in Akkadian poetry*

In the absence of a modern, comprehensive account of metre in Assyro-Babylonian verse it would be premature to give more than a brief note here. Böhl, whose treatment is now over twenty years old,[24] makes the point that purely accentual metre applies more to spoken Akkadian than to Hebrew. According to Böhl, the normal metrical pattern is 2 + 2 // 2 + 2, and allowance must be made for anacrusis. Verses usually end in a trochee (as established by Landsberger, though recently this 'law' has been questioned, e.g. by Hecker). Prepositions, particles and even prepositional expressions have no stress; case-endings can be elided; there can be intervocalic elision and stress can be shifted to the penultimate. This account has now to be updated by Knudsen's recent paper on stress.[25] According to Hecker,[26] metre comprises a fixed set of stresses in combination with an indeterminate number of unstressed syllables. This is termed free rhythm. Metre, therefore, cannot be quantitative; it is accentual. Verse-lines occur with one, two, three and four components (stress-units) of which the last-mentioned is the most frequent while one-word lines are extremely rare. The subdivision of lengthier lines is often uncertain. Since stress-units can comprise nouns in bound form (sets of nouns connected by the construct state) and since particles (prepositions, negatives, enclitics, etc.) have no stress, even very long lines can count as few as four stresses.[27] Hecker observes that while on the one hand no literary form has its typical metre, on the other, no single composition (with the exception of the Babylonian Theodicy) uses a constant metre throughout.[28]

Very recently von Soden gave a talk on metre in Babylonian epic in which he suggested that 'rhythmical variation' was operative for a certain period.[29] Another account based on modern linguistic theory,

---

24. Böhl: 1961.

25. Knudsen: 1980.

26. Hecker, *Epik*, 101ff.

27. Hecker, *Epik*, 117-118, quotes two eight-'word' lines, each with only four stresses.

28. See the table in Hecker, *Epik*, 119. Hecker observes that two otherwise identical lines, one with and one without a formulaic expression, seem at times to be metrically equivalent. For a range of metrical patterns cf. Hecker, *Epik*, 120-138.

29. 'Rhythmical variation is operative for verses of differing lengths in such a way that every poem has a "normal" verse-length. Verses could be made up of trochees (stress-unstress) or of three-syllable feet (dactyl and amphibrach). Most types of verse had trochaic endings. Two and three-syllable feet could be mixed within a verse' (von Soden: 1976).

has been provided by Kuryłowicz.[30] Evidently no satisfactory description of Akkadian/Babylonian metre is available, but some points emerge as fairly well established. We know the stress-laws for prose;[31] whether the same laws were operative in poetry is not entirely clear. In any case we must allow for change and development over the centuries. Both syllable count and number of stresses were metrically significant. Generally speaking, metre tended to be mixed —which incidentally did not tire either reciter or his audience. Fuller details will be available once von Soden's lecture is published.[32]

### BIBLIOGRAPHY

Böhl, F.M.T. de Liagre, 'Bijbelse en babylonische Dichtkunst. Een metrisch Onderzoek', *JEOL* 5 (1958) 133-153.
—'La métrique de l'épopée babylonienne', *Gilgameš et sa légende*, ed. P. Garelli (Paris, 1960) 145-152.
Knudsen, E.E. 'Stress in Akkadian', *JCS* 32 (1980) 3-16.
Soden, W. von 'Rhythmische Variation in babylonischen Epen' (unpublished lecture given at the Rencontre Assyriologique Internationale, Birmingham, 1976; kindly made available to me by the author).
Also von Soden, *ZA* 40 (1950) 153-155; *ZA* 68 (1968) 53; Lambert, *BWL*, vi. 65; Kuryłowicz: 1972, 177-187.

### Metre in Ugaritic poetry

No consistent theory has yet been proposed to account for the metre of Ugaritic poetry, or even to accurately describe it. This is in part due to the nature of the texts which are written in a consonantal script with the exception of the three vocalic alephs (*a*, *i* and *u*) and a scattering of vowel-letters.[33] As has been seen, Young expressed scepticism that regular metre was used in Ugaritic poetry.[34] Margalit has put forward a detailed explanation of Ugaritic metre[35] but there

---

30. Kuryłowicz: 1972.
31. Knudsen: 1980.
32. See, now *ZA* 71 (1982) 161-204. See also B. Groneberg, Untersuchungen zum hymnisch-epischen Dialekt der altbabylonischen literarischen Texte (unpublished dissertation, Münster, 1971).
33. There are also the Akkadian transcriptions of Ugaritic words in the syllabic texts from Ras Shamra.
34. Young: 1950.
35. Margalit: 1975. In brief, Margalit's six principles of scansion are: (1) The verse-unit is the word (nouns and verbs but not particles, prepositions, conjunctions or relative pronouns); to qualify as a verse-unit a word must have between two and five syllables, though certain monosyllables also count. (2) Words or word-clusters of over

are too many inconsistencies[36] for it to be totally acceptable. The nearest approach is the letter-counting system advocated by Loretz,[37] but this he regards as a *pre*-metrical theory. Even if a consistent, linguistically correct theory of Ugaritic metre were to hand it would not be of direct help towards understanding Hebrew metre which is based on stress.[38]

Recently, de Moor has proposed a non-metrical account of Ugaritic poetry.[39] The basic component of verse was the *foot*, comprising a word or word-cluster bearing the main stress. (It is crucial to note the equation, in terms of rhythm, of word and word-cluster.[40]) There was neither free metre nor even a fixed metre, but there was *free rhythm*. In other words, there was no tradition of reciting (or singing) every line within a set stretch of time irrespective of the number of syllables, meaning that longer lines would have to be recited faster 'to get them in', because there was too great a difference between very short lines and very long lines. By the same token (some lines short, others long), it makes no sense to speak of fixed metre. This leaves open the possibility of free rhythm.

The idea of free rhythm can only be understood in the context of sung verse.

> Music with a free rhythm is nearly always monodic, which means
> that there is one leading voice to which any accompanying music

---

five syllables count as two verse-units. (3) In the bound state two monosyllabic words are equivalent to one verse-unit. (4) Three-word clusters count as two verse-units, (5) two-word clusters as one verse-unit. (6) Short particles and prepositions count as one verse-unit, or less.

36. For instance, he posits the existence of monosyllables which is impossible in a language with case-endings.

37. Discussed below.

38. 'In Ugaritic (as in Arabic) vowel quantity is distinctive and the stress is attracted to a penultimate or previous open syllable containing a long vowel (or its equivalent, a closed syllable containing a short vowel)'; accordingly, 'syllable counting may be a viable undertaking for Ugaritic where differences in vowel quantity are phonologically relevant, but is hardly meaningful in the case of a stress-orientated language like Hebrew' (Gibson, *CML*, 140).

39. De Moor: 1978. He enumerates the difficulties involved (pp. 120-121) but they are not so formidable as he suggests. The principal problem is our uncertainty regarding the pronunciation of Ugaritic. Unlike Hebrew, Ugaritic retained its final short vowels, and stress was retracted either to the long syllable closest to the end of the word, or in the absence of any such syllable (CVC or C + long V), right to the initial syllable. For details, see de Moor: 1978, 122 and n.16; also Gibson, *CML*, 140.

40. So Parker: 1974; Margalit: 1975 and de Moor: 1978.

adapts itself. In practice the soloist, usually a singer, is very often at the same time the conductor of the orchestra and/or the choir.[41]

The stichoi of ancient West Semitic poetry are very short, often counting only two or three words. Because a verse could consist of as much as three equivalent stichoi of five words each, it must be assumed that the natural breathing space fell after each stichos. If, however, the rhythm of singing had approximated that of speaking, the musical phrases would have been much too short. The singer would have felt the need of taking a breath ... Therefore it is likely that more notes were sung to the same syllable.[42]

In singing, the stressed syllables played a prominent part, though not with regard to metre. Probably their prominence was expressed by drawing out the notes or by singing more than one note to the syllables bearing the accent.[43]

The question then arises, if there is no metre in Ugaritic verse, how is it that there is a tendency for verse-lines to have three stresses? Or, to put it another way, which is at the same time more general, how is it that lines of Ugaritic poetry tend to be balanced (with regard to length, number of stresses, etc.)? The answer, it would appear, is that such balance and regularity is a direct result of a love for *symmetry*. Symmetry comes first as a prime requirement; its corollary, particularly in sets of parallel couplets, is what appears to be regularity of stress-patterns (which in turn gives the illusion of metre). Some examples will show what is meant.

Contrast the two-beat lines:

| | |
|---|---|
| *šṣat btlt-ʿnt* | Virgin-Anath released |
| *krḥ npš* | like-wind his-breath, |
| *kiṯl brlth* | like-spittle his-life, |
| *kqṯr baph* | like-incense from-his nose. |
| | (*CTA* 19 ii 91-93) |

with lengthier

| | |
|---|---|
| *ik tmtḥṣ ʿm aliyn bʿl* | How can you fight with omni-potent Baal, |
| *ik al yšmʿk ṯr il abk* | how indeed shall the bull El your father hear you? |
| | (*CTA* 6 vi 24-27) |

41. De Moor: 1978, 129.
42. De Moor: 1978, 130.
43. De Moor: 1978, 131-132.

As noted, the usual pattern is a three-beat line:

| | |
|---|---|
| *tbʻ ktr lahlh* | Kutharu departed to-his-tent, |
| *hyn tbʻ lmšknth* | Heyanu to-his-residence departed. |
| | (*CTA* 17 v 31-33) |

Pardee prefers not to use the term 'metre', opting instead for the claim that 'parallelism was the primary structural principle of Ugaritic poetry'.[43a]

Evidently, then, there is no unanimity concerning the nature of Ugaritic poetry: whether it is metrical or not, and, if metrical, what the nature of the metre involved might be.

### BIBLIOGRAPHY

Margalit, B. 'Introduction to Ugaritic Prosody (Studia Ugaritica I)', *UF* 7 (1975) 289-313.

Moor, J.C. de 'The Art of Versification in Ugarit and Israel. I: The Rhythmical Structure', *Loewenstamm FS* (1978) 119-139.

Pardee, D. 'Ugaritic and Hebrew Metrics', *Wisconsin Symposium*, 113-130.

Parker, S.B. 'Parallelism and Prosody in Ugaritic Narrative Verse', *UF* 6 (1974) 283-294.

Patton, J.H. *Canaanite Parallels in the Book of Psalms* (Baltimore, 1944) 5-11.

Young, G.D. 'Ugaritic Prosody', *JNES* 9 (1950) 124-133.

Also, Margalit, *AMOLAD*, 219-228 [Excursus: The Principles of Ugaritic Prosody].

## 5.3 *The Stress (Accentual) Theory of Hebrew Metre*

### *Description*

Before going into the polemics surrounding this particular theory of Hebrew metrics (see below), it seems logical to set out a descriptive account of the theory, with explanations and illustrative examples.

The stress-pattern (metre) of a line of Hebrew verse is as follows:

קוֹלִי אֶל־יְהוָֹה אֶזְעָק     With my voice to Yahweh do I yell. (Ps 142,2a)

There are three stresses—intervening syllables and secondary stresses are ignored. The normal unit of Hebrew verse, though, is the couplet, for example:

| | |
|---|---|
| רָאוּנִי נְעָרִים וְנֶחְבָּאוּ | The young men saw me and hid, |
| וִישִׁישִׁים קָמוּ עָמָדוּ | the old men rose and stood. (Job 29,8) |

---

43a. Pardee: 1981, 126.

Here the number of (metrical) stresses in each line is again three and
the metre of such couplets is conventionally represented as 3 + 3.
Some couplets are shorter as in

קֹמוּ הַשָּׂרִים      Get up, O princes,

מִשְׁחוּ מָגֵן      oil a shield. (Isa 21,5)

which is 2 + 2. Others can be longer: 4 + 4 is quite common:

אֱלֹהִים בְּקִרְבָּהּ בַּל־תִּמּוֹט      With God within her she'll not be toppled,

יַעְזְרָהּ אֱלֹהִים לִפְנוֹת בֹּקֶר      he will help her at break of dawn. (Ps 46,6[44])

The number of stresses in each line is by no means always
identical. Patterns such as 3 + 4 (Dt 32,7a; Job 17,12) and 4 + 3
(Job 3,20; 17,14) occur, as does the pattern 3 + 2. This last metrical
pattern is known as *qinah* metre since it is frequent in laments (*qinah*
= 'lament') though it is also found elsewhere. A typical example is
Lam 2,21:

שָׁכְבוּ לָאָרֶץ חוּצוֹת      Lying on the ground in the streets

נַעַר וְזָקֵן      were man and boy.

Also 1,13b; 2,5a.7a; 3,19; etc.—and outwith laments: Dt 33,18; Ps
96,13b and so on. The reverse form (2 + 3) also occurs, e.g.
Dt 32,10b. Lengthier metrical patterns are used as well: 5 + 5
(Ps 71,22); 5 + 4 (Ps 64,7) and 4 + 5 (Song 5,9); etc.

Some of the commoner metrical patterns in tricola can be listed
here. Symmetrical are 3 + 3 + 3 (Ps 24,7); 4 + 4 + 4 (Song 4,1) and
the staccato-like 2 + 2 + 2 (Nah 3,18b). Asymmetrical are such
patterns as 4 + 4 + 3 (Job 19,29), 3 + 2 + 2 (Nah 1,11) and the like.[45]

### Comment

The most noticeable aspect of Hebrew metre when described in
accentual terms (aside from different ways of scanning by scholars) is
that no single poem is consistently written in one metrical pattern.
Even Lamentations does not use the *qinah* (3 + 2) metre throughout.
True, certain stretches of verse use one metrical pattern—for example,
Ps 29,1-2 is in 3 + 3—but soon the metre changes and then it changes
again. It is this *lack of regular metre* which jars those brought up on
(Indo-) European verse and it has to be accepted as part and parcel of
Hebrew verse tradition. Some poems do exhibit a degree of regularity
(see on Mic 3,9-12 below), but these are exceptional.

---

44. Translation following Dahood, *Psalms I*, 277.
45. See, conveniently, Gray, *Forms*.

*Indicators of stress*

1. Normally, stress is on the *final* syllable (or ultima) as in מוֹרָא, 'fear'; יָדְעוּ, 'they knew'.

2. Commonly enough, stress is on the last syllable but one (penultima) as in the segholates, e.g. כֶּלֶב, 'dog'.

Stress on the ante-penultimate only occurs in two adverbs with the locative *h*: הָלְאָה, 'out there' and אֹהֱלָה, 'into the tent'. Normal stress can be *retracted* when two words co-occur which would result in two stressed syllables in succession (e.g. קָרָא לַיְלָה, 'he named "Night"' [Gen 1,5] for קָרָא לַיְלָה).[46] Pausal forms have special rules.[47]

*Arguments in favour of the stress theory of metre*

Although scholars are by no means agreed that Hebrew metre is accentual in character, there are certain considerations which point in that direction. To begin with, *stress is phonemic* in Hebrew; it makes בָּנוּ, 'they built' (with final stress) distinct from בָּנוּ, 'in us' (with penultimate stress); similarly, שָׁבָה, 'she returned' and שָׁבָה, 'returning' (fem. ptc.). These are minimal pairs. Since stress is phonemic it must be significant in Hebrew metre.[48]

In favour of the accentual theory, too, is the well-attested presence of *silent stress*, particularly in the pivot-patterned couplet (see PIVOT PATTERN). For example, the stress pattern in Ps 59,2 is 3 + 2:

| | |
|---|---|
| הצילני מאיבי אלהי | Rescue me from my foes, God, |
| ממתקוממי תשגבני | against my attacker be my bulwark. |

Closer inspection, though, shows that an equivalent to אלהי is lacking in the second line and the stress-pattern is, in reality,

46. See J. Blau, *A Grammar of Biblical Hebrew* (Wiesbaden, 1976), 19 (5.2). For a more detailed approach see J.C.L. Gibson, 'Stress and vocalic change in Hebrew: a diachronic study', *JL* 2 (1966) 35-56; 'The Massoretes as Linguists', *OTS* 19 (1974) 86-96; 'On the Linguistic Analysis of Hebrew Writing', *AL* 17 (1969) 131-160.

47. Note particularly E.J. Revell, 'Pausal forms in biblical Hebrew: their function, origin and significance', *JSS* 25 (1980) 165-179.

48. This was pointed out to me by John Gibson and is implied in the articles listed in note 46. Of particular significance is that with the loss of final vowels in Hebrew (approx. 1000 BC) stress became free and so it—rather than vowel quantity—became distinctive (see Gibson: 1966, 39). For the history of stress in classical Hebrew, cf. Blau: 1976, 16, n.48.

where ∅ represents silent stress. An example nearer home in the form of a limerick will perhaps illustrate silent stress better:

> Hebrew poems are not just a mess,
> nor is this, we hope, a mere guess.
> They may not have rhyme,
> but you'll find every time
> that the poets composed under stress.

If scanned correctly, lines 3 and 4 will be found to end with silent stress.

Hebrew poets could not exploit metre in this way if it were not stress-based.

*Unusual word-order* is yet another indication that stress was metrically significant. The broken construct chain, for example,[49] is a means of creating additional stress. In Isa 19,8 the three stresses of the first line are balanced by three in the second:

ואנו הדיגים ואבלו    Groan shall the fishermen, and lament
כל משליכי ביאור חכה    all casting hook into the Nile.

The broken construct chain replaced normal word sequence which would have been כל משליכי חכה ביאור with only two stresses.

Yet another pointer towards stress as metrically important is its conscious *use in a chiastic pattern*, directly contravening the principle that two accents should not follow each other directly. The case in question is Prov 10,9:

הוֹלֵךְ בַּתֹם יֵלֶךְ בֶּטַח    Who walks unsullied walks secure,

with the pattern o / o / / o / o, although the presence of two contiguous stresses is alleviated by a slight caesura or pause between the two phrases.[50]

## Determining metre

The following steps should be undertaken in determining metrical patterns.

1. Note where *expected* lenition (after a word ending in a vowel) is *not* present. This shows which words have primary stress.

(Jer 5,1b) ובקשו ברחובותיה

---

49. For other examples see D.N. Freedman, 'The Broken Construct Chain', *Bib* 53 (1972) 534-536; A. Frendo, *Bib* 62 (1981) 544-545, with bibliography 545, n.8.

50. Other indications of metre may be the preservation of archaic case-endings and the variation of standard parallel word-pairs.

2. Note the maqqefs joining the words to form metrical feet with only one (primary) stress.

ולא־חלו (Jer 5,3)

3. Note other word-groups, particularly noun in bound state + following noun (construct relationships) and preposition + noun combinations.

דרך יהוה (Jer 5,5)

4. Mark off stresses within each line (see presently for full example). *Mic 3,9-12* is a good illustration since it exhibits a regular metrical pattern, has no philological problems and provides at least six examples of dagesh lene after a vowel.[51]

|  |  |  | number of stresses |
|---|---|---|:---:|
| שמער־נא זאת | 9a | I | 2 |
| ראשי בית יעקב | b |  | 2 |
| וקציני בית ישראל | c |  | 2 |
| המתעבים משפט | d |  | 2 |
| ואת כל־הישרה יעקשו | e |  | 2 |
| בנה ציון בדמים | 10a |  | 2 |
| וירושלם בעולה | b |  | 2 |
| ראשיה בשחד ישפטו | 11a | II | 3 |
| וכהניה במחיר יורו | b |  | 3 |
| ונביאיה בכסף יקסמו | c |  | 3 |
| ועל־יהוה ישענו לאמר | d |  | 3 |
| הלוא יהוה בקרבנו | e |  | 3 |
| לא־תבוא עלינו רעה | f |  | 3 |
| לכן בגללכם | 12a | III | 2 |
| ציון שרה תחרש | b |  | 2 |
| וירושלם עיין תהיה | c |  | 2 |
| והר הבית לבמות יער | d |  | 2 |

51.  Bee, who deals with the frequency of maqqefs in this text concludes to the date 700 BC; cf. *JSOT* 11 (1979) 29. For other worked examples see A.S. Cooper, Biblical Poetics: A Linguistic Approach (Yale thesis, 1976) 112-139 (Prov 8,22-31); J. Kuryłowicz, *Metrik und Sprachgeschichte* (Warsaw, 1975) 222 (Ps 44) and Longman: 1982 (Dt 33; Jer 12). Longman, whose references these are, points out how few such analyses have been made as yet.

102 *Classical Hebrew Poetry*

I   9   Hear this, please,
chiefs of House Jacob,
and leaders of House Israel,
who putrefy justice,
making all uprightness deviant,

    10   building Zion with their blood,
and Jerusalem with wrongfulness:

II   11   'Her chiefs: for a bribe do they judge;
her priests: for a price do teach;
her prophets: for money do divine.

But on Yahweh they rely, saying:
"Surely Yahweh is among us!
To us no evil can happen!"

III   12   Just because of you, then,
Zion like a field shall be ploughed[52]
and Jerusalem rubble will become,
and the temple-hill thicket-covered heights.'

The metre, as indicated by the stress-marks in the Hebrew text, is suggested by the following.

1. The *presence of dagesh lene immediately after a vowel* in 9b, 9c, 11abce and 10a. In 9b and c the spelling בית occurs (after וקציני and ראשי respectively). In 11abc, the preposition בֿ has the dagesh lene in spite of the foregoing suffix (ה־) used three times in succession—and similarly in 11e with בקרבנו after *yahweh*. Note, too, that 10a must be metrically distinct from 9e since that colon ends with a vowel (יעקשו) and 10a opens with dagesh lene (בנה).

In each of these cases the presence of dagesh lene marks a break between the word beginning with a begadkepat letter and the word just before it—each word, then, has its own stress, e.g. 9b:

ראשי בית יעקב

2. The *absence* of dagesh lene immediately after a vowel—as expected—shows a word-group to have only a single stress. The only instance is in 12b: שרה תחרש.

3. The *maqqef* connecting words in 9a (שמעו־נא), 9e (כל־הישרה) and 11f (לא־תבוא) which again shows each particular word-group to have only one stress.

---

52. 'Like a field'—an adverbial accusative (שרה). The allusion here is to 'Virgin Zion' now subject to rape. 12bce also occurs in the prose passage Jer 26,18.

4. The inverted sequences (Subj.—Verb) in 12b and c.

### 5.4 *Other Theories: Survey and Critique*

*Introductory*

The rapid survey presented here provides brief accounts of rival theories put forward to explain Hebrew metre. Each account will be followed by a critical comment. At the end, some space will be devoted to the current opinion that Hebrew poetry does not exhibit metre. This section will show, in a negative way, that only an accentual (stress-based) theory can account for Hebrew metre.

#### 1. *Alternating (stress) metre*

Proposed by Segert,[53] this theory maintains that in Hebrew poetry a stress comes before (or follows) *one* unstressed syllable, permissible patterns being

$$\_\bot\_\bot\_\bot \quad \text{and} \quad \bot\_\bot\_\bot\_$$

Excluded, therefore, is a sequence of two unstressed syllables, whether before or after the stress ( $\_\_\bot$ or $\bot\_\_$ ), though two consecutive stresses are possible, if exceptional (syncope).

Segert based his explanation largely on a comparison between Hebrew verse and late (Aramaic and Syriac) poetry. This means that it should fit MT as handed down to us and not a hypothetically reconstructed vocalisation as he would argue.[54] A double contradiction would be involved: fitting the metre of late poetry to an earlier text and altering the traditional text (at least in respect of its vowels) to suit a metrical theory.

In any case, alternating stress is hardly the rule in Hebrew poetry. It fails to take word-complexes into account and cannot explain texts such as Isa 9,3 which has five unstressed syllables before the tone:[55]

כי את־על סבלו

#### 2. *The word-foot*

In an attempt to avoid the problems incurred by counting either

53. S. Segert, 'Versbau und Sprachbau in der althebräischen Poesie', *MIO* 15 (1969) 312-321; cf. 'Vorarbeiten zur hebräischen Metrik, I-II', *ArOr* 21 (1953) 481-542; 'Die Methoden der althebräischen Metrik', *CV* 1 (1958) 233-241; 'Problems of Hebrew Prosody', *VTS* 7 (1960) 283-291.
54. E.g. *šᵉwa mobile* is considered a full syllable; certain vowels undergo syncope.
55. I owe this example to John Gibson.

vowels or stresses, the word-unit theory assumes that there are a set number of 'word-feet' or word-units in every verse-line. For example, Dt 32,43

ונקם ישיב לצריו     With vengeance he requites his foes

has three word-feet.[56]

Unfortunately, the problem of what counts as a 'word' is difficult to solve.[57] Should separate prepositions such as מן or particles such as כל be counted as words or not?[58] Though superficially very attractive, this theory is difficult to apply. Furthermore, metre is a phonological construct while 'word' is a grammatical element. Such mixing of levels discounts the word-unit theory as contrary to basic principles in linguistics.

### 3. *The thought-unit*
According to this theory each 'thought-unit' represents one stress in Hebrew poetry.[59] It is an extension of the previous theory and suffers from the same defects (mixing of levels chiefly) compounded by a vague semantic component.

### 4. *Syllable-counting*
Though not strictly a metrical theory, this approach can be conveniently discussed here. The method used is this: the number of syllables per line is counted without considering vowel length, or whether syllables are closed or open. It is, in effect, a mechanical reckoning of the number of vowels per colon. An example is Lam 4,15:

|  | syllables |  |
|---|---|---|
| sūrū ṭāmē' qārᵉ'ū lāmō | 9 | 'Depart, you unclean' they cried to them, |
| sūrū sūrū 'al- tiggā'ū | 8 | 'Depart! depart! do not trespass!' |

---

56. J. Ley, *Leitfaden der Metrik der hebräischen Poesie* (Leipzig, 1887); E. Isaacs, 'The metrical basis of Hebrew poetry', *AJSL* 35 (1919) 20-54; H. Kosmala, 'Form and Structure in Ancient Hebrew Poetry', *VT* 16 (1966) 152-180; T.H. Robinson, 'Some Principles of Hebrew Metrics', *ZAW* 54 (1936) 28-43; cf. J. Nist, 'The Word-group Cadence: Basis of English Metrics', *Ling* 6 (1964) 73-82.

57. See discussion in glossary.

58. The presence of maqqef is too inconsistent for more than an approximation.

59. R. Gordis, *The Book of God and Man. A Study of Job* (Chicago, 1965) 160; Boadt, *CBQ* 35 (1973) 22.

|                      | syllables |                                |
|----------------------|-----------|--------------------------------|
| *kī nāṣū gam nā'ū*   | 6         | For they are homeless, even wanderers, |
| *'ām^erū baggōyīm*   | 6         | they said among the nations.   |
| *lō' yōsīpū lāgūr*   | 6         | They shall not stay any longer.[60] |

Syllable-counting has many advocates and is no new approach.[61] Its principal drawbacks are that it relies on reconstructing the vowels and that it ignores stress. At best it is useful for lineation.[62]

## 5. Letter-counting

Again, like syllable-counting, not a metrical theory; in fact it has been labelled a 'pre-metrical theory'.[63] Using Ugaritic as a model, where few vowels have been transmitted, this method relies on counting the number of consonants or letters per line. For example, Ps 117 is presented as follows:[64]

| *hllw 't yhwh kl gwym* | (16) | Praise Yahweh, all nations,        |
| *šbḥwhw kl h'mym*      | (13) | laud him, all peoples.[65]          |
|                        |      |                                    |
| *ky gbr 'lynw ḥsdw*   | (14) | For strong is his mercy towards us, |
| *w'mt yhwh l'lm*       | (13) | and Yahweh's truth is everlasting.  |
|                        |      |                                    |
| [*hllw yh*]            | (6)  | [liturgical insert].               |

---

60. So D.N. Freedman, *Poetry, Pottery, and Prophecy: Studies in Early Hebrew Poetry* (Winona Lake, 1980) 64-65.

61. An early proponent (if not the earliest) was G. Bickell, 'Die hebräische Metrik', *ZDMG* 34 (1880) 557-563. Apart from Freedman's studies (collected in Freedman: 1980; see previous note) see R.C. Culley, 'Metrical Analysis of Classical Hebrew Poetry' in Wevers, ed., *Essays on the Ancient Semitic World* (Toronto, 1970) 12-28.

62. Since the above was written M. Halle—J.J. McCarthy, 'The Metrical Structure of Psalm 137', *JBL* 100 (1981) 161-167, has appeared. They come to the following conclusions. The approach that 'seems most productive of insights' is syllable counting. While not necessarily valid for all or any of the OT 'this proposal holds true for Psalm 137'. Syllables following the last stress in a line are regarded as extra-metrical (confirmed by retraction of stress to reduce syllable count by one). See, also, Longman: 1982.

63. So Loretz, *UF* 7 (1976) 265-289.

64. Following Loretz, *Psalmen II*, 197-198.

65. For discussion of this difficult word cf. Dahood, *Psalms III*, 152-153. As he points out it is not unknown for a f. noun to have a morphologically m. plural ending, as here.

Evidently, the average length of the long line here is (14), so that the final line (הללו יה) stands outside the prevailing pattern. It is therefore additional (a liturgical addition) and should not be reckoned with in a metrical analysis of the poem.

So far, so good. However, there is a tendency to make the material fit the pattern—by excision of glosses, later additions, editorial corrections and the like[65a]—which ultimately results in a reconstructed text. In any case, consonant counting is too mechanical to be more than a check on lineation (stichometry) and cannot be included within a serious discussion of metrical theory.[66]

Even today Cobb's critique remains a useful survey of many theories propounded concerning Hebrew metre.[67]

Before concluding this section two further explanations must be looked at. They are too important and too novel to be included among theories which have been rejected (i.e. theories not based on stress) and they will be described as much as possible in the terms used by their proponents.

### Metre and syntactic analysis

Two recent and very important books on Hebrew poetry[68] have approached the problem of Hebrew metre as a problem in the field of syntactic analysis. In this they follow Kiparsky; see, for instance, his assertion that

> The most important, virtually unbreakable constraints on metre in English involve the grammatical structure of the verse, notably the phrase and word units of which it is made up.[69]

Curiously, though, they do not come to the same conclusions concerning Hebrew metre; in fact, not to mince words, they hold diametrically opposing views.

Collins makes the point that

---

65a. See Loretz's writings, passim. For Ugaritic examples see his writings, too.

66. S.T. Byington, 'A Mathematical Approach to Hebrew Meters', *JBL* 66 (1947) 63-77, used a comparable approach, but concluded that 'Hebrew has a quantitative meter' (74).

67. Cobb: 1905.

68. Collins, *Line-forms*; O'Connor, *Structure*.

69. P. Kiparsky, 'Stress, syntax and meter', *Lang* 51 (1975) 576-616; quote from 579.

the fact that no system has emerged from all the laborious studies
of stress patterns and syllable counts does not mean that there is no
system. However, it does suggest that we probably ought to be
looking for it somewhere else.[70]

He goes on to argue that 'an analysis of lines based on grammatical
structures' is the best approach. After presenting his line-form
analysis, he concludes at the end of his book:

in the formation of Hebrew verse-lines it is the line-forms that are
the basic framework which can be adapted to produce the required
rhythmic pattern.[71]

As an example he cites Ez 19,1-9, where the line-forms appear to
have been selected in order to fit (or produce) *qinah* metre.[72]

Only the first two verses (except for the first sentence) will be set
out:

|  |  | *line-type* |
|---|---|---|
| רבצה בתוך כפרים | She crouched among the cubs, | (IV) |
| רבתה גוריה | she reared[73] her whelps. | |
| ותעל אחד מגריה | One of her whelps she raised, | (IV) |
| כפיר היה | he was a cub. | |
| וילמד לטרף־טרף | He learnt to tear prey; | (II) |
| אדם אכל | man he devoured. | |

Collins comments:

1. 'The most noticeable thing about it from the structural point of
view is the fact that lines of Type I are not dominant in the way that
is characteristic of Ezekiel ... the author goes out of his way to
include line-types with a strong central caesura. This would appear
to be a requirement of the *qinah* style, and one which can be catered
for by the choice of line-types.'

2. 'There appears to be deliberate manipulation of the line-forms to
produce lines in which the second hemistich is shorter than the
first—usually in the ratio of three words to two.' An example is the
redundant טרף (in the fifth line, above), and there are others.

He concludes that: 'in the formation of Hebrew verse-lines it is the
line-forms that are the basic framework which can be adapted to

70. Collins, *Line-forms*, 7.
71. Collins, *Line-forms*, 273.
72. Collins, *Line-forms*, 271-273.
73. Or 'she had many cubs'; cf. NEB.

produce the required rhythmic pattern'; but he fails to see the implication of this argument. It is this: if the poet chose his line-forms to fit a pre-conceived pattern, *then it is this pattern* and not the line-forms *which is basic*. In this instance, the poet chose qinah metre—a rhythm comprising 3 + 2 stresses—and then fitted in his words. True, his line-forms are standard, but they presuppose metre. Conversely, line-form analysis cannot be used to determine metre.[74]

O'Connor also uses syntactic analysis in his discussion of Classical Hebrew poetry, but denies that it is metrical.[75] Instead he prefers to speak of 'constraints' and provides, in summary form, what he considers to be the constraints on Hebrew poetry (based on a restricted corpus).[76] He sets out six rules, as follows:

1. No line has more than 3 *clause predicators*,[77] e.g. Dt 32,15b.
2. No line has fewer than 1 or more than 4 *constituents*,[78] e.g. Ps 106,7a.
3. No line has fewer than 2 or more than 5 *units*,[79] e.g. Ps 106,46.
4. No constituent has more than 4 units (cf. Ps 106,40a).
   – 4-unit constituents occur in lines without a clause predicator;
   – 3-unit constituents occur alone in lines with no clause predicator (Ps 106,38b) or as one of two constituents in 1-clause lines (v. 48a).
5. No line of 3 clause predicators contains any *dependent nominal clauses* (in lines with 2 clause predicators, only one has dependent nominal clauses).
6. If a line contains more than one clause predicator, it contains only nominal phrases dependent on them.

74. See Collins, *Line-forms*, 271-273.
75. 'No consensus has ever been reached in the matter of Hebrew meter because there is none', O'Connor, *Structure*, 138.
76. Gen 49; Dt 32-33; Nb 23-24; 2 Sm 1; Ex 15; Pss 78; 106; 107; Hab 3; Jgs 5; Zeph 1-3.
77. A clause predicator = finite verb
   non-absolute infinitive
   infinitive governing only an agent
   non-absolute participle
   participle governing agent/object/possessor
   zero-predicator of verbless clause
   vocative/focus marker
78. Constituent = verb; an argument of a predicator.
79. Unit = verb; individual nomen.

Finally, the *dominant line form* comprises:
1 clause (Ex 15,7b; Zeph 2,8a; Ex 15,15c; Ps 78,9a; Dt 32,36a;
Nb 23,10c; Ex 15,4c; Ps 107,6a; Zeph 3,11d);
2 or 3 constituents, of 2 or 3 units (Ps 106,6b.47a).[80]

Though not entirely side-stepping the problem of Hebrew metre,
O'Connor has at least attempted an approach which is independent
of metrical analysis. It remains to be seen whether he has succeeded.[81]

### Hebrew poetry as non-metrical

Unwittingly using words almost identical with O'Connor's, Kugel
comes to the conclusion that 'no meter has been found in Hebrew
poetry because none exists',[82] adding 'or, as others have urged,
parallelism is the only meter of biblical poetry'.[83] This is a corollary
to his contention 'that the concepts of poetry and prose correspond to
no precise distinction in the [Hebrew] Bible, and that their sustained
use [by scholars] has been somewhat misleading about the nature
and form of the Bible, and about the phenomenon of parallelism'.[84]
He prefers, instead, to use terms such as 'high style' or 'rhetorical
style'. As Barr convincingly argues, though,[85] if the metre of Hebrew
verse is reduced to parallelism in this way then it has no distinctive
character since parallelism is transparent even in translation. Surely
the original Hebrew had some additional 'native' component (metre?)
which is filtered out in a rendering.

### Postscript

Longman [85a] discusses both the syllable-counting method and what
he terms the 'syntactic accentual approach'. The first he judges to be,
at least, a way of providing 'insights into the stylistic structure of the
poem'. The second, which results in more balanced patterns (though
anomalies remain), has yet to define 'what exactly constitutes a word
complex which carries the metrical stress'. Also, (non) spirantisation
of begadkepat letters (as discussed above) is too infrequent to be valid

---

80. O'Connor, *Structure*, 86-87, for all the above; see, too, 317ff.
81. For a critique of O'Connor's view cf. Kugel, *Idea*, 315-323.
82. Kugel, *Idea*, 301.
83. Kugel, *Idea*, 301—see his additional comments. Also, 171-203 and 287-304.
84. Kugel, *Idea*, 302.
85. J. Barr, *TLS* 1506 (Dec. 1981) = review of Kugel, *Idea*.
85a. T. Longman, 'A Critique of Two Recent Metrical Systems', *Bib* 63 (1982) 230-254.

as a criterion. He opts, instead, for the syntactical parallelism
proposed by Collins.

## 5.5 Anacrusis

*Anacrusis*

Anacrusis is 'a syllable at the beginning of a line, before the just
rhythm'[86] or, put simply, an extra-metrical word. The term derives
from Greek, meaning 'the striking up of a tune'[87] and so is clearly a
strophe- stanza-, or poem-opener. For example, Ps 33,9

| כי | For, |
| הוא אמר ויהי | he spoke and it was, |
| הוא צוה ויעמד | he commanded, and it stood; |

where the word כי comprises anacrusis. There is a whole series of
such words used to open a segment of poetry—though, in theory,
almost any word could fulfil this function. Examples include הן / הנה,
'behold'; לכן, 'therefore'; הוי, 'woe'; עתה, 'now'; Robinson grouped
them into introductory elements (mostly from אמר, 'to say'); inter-
jections, pronouns and particles.

Anacrusis is present, too, in Ugaritic and Akkadian poetry. For
example (*CTA* 24:45-47)

| hn | See! |
| bpy sprhn | In my mouth their number; |
| bšpty mnthn | on my lips, their counting, |

with anacrusis of *hn*, 'Behold'. In Akkadian: Gilg Y iii 3 (=18-20
etc.):

| Ḫumbaba | Humbaba, |
| rigmašu abūbu | the Flood is his roar, |
| pīšu girrumma | fire is his mouth, |
| napissu mūtu | death is his breath.[87a] |

*Significance*

It is important to recognise anacrusis for several reasons. First and
foremost, of course, for determining the correct metre; little more
need be added on this point. Secondly, it can help establish secondary

86. Robinson: 1936, 37.
87. *PEPP*, 33.
87a. See *CAD* M/2, 251 for Gilg. V i 6.

patterns, notably the quasi-acrostic. This involves sequences of lines (though often not more than two) beginning with the same letter. The example just quoted (Ps 33,9) was a good illustration since each line begins with ה, a feature which would have been obscured if anacrusis had gone unnoticed. Another example is Isa 55,13

| | |
|---|---|
| והיה | It shall be: |
| ליהוה לשם | a name for Yahweh, |
| לאות עולם לא יכרת | a perpetual, imperishable sign. |

Both lines begin with ל (approximated by the use of line-initial *a* in translation, here), as is evident once anacrusis of והיה is discerned. Finally, use of anacrusis is a stylistic trait, frequent in some poems but rare in others. Examples of its common use are Isa 5,8-23[88] and Job 4-5 (Eliphaz speeches).

BIBLIOGRAPHY

Robinson, T.H. 'Anacrusis in Hebrew Poetry', *BZAW* 66 (1936) 37-40.
For Akkadian cf. Böhl: 1961, 148-149.

## 5.6 *Functions of Metre*

*Introductory*

A writer or poet chooses to compose in metrical lines (or verse) for definite reasons, and in particular, certain functions dictate his choice of one metrical form rather than another. The most obvious example for Hebrew verse is qinah metre (3 + 2 stresses) which is characteristic of laments: it occurs either in genuine laments (as in the Book of Lamentations) or in mock dirges (Isa 23,16). The following enumeration of functions, based very much on Chatman,[89] will be illustrated by examples from the Hebrew tradition only.

*Functions*

(a) *Metre indicates tempo and texture.*

Metre sets the speed at which a poem should be uttered—to be precise, its tempo. A dirge will be slow and measured (Lam 5); a victory song, quick and lively (Ex 15; Ps 29). The effect of slowness can be conveyed by the use of very long cola (Ps 19,8-10), judicious

---

88. Alonso-Schökel, *Estudios*, 193.
89. Chatman: 1965, 184-224.

placing of caesura (Job 9,16)[90] or the presence of long words (Lam 3,6a.15a). Rapidity, instead, is felt in two-beat staccato verse (Jer 46,3ff) or a succession of polysyllabic words (Jgs 5,22b). Akin to tempo is texture:

> Individual poets achieve distinctive 'textures' through their manipulation of language within a chosen metre, and such texture is not captured by an analysis which reveals only which syllables are metrically stressed. A poem full of multisyllabic words (for example) is quite different from one which largely utilizes monosyllables and disyllables, different in ways which go beyond the selection of diction. There is . . . a metrical difference, because there is an inevitable phonological difference.[91]

An example is Prov 20,18.

(b) *Metre sets up a regular pattern.*
By adopting a particular metre the poet casts his work in a specific form. This assists him as a composer by providing a framework within which he can create, and at the same time sets up a listening pattern for his audience.[92] The way is then paved for changes in the pattern, or special effects (defeated expectancy). The stricter the metre, the more effective is any abrupt alteration in its flow (Isa 28,9ff).

(c) *Metre as a measure of the poet's skill.*
Having selected his metre, the poet must then sustain it, which may require all his skill and language control. The audience will appreciate his talent when he is successful.[93]

(d) *Metre disautomatises language.*
In his search for language to suit the metre a poet is forced to break away from stock expressions, everyday vocabulary and normal syntax.[94] Archaisms are more frequent than in standard language and language is used in a fresh way.

---

90. See P. Vetter, 'Die Metrik des Buches Job', *Biblische Studien* (Freiburg, 1897) 57ff., for caesura.
91. Fowler: 1968, 282-283.
92. Termed 'metrical set' by Chatman: 1965, 121; see also Fowler: 1968, 293-294.
93. Perhaps this is why there is so much 'mixed metre' in Hebrew: it was too difficult to maintain metre of one type.
94. This topic is explored by D.R. Hillers, 'Observations on Syntax and Meter in Lamentations', *Myers FS*, 265-270.

(e) *Metre implies the unusual.*

The mere fact that metre is used in poetry indicates its content to be totally different from everyday life.[95] This explains why the Hebrew prophets used verse: it marked their words as being authentic and as conveying a special message. Wisdom sayings and poems (Prov, Job) and liturgical poetry (Pss) are in verse for the same reasons.

(f) *Metre assists memorisation.*

Perhaps this function could be better expressed by saying that texts in metrical form are more easily committed to memory, exemplifying the foregrounding function of verse where the words themselves are as important as the content. It also explains why ancient poetry could be transmitted relatively unchanged over long periods.

95. Called the framing effect.

# 6

## PARALLELISM

### 6.1 *Introductory*

*Parallelism*
Parallelism is universally recognised as *the* characteristic feature of biblical Hebrew poetry although it is also used extensively in kindred Semitic verse (notably Akkadian) as well as elsewhere.[1] Most introductions to Hebrew poetry, for instance, Gray's *The Forms of Hebrew Poetry*, provide a brief description of parallelism and then proceed to give a detailed classification of its sub-types: synonymous, antithetic, synthetic[2] and so on. My presentation here will be very different from the standard not simply to avoid dupliation or out of sheer love of novelty but because the study of parallelism has been affected, recently, on two levels, both related to theory. Accordingly, a few basic notions of theory with particular reference to parallelism must now be set out, as a preliminary to what is to follow. The first paragraph will deal, in a very simplified way, with the notion of parallelism as a mathematical concept; the second (which to most will appear more relevant) is an explanation of grammatical parallelism in the strict sense.

*Symmetry, asymmetry and parallelism*
To talk about parallelism is to use an analogy based on mathematical (or, rather, geometrical) concepts and scholars have failed to see the deeper implications resulting from this commonly accepted notion. At the risk of alienating the reader, certain points of theory must be established before any critique of existing misconceptions is possible.[3]

---

1. For a good survey, see Jakobson: 1966.
2. Strictly speaking such 'parallelism' is structural or a form of enjambment; see below.
3. Most of what follows derives from Laferrière and Shapiro, who in turn depend on

When we analyze poetry we consider it as two-dimensional space (say, a rectangle) which corresponds to the time taken in reading the poem through:

This is how most poems look on a page—since we are so used to seeing poems printed out—but, in fact, a poem is read, either silently or aloud, and so constitutes *discourse*. Discourse, in its turn, involves the passage of time. Since we cannot deal adequately with an abstract like *time*, we have to represent it as *space* (the rectangle in our example) but always with the proviso that this is an *analogy*.[4]

Once we are aware that we are dealing with *space* (as representing time) then we must keep to its inherent laws, namely, those of geometrical structure and more specifically, those of symmetry. What, then, is symmetry? (This requires a further sidetrack, but its significance is such that it must be made clear before proceeding further.)

If we consider, as an example, a cat in front of a mirror:

---

the basic insights of Weyl. Though this section seems disappointingly long, abbreviation would result in lack of clarity. The conclusions have not been applied throughout the book and it is left to the reader to do so.

4. 'The analysis of poetry always presupposes spatialization of the temporal (dynamic, unidimensional, unidirectional) discourse . . . Poeticists have simply grown accustomed to "looking" at the poem, as if it really were an object which the poet writes down in a plane. The spatial analogy is indispensable, but it *is* nevertheless an analogy' (Laferrière: 1978, 16).

its reflection (CAT$_1$') will be equidistant from the mirror on its other side and in the same plane, but the image will be reversed:

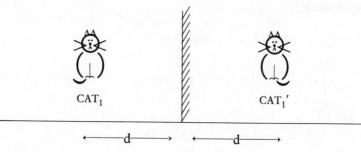

The important point to notice is that CAT$_1$ and CAT$_1$' are symmetrical (or, if you like, balance each other) only when considered *together* as a pair. Either 'cat' on its own cannot be symmetrical since symmetry is a *relationship*. Symmetry, then, is a relation between two (or more) items and is, strictly speaking, only one of several types of 'automorphism'.[5]

Let us now take another example, this time of two cats in front of a mirror:

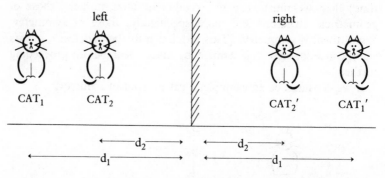

The group to the left plus the group to the right of the mirror are symmetrical—the difference between the cats and their reflections being the reversal in the images (image-tails to the right)—the distances d$_1$ and d$_2$ being fixed by the laws of reflection in a plane. This illustrates two essential notions: *sequence* and *sign*. Sequence is

5. An automorphism is a transformation which preserves the structure of space; the ensuing discussion will, it is hoped, clarify this point.

indicated by the subscript numbers ($CAT_1$, $CAT_2$, etc.), and sign by the directions of the tails. If we ignore the mirror and play around with the four-cat arrangement (always preserving the distances between them)[6]—four possible sets emerge, corresponding to the interplay between two variables (sign and sequence):[7]

1:—ignoring the tails:

2:—with tails included:

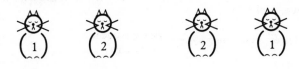

3:—ignoring the tails and switching the cats on the right:

4:—switching the cats (as above) but including the tails as well:

or, schematically:

| | | | | | |
|---|---|---|---|---|---|
| 1: | $a_1$ | $a_2$ | // | $a_2$ | $a_1$ | (reflexive congruence) |
| 2: | $a_1$ | $a_2$ | // | $-a_2$ | $-a_1$ | (reflexive anti-congruence) |
| 3: | $a_1$ | $a_2$ | // | $a_1$ | $a_2$ | (parallelism) |
| 4: | $a_1$ | $a_2$ | // | $-a_1$ | $-a_2$ | (proper anti-congruence) |

6. These combinations and permutations apply to sets larger than 4-component sets—but for clarity only 4 are used.

7. Using the simplified notation $CAT_1 = 1$, etc.

Parallelism, it is now evident, belongs within a larger group of mathematical analogues and cannot be exalted to the rank of 'the characteristic of Hebrew poetry', quite irrespective of the fact that it is by no means the only form in which such poetry is cast.[8] The significance of what has been set out is that it accounts for chiastic patterns as well as parallelism, and sets parallelism in its proper context. Some examples will help illustrate the theoretical notions set out above.[9]

1. *Parallelism (proper congruence)*: $\begin{cases} \text{same sequence} \\ \text{same sign} \end{cases}$

$$a_1, a_2, a_3, \ldots // a_1, a_2, a_3, \ldots$$

for example, Jer 51,27:

| | | | |
|---|---|---|---|
| שאו־נס בארץ | Raise | a standard | in the land; |
| תקעו שופר בגוים | blow | a trumpet | among the nations. |

Similarly, Job 8,3.

2. *Chiasmus or mirror symmetry (reflexive congruence)*: $\begin{cases} \text{same sign} \\ \text{opposite sequence} \end{cases}$

$$a_1, a_2, a_3, \ldots // \ldots a_3, a_2, a_1$$

for example, Ps 107,16:

| | | |
|---|---|---|
| כי | For | |
| שבר דלתות נחושת | he has shattered | doors of bronze; |
| ובריחי ברזל גדע | and bars of iron | he has snapped. |

3. *Proper anti-congruence*: $\begin{cases} \text{same sequence} \\ \text{opposite sign} \end{cases}$

$$a_1, a_2, a_3, \ldots // -a_1, -a_2, -a_3, \ldots$$

for example, Ps 85,12 (with gender and semantic reversal):

| | |
|---|---|
| אמת מארץ תצמח | Fidelity (f) from the earth (f) will spring up (+), |
| וצדק משמים נשקף | and justice (-f) from the sky (-f) will peer down (–). |

8. The outstanding exception is, of course, the monocolon, but enjambment, too, can be mentioned.

9. Note: there are two variables, *sequence* (the subscripts in $a_1$, $a_2$, etc.) and *sign* or polarity (+ understood as present if not written, and –; polarity can be semantic or can be, say, of gender). Grammatical categories are not polar, however.

4. *Reflexive anti-congruence (chiastic)*: $\begin{cases}\text{reversed sequence} \\ \text{opposite sign}\end{cases}$

$$a_1, a_2, a_3, \ldots // -a_3, -a_2, -a_1$$

for example, Ps 37,30:

| פי צדיק יהגה חכמה | The just man's mouth | mutters | wisdom[10] |
|---|---|---|---|
| | (m) | (m) | (-m) |
| ולשונו תדבר משפט | his tongue | speaks | justice. |
| | (-m) | (-m) | (m) |

It is important to notice that very often there are *invariants outside* a particular set, which are not affected by changes within the set.[11] An example was the initial *kî* in Ps 107,16 given above.[12] This accounts for partial patterns or subgroups which can then be assigned to one of the four basic types described above.

## Line-forms and grammatical parallelism

The standard handbooks all give lists of the various kinds of parallelism in Hebrew verse—and classification along similar lines will be attempted here, too. Underlying such systems, though, which tend to be impressionistic rather than precise,[13] is grammatical analysis of each verse-line. Up to recently such analysis has only been *implicit*, but a newly published book of great significance has pointed the way towards a more overt and a more precise approach to poetry. The book in question is Collins' *Line-forms in Hebrew Poetry* and is considered in detail elsewhere; here I will only deal with its implications for parallelism.

Very briefly, Collins has shown that by breaking down sentences into their components—subject, object, verb and verb-modifier[14]—*four basic sentences* emerge:

---

10. With '-m' standing for its polar opposite, 'f' (= feminine).
11. After determining the group of automorphisms, 'you may start to investigate symmetric configurations of elements, i.e. configurations which are invariant under a certain subgroup of the group of all automorphisms; and it may be advisable, before looking for such configurations, to study the subgroups themselves, e.g. the subgroup of those automorphisms which leave one element fixed, or leave two distinct elements fixed, and investigate what discontinuous or finite subgroups there exist, and so forth' (H. Weyl, *Symmetry* [Princeton, 1952] 144).
12. Anacrusis, in a sense, though strictly the term refers to metre.
13. And often highly inaccurate since the standard abc // a'b'c' system cannot be correctly applied to many passages.
14. '"Subject": includes pronouns, nouns, noun phrases (e.g. construct chains, noun

A  $NP_1$–V
B  $NP_1$–V–M
C  $NP_1$–V–$NP_2$
D  $NP_1$–V–$NP_2$–M

These basic sentences, in their turn, yield *four general line-types*,[15] of which only types II and III are significant, directly, for parallelism: Of the 40 specific line types available to the Hebrew poet[16]—not including variations such as the use of extra verbs, let alone nominal sentences—only about half can be called parallel. For example:

| ושפט בין הגוים | He'll judge among the nations, |
| והוכיח לעמים רבים | and reprove the many peoples. |

(Isa 2,4)

This can be analysed as

V     M
V     M

—two lines with evident grammatical parallelism (as well as semantic parallelism).[17]

In his recent book on Hebrew poetry,[18] Kugel describes parallelism as follows.

> The basic feature of biblical songs—and, for that matter, of most of the sayings, proverbs, laws, laments, blessings, curses, prayers, and speeches found in the Hebrew Bible—is the recurrent use of a relatively short sentence-form that consists of two brief clauses.

> The clauses are regularly separated by a slight pause—slight because the second is ... a continuation of the first and not a wholly new beginning. By contrast, the second ends in a full pause.

---

+ adjective) and noun clauses ($= NP_1$). "Object": includes the same ($= NP_2$). "Verb": this may be a finite verb, a participle or an infinitive ($= V$). "Modifiers of the verb": these may be adverbs, prepositional phrases, locatives, etc. ($= M$)' (quoted substantially from Collins, *Line-forms*, 23).

15. The four general line types are: I. contains one basic sentence; II. two basic sentences of the same kind, in such a way that all the constituents in the first half-line are repeated in the second, though not necessarily in the same order; III. two similar basic sentences with ellipsis in the second; IV. two different basic sentences. See Collins, *Line-forms*, 23-24.

16. See the table in Collins, *Line-forms*, 25.

17. Collins, *Line-forms*, 106.

18. Kugel, *Idea*. Note the title of his first chapter: 'The Parallelistic Line: "A is so, and *what's more*, B"'.

The structure might thus be schematized as

_____/_____//

with the single slash representing the pause between the clauses (short) and the pair of slashes representing the final pause (long).[19]

He terms the two halves of the standard couplet 'A and B', and after discussing various types of parallelism,[20] he goes on to consider the 'essence of biblical parallelism' which is 'basically a sequence: first part-pause-next-part-bigger pause'. 'What those pauses actually embody is the subjoined, hence emphatic, character of B.' He concludes:

> B, by being connected to A—carrying it further, echoing it, restating it, it does not matter which—has an emphatic, 'seconding' character, and it is this, more than any aesthetic of symmetry or paralleling, which is at the heart of biblical parallelism.[21]

This description (which is better appreciated in the larger context of Kugel's book) should be compared with what has been set out above and complemented by Collins' approach.

## BIBLIOGRAPHY

Here only the bibliography for parallelism in general will be given; for specific types of parallelism see appropriate sections.

(a) *General.*

Austerlitz, R. *Ob-Ugric Metrics* (FFC 70.174; Helsinki, 1958).

Gräf, H. *Der Parallelismus im Rolandslied* (Wertheim, 1931).

Hiatt, M. 'The Prevalence of Parallelism: A Preliminary Investigation by Computer', *LS* 6 (1973) 117-126.

Hightower, J.R. 'Some Characteristics of Parallel Prose', *Karlgren FS*, 60-91.

Jakobson, R. 'Grammatical Parallelism and its Russian Facet', *Lang* 42 (1966) 399-429.

Laferrière, D. *Sign and Subject* (Lisse, 1978).

Levin, S. *Linguistic Structures in Poetry* (The Hague, 1962.1973).

Sebeok, T.A. 'Grammatischer Parallelismus in einem tscheremissischen Segen', *UAJb* 39 (1967) 41-48.

Shapiro, M. *Asymmetry: an inquiry into the linguistic structures of poetry* (North-Holland linguistic, 26; Amsterdam, 1976).

19. Kugel, *Idea*, 1.
20. See Kugel, *Idea*, 4-7.54-55, etc.
21. Kugel, *Idea*, 51. See the comments by Barr in his review, *TLS* Dec. 25, 1981, 1506 (brought to my attention by Dr David Wasserstein).

Stalker, G.H. 'Some Notions of "Similarity" Among Lines of Text', *CompHum* 11 (1978) 199-209.

Steinitz, W. *Der Parallelismus in der finnisch-karelischen Volksdichtung* (FFC 115; Helsinki, 1934).

(b) *Semitic*

Baker, A. 'Parallelism: England's Contribution to Biblical Studies', *CBQ* 35 (1973) 429-440.

Begrich, J. 'Der Satzstil im Fünfer', *ZSem* 9 (1933-34) 169-209.

Berlin, A. 'Grammatical Aspects of Biblical Parallelism', *HUCA* 50 (1979) 17-43.

Boling, R.G. '"Synonymous" Parallelism in the Psalms', *JSS* 5 (1960) 221-225.

Broadribb, D. 'A Historical Review of Studies of Hebrew Poetry', *AbrN* 13 (1972-73) 66-87.

Casanowicz, I.M. 'Parallelism in Hebrew Poetry', *The Jewish Encyclopaedia* (London, 1916), vol. 9, 520-522.

Collins, *Line-forms*.

Donald, T. Parallelism in Akkadian, Hebrew and Ugaritic (unpublished thesis, Manchester, 1966; cf. *BSOAS* 36 [1973] 641 and *JSS* 10 [1965] 99-101).

Geller, S.A. *Parallelism in Early Biblical Poetry* (Harvard, 1979).

Gevirtz, *Patterns*.

Gevirtz, S. 'Evidence of Conjugational Variation in the Parallelization of Selfsame Verbs in the Amarna Letters', *JNES* 32 (1973) 99-104.

Held, M. 'The *yqtl-qtl (qtl-yqtl)* Sequence of Identical Verbs in Biblical Hebrew and Ugaritic', *Neuman FS*, 281-290.

—'The Action-Result (Factitive-Passive) Sequence of Identical Verbs in Biblical Hebrew and Ugaritic', *JBL* 84 (1965) 272-282.

Holladay, W.L. 'The Recovery of Poetic Passages of Jeremiah', *JBL* 85 (1966) 401-435, esp. 406-412.

Isaacs, E. 'The origin and nature of parallelism', *AJSL* 35 (1919) 113-127.

Kaddari, M.Z. 'A Semantic Approach to Biblical Parallelism', *JJS* 24 (1973) 167-175.

Kugel, *Idea*.

Maeso, D. 'Contribución al estudio de la métrica bíblica: sobre la verdadera significación y alcance del "paralelismo" ', *Sef* 3 (1943) 3-39.

Newman, L.I.—Popper, W. *Studies in Biblical Parallelism* (Berkeley, 1918).

Parker, S.B. 'Parallelism and Prosody in Ugaritic Narrative Verse', *UF* 6 (1974) 283-294.

Ringgren, H. 'The omitting of *kol* in Hebrew parallelism', *VT* 32 (1982) 99-103.

Robinson, T.H. 'Basic Principles of Hebrew Poetic Form', *Bertholet FS*, 438-450.

—'Hebrew Poetic Form', *VTS* 1 (1953) 128-149.

Yoder, P.R. 'Biblical Hebrew', Wimsatt, *Versification*, 52-65.

## 6.2 *Gender-matched Parallelism*

*Description*

First identified in Ugaritic poetry by Cassuto,[22] gender-matched parallelism is a type of parallelism where the gender of the nouns involved is the basic component.[23] An example from classical Hebrew poetry will make this clear. In Isa 49,22,

| | |
|---|---|
| וחביאו בניך בחצן | They shall bring your sons in their embrace (m.), |
| ובנתיך על כתף תנשאנה | and your daughters shall be carried on their shoulder (f.), |

a masculine noun ('sons') is used in connection with 'embrace', which is also masculine, in the first colon while in the parallel line both nouns ('daughters', 'shoulder') are feminine. The *genders* of the nouns in each colon *match*—masculine and feminine genders occurring in *parallel* lines—which accounts for the designation 'gender-matched parallelism'.

As mentioned, the device is used, too, in Ugaritic poetry, and one illustration will be enough in the present context.[24] It is as follows:

| | |
|---|---|
| *bph rgm lyṣa* | Scarcely had his word (m.) issued from his mouth (m.), |
| *bšpth hwth* | from his lips (f.), his word (f.). |

To complete the picture, a single example can be cited from Akkadian literature:

| | |
|---|---|
| *ina āli ardatu zamārša šani* | In the city the young girl's song (m.) is altered; |
| *ina āli eṭlu nissassu šanāt* | in the city the man's tune (f.) is altered. |

In fact the gender-pattern in this text[25] is slightly different from the previous two passages and anticipates a later paragraph of this section.

---

22. Cassuto, *Anath*, 44-46.
23. For the theoretical background see the preceding section on SYMMETRY, ASYMMETRY AND PARALLELISM.
24. The passage cited is *CTA* 19 iii 113 (and parallels). For a score or so of examples cf. Watson: *UF* 13 (1981) 181-187.
25. Cited in *CAD* E, 410 and *CAD* N/2, 274.

The straightforward m. + m. // f. + f. pattern appears to be the point of departure for a whole series of variations and these can now be set out.

### 1. *Straightforward patterns*

m. + m. // f. + f.
already illustrated; also: Gen 49,11; 2 Sm 22,7; Isa 5,7; Joel 2,16; Ps 91,7; Job 10,12; Lam 5,3; etc.

f. + f. // m. + m.
For example, Jer 48,37:

| | |
|---|---|
| על כל ידים גדרת | On every pair of hands (f.) a slash (f.), |
| ועל מתנים שק | on every pair of hips (m.), sackcloth (m.). |

Also Isa 5,29; Jer 13,27; Hab 2,5; Ps 147,15; etc.

The same patterns occur, too, within construct chains as m.-m. // f.-f. (Dt 33,29; Isa 18,6; Hos 7,1; Job 20,24; Song 4,6; etc.) and as f.-f. // m.-m. (Dt 33,14 and Ps 107,16 only).

### 2. *Inverted patterns*

A deliberate variation on the device: instead of a noun corresponding in gender with its companion noun, a noun of the *opposite* gender is chosen. This results in the following patterns:

m. + f. // m. + f., as in

| | |
|---|---|
| יתן כעפר חרבו | Who makes them like dust (m.) with his sword (f.), |
| כקש נדף קשתו | like chaff (m.), drives them with his bow (f.)? |

Isa 41,2; and Joel 2,1; Nah 2,14; Job 11,14; Prov 3,22; 26,13, etc.

f. + m. // f. + m., e.g. Isa 62,1:

| | |
|---|---|
| עד יצא כנגה צדקה | Till her vindication (m.) emerges like brightness (f.), |
| וישועתה כלפיד יבער | and like a torch (m.), her victory burns (f.). |

Also Isa 28,15; Job 5,9; Prov 5,5; etc. There appear to be no examples of this type within construct chains.

### 3. *Chiastic gender patterns*

m. + f. // f. + m., as in Ps 37,30:

| | |
|---|---|
| פי צדיק יהגה חכמה | A just man's mouth (m.) utters wisdom (f.), |
| ולשונו תדבר משפט | and his tongue (f.) speaks justice (m.). |

Further: Isa 33,6; Ps 73,7; Prov 10,15; Lam 3,47; etc.

f. + m. // m. + f., e.g. Isa 66,8:

| | |
|---|---|
| היוחל ארץ ביום אחד | Is a land (f.) born in one day (m.)? |
| אם יולד גוי פעם אחת | Can a nation (m.) be brought forth in one moment (f.)? |

And Gen 49,15; Isa 29,4; Ps 128,3; Job 16,18; Song 7,7; etc.

The same chiastic gender patterns occur within construct chains m.—f. // f.—m.: Prov 8,20; f.—m. // m.—f.: Dt 32,14; Isa 24,18; Job 29,13; etc.

Having classified the patterns within gender-matched synonymous parallelism, the next step is to look at its *functions*: why does a particular passage use parallelism of this kind? What did the poet have in mind?

Approximately five or six different functions can be identified and a brief look at each, with illustrative texts, will suffice as a basis for further study.

*Functions*
The following functions can be listed:

1. *To express merismus.*
The main function of gender-matched parallelism (in both its 'normal' and reversed forms) is to present a global picture, as in Jer 46,12:

| | |
|---|---|
| שמעו גוים קלונך | The nations (m.) have heard your cry (m.), |
| וצוחתך מלאה הארץ | and the earth (f.) is filled by your shout (f.), |

implying everyone was aware of Judah's plight. Similarly: Nb 21,29; Hab 2,5; Ps 32,2; Lam 1,20. Merismus is the function, too, when there is mismatch of gender: Isa 41,4; Jer 16,3; Prov 22,17.

2. *To heighten antithesis.*
Gender-matching can also be used to reinforce antithesis or contrast; examples include Isa 3,24a; Prov 15,6 and

| | |
|---|---|
| גם בשחק יכאב לב | Even in laughter (m.) a heart (m.) may grieve, |
| ואחרית השמחה תוגה | and the end of joy (f.) be sorrow (f.). (Prov 14,13)[26] |

---

26. The gender of two nouns in a construct chain ($N_1 N_2$) is that of the first ($N_1$)—here f.

With reversal of gender concord the contrast is even stronger: Ps 73,7; Prov 20,9; etc.

### 3. *To express harmony.*

By matching the genders within each line, a poet can express harmony, as in Ps 122,7:

| | |
|---|---|
| יהי שלום בחילך | Let there be peace (m.) within your ramparts (m.), |
| שלוה בארמנותיך | tranquillity (f.) within your fortress (f.). |

Also Ps 128,3 and Sir 3,29.[27]

### 4. *To improve parallelism.*

Occasionally, the poet chooses synonyms of one or other gender to achieve better parallelism; for instance Sir 3,29:

| | |
|---|---|
| לב חכם יבין משלי חכמים | A wise mind (m.) will understand wise proverbs (m.), |
| ואזן מקשבת לחכמה תשמח | and an attentive ear (f.) rejoices in wisdom (f.). |

Also: Joel 1,6; Job 28,2; Lam 5,3; etc. The same effect is produced even when nouns of opposite gender occur within each line: Prov 30,19b; Song 7,8.

### 5. *For emphasis.*

Emphatic denial or affirmation can be expressed by gender-matched parallelism: Gen 49,6a; Ps 88,13; Sir 32,20; etc.

### 6. *To express inevitability.*

This kind of parallelism is sometimes used to imply inevitability; so Sir 42,13:

| | |
|---|---|
| כי מבגד יצא עש | For out of clothes (m.) comes a moth (m.), |
| ומאשה רעת אשה | and from a woman, a woman's wickedness (f.). |

Precisely the reverse is true when the genders are switched, for then what is expressed is unexpectedness, or surprise:

| | |
|---|---|
| טמון בארץ חבלו | Hidden in the ground (f.) is a rope (m.) for him, |
| ומלכדתו עלי נתיב | and a trap (f.) for him is on the path (m.). |
| | (Job 18,10) |

Also: Dt 32,14; Prov 18,7; etc. Other functions could be mentioned, but they are not so common as those already listed.[28]

---

27. Curiously, the same function may be discerned in texts such as Isa 11,4; Ps 25,13; Prov 8,20, where there is gender reversal.

28. To express poetic justice (Ps 59,13; Job 20,24), abundance (Pss 72,3; 144,12), etc.

Peculiar to inversion of gender-matching are three special and related functions:

(a) To emphasise an unusual event; for example Isa 43,16:

הנותן בים דרך     Who sets a road (f.) in the sea (m.),
ובמים עזים נתיבה     in the mighty waters (m.), a path (f.).

Also Isa 28,8; Ez 11,18-20; Joel 4,3.10; etc.

(b) To denote destruction as in Nah 2,14:

והבערתי בעשן רכבה     I will burn your chariots (f.) in smoke (m.),
וכפיריך תאכל חרב     and the sword (f.) will devour your cubs (m.);

as well as Isa 41,2; Job 18,15.

(c) To portray inversion of state; for example Ps 44,14:

תשימנו חרפה לשכנינו     You have made us a taunt (f.) to our fellow-
                        citizens (m.),
לעג וקלס לסביבותינו     derision and scorn (m.) to our neighbourhood (f.).

Further: Isa 28,8; Job 11,14; Sir 5,29; etc.

*For study*
—Identify the gender patterns in the following texts:
    Nb 21,29; Isa 3,24a; 24,2; 28,17; 34,13; 40,3; 59,9b; 61,10; Jer 46,12; 48,46; Nah 2,13; Hab 3,3; Pss 31,11; 32,2; 119,55; Job 5,20; 8,2; Lam 1,15b.
    Isa 65,18c; Pss 57,5; 85,12; Lam 1,20.
    Isa 54,2; Jer 16,4; Joel 1,6; Pss 18,16; 109,14; Job 31,16; Song 6,31; Sir 6,31.
    Gen 49;6a.17a; Isa 42,4; 43,16; 44,3b; Pss 57,6; 104,2; 105,27; 135,6; Job 18,10.15; Prov 22,17; 29,3.
—What are the *functions* of gender-matched parallelism in the following passages:
    Jer 13,27; Isa 42,4; Job 5,20; Ps 125,3; and Job 10,12; Prov 15,13; Hab 3,3; Joel 2,16; Prov 3,22?

*Cross-references*
CHIASMUS, STANZA.

### BIBLIOGRAPHY

Berlin, A. 'Grammatical Aspects of Biblical Parallelism', *HUCA* 50 (1979) 17-43, esp. 27-30.

128 — *Classical Hebrew Poetry*

Watson, W.G.E. 'Gender-Matched Parallelism in Ugaritic Poetry', *UF* 13 (1981) 181-187.
—'Gender-matched Synonymous Parallelism in the OT', *JBL* 99 (1980) 321-341.

### 6.3 *Parallel Word-pairs*

*Terminology and definitions*
Narrowly considered, the parallel pair is mostly used in a bicolon or couplet, with one member of the pair in the first line and the second member in the parallel line. For example (Prov 26,1):

| כשלג בקיץ | Like *snow* in summer, |
| וכמטר בקציר | and like *rain* at harvest |

where the synonymous word-pair is שלג // מטר.

A whole series of terms is on hand to refer to such pairs: 'standing pairs', 'fixed pairs', 'A-B pairs', 'parallel pairs' and so on, which tend to be used interchangeably by modern scholars, each term emphasising a particular aspect of these pairs (as will become evident later on). The use of 'fixed pair' (or the less frequent 'standing pair') is not recommended since there is a certain amount of flexibility in these pairs, the stock sequence occasionally being reversed ('orphan // widow' rather than 'widow // orphan', for instance), or the second component being varied. Accordingly, 'parallel pair' is preferable or, as in this section heading, 'parallel word-pair' (occasionally, simply 'word-pair' for brevity or because parallelism does not always obtain).[29]

*Criteria*: Parallel word-pairs can be recognised as such if they fit the following requirements:[30]
1. each must belong to the same grammatical class (verb, noun, etc.);
2. the components must occur in parallel lines;
3. such word-pairs must be relatively frequent.
An example is the word-pair עלה // ירד, 'to ascend // to descend' as used in Ps 107,26:

|  |  | *analysis* |
| יעלו שמים | They go up to the sky | V-M |
| ירדו תהומות | they go down to the ocean. | V-M |

29. See the apposite remarks of Dahood, *RSP* I, 73. For the underlying semantic theory cf. A. Lehrer, *Semantic Fields and Lexical Structure* (Amsterdam, 1974).
30. Following Yoder: 1971, 472.

Both components are verbs, as shown in the 'analysis' column (criterion 1), they comprise parallel lines (as part of a tricolon: criterion 2) and the word-pair recurs several times in Hebrew (Isa 14,14-15; Jer 48,5; Am 9,2; Ps 104,8 [criterion 3]).

*Sequence*: Generally speaking, the first element of a parallel word-pair (referred to as the *A-word*) is more frequent and more well known than its counterpart in the second colon (the *B-word*).[31] So, in Ps 7,17

| | |
|---|---|
| ישוב עמלו בראשו | May his sin redound on his *head*, |
| ועל קדקדו חמסו ירד | and upon his *pate* may his violence descend |

the poet uses the rare noun קדקד as a B-word in tandem with common or garden ראש (the A-word). This explains why the same A-word may be used with a variety of synonymous B-words: there are fewer common words for the same thing, but a variety of rare or esoteric words. As will be seen, though, the normal A // B sequence is sometimes deliberately reversed for special effects.

### Lists of parallel word-pairs

Although it has long been known that Hebrew poets used a selection of stock word-pairs, it was not until scholars had studied Ugaritic literature that they became aware of the extent to which such word-pairs actually occurred. This was because Ugaritic poetry, too, used a whole range of parallel word-pairs; not only that: a high percentage of these pairs are identical with Hebrew word-pairs. For example,

| | |
|---|---|
| *bḥyk abn nšmḫ* | In your life, father of ours, we *rejoice*, |
| *blmtk ngln* | in your non-death we *exult*. |

(*CTA* 16 ii 98-99)

where the Ugaritic word-pair *šmḫ* // *g(y)l* exactly matches Hebrew גיל // שמח (e.g. Isa 9,2; Hos 9,1) with the same meaning.

Such correspondences have led scholars to compile lists of word-pairs common to Ugaritic and Hebrew (notably in *RSP* I, II and III).[32] Identical (or corresponding) word-pairs have also been found in other languages cognate with Hebrew and a project is in hand, in Jerusalem, to provide complete lists of all word-pairs in Hebrew,

31. See, particularly, Boling, Held and Yoder. For a particular study see my article 'The Hebrew Word-pair *'sp//qbṣ*', in *ZAW* [in press].

32. A fourth volume is in preparation, but note the critiques mentioned in the bibliography.

Ugaritic, Akkadian and Aramaic.[33] Phoenician, too, has also been
studied with this in mind.[34] However, certain cautionary remarks
are in order. First, no totally exhaustive list of Hebrew word-pairs
has yet been drawn up (partly because the bulk of scholarly effort has
been on making lists of pairs *common* to Ugaritic and Hebrew). Since
only partial listings are available, assured results regarding, say,
statistical frequency are not possible and much that has been asserted
so far has been through extrapolation. Secondly, parallel word-pairs
are not confined to Ugaritic and Hebrew: they occur, too, in other
languages (notably, Akkadian), but to date full listings have not yet
been drawn up for the related languages. Therefore, pending the
availability of these lists it is difficult to evaluate the significance of
data collected so far. It does seem that there was a common core of
word-pairs for several of the languages concerned, but the extent of
this core has not yet been determined.

*Types of parallel word-pairs*
In classifying parallel word-pairs[35] two factors are significant. The
first is the *semantic* element—for example, the pair 'father // mother'
belongs to the semantic class PARENT. The second is the *restrictive
context* of two parallel lines. It is at the intersection of these two
components that the various categories (to be listed) arise. The
second component (parallelism within a couplet) is necessary, otherwise the semantic class of a particular word-pair would be undeter-
mined. To take our example: 'father // mother' could also be
hyponyms of the classes SEX (as male // female), ADULT (contrasted
with CHILD) and so on. The second co-ordinate fixes the class by
narrowing the context and determining which 'rhetorical relationship'
is operative between components of a particular pair.[36]

   However, although such considerations must be kept in mind, we
are here dealing with the use of poetic technique in practice.

33.  See Watters, *Formula Criticism*, 27.
34.  Avishur: 1975.
35.  For attempts at classifying word-pairs see Watson, *Or* 45 (1976) 434-436, and
Geller, *Parallelism*, 31-41.
36.  The phrase is Geller's. He writes: 'It is necessary to combine the concept of
semantic paradigm with the recognition that the relationship of the B line term to its A
line parallel involves in every case what might be called a "rhetorical relationship", that
is, one which is intended to produce a certain literary effect', and 'in the context of
parallelism only two members of a given paradigm can be present, and what is most
significant is the rhetorical relationship between them' (Geller, *Parallelism*, 32 and 33).

Accordingly, rather than remain at the theoretical level, it makes more sense to categorise the different kinds of parallel word-pairs in line with the way poets employ them. (This, in fact, is what Geller means by rhetorical relationship.) Whatever classification is adopted or posited there will inevitably be some overlap: a particular pair may belong under two or more heads, or the same class type may apply to more than one kind of word-pair. With such provisos, the following classification can be set out.

1. *Synonymous word-pairs* comprise a large class with a broad spectrum in which many of the other types would fit. Its components are synonyms or near-synonyms and therefore almost interchangeable in character (hence the possibility of reversal, on which see later on). Since Hebrew poetry has a high percentage of synonymously parallel (or semantically parallel) lines, there is a correspondingly large number of such synonymous word-pairs. A short list will indicate the nature of such pairs:

| | |
|---|---|
| ארץ // עפר | 'earth // dust' |
| בין // ידע | 'to understand // to know' |
| ים // נהר | 'sea // river'. |

Of course these couples could also be considered as hyponyms of a more general category; for example, 'to understand' and 'to know' are hyponyms of verbs denoting the use of one's mental powers. The adjective 'synonymous' has been kept as it is in more general use.

A subset of this type comprises the *list* or catalogue, for example

| | |
|---|---|
| אכל // שתה | 'to eat // to drink' |
| מטר // טל | 'rain // dew'. |

'Members of this category . . . are related by an understood common denominator and are not logically interchangeable, even in the most general way. The rhetorical effect is . . . enumerative and impressionistic.'[37]

2. *Antonymic word-pairs* are made up of words opposite in meaning and are normally used, not surprisingly, in antithetic parallelism. Examples are:

| | |
|---|---|
| יש // אין | 'there is // there is not' |
| ימין // שמאול | 'right // left'. |

---

37. Geller, *Parallelism*, 35.

The possibility of overlap with other groups is apparent in such pairs as

ארץ // שמים    'earth // heaven'
שמש // ירח    'sun // moon',

where the components are correlative (see below).

3. *Correlative pairs* can be correlated synonyms,[38] for instance,

עור // פסח    'blind // lame',

both indicating a crippled person.[39] Others indicate a progression, notably

זרע // אכל    'to sow // to eat' (Isa 55,10).[40]

To the same class belong pairs of the MALE // FEMALE order, e.g.

אב // אם    'father // mother'.[41]

Pairs of this kind may also be associative, being formed by simple association of ideas, for instance:

אור // חשך    'light // darkness'.[42]

4. *Augmented word-pairs* are characteristic of Canaanite poetry. Symbolised as A//AB, they differ from repetitive or identical pairs (A//A, see below) by the addition of the modifier B to the repeated element, hence the name 'augmented'.[43] For example

קול יהוה יחיל מדבר    Yahweh's voice makes *the desert* writhe,
יחיל יהוה מדבר קדש    Yahweh('s voice) makes *the holy desert* writhe
(Ps 29,8),

where the word מדבר is augmented in the parallel colon by the addition of קדש (מדבר now being in the construct state): מדבר קדש. Other examples are ים // ים סוף 'sea // reed sea' (Ex 15,4) and ארזי ארזים // הלבנון 'cedars // cedars of Lebanon' (Ps 29,5). The function of such augmented pairs is metrical, serving to fill out the line as expletives.[44]

---

38. The term used by Cassuto, *Anath*, 25.
39. Alternatively, they are hyponyms for 'cripple'.
40. A different example: Isa 66,1.
41. As pointed out to me by A. Berlin; see the section on gender parallelism.
42. So Watters, *Formula Criticism*, 75ff.
43. Freedman-Hyland, *HTR* 66 (1973) 248, prefer 'expanded repetition'.
44. See BALLAST VARIANT.

5. *Epithetic word-pairs* are usually of the pattern $PN_1$ // son of $PN_2$ as in

ושלחתי אש בבית חזאל    I shall send a fire against the house of *Hazael*,
ואכלה ארמנות בן־הדד    and it shall consume *the son of Hadad*'s palaces.

(Am 1,4)

Also: 'Barak // son of Abinoam' (Jgs 5,12); 'David // son of Jesse' (2 Sm 20,2) and 'Balaq // son of Zippor' (Nb 23,18). Evidently this type is closely akin to the preceding (augmented word-pairs).[45]

6. *Figurative word-pairs* include metaphorical words in parallel and metonymic pairs such as abstract nouns in parallel with concrete and synecdochic couples.[46] Some examples will illustrate what is meant.

In Prov 5,3 the metaphorical word-pair 'honey // oil' is used, to good effect:

כי נפת תטפנה שפתי זרה    For the lips of a loose woman drip *honey*,
וחלק משמן חכה    and her palate is smoother than *oil*.

See, too, Job 20,17; Gen 27,28.39; etc. When used in parallel with a concrete noun an abstract noun, too, takes on a concrete meaning as in Ps 54,9:

כי מכל צרה הצילני    For you have delivered me from every *foe*,
ובאיבי ראתה עיני    and my eye has looked triumphantly at my *enemies*.

Finally, a synecdochic pair is יום // ירח 'month // day' (Job 29,2) with a term for a whole in parallel with a part of that whole.

The next four types could be considered as a group where position (or the structural factor) is the most significant feature.

7. *Identical or repetitive pairs* use exactly the same word in each line of the couplet (symbolised as A//A). About 150 such pairs have

---

45. The origin of such word-pairs is stock legal phraseology in the form '$PN_1$ son of $PN_2$' with the components being 'broken up' and distributed over parallel cola (see BREAK-UP OF STEREOTYPE PHRASES). The same parallelism is found in Ugaritic, for example:

    *šrd bʻl bdbḥk*      By your sacrifice cause *Baal* to come down,
    *bn dgn bmṣdk*      by your game, *the son of Dagan*. (*CTA* 14 ii 77-79)

For a different aspect cf. D.J.A. Clines, 'X, X *ben* Y, *ben* Y: Personal Names in Hebrew Narrative Style', *VT* 22 (1972) 286-287.

46. Metonymy is the use of one word for another; synecdoche is the part for the whole or the species for the genus (and the other way round, too).

been identified in Hebrew, and they are common, too, in Ugaritic.[47] One example will be enough (Jer 2,9):

לכן עד אריב אתכם    Therefore, *I* still *contend* with you,
ואת בני בניכם אריב    and with your children's children *will I contend*.

8. *'Fixed + variant'* word-pairs are parallel pairs in which the first element is unchanging while the second is varied (symbolised as A // $B_1$, $B_2$, $B_3$, etc.). For example, the following series is based on the common (A) word יין, 'wine':

יין // זבח    'wine // sacrifice' (Hos 9,4).
דם ענבים    'grape blood' (Gen 49,11).
שכר    'strong drink' (Isa 5,20; Prov 20,1; etc.).
שמן    'oil' (Am 6,6; Ps 104,15; Song 4,10).
תרוש    'must' (Sir 31,25; rev. Mic 6,15).
יין    'wine' (Isa 28,7; Jer 13,12).

Similarly, a series based on ספר // הגה, ידע, מנה: ספר.[48]

A variation on this type is where the second (B) elements are themselves combined to form a new pair, for example תורה // תפלה in

מסיר אזנו משמע תורה    If someone averts his ears from listening to *instruction*,
גם תפלתו תועבה    even his *prayer* is an abomination. (Prov 28,9)

and the pair תורה // אמרי פה in Ps 78,1,

האזינה עמי תורתי    Listen, my people, to my *instruction*,
הטו אזנכם לאמרי־פי    bend an ear to *the words of my mouth*,

results in the formular pair תפלה // אמרי פה as used in Ps 54,4.[49]

9. *Distant word-pairs* are pairs which normally occur in consecutively parallel lines, but are occasionally found in lines which are distant from each other.[50] The recognition of these pairs is dependent on establishing straightforward word-pairs (perhaps even in a different literary tradition such as Ugaritic) and on being able to determine correct stichometry. An example is the pair פרר // שבר 'to break // to

---

47. In an unpublished thesis by R. Bornemann (cited in *RSP* I, 76).
48. References in *RSP* I. For a full study see Boling: 1960.
49. This is an original insight of Yoder: 1971, 484-487; the examples are his.
50. See Dahood, *RSP* I, 80-81. Dahood points to word-pairs whose elements in Ugaritic are sequential but which in Hebrew occur at a distance, and he gives examples. See also Talmon, *ScrH* 8 (1961) 335ff., and the section on BREAK-UP.

crush' common to Hebrew and Ugaritic and found in lines separated from each other in Qoh 12,5-6:[51]

> (Remember God) . . .
> when the blossom whitens on the almond tree,
> the locust stuffs itself,
> and the caper-berry *bursts* (תפר).
> For man marches to his eternal home,
> and mourners moon round the streets
> until (his) strength is far away.
> (Until) <snapped is> the silver cord
> and the golden bowl crushed
> and the pitcher *is shattered* (שבר) at the spring,
> and the basin crushed at the well.

10. *Reversed word-pairs* use an inverted sequence of the normal A//B order, whether synonymous, antonymic, correlative, augmented (AB//A). There seems to be no reversal for either epithetic word-pairs or numerical pairs. Since the topic of inversion is considered elsewhere (INVERSION), only a few remarks are required here.

Inversion of word-pairs occurs for a variety of reasons. Occasionally it is for the sake of varying the monotony of the stock sequence. It can also be used simply for emphasis (e.g. Isa 41,8)[52] or to portray the reversal of an event (e.g. Gen 27,28 and 39).[53] Chiastic patterns can be produced in this way (e.g. Prov 18,6-7).[54] The acrostic element of a poem may demand change of the accepted sequence (e.g. Ps 145,21),[55] or the inversion may effectively portray merismus.[56]

It is important to note that in complete alphabetical listings of word-pairs, a word-pair and its inverted form are not two separate entries.

11. *Numerical word-pairs* are discussed in the section on NUMBER PARALLELISM (6.4).

---

51. The example is given in *RSP* I, 316; the pair is found in Ps 74,13 and in Ugaritic. For the problems of translation cf. C.F. Whitley, *Koheleth* (Berlin, 1980) 99-101, and W.G.E. Watson, 'Gender-patterns in Qoheleth' [forthcoming].

52. So Boadt, *CBQ* 35 (1973) 27-28.

53. J.P. Fokkelman, *Narrative Art in Genesis: specimens of stylistic and structural analysis* (Studia Semitica Neerlandica 17; Assen, 1975) 111. Also, Gevirtz, *Patterns*.

54. Dahood, *RSP* I, 78. See Miller, *HTR* 73 (1980) 79-89.

55. As noted by Boling, *JSS* 14 (1969) 241. Also in Ps 25.

56. See particularly J. Krašovec, *Der Merismus im biblisch-Hebräischen und Nord-westsemitischen* (Rome, 1977).

*Parallel word-pairs and oral poetry*
Having looked at several examples of different types of word-pairs in
various contexts, it is now possible to outline some theoretical
considerations which will explain, among other things, why recognition of word-pairs is important to understanding Hebrew poetry.
One of the principal points to evaluate is the relationship of parallel
word-pairs to the oral origins of Hebrew verse.[57]

1. It would seem that the word-pair played the same role in
Hebrew poetry as did the *formula* (in the Parry-Lord sense)[58] in
classical Greek verse. The fixed pair—which could, of course, be
varied to a certain extent by the poet—was a ready-made item for use
in oral composition.

> What scholars have called A-B terms or fixed word-pairs in
> Hebrew poetry fit Parry's definition of a formula... In the
> Hebrew poetic tradition the formal requirement which had to be
> met by the poet was *parallelism* instead of meter. To create
> parallelistic poetry, the poet had first to link together at least two
> cola to form a line, since the words of a colon without a partner
> could not enter into parallelism. Secondly and concomitantly, he
> had to produce B cola whose words formed parallels to the words
> used in the A cola. It was to meet these two exigencies that the
> traditional word-pairs arose; for if two cola contained a traditional
> word-pair, it would be clear that the poet intended these two cola
> to form a line. Likewise, if words have their traditional parallels,
> when a poet composed the A colon of a line, he could readily
> compose a parallel B colon by filling it with the traditional,
> recognized B counterparts of the words he used in the first colon.

Yoder[59] proceeds to illustrate his point: if a poet uses the A word הר
in the first colon, he must use the corresponding B word (גבעה) in the
second, not for its semantic content, but because the combination of
these two words in parallel constitutes a *formula*. (This aspect is
considered below.)

Although, as Culley has shown,[60] a whole series of stereotyped
expressions which occur in Hebrew poetry also fit the (Parry-Lord)
definition of formula, this does not exclude the parallel word-pair as
being formulaic as well. It simply means that Hebrew poets had to

---

57. See particularly the studies of Gevirtz, Watters, Whallon and especially Yoder.
58. Discussed in chapter 4: ORAL POETRY.
59. Yoder: 1971, 480-481.
60. Culley, *Oral Formulaic*.

hand two different sets of traditional fixed components: stock expressions and the fixed pair, both fitting the requirements of the formula. That is to say, both were (a) *ready-made* and already existing in tradition; and (b) *useful* as particularly suited for the composition of poetry. Since Hebrew poetry is very largely (but by no means exclusively) written in parallel couplets, the parallel word-pair would seem to be more apt as the equivalent of Homeric formulae.

2. A high percentage of word-pairs in a particular passage is a strong indication that the text originated orally, although it does not automatically follow that poems with such high ratios were necessarily orally composed. Yoder's example of Ps 54 will provide a convenient illustration of such a poem.[61] It will be set out as follows: beside each couplet the corresponding word-pair will be given with references to its occurrence elsewhere (since one characteristic of a word-pair is recurrence):

*Psalm 54*

| Text | | Word-pair |
|---|---|---|
| אלהים בשמך הושיעני | 3 | שם // גבורה[62] |
| ובגבורתך תדינני | | הושיע: שפט // דין[63] |
| אלהים שמע תפלתי | 4 | שמע // האזין[64] |
| האזינה לאמרי-פי | | תפלה: תורה // אמרי-פה[65] |
| כי | 5 | |
| זרים קמו עלי | | זר // עריץ[66] |
| ועריצים בקשו נפשי | | קום על // בקש נפש[67] |
| לא שמו אלהים לנגדם | | |
| הנה | 6 | |
| אלהים עזר לי | | אלהים // אדון[68] |
| אדני בסמכי נפשי | | עזר // סמך[69] |
| ישוב הרע לשררי | 7 | שוב(- און) // הצמית[70] |
| באמתך כ-הצמיתם | | |
| בנדבה אזבחה-לך | 8 | זבח // (קרא) שם[71] |
| אודה שמך יהוה כי-טוב | | |
| כי מכל-צרה הצילני | 9 | צרה // אויב[72] |
| ובאיבי ראתה עיני | | |

61. Yoder: 1971, 473-474 and 486-487. Van der Lugt, *Strofische Structuren*, 282-284, ignores this aspect and divides the poem into two stanzas (vv. 3-5 and 6-9) on the basis of content.

62. Jer 16,21; Ps 106,8.
63. Ps 70,4 and 9,9; cf. Prov 31,9; Ps 7,9.
64. Pss 39,13; 49,2; 80,9.
65. Prov 28,9 and Ps 88,1 (cf. Job 22,22).
66. Isa 25,5; 29,5.
67. Ps 86,14.
68. Pss 68,18; 104,7.
69. Isa 63,5.
70. Ps 94,23.
71. Ps 116,17.
72. Ps 138,7; etc. (also in Ugaritic).

*Psalm 54*

3  God, by your *name save* me,
   and by your *might defend* me.

4  God, *hear* my *prayer*,
   *give ear* to the *words of my mouth*.

5  For
   *foreigners have risen up against* me,
   *vicious men seek* my *life*.

6  See!
   *God* is my *helper*;
   the *Lord* really is the *supporter* of my life.

7  Making *evil recoil* on my slanderers,
   in truth, he really *destroyed* them.

8  For generosity I will *sacrifice* to you,
   I will *praise* your *name*, Yahweh, for it is good.

9  For,
   from all my *enemies* he rescued me,
   and my eyes gloated over my *foes*.

3. The *functions* of word-pairs will be considered in detail below; here discussion of their function in oral poetry need only be brief. The improvising poet with an extensive repertoire of word-pairs at his command could produce oral poetry with ease. At the same time, aware that his audience too was familiar with a large number of these pairs, the poet could alter the established pairs by inverting the accepted sequence to produce special effects, or by inventing variations to show his versatility. If audience and bard did not share the same set of parallel word-pairs, such variations would have been meaningless. By the same token a rapport would be quickly established between composer and audience (both, in effect, speaking the same 'language') enabling them to concentrate more on the verse.

4. So-called '*dictionaries*' of word-pairs evidently existed; by this is meant, of course, not written reference books, but lists of pairs handed down through tradition and known to both poet and audience.

> The stock of formulas which a poet has at his disposal is the result of a poetic tradition which hands these formulas on generation after generation because they are useful and pleasing. Individual poets may add to the inherited stock of formulas but these

additions will be few, since the tradition is the work of many hands.[73]

It seems clear, too, that poets in both the Ugaritic and Hebrew traditions shared a common stock of word-pairs (discussed above). It is also evident—and this must be stressed—that each tradition went its own way as well, one particular tradition using formulas (= word-pairs) unknown to another. The interchange of knowledge is easily explained by assuming the existence of wandering singers.

5. Quite often *only one element of a word-pair is intended* by the author, its companion being used merely for the sake of parallelism.[74] This is a characteristic of the ready-made formula in oral poetry where a stock formula may be used simply out of habit even if contradicted by the context. This, then, is yet another argument in favour of equating the parallel (fixed) word-pair with the formula of oral poetry.[75] In Prov 4,3 for example, *only the first element* is intended:

| | |
|---|---|
| כי בן הייתי לאבי | For I was a son to my *father*, |
| רך ויחיד לפני אמי | tender and alone before my *mother*. |

even though the word-pair 'father // mother' is used since it is really the male parent that is in focus—the next verse, in fact, begins 'He taught me'.[76] Conversely, in Am 6,1 where the prophecy is directed against Samaria, only the *second element* in the word-pair is significant:

| | |
|---|---|
| הוי השאננים בציון | Woe to those who are at ease in *Sion*, |
| והבטחים בהר שמרון | and to those feeling secure on *Samaria*'s mountain. |

Other examples are Ps 81,4 and Prov 24,30.[77] In both these types the accompanying word is there for reasons of versification and with no regard for its actual meaning. Similar strictures are valid for the numerical word-pairs (see separate paragraph).[78]

## Functions of parallel word-pairs

This topic has already been touched on but it merits extensive

---

73. Yoder: 1971, 478; see also 478, n.3, on idiosyncratic formulaic word-pairs in Am.
74. Haran: 1972.
75. However, see Culley, *Oral Formulaic*.
76. Also: Jgs 5,25; Prov 1,8; 6,20; 23,22; Lam 5,6.
77. The examples derive from Haran: 1972.
78. For the relationship between word-pairs and hendiadys see Aalto: 1964 and Avishur: 1972.

treatment in view of its importance. Two principal functions relate to composition and to inner-strophic cohesion; a secondary function concerns audience participation.

1. From the poet's point of view the main function of parallel pairs was *to assist him in composing verse*. Since this aspect has been considered in the section on oral poetry, there is no need for illustration here. It must be noted, though, that use of word-pairs is not exclusive to oral poetry; the writing prophets, for example, though well schooled in the traditions of oral poetry, were able to use word-pairs with a certain degree of freedom betokening mastery.

2. The word-pair effectively slowed down the flow of verse-making and at the same time reiterated keywords in each line, *enabling the audience* (or reader) *to follow the meaning better*. Also, as bard and listeners (or readers) shared the same traditional stock of word-pairs—though, of course, the poet's repertoire was very much larger than that of the average person—*communication became easier* not least because of the rapport which must inevitably have been created between them. There does not seem to be much support for the view that word-pairs, in themselves, were ever props to the memory of either poet or audience.

3. The third function of parallel word-pairs, operative at a linguistic level, is *cohesion*: the use of stock word-pairs helps bind together the parallel lines of couplets. Lexical cohesion 'is achieved through the association of lexical items that regularly co-occur'.[79] This is collocation.

> There is cohesion between any pair of lexical items that stand to each other in some recognizable lexicosemantic (word meaning) relation. This would include not only synonyms and near-synonyms such as *climb . . . ascent, beam . . . rafter, disease . . . illness*, and superordinates such as *elm . . . tree, boy . . . child, skip . . . play*, but also pairs of opposites of various kinds, complementaries such as *boy . . . girl, stand up . . . sit down*, antonyms such as *like . . . hate, wet . . . dry, crowded . . . deserted*, and converses such as *order . . . obey*. It also includes pairs of words drawn from the same order series . . . or from unordered lexical sets . . . The members of such sets often stand in some recognizable semantic relation to one another; they may be related as part to whole . . . or as part to part; they may be members of the same more general class; and so on. The members of any such set stand in some kind of semantic

79. M.A.K. Halliday and R. Hasan, *Cohesion in English* (London, 1976) 284.

relation to one another, but for textual purposes it does not matter what this relation is. There is always the possibility of cohesion between any pair of lexical items which are in some way associated with each other in the language.

These comments of Halliday and Hasan concerning cohesion by collocation in the English language[80] are equally valid for Hebrew (and Ugaritic). The quoted extract is perhaps lengthy, but it does explain the cohesive power of parallel word-pairs and hence their almost universal use in Hebrew poetry.

*Concluding remarks*

Study of parallel word-pairs in Hebrew (and Ugaritic) poetry has led to the realisation that much of that poetry is oral in origin, or is at the very least indebted to oral techniques of composing verse. This in itself is obviously of value. Further, correct recognition of word-pairs can have consequences with respect to textual changes and meaning.[81] One example will be sufficient to illustrate this point. In Ps 72,1 there is evidently an epithetic word-pair modelled on the 'PN$_1$ // PN, son of PN$_2$' type,

| | |
|---|---|
| אלהים | O God, |
| משפטך למלך תן | give your justice to *the king*, |
| וצדקתך לבן מלך | and your honesty to *the son of the king*, |

where both terms מלך and בן מלך designate one and the same person, not the reigning king and the crown prince.

*Extensions of the word-pair* are also very much used in Hebrew poetry, notably the triple synonym (in various forms) and the 'tour' or long series of words with similar meaning. The second topic is dealt with in Chapter 12 under EXTENSION.

80. Quoted (with some abbreviating) from Halliday-Hasan: 1976, 285; for fuller theoretical analysis see 274-292; on 292 a short poem is discussed from this point of view.

81. See Dahood, *RSP* I, 78-79 for examples. Recent articles on word-pairs include W. Brueggemann, 'A Neglected Sapiential Word-Pair', *ZAW* 89 (1977) 234-258; cf. *CBQ* 32 (1970) 532-542. Also, N. Tidwell, 'A Road and a Way. A Contribution to the Study of Word-Pairs', *Semitics* 7 (1980) 50-80.

EXAMPLE: Isa 40,28-31—*Parallel word-pair used as key component in a poem*

*introduction*

| | |
|---|---|
| הלוא ידעת | Don't you know? |
| אם לא שמעת | Haven't you heard? |

--------

| | | |
|---|---|---|
| אלהי עולם יהוה | A | Eternal God, Yahweh, |
| בורא קצות הארץ | | creator of the world's ends, |
| לא ייעף | | does not grow WEARY, |
| ולא ייגע | | does not grow FAINT; |
| אין חקר לתבונתו | | there is no fathoming his understanding. |
| נתן ליעף כח | B | He gives strength to the WEARY, |
| ולאין אונים עצמה ירבה | | increases the force of the powerless. |
| ויעפו נערים ויגעו | C | Do WEARY—young men and do FAINT, |
| ובחורים כשול יכשלו | | vigorous lads just stumble. |
| וקוי יהוה יחליפו כח | B′ | But those dependent on Yahweh will acquire strength, |
| יעלו אבר כנשרים | | they'll grow wings like eagles. |
| ירוצו ולא ייגעו | A′ | They will run—and not grow WEARY; |
| ילכו ולא ייעפו | | they will march—and not grow FAINT. |

This five-strophe poem (not counting the introductory couplet) is built around the key word-pair יעף//יגע, 'to be weary // to be faint',[82] which not only comprises the basic building block, but the main component of the chiastic (ABCBA) pattern. The parallel word-pair has not been used in an automatic way: there are variations in the B-strophe (where for alliterative assonance the synonymous expression אין אונים has been substituted) and in the corresponding B′-strophe. In strophe C, the central element in the composition, the members of the word-pair have been almost juxtaposed in an aba′ chiastic line, again probably for variation. The basic thrust is the *negation* of the word-pair 'weary // faint'—negative particles occur no less than six times—laying the emphasis on strength, which is probably to be equated with wisdom (end of A-strophe).[83]

--------

82. The word-pair also occurs in Jer 51,58.
83. For a form-critical analysis of these verses see R. Melugin, *The Formation of Isaiah 40-55* (*BZAW* 141, Berlin, 1976) 535-536 and 90-93; he notes 'these verses are a disputation calculated to overcome the complaint quoted in v. 27', so that v. 27 may be an integral part of the poem. See, too, R. Melugin, 'Deutero-Isaiah and Form-Criticism', *VT* 21 (1971) 326-337, esp. 334-335.

*For study*
Prov 12,17 (contrast 14,5.25; 19,5.9 and Hab 2,3; cf. Janzen, *HTR* 73 [1980] 56-57).

BIBLIOGRAPHY

(a) *General*
Aalto, P. 'Word-pairs in Tokharian and Other Languages', *Ling* 5 (1964) 61-78.
Emeneau, M.B. 'The Songs of the Todas', *PAPS* 77 (1937) 543-600.
—'Oral Poets of South India—the Todas', *JAF* 71 (1958) 312-324.
—'Style and meaning in an oral literature', *Lang* 42 (1966) 323-345, esp. 343ff.
Malkiel, Y. 'Studies in Irreversible Binomials', *Lingua* 8 (1959) 113-160.
Sayce, R.A. 'The Style of Montaigne. Word-Pairs and Word-Groups', Chatman, S. (ed.), *Literary Style: a Symposium* (London/New York, 1971) 383-405.

(b) *Lists of word-pairs common to Hebrew, Ugaritic, Akkadian and Phoenician*
Avishur, Y. 'Word-pairs common to Phoenician and Biblical Hebrew', *UF* 7 (1975) 13-47.
—'Pairs of Synonymous Words in the Construct State (and in Appositional Hendiadys) in Biblical Hebrew', *Semitics* 2 (1971-72) 17-81.
Boling, R.G. '"Synonymous" Parallelism in the Psalms', *JSS* 5 (1960) 221-225.
Cassuto, U. 'Parallel Words in Hebrew and Ugaritic', *Biblical and Oriental Studies II: Bible and Ancient Oriental Texts* (Jerusalem, 1975) 60-68; originally: *Lesh* 15 (1943) 97-102 [in Hebrew].
Dahood, M.J. 'Additional Pairs of Parallel Words in the Psalter', *Ziegler FS*, II, 35-40.
Also, *RSP* I, II and III, with their bibliographies.
Gevirtz, S. 'The Ugaritic Parallel to Jeremiah 8:23', *JNES* 20 (1961) 41-46.
—*Patterns* (revised edition, 1973, with index of word-pairs, 101, compiled by D. Pardee).
Salo, V. *Phönizisch-Hebräische Wortpaare* (StPohl; Rome [in press]).
Watson, W.G.E. 'Fixed Pairs in Ugaritic and Isaiah', *VT* 22 (1972) 460-468.
—'Reversed Word-Pairs in Ugaritic Poetry', *UF* 13 (1981) 189-192.
Watters, *Formula Criticism*.

(c) *Critical comments on word-pair list and notes on theory*
Craigie, P.C. 'A Note on "Fixed Pairs" in Ugaritic and Early Hebrew Poetry', *JTS* 22 (1971) 140-143.
—'Parallel Word-Pairs in the Song of Deborah (Judges 5)', *JETS* 20 (1971) 15-22.
—'The problem of parallel word-pairs in Ugaritic and Hebrew poetry', *Semitics* 5 (1977) 48-58.

Haran, M. 'The Graded Numerical Sequence and the Phenomenon of "Automatism" in Biblical Poetry', *VTS* 22 (1972) 238-267.
Loewenstamm, S.E. 'Ugarit and the Bible, I', *Bib* 56 (1975) 103-119.
—'Ugarit and the Bible, II', *Bib* 59 (1978) 100-122.
Moor, J.C. de—Lugt, P. van der 'The Spectre of Pan-Ugaritism', *BO* 31 (1974) 3-26.
Watson, W.G.E. 'Ugarit and the OT: Further Parallels', *Or* 45 (1976) 434-442.
Yoder, P.B. 'A-B Pairs and Oral Composition in Hebrew Poetry', *VT* 21 (1971) 470-489.
Also, O'Connor, *Structure*, 96-109.

### 6.4 *Number Parallelism*

*Theory*
Basically, number parallelism of the type 'seven // eight' is a variant of the synonymous word-pair already discussed. Since no number can have a synonym[84] the only way to provide a corresponding component is to use a digit which is higher in value than the original. Normally the increase is by one, the next digit along the scale being chosen, as in '7 // 8' which = '7 // 7 + 1', or formulaically, 'n // n + 1'. For example Mic 5,4

| | |
|---|---|
| והקמנו עליו שבעה רעים | then we will raise against him SEVEN shepherds, |
| ושמנה נסיכי אדם | EIGHT chiefs of men, |

where the value for 'n' is of course 'seven'.[85] As will be seen, this type of numerical parallelism is by no means confined to Hebrew poetry.

Occasionally the whole ratio is multiplied by the factor 10 to give '70 // 80'—or even by 11, to give '77 // 88'. Examples are given below.[86] Other variations, too, occur.

*Number parallelism in Ugaritic and Akkadian*
The 'graded numerical sequence'[87] or number parallelism is found in a number of languages including Sumerian and Aramaic. Here, in accordance with the practice followed in the rest of the book, examples will be given only for Ugaritic and Akkadian.

---

84. Exceptions, and very rare exceptions at that, are the plural form שנים, 'two', and possibly אחדים, 'a pair', if Shaffer, *JAOS* 99 (1979) 5, is correct concerning Gen 11,1.
85. For translation cf. Cathcart, *Bib* 59 (1978) 38-48.
86. Symbolically: 10 (n // n + 1) and 11 (n // n + 1).
87. To use Haran's term; see Haran, 1972.

From the Baal Epic comes the following couplet:

| | |
|---|---|
| *'mk šb 't ǵlmk* | (Take) with you your seven 'pages', |
| *ṭmn ḫnzrk* | your eight 'boars', (*CTA* 5 v 9[88]) |

and similarly in the Aqhat Tale (*CTA* 19 i 42-44) as well as elsewhere.[89]

The same device is used in Akkadian incantations (rarely elsewhere):

| | |
|---|---|
| 6 *riksīšina* | SIX are their bindings, |
| 7 *piṭrūa* | SEVEN my loosenings.[90] |

### Hebrew
Occurrences of the 'n // n + 1' pattern in Hebrew poetry are as follows:

1 // 2   Jgs 5,30; Dt 32,30; Ps 62,12; Job 33,24; 40,5; Sir 38,17.
2 // 3   Hos 6,2; Sir 23,16; 26,28; 50,25 (cf. Isa 17,6).
3 // 4   Am 1,3.6.9.11.13; 2,1.4.6; Prov 30,15.18.21.29; Sir 26,5.
4 // 5   Cf. Isa 17,6.
6 // 7   Job 5,19; Prov 6,16.
7 // 8   Mic 5,4; cf. Qoh 11,2.
9 //10   Sir 25,7.

### Origins and development of number parallelism
As with other parallel word-pairs the 'n // n + 1' type apparently developed from such casual prose utterances as שלשה סריסים שנים, 'two or three eunuchs' (2 Kgs 9,32). Similar expressions occur in Ugaritic narrative poetry.[91] In poetry, the first number was then used in the first colon, the second in the second colon—an application of the process known as 'break-up of a stereotype phrase' (see BREAK-UP).

Variations of the 'n // n + 1' pattern include multiplication by *eleven*, as in Gen 4,24

| | |
|---|---|
| כי שבעתים יקם קין | For, SEVENFOLD is Cain avenged, |
| ולמך שבעים ושבעה | but Lamech, SEVENTY-SEVEN times, |

which has its equivalent in Ugaritic (*CTA* 4 vii 9-10):

| | |
|---|---|
| *ṭṯ lṭṭm aḫd 'r* | SIXTY-SIX cities did he seize, |
| *šb'm šb' pdr* | SEVENTY-SEVEN towns. |

---

88. For the precise meaning of this passage cf. Day, *VT* 29 (1979) 143-151.
89. See list in *RSP* I, 345.
90. *Maqlû* IV 109—adduced by Gevirtz, *Patterns*, 21; see there for additional examples.
91. *ym ymm*, 'one day, two days' (*CTA* 6 ii 26, etc.); *išt ištm*, 'a fire, two fires' (2 i 32).

In Akkadian, instead, the multiplicand is *ten*, for example Gilg XI 300-301[92]:

| | |
|---|---|
| *ana 20 [bēr] iksupū kusāpa* | After TWENTY [double-hours] they broke off a bite, |
| *ana 30 bēr iškunū nubatta* | after THIRTY double-hours they encamped for the night. |

It is difficult to decide whether the word-pair 'a thousand // ten thousand' belongs here, or is simply lexical.[93] It is used in Ugaritic, e.g.:

| | |
|---|---|
| *alp kd yqḥ bḥmr* | He took a THOUSAND pitchers of wine, |
| *rbt ymsk bmskh* | TEN THOUSAND he mixed in his mixture, |

and over a dozen times elsewhere.[94] The word-pair occurs almost as often in Hebrew, e.g. Mic 6,7

| | |
|---|---|
| הירצה יהוה באלפי אילים | Shall Yahweh be pleased with THOUSANDS of rams, |
| ברבבות נחלי שמן | with TENS OF THOUSANDS of oil-wadis? |

and Dt 32,30; Ps 91,7; Dt 33,17; Gen 24,60; Ps 68,18; etc.[95]

A further development was the *extension* of the numerical pair to a set of three using the formula n // n + 1 // 'all'.[96] Unfortunately, there are no clear examples of the 'pure' form,[97] but one passage in Ugaritic and one in Hebrew use multiplicands. The first text in *CTA* 12 ii 49-52:

| | |
|---|---|
| *kšb't lšb'm aḫh ym[ẓah]* | His 77 brothers reach him, |
| *wtmnt ltmnym šr aḫyh mẓah* | his 88 siblings reach him, |
| *wmẓah šr ylyh* | his kinsmen reach him.[98] |

---

92. Adduced by Gevirtz, 1973: 168; *Patterns*, 22. However, the text continues: '50 "double-hours" they travelled the whole day' which shows that the numbers were added. See also 'the porters bring me ice from a distance of *ten* miles, even from *twenty* miles' (*ARM* I 21 r.10').

93. See the extensive discussion by Gevirtz, *Patterns*, 15-24.

94. References in *RSP* I, 114, with bibliography.

95. Also 1 Sm 18,7; 21,12; 29,5; 18,8—not always in the same sequence.

96. Gevirtz: 1973, 167-170.

97. Except in prose: letters from Amarna (see preceding note) and Jer 36,23 (as 'three . . . four . . . all').

98. Translation as by Gevirtz; the text is difficult.

and the other is Song 6,8:[99]

| | |
|---|---|
| ששים המה מלכות | 60 queens are they, |
| ושמנים פילגשים | 80 concubines, |
| ועלמות אין מספר | girls without number. |

## Comparison between Hebrew and other poetic traditions

Although number parallelism of the types presented above occurs in many poetic traditions, some of them ancient,[100] there are differences which cannot be ignored. As has been seen, both Ugaritic and Hebrew poetry use numerical parallelism extensively and in a wide variety of forms. (A glance at the list given above shows that only the sets '5 // 6' and '8 // 9' are missing.) By contrast, the graded numerical sequence is very rare in Akkadian poetry and is almost exclusively used in incantations. This may be due to chance, but such an explanation does not account for the complete absence of the device in the long Epic of Erra and its extreme rarity in the 12-tablet Epic of Gilgamesh. On the other hand, since magic and numbers tend to go hand in hand, the presence of numerical word-pairs in incantations is not surprising. On the whole, then, Ugaritic and Hebrew poetry share a common tradition in this regard and are to be distinguished from Akkadian versification.

## Functions and meaning of the device

Generally speaking, the graded numerical sequence *provides a frame* within which a list of items can be given. This helps disparate items to form a coordinated whole. Numerical word-pairs, too, share the functions of the synonymous word-pair (dealt with elsewhere) and overlap, to a certain extent, with gender parallelism.

It is not always clear what meaning should be attached to the members of a graded numerical sequence, whether considered singly or as a complete unit. In prose texts, in expressions such as 'Nor is this work for one day or two' (Neh 10,13) an indefinite number is obviously intended. In other passages, though, a precise figure is meant, as in Ex 20,5 'I punish the children for the sins of the fathers to the third and fourth generations of those who hate me'. Further, as with word-pairs in general, the intended meaning may be restricted

99. See Watson, *Or* 45 (1976) 434 n.3. For a neo-Assyrian parallel cf. Sasson, *Maarav* 1/2 (1979) 195, who cites an oracle concerning Esarhaddon (*ANET*, 450, lines 12-16).
100. Notably Sumerian, Hittite and Aramaic.

to either member of the pair.[101] Finally, a climactic sequence may be operative. These meanings and functions will now be illustrated.
—*Indefinite number.*

| יחינו מימים | After two days he will revive us, |
| ביום השלישי יקמנו | on the third day he will raise us up. (Hos 6,2) |

Cf. Sir 38,17 (sequential use of word-pair) and Qoh 11,2 (ditto).
—*Only one number of the pair intended.* Examples of the first number (n) only being intended include Mic 5,4 (cited above), Job 33,14 and Ps 62,12. Examples of the second number (n + 1) only being intended can be subsumed under the heading 'enumeration' (see immediately).
—*For enumeration.* These texts are almost completely confined to Prov and Sir (and perhaps Am 1-2). For example, Sir 50,25f:

| בשני גוים קצה נפשי | TWO nations I detest, |
| והשלישית איננו עם | and the THIRD is no nation at all: |
| יושבי שעיר ופלשת | (1) the inhabitants of (Mount) Seir, |
| | (2) and the Philistines, |
| וגוי נבל הדר בשכם | (3) and the senseless folk living at Shechem. |

—*For climactic effect.* In most of the enumerations, it is the last item which is the focus of attention since it comprises the climax of the series. For instance, Prov 30,18-20:

| שלשה המה נפלאו ממני | Three things are too wonderful for me, |
| וארבע לא ידעתים | four I do not understand: |
| דרך הנשר בשמים | (1) the way of a vulture in the sky; |
| דרך נחש עלי צור | (2) the way of a serpent on a rock; |
| דרך אניה בלב ים | (3) the way of a ship out at sea; |
| ודרך גבר בעלמה | (4) and the way of a man with a maiden. |

The three 'ways' listed simply lead up to the principal paradox under inspection here, namely the attraction of the sexes. Other examples are Job 5,19-20; Prov 30,15-16; 30,21-23; 30,29-30; 6,16; Sir 23,16; 26,28; 25,7-10; 26,5-6 and Am 1-2.
Other passages use numerical parallelism *to denote abundance*, e.g. Jgs 5,30:

| הלא ימצאו יחלקו שלל | They must be finding spoil, |
| | taking their shares, |
| רחם רחמתים לראש גבר | a wench, *two* wenches to each warrior, |

101. See Haran: 1972.

שלל צבעים לסיסרא    booty of dyed stuffs for Sisera,
שלל צבעים    booty of dyed stuffs:
רקמה צבע    one length of striped stuff,
רקמתים לצואר שלל    two lengths, for the spoiler's neck.

Just as a man needs only one 'wench', so his neck needs only one length of cloth—the number sequence here conveys the image of plenty of spoil. Note the combined use of two sets of number parallelism in Dt 32,20.

*For study*

What functions can be assigned to number parallelism in Mic 6,7; Ps 62,12; Sir 38,17? Provide an explanation for the clustering of this pattern in Prov 30 and Sir 26 and compare its use in Am 1-2. What function is evident in Sir 25,7-11 (9-15)?

*Cross-references*
STANZA, WORD-PAIR.

BIBLIOGRAPHY

Cassuto, *Anath*, 138-139.
Freedman, D.N. 'Counting Formulae in the Akkadian Epics', *JANES* 3 (1971) 65-81, esp. 75ff.
Gevirtz, S. *Patterns*, 15-24.29-30.
—'On Canaanite Rhetoric: The Evidence of the Amarna Letters from Tyre', *Or* 42 (1973) 162-177, esp. 167-169.
Haran, M. 'The Graded Numerical Sequence and the Phenomenon of "Automatism" in Biblical Poetry', *VTS* 19 (1971, pub. 1972) 238-267.
Lee, J.T. The Ugaritic Numeral and its Use as a Literary Device (University Microfilms, 1973; cf. Pardee, *BO* 37 [1980] 280 for this reference).
Pope, M.H. 'Number', *IDB*, vol. K-Q, 561-567, esp. 563-564.
Roth, W.M.W. 'The numerical sequence x/x + 1 in the OT', *VT* 12 (1962) 300-311.
—*Numerical Sayings in the OT. A Form-Critical Study*, VTS 13, 1965.
Rüger, H.-P. 'Die gestaffelter Zahlensprüche des Alten Testaments und aram. Achikar 92', *VT* 31 (1981) 229-234.
Sauer, G. *Die Sprüche Agurs* (Stuttgart, 1963) 49-70.
Weiss, M. 'The Pattern of Numerical Sequence in Amos 1-2. A Re-Examination', *JBL* 86 (1967) 416-423.

### 6.5 *Staircase Parallelism*

*Definition*

Staircase parallelism, as its name implies[102] is a form of couplet (or tricolon) which proceeds in steps. For example,

| | |
|---|---|
| סורה אדני | Turn aside, O sir, |
| סורה אלי | turn aside towards me. (Jgs 4,18) |

A sentence is started, only to be interrupted by an epithet or vocative. The sentence is then resumed from the beginning again, without the intervening epithet, to be completed in the second or third line. Three components, then, go to make up the pattern:

1 *the repeated element*: 'turn aside' (סורה);
2 *the intervening element*: 'O sir' (אדני);
3 *the complementary element*: 'towards me' (אלי).

As will be seen, there are more complex cases, but the components remain basically the same.

*Comparison with kindred patterns*

Some confusion is possible with related poetic patterns such as the 'pivot pattern' and the terrace. Similar, too, are the *aba*-monocolon and simple anaphora (see REPETITION). The differences are best illustrated by a simple diagram:

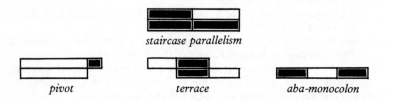

staircase parallelism

pivot          terrace          aba-monocolon

*Typology*

Staircase parallelism occurs comparatively often in Ugaritic verse, and some forty to fifty examples have been identified in Hebrew.

---

102. The term 'staircase parallelism' has been adopted here, following Greenstein and Cohen. Other designations are 'climactic parallelism', 'repetitive parallelism' used by Albright and others. Loewenstamm coined the expression 'expanded colon', but this is to be rejected both for its unwanted medical overtones and for its vagueness. Another possible designation is 'incremental repetition', on which see F.B. Gummere, *The Popular Ballad* (London, 1907) 117-134 and passim.

Strangely, the pattern has not yet turned up in Mesopotamian poetry,[103] suggesting it to be 'Canaanite' in origin.

*Two main types* can be differentiated: 2-line and 3-line staircase parallelism. It is not certain which evolved from which.[104]

—*Two-line staircase parallelism* is a self-contained unit, as in the Ugaritic example

| | |
|---|---|
| *ytb ly ṯr il[aby]* | Turn to me, Bull El, my father, |
| *yṯb ly wlh [aṯb]* | turn to me, and to him will I turn. |

(CTA 3E iv 7-8[105])

It occurs some twenty times in Hebrew,[106] for instance:

| | |
|---|---|
| שובי בתולת ישראל | Return, O Virgin Israel, |
| שובי אל עריך אלה | return to these your cities. (Jer 31,21) |

The fact that it can be used as a refrain (see below) is argument enough that the unit is a bicolon and not part of a tricolon.

—*Three-line staircase parallelism*, a pattern common in both Ugaritic and Hebrew; so

| | |
|---|---|
| *p'bd an 'nn aṯrt* | Am I a slave, then, Athirat's menial? |
| *p'bd ank aḫd uḷt* | Am I a slave, then, handling the trowel? |
| *hm amt aṯrt tlbn lbnt* | Athirat's slave-girl making the bricks? |

(CTA 4 iv 59-62[107])

and

| | |
|---|---|
| ראוך מים אלהים | When the waters saw you, God, |
| ראוך מים יחילו | when the waters saw you they trembled, |
| אף ירגזו תהמות | even the deeps shook in fear. (Ps 77,17[108]) |

Other typologies have been proposed but they do not need to be discussed here.[109]

---

103. An Arabic example may be identifiable. The occurrence of the verse-pattern in the Egyptian story of the Shipwrecked Sailor has been construed as a Canaanitism: see van Selms, *UF* 3 (1971) 251; also O'Callaghan, *Or* 21 (1952) 39 and n.1.

104. Loewenstamm would argue that the simpler form became more complex; Greenstein doubts this. Such problems do not affect the matter in hand which is largely to do with form and function.

105. See the quasi-parallel passage *CTA* 17 vi 42. No other examples occur.

106. Ex 15,6-7a.11.16; Jgs 4,18 (quoted above); 5,3.12.30; 15,16; Pss 67,4 (= 6); 94,1.3; 124,1-2; 129,1-2; Song 4,8; 5,9; 7,1; Lam 4,15; Qoh 1,2.

107. See Watson, *UF* 9 (1977) 284, and for the translation *CML*, 60.

108. As translated by Dahood, *Psalms II*, 224.231-232.

109. Loewenstamm distinguishes three types: 1. those where 'the first colon requires

*Characteristics of the pattern*

Most of the characteristics of staircase parallelism occur in both Ugaritic and Hebrew (except for one);[110] accordingly, only Hebrew examples will be set out in illustration.

—*3-fold repetition of same word*

| | |
|---|---|
| נאם בלעם בנו בער | *Oracle* of Balaam, son of Beor, |
| ונאם הגבר שתם העין | *oracle* of the warrior, with perfect eye, |
| נאם שמע אמרי אל | *oracle* of a listener to El's sayings. |

(Nb 24,3 [= 24,15])

Similarly: Pss 29,1-2 (הבו); 96,7-9 (הבו); Sir 31,13 (רעה); cf. Prov 31,2; Song 6,9.[111]

—*Ellipsis*: often the expected repetition of the initial word in the third line is missing, but is evidently understood as being present:

| | |
|---|---|
| אל למלכים למואל | It is not for kings, Lemuel, |
| אל למלכים שתו יין | it is not for kings to drink wine, |
| ולרונים או שכר | and (it is not) for chieftains to crave liquor. |

(Prov 31,4)

Likewise: Gen 49,22 (discussed below); Pss 29,7-8 (see below); 92,10 and Song 4,9.[112] Recognition of this feature can lead to a correct understanding of a difficult verse, as will be seen. Ellipsis is also operative in the last line of two-line staircase parallelism:

---

a complement by the very nature of its grammatical structure' (Ex 15,6; Ps 29,1; etc.); 2. those where a complement is required by the context only (Jgs 5,12; Isa 26,15; etc.); 3. those with two parallel and complete cola (Ex 15,16; Jgs 5,7).

Greenstein proceeds from the findings of psycholinguistics and proposes three kinds of staircase parallelism: 1. suspended analysis, where the listener does not analyse the sentence until it has been completed (Ps 93,7; Hab 3,8); 2. re-analysis: once the full sentence has been heard, the listener corrects his analysis of the first part (Pss 77,17; 92,10); and 3. additive, when a clause or phrase is added to the first colon without involving syntactical change (Ex 15,11; Song 4,9). For the debate between these two scholars see the bibliography.

110. Namely, the use of this pattern in combination with the terrace, as in *CTA* 3 v 27-29; 10 ii 13-15.21-23.26-28; *KTU* 1.161 20-22; etc.

111. Ugaritic examples: *CTA* 2 iv 8-9; 4 iv-v 112-119; 17 i 12-16 (cf. v 37-38); *Ugar. 5 7* 70-71.

112. This feature was recognised by Gevirtz, *HUCA* 46 (1975) 40-41. Ugaritic texts: *CTA* 14 i 21-25; 16 vi 54-57; 17 vi 26-28; *Ugar 5 7* 71-72; cf. *CTA* 6 i 63-65. For a different translation of the passage given as an example cf. D.T. Tsumura, 'The Vetitive Particle אי and the Poetic Structure of Proverbs 31:4', *AJBI* 4 (1978) 23-31. He prefers: '(Let there be) not for kings, O Lemuel, (Let there be) not for kings (any) drinking of wine, Yea, for rulers (let there be) no (drinking of) strong drink'.

עד שקמתי דבורה    Until you arose, Deborah,
שקמתי אם בישראל    (until) you arose as a mother in Israel. (Jgs 5,7)

Note ellipsis of the third word ('among the gods') in the second colon of Ex 15,11.

—*Variation*: already in Ugaritic there is a tendency to move away from rigid adherence to a standard pattern; for instance, instead of simply repeating the same initial word in the last line, *a parallel word* is used:

| | |
|---|---|
| *aṭt tqḥ ykrt* | The wife you take, O Keret, |
| *aṭt tqḥ btk* | the wife you take into your house, |
| *ǵlmt tš'rb ḥẓrk* | the wench you introduce into your court. |
| | (*CTA* 15 ii 21-23[113]) |

In Hebrew, the same word may be used but with either the tense altered, or the mood:

עורה כבדי    Awake, my inmost being,
עורה הנבל וכנור    Awake, with harp and lyre,
אעירה השחר    Let me wake up the dawn! (Ps 57,9)

Also Ps 93,3.

Synonyms are used more often in Hebrew, as in

אנה הלך דודך היפה בנשים
אנה פנה דודך ובקשנו עמך

Whither *has gone* your love, O fairest among women,
Whither *has turned* your love, that we may look for him with you?

(Song 6,1)

This example illustrates an additional tendency in Hebrew: the lines become quite long; this is evident from Pss 124,1-2; 129,1-2; Song 5,9.

—*Clustering*: the tendency for several examples of the pattern to occur in the same poem, even consecutively, is evident in Ugaritic (*CTA* 10) and seems to have run over into Hebrew: Ps 94,1 and 3; Song 4,8-9.

*Functions*
In Ugaritic, staircase parallelism is used *to open a speech*, comprising

---

113. Also *CTA* 6 iii-iv 25-27 and 4 iv 59-62 (cited above).
114. *CTA* 2 i 36-37; 3 E v 27-29; 4 iv-v 59-62; etc. Note, however, texts such as 6 i 63-64 which open *action* rather than speech.

either the actual opening lines, or following immediately after an introductory couplet.[114] In general this accords with the effect of the pattern which is *to increase tension* in the listener.[115] Once his attention and curiosity have been aroused by the incomplete nature of the first line, the listener feels compelled to learn the outcome.

In Hebrew, this *speech-opening* function is operative in much the same way. It has been extended, besides, to fulfil two other functions: it can close a section of poetry and it can act as a refrain. This extension is easily explained as an application of the segmenting character of staircase parallelism. These three main functions will now be looked at, with examples.

—*To open a section.* The longest section in Gen 49 opens at v. 22 with staircase parallelism; the whole book of Qohelet begins:

| הבל הבלים אמר קהלת | Utter futility, says Qoheleth, |
| הבל הבלים הכל הבל | Utter futility; all is futility! |

Likewise: Nb 24,3 (= 5); Jgs 5,12; Hos 9,1; Pss 29,1-2.7-8; 77,17; 94,1; 96,7-9; 124,1-2; 129,1-2; Prov 31,4; Song 7,1. A sub-category of this function is staircase parallelism as *speech-opener*: Jgs 4,18; 5,3; Lam 4,15.

—*To close a section.* Here belong Jgs 5,30; Hos 12,6; this function is unknown in Ugaritic. See, also, Qoh 12,8.

—*As a refrain.* In Ex 15 the pattern is used as a variant refrain three times: vv. 6-7a.11 and 16. It occurs twice, unchanged, in Ps 67

| יודוך עמים אלהים | The peoples praise you, God, |
| יודוך עמים כלם | the peoples praise you with their tool.[116] |

*The value of recognising this pattern*

Recognition of staircase parallelism can assist the *segmentation* of a poem into stanzas: its main function, as has been seen, is as a stanza-marker. This is true of it even when used as a refrain. At a lower level, it can determine the *correct stichometry* of a strophe. An example is Ps 17,14:

| ממתם ידך יהוה | Slay them with your hand, O Yahweh, |
| ממתם מחלד | Slay them from the earth, |
| חלקם בחיים | Make them perish from the land of the living. |

---

115. As expounded by both Loewenstamm, and with more detail, Greenstein.
116. For the meaning of Heb. *kl* cf. Akk. *kullu*, 'hoe', here perhaps an allusion to 'our plough' in v. 1.

This version by Dahood[117] contrasts with RSV: '(Deliver my life) from men by thy hand, O Lord, from men whose portion in life is of the world'—which is a couplet. See also Pss 57,9 (cited above); 124,1-2 and 129,1-2 (couplets, not tricola); etc.

*Prose* can be distinguished from poetry, e.g. Jgs 4,18. In Jgs 5,3 the particle ל is shown to be *vocative*:

| | |
|---|---|
| אנכי ליהוה | I, *O* Yahweh, |
| אנכי אשירה | I will sing. |

Since *ellipsis* is a feature of staircase parallelism, certain passages become intelligible, once this is adverted to. Gevirtz has explained Gen 49,22 by positing the ellipsis of 'son of' in the last line, as in comparable Ugaritic passages:

| | |
|---|---|
| בן פרת יוסף | Son of a wild she-ass is Joseph, |
| בן פרת עלי עין | Son of a wild she-ass at a fountain, |
| בנות צעדה עלי שור | (*Son of*) wild asses by a (?) well.[118] |

Note, further, Hab 3,8, with ellipsis of the verb חרה, as part of the stock expression חרה אף, 'to burn with anger', occurring in the second line,[119] and by extension, the third.

| | |
|---|---|
| הבנהרים חרה יהוה | Against the rivers was kindled, Yahweh, |
| אם בנהרים אפך | Against the streams (*was kindled*) your anger, |
| אם בים עברתך | Or against the sea, your wrath? |

Finally, Ps 29,7-8 can be better understood once *ellipsis* is seen to operate in the third and last cola and, perhaps more importantly, once the phrase '(who) cleaves with fiery flame' is understood as referring to *Yahweh*, and not to 'the voice of Yahweh'.[120] The resulting version is:

| | |
|---|---|
| קול יהוה חצב להבות אש | The voice of Yahweh, who cleaves with fiery flame, |
| קול יהוה יחיל מדבר | The voice of Yahweh convulses the steppe, |
| יחיל יהוה מדבר קדש | (*The voice of*) Yahweh convulses the steppe of Qadesh, |
| קול יהוה יחולל אילות | The voice of Yahweh makes hinds writhe, |
| ויחשף יערות | (*The voice of Yahweh*) strips forests. |

---

117. Dahood, *Psalms I*, 98-99.
118. For details see Gevirtz, *HUCA* 46 (1975) 33-49.
119. Note the variations of the interrogative particles.
120. In the same way in Ex 15,6-7a 'might in strength' refers not to the divine hand, but to God himself; cf. Cohen: 1975, 13-17.

*For study*

'Now these [i.e. forms of staircase parallelism], and other repetitions, may be mere variations on a single principle, though the peculiar prominence of the interruptive vocative suggests this may indeed have been a particular *type*, a sort of formula (but note the use of interruptive vocatives without repetition, as in Psalms 50:22, 127:2). However, it is probably unwise to see this formula as the archetype from which the others "developed", as one writer [Loewenstamm: 1969] has proposed. Indeed, the whole notion of an "original" form of repetitive parallelism is highly questionable.' In the light of the foregoing discussion, is this quote from Kugel, *Idea*, 36, at all valid?

*Cross-references*

MONOCOLON, PIVOT, REPETITION, TERRACE-PATTERN, TRICOLON.

BIBLIOGRAPHY

Albright, W.F. 'The Psalm of Habakkuk', *Rowley FS*, 1-8.
—*Yahweh and the Gods of Canaan* (London, 1968) 5-7.
Avishur, Y. 'Addenda to the Expanded Colon in Ugaritic and Biblical Verse', *UF* 4 (1972) 1-10.
Cohen, C. 'Studies in Early Israelite Poetry I: An Unrecognized Case of Three-Line Staircase Parallelism in the Song of the Sea', *JANES* 7 (1975) 13-17.
Greenstein, E.L. 'Two Variations of Grammatical Parallelism in Canaanite Poetry and Their Psycholinguistic Background', *JANES* 6 (1974) 87-105.
—'One More Step on the Staircase', *UF* 9 (1977) 77-86.
Loewenstamm, S.E. 'The Expanded Colon in Ugaritic and Biblical Verse', *JSS* 14 (1969) 176-196.
—'The Expanded Colon Reconsidered', *UF* 7 (1975) 261-264.
Watson, W.G.E. 'A Note on Staircase Parallelism', *VT* [in press].
Also: Ginsberg, *JPOS* 15 (1935) 127; *Or* 5 (1936) 180; Gevirtz, *HUCA* 46 (1975) 40-41; Kugel, *Idea*, 35-40; Pope, *Song*, 51-52; Watson, *UF* 7 (1975) 492, n. 54; *UF* 9 (1977) 284; Whitley, *UF* 7 (1975) 501-502. For references to Rashbam and Yellin, who were among the earliest to recognise this pattern in Hebrew, cf. Loewenstamm: 1969, 176-177. Also, Wansbrough, *BSOAS* 45 (1982) 425-433.

## 6.6 *Other Types of Parallelism*

There is no space to consider more than briefly four other forms of parallelism. They are synonymous-sequential, noun-verb, vertical and 'Janus' parallelism.

## Synonymous-sequential parallelism

In this form of parallelism, identified by Miller,[121] there is

> a quite explicit combination of parallel and non-parallel elements, or more specifically, cola, in which some elements are synonymously parallel and some are sequential or continuous with one another.

For example, Mic 7,3 can be set out in the following way:

| *continuous* | – | *parallel* | | *parallel* | – | *continuous* |
|---|---|---|---|---|---|---|
| שאל | | השר | | The prince | | asks |
| בשלום | | והשפט | | and the judge | | for a payment. |

Pss 18,42; 19,15; 22,22; 77,2; 88,2; 135,5 and 136,7-15 follow the same pattern.[122]

## Noun-verb parallelism

Finite verbs can function as parallel members to nouns in classical Hebrew, which is not surprising in view of widespread nominalisation in this language. Grossberg first recognised noun-verb parallelism in Hebrew poetry[123] and according to him there are three sub-types. The first follows the pattern *construct* + genitive // *construct* + finite verb as in Job 29,2:

| מי יתנני כירחי קדם | Would that I were in the months of an earlier time, |
|---|---|
| כימי אלוה ישמרני | in the days of 'God-watched-over-me', |

where the clause in quotes is equivalent to a nominal clause. Also Isa 57,3; 58,5; Job 18,21. Sub-type two is equally symmetrical: *preposition* + noun // *preposition* + finite verb, exemplified by Jer 2,8:

| והנביאים נבאו בבעל | The prophets prophesied by Baal, |
|---|---|
| ואחרי לא יועלו הלכו | and after 'they-do-not-avail' they went. |

As Grossberg points out, the last line is in fact climactic to a five-line strophe (or pentacolon) which 'varies from the pattern established in the first four'.[124] Sub-type three of noun-verb parallelism consists

---

121. P.D. Miller, 'Synonymous-Sequential Parallelism in the Psalms', *Bib* 61 (1980) 256-260. See section 11.3 on BREAK-UP.

122. A Ugaritic example may be *CTA* 2 i 18-19. An inverted form of the pattern occurs in Ps 18,42.

123. D. Grossberg, 'Noun/Verb Parallelism: Syntactic or Asyntactic?', *JBL* 99 (1980) 481-488.

124. Grossberg: 1980, 486. Also Ez 13,3 and Ps 71,18. All the examples mentioned in this paragraph are his.

of an infinitive or participle in parallelism with a finite verb. So, in Prov 2,16

לְהַצִּילְךָ מֵאִשָּׁה זָרָה    To save you from the foreign woman,
מִנָּכְרִיָּה אֲמָרֶיהָ הֶחֱלִיקָה    from a stranger 'who-made-smooth-her-words',

the final verb functions as a noun. Similar are Am 5,12; Mal 2,16; Ps 144,2 and Prov 2,17. Other patterns are *preposition* + noun + noun // *preposition* + noun + verb (Isa 51,2); *imperative* + noun + noun // *imperative* + verb (Isa 54,1) and *adverb* + verb + noun // *adverb* + verb + verb (Song 8,5). See, too, Jer 2,27.

*Vertical parallelism*
In vertically parallel lines,[125] usually extended beyond the couplet, the correspondence between components is up and down rather than across as is the norm. Vertical parallelism is present in 2 Sm 1,23

שָׁאוּל וִיהוֹנָתָן    Saul and Jonathan,
הַנֶּאֱהָבִים וְהַנְּעִימִם    most loved and most pleasant,
בְּחַיֵּיהֶם וּבְמוֹתָם    in their life and in their death
לֹא נִפְרָדוּ    were not separated.

Schematically, the first three lines can be set out as

a  a′
b  b′
c  c′

instead of the more usual

a  b  c
a′  b′  c′

and the like. The pattern is used elsewhere (Jer 1,10; 2,19; 2,26b; 3,24cd; 5,17; 8,16; Hos 3,4; Ps 135,6) as well as in Ugaritic. The clearest example is *Ugar 5* 2,3-4:

*dyšr wyḏmr*    Who sings and chants
*bknr wṭlb*    to lyre and flute,
*btp wmṣltm*    to tympanum and cymbals.

See, too, *CTA* 23:51-52 and 17 vi 30-32. There is some overlap with the LIST (on which see 12.2).

---

125. For the term see Watson, *Bib* 61 (1980) 582 (review of Collins, *Line-forms*).

## '*Janus*' parallelism

As Gordon notes:

> One kind of parallelism is quite ingenious, for it hinges on the use of a single word with two entirely different meanings: one meaning paralleling what precedes, and the other meaning, what follows.[126]

Illustration comes from Ugaritic (*CTA* 3B ii 24–26):

| | |
|---|---|
| *mid tmtḫṣn wt'n* | Hard did she fight and look; |
| *tḫtṣb wtḥdy 'nt* | do battle and GLOAT did Anath; |
| *tġdd kbdh bṣḥq* | her belly swelled with laughter, |
| *ymlu lbh bšmḫt* | her heart was filled with happiness. |

The verb *ḥdy*, 'to gaze', in the second line is parallel with *'ny*, 'to see', of the opening line; at the same time—with the meaning 'to rejoice'—it is parallel with the final two lines of the quatrain.[127] Since it faces both ways, *ḥdy* here is in Janus parallelism within these lines. Examples in Hebrew include Gen 49,26,[128] Job 9,25,[129] Song 2,12 and Jer 2,14–15:

| | |
|---|---|
| העבד ישראל | Is Israel a slave? |
| אם יליד בית הוא | Is he a house-boy? |
| מדוע היה לבז | Why has he become SPOIL? |
| עליו ישאגו כפרים | Over him do roar cubs |
| נתנו קולם | (and) give out their growl. |

Here בז means 'contempt' in retrospect, but prospectively must mean 'prey'.[130]

126. Gordon, *BASP* 15 (1978) 59; cf. Gordon, *JAOS* 100 (1980) 356 (both are comments on Song 2,12, on which see 13.4, below).

127. For further details cf. Watson, *VT* 31 (1981) 94. For the translation 'belly' of *kbd* cf. Gevirtz, *HUCA* 52 (1981) 101–110.

128. G. Rendsburg, 'Janus Parallelism in Gen 49:26', *JBL* 99 (1980) 291–293; the two-way expression there means both 'my progenitors of old' and 'mountains of old'. See, too, W. Herzberg, Polysemy in the Hebrew Bible (Diss., New York, 1979) in *DissAbsInt* 40 (1979–80) 2631f-A. Also, G. Rendsburg, 'Double Polysemy in Genesis 49:6 and Job 3:6', *CBQ* 44 (1982) 48–51.

129. E. Zurro, 'Disemia de *brḥ* y paralelismo bifronte en Job 9,25', *Bib* 62 (1981) 546–547.

130. Perhaps the original (regional or dialect) pronunciation has been obscured in MT. For other types of parallelism cf. A. Berlin, 'Grammatical Aspects of Biblical Parallelism', *HUCA* 50 (1979) 17–43.

# 7

## STANZA AND STROPHE

### 7.1 *The Stanza*

*Introduction*

One of the problems inherent in discussions of whether or not there are strophes or stanzas in Hebrew poetry (or, for that matter, in Ugaritic and Akkadian) concerns *terminology*. Different scholars use the same terms to mean different things, some referring to a major subdivision in a poem as a 'strophe', others as a 'stanza'. The result has been that these terms have become almost interchangeable, adding to the confusion. Accordingly, exact definitions are a necessary preliminary so that, at the outset, we know what we are talking about. Another source of confusion is the preconception (based on Greek classical poetry) that the structure of strophes and stanzas has to be *regular*. It would seem that the poets we are considering had a greater degree of freedom in this matter; once that is conceded a great deal of misunderstanding can be removed at one go. (Ultimately, this aspect too is a question of terminology: should one refer to irregularly structured blocks of verse as strophes and stanzas or not? If the answer is yes, then we can carry on from there.)

Before setting out the appropriate definitions a few words are in order concerning recent research on the stanza. The most valuable study to date (and one of the most recent) is undoubtedly E. Häublein's *The Stanza*, a short, clearly written book with a useful, annotated bibliography which develops ideas first set out in Smith's work on closure.[1] The only comprehensive survey for Hebrew (Semitic) poetry remains Kraft's 1938 monograph[2] which he partially

---

1. Smith, *Closure*.
2. Kraft: 1938. See note 4.

updated with a discussion of the stanza in Ugaritic.[3] There have been other, sporadic studies (see bibliography), the most significant being de Moor's pioneering paper[4] to which fuller reference will be made later.

*Definitions*

The stanza is a subunit within a poem, and a strophe is a subunit within a stanza. This is the basic principle underlying the definitions to be set out, the axiom from which further explanations derive. A poem can be considered as the starting-point (or unit); within that unit are one, two, three or more stanzas which comprise the poem as a whole. And each stanza, in its turn, is made up of strophes (and, of course, the strophes consist of varying numbers of verse-lines). A diagram will make this clear:

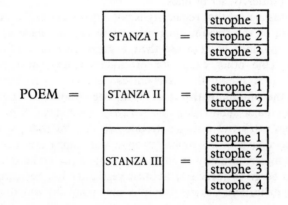

The *stanza* can be broadly defined as a subdivision of a poem—or better, a major subdivision of a poem—which comprises one or more strophes. Intentionally, the aspect of regularity is omitted from the definition; it is not excluded nor yet is it prescribed. From the range of definitions surveyed by Häublein,[5] his own is perhaps the best: 'The Italian etymology (a room of a house) implies that stanzas are

3. C.F. Kraft, 'Some Further Observations Concerning the Strophic Structure in Hebrew Poetry', *Hobbs FS*, 62-89.

4. De Moor, *UF* 10 (1978) 187-217; note his remarks on regularity, 196-197. Van der Lugt, *Strofische Structuren*, only became available after the present work was in its final stages.

5. Häublein, *Stanza*, 1-17.

subordinate units within the more comprehensive unity of the whole poem'.[6]

If this analogy is insisted on, then stanza = room and poem = house; it follows that stanzas can all have the same form (corresponding to a house constructed of totally uniform rooms), or can have varying shapes and sizes. In other words, stanzas can be regular, but need not be.

The *strophe* is a group of one or more lines forming a subdivision of a stanza.[7] Extending the analogy already referred to: poem = house; stanza = room; strophe = furniture. Again, every room may contain exactly the same furniture arranged in precisely identical patterns, but this is not always the case. Similarly, every strophe may consist, let us say, of three lines, with no deviations from that norm. It is just as likely, though, in ancient Semitic poetry, that each strophe can number a different set of lines.

Once it is agreed that regularity is not a necessary factor in either the stanza or the strophe (just as a poem can be made up of an arbitrary number of stanzas) then a great deal of confusion is removed. One other cause for misunderstanding must now be removed. It is simply this: a poem can comprise any number of stanzas, the minimum therefore being one. And, in a one-stanza poem, the major subdivisions are *strophes*, not stanzas. Similarly, a stanza can consist of a single strophe—so that for that poem, that particular stanza = a strophe (strophe and stanza are identified). This is a major difficulty in analyzing poetry since no hard and fast rules can be given (precisely because regularity has been excluded from our definitions). Some examples may point the way to correct analysis.

As part of an 8-stanza poem, Am 1,13-15 is a stanza which comprises an introductory monocolon, two quatrains, a closing tricolon and another monocolon (which may be additional), in all four or five strophes:

6.  Häublein, *Stanza*, 5, following Samuel Johnson. For the equivalent terms 'batch' and 'stave', see O'Connor, *Structure*, 529-533 and 527-528. According to Krahmalkov, *RSF* 3 (1975) 197, the corresponding term in Phoenician is *bt*, 'house'—a tradition preserved in later Hebrew.

7.  The word *strophe* is Greek for 'turn': after completing a strophe, the poet goes back to the beginning and starts another one (cf. Häublein, *Stanza*, 4, quoting J.P. Titz).

| | | |
|---|---|---|
| 13 | כה אמר יהוה | (1) So says Yahweh: |
| | על־שלשד פשעי בני־עמון<br>ועל ארבעה לא אשיבנו<br>על בקעם הרות הגלעד<br>למען הרחיב את־גבולם | (2) For three crimes of the Ammonites<br>and for four I'll not reprieve him:<br>for their invading of Gilead's slopes<br>to enlarge their territory. |
| 14 | והצתי אש בחומת רבה<br>ואכלה ארמנותיה<br>בתרועה ביום מלחמה<br>בסער ביום סופה | (3) I will make Rabbah's wall blaze with fire<br>and it will consume its palaces,<br>during the shout on battle-day,<br>during a whirlwind in a stormy day. |
| 15 | והלך מלכם בגולה<br>הוא ושריו יחדו | (4) Their king will march into exile,<br>he and his officers together. |
| | אמר יהוה | (5) Says Yahweh. |

By contrast, Ps 117 is a one-stanza poem and Isa 12 is in fact a set of three poems (vv. 1-3; 4-5a and 5b-6).

## Dividing poems into stanzas

It is generally agreed that (a) stanza division tends to be based on content, (b) that there are certain stanza-markers showing where stanzas begin and/or end (see presently) and (c) there are no hard and fast rules which can be applied. It is, to some extent, a matter of feel.

The broad divisions of poetic texts can be fairly easily determined by seeing where the subject matter changes. For example, in Gen 49 and Dt 33 the stanza division coincides with the sequence of oracles concerning Reuben, Judah, Levi, Benjamin and so on. Evidently there is no fixed length for a stanza since, for example, two lines are enough for Reuben (Dt 33,6) while Joseph is worth some twenty (Dt 33,13-17).

Stanza-markers include the following:

The most obvious is the *refrain* since it breaks up a poem into groups of strophes (i.e. stanzas); for example, Ps 67 where the refrain repeated in v. 4 and v. 6 indicates the stanza division to be:

| | |
|---|---|
| I | vv.2-3 |
| II | 5 |
| III | 7. |

Also, Job 28; for a fuller discussion see section on REFRAIN.

Certain *acrostic* poems can be divided into stanzas with no difficulty, the classic instance being Ps 119 with its unmistakable division of 22 eight-line stanzas; for further details, see ACROSTICS.

*Keywords*, too, can indicate where stanza division occurs—a topic dealt with in the section on KEYWORDS. Cf. Mic 7,8-10.

The use of *certain particles* such as הנה, 'See!', כי, 'For, because', לכן, 'Therefore', and the like can confirm that a particular stanza division is probably correct. In themselves, though, they are not independent markers.

*Gender patterns* can also help to mark off a poem into stanzas, e.g. Jgs 9; Jer 2,2-3[8] and Mic 7,8-10.

An *overall chiastic* or concentric *pattern* very often closes off a set of strophes as a stanza—examples: see the paragraph on CHIASMUS.

*Introductory formulae* such as כה אמר יהוה, 'This is what Yahweh said' (e.g. Isa 56,1) or נאם יהוה, 'Oracle of Yahweh' (e.g. Jer 5,9) and the frequent והיה ביום ההוא, 'What will happen on that day is . . .'— whether used singly or in combination (cf. Jer 4,9) and even if later editorial insertions—can help show where major structural segments are demarcated. Of course, such formulae can also indicate stanza closure (see presently).

Another way that stanza segmentation is shown is by *change of speaker* as in Ps 24 where question and response alternate throughout. Mere change of speaker is not enough, though, to be a guide for dividing a poem into stanzas as is evident from the book of Job where each speaker has a poem (or set of poems) to himself, and within these poems there is the possibility of further subdivision (into stanzas).

Particular *strophic patterns* also help in determining where stanzas begin and/or end; examples are the tricolon, the pivot-patterned couplet, chiastic strophes—or, generally speaking, a change in the dominant strophic pattern of a stanza. (See appropriate sections for details and examples.)

*Stanzaic unity: opening and closure*

The stanza is a self-contained unit on its own, but it is, at the same time, part of a larger whole: the poem. Here, the stanza will first be looked at as a semi-independent unit; the next paragraph will discuss its relationship to the poem (and, of course, the relationship of stanza to stanza within a poem).

A stanza can be considered as a miniature poem, with an opening,

---

8. W.G.E. Watson, 'Symmetry of Stanza in Jer 2,2b-3', *JSOT* 19 (1981) 107-110.

a central section and a closing section. Evidently, the middle part of a stanza is peculiar to that stanza, but both opening and closing components tend to have certain common characteristics. Some of these have already been outlined, briefly, in the foregoing paragraph and what has been said will not be repeated.

A stanza may *open* by arousing interest: this can be effected by posing a question or setting out a hypothetical case. An example is Jer 3,1

הן ישלח איש את־אשתו    If a man divorces his wife.

See further Jer 18,13; Pss 74,1 and 10-11.

Another method of starting a stanza is to imply precisely that: a start or a beginning, for example, Jer 1,17; 10,17.22; 49,28b.30.31 and Job 6,8; 4,12:

ואלי דבר יגנב    And to me a word came stealthily,
ותקח אזני שמץ מנהו    and my ear caught its whisper.

Similarly, a stanza may *close* in a variety of ways: with a *quotation* or saying (Hos 13,2; Joel 2,17; Job 4,21); with a line that is extra *long* (Nah 2,14) or extremely *short* (Nah 2,1); by referring to *finality* in some way (Job 4,11.21); by *change of speaker* (Song 6,1.2-3.4-8; etc.) and so on. Many of these devices also serve to close a poem (see CLOSURE) and can co-occur. Structural devices such as chiasmus, envelope figure, refrain, acrostics are considered elsewhere.[9]

### Stanzaic mobility

In some poems the sequence of stanzas is unalterable for one reason or for several. For example, in the *blasons* (descriptions of lover's body) that occur so often in Song, the arrangement of topics is predetermined by the set order 'head to toe' (e.g. Song 4,1-7: eyes, hair, teeth, lips, mouth, brow, neck, breasts, vulva). In other poems, the arrangement of stanzas depends on the development of a theme (Jer 14,17-22) or on ancient history (Ps 105). Often enough, though, the stanzas are practically *interchangeable*—or, at the very least, the

---

9. 'Features of stanzaic closure may impress the reader more strongly than openings because they delimit stanzas *ex posteriori*. It is essential to realize that retrospective patterning is not only performed between several stanzas but also within individual stanzas . . . The fact, however, that stanzaic closure does involve retrospection explains the predominance of terminal over initial devices, although some of them may occur in both functions' (Häublein, *Stanza*, 53).

sequence handed down to us is not immutable. The classic and most obvious example is Ps 119 with its succession of almost disconnected lines (in acrostic patterns); in fact, recently a scholar has proposed reshuffling the traditional sequence into a more logical arrangement[10]—and, whether he is correct or not, it remains true that the poem's stanzas and their components seem to have no fixed order. Another example is Am 1,3–2,5 (or 2,6), a set of eight oracles against Damascus, Gaza, Tyre, Edom, Ammon, Moab and Judah. Evidently the last stanza could not be re-positioned—the other seven stanzas acting as a lead-in to the climactic oracle against Judah—but the same seven stanzas could be set out in different sequences without dramatic loss.[11] Again, the twin blessing-poems on the 'twelve' tribes (Gen 49 and Dt 33) differ not only in sequence of tribe but in the names of the tribes that are included: Gen 49 lists Reuben, Simeon and Levi, Judah, Zebulun, Issachar, Dan, Gad, Asher, Naphtali, Joseph and Benjamin; in Dt 33 the tribes mentioned are Reuben, Judah, Levi, Benjamin, Joseph, Zebulun, Gad, Dan, Naphtali and Asher.[12] Häublein, who discovered the principle of stanzaic mobility, comments:[13]

> A poem containing only mobile stanzas belongs to a different structural category. Whereas its individual stanzas are all tightly closed, the whole poem is basically open. All exchangeable stanzas can claim equal logical status within the whole. Stanzas may be added or taken away anywhere.

*Literary forms*

Although the subject of literary form is integral to a consideration of poetic structure, it covers an area so vast that it would merit another book.[14] A few words are needed here, though, to provide perspective. (See above, chapter 4 under 4.5: SOCIAL SETTINGS.)

The two main forms used in the psalms (and carried over into the prophetic and wisdom traditions) were those of *praise* and of *lament*.

---

10. S. Bergler, 'Der längste Psalm—Anthologie oder Liturgie?', *VT* 29 (1979) 257-288.

11. See Häublein, *Stanza*, 82-100.

12. For the problems involved see A.D.H. Mayes, *Deuteronomy* (NCB; London, 1979), 396-397; he points out that the order followed in Dt 33 may have a geographical basis.

13. Häublein, *Stanza*, 90.

14. See conveniently J.H. Hayes, ed., *Old Testament Form Criticism* (San Antonio, 1974).

The category of hymn is not a literary unit.[15] Individual psalms of praise, such as Pss 18; 30; 40; 66,13-20, had the structure:

proclamation
summary
flashback
report
vow
praise.

The communal praise-psalms (Pss 126,3-4; 144,1-10; etc.) had no such clear articulation. The laments, both of the individual (Pss 74; 79; 80) and of the community (Pss 27B; 102; 143), followed a common pattern:

address
lament
statement of trust
petition
vow of praise.

There is a large number of other categories (victory songs, declarative psalms of praise, imperative psalms and so on), a discussion of which is outside the present terms of reference.[16] It is noteworthy that analysis of this kind, based on content and meaning, complements the study of form and structure followed elsewhere in this book.

BIBLIOGRAPHY

(a) *General*
Häublein, *Stanza* (an excellent introduction only 125 pages long, with a good annotated bibliography [118-121]).
Smith, *Closure*.

(b) *Semitic*
Beaucamp, E. 'Structure strophique des Psaumes', *RSR* 56 (1976) 199-223.
Condamin, A. *Poèmes de la Bible. Avec une introduction sur la strophique hébraïque* (Paris, 1933, 2nd ed.).

15. So C. Westermann, *The Praise of God in the Psalms* (London, 1965) 30. His table, 156-157, is particularly useful.
16. See now C. Westermann, *The Psalms. Structure, Content and Message* (Minneapolis, 1980; translation by R.D. Gehrke of *Der Psalter* [Stuttgart, 1967]), and B. Feininger, 'A Decade of German Psalm Criticism', *JSOT* 20 (1981) 91-103, with extensive bibliography. Also, G.M. Tucker, *Form Criticism and the Old Testament* (Philadelphia, 1971).

Fullerton, K. 'The Strophe in Hebrew Poetry and Psalm 29', *JBL* 48 (1929) 274-290.

Gray, G.B. 'The Strophic Division of Isaiah 21:1-10 and Isaiah 11:1-8', *ZAW* 32 (1912) 190-198.

Kelly, F.T. 'The Strophic Structure of Habakkuk', *AJSL* 18 (1902) 94-119.

Kraft, C.F. *The Strophic Structure of Hebrew Poetry as Illustrated in the First Book of the Psalter* (Chicago, 1938).—a comprehensive survey

—'Some Further Observations Concerning the Strophic Structure in Hebrew Poetry', *Irwin FS*, 62-89 [deals largely with Ugaritic poetry].

Lugt, van der *Strofische Structuren*—the fullest account available.

Montgomery, J.A. 'Stanza-Formation in Hebrew Poetry', *JBL* 64 (1945) 379-384.

Moor, J.C. de 'The Art of Versification in Ugarit and Israel II: The Formal Structure', *UF* 10 (1978) 187-217.

Skehan, P.W. 'Strophic Patterns in the Book of Job', *CBQ* 23 (1961) 125-142.

Smith, J.M.P. 'The Strophic Structure of the Book of Micah', *AJSL* 24 (1908) 187-208.

Also Wahl, T.P. Strophic structure of individual laments in Psalms Books I and II (New York, 1977)—unavailable to me; see van der Lugt, *Strofische Structuren*, 109-113.

For Akkadian cf. Reiner, *JNES* 33 (1974) 221-236.

## 7.2 Strophic Patterns: Introduction

In the following pages certain mainline strophic patterns will be described in full. They are the monocolon (7.3), the abc // b′ c′ couplet (7.4), the tricolon (7.5), the quatrain (7.6) and the pentacolon (7.7). There are higher units (7.8) but they do not occur with enough frequency for rules to be established. Finally comes the alphabetic acrostic (7.9) which can determine a strophe, a stanza or a complete poem.

## 7.3 The Monocolon

### The monocolon in general

By definition a monocolon or 'isolated line' is a single colon which does not closely cohere with another colon in the same sub-section of a poem. Athough, strictly speaking, all the lines of a poem cohere in some way (or else they would not form part of the poem), it is meaningless to deny that monocola exist.[17] More simply defined,

---

17. As does Jakobson, *Lang* 42 (1966) 429, who writes: 'Orphan lines in poetry of pervasive parallels are a contradiction in terms, since, whatever the status of a line, all its

they are *one-line strophes*—a strophe forming part of a stanza, and therefore, of a poem. Other terms are current for monocolon, such as 'anacrustic line',[18] 'orphan line', 'isolated line', and the like.[19] For the sake of consistency, 'monocolon' will be used here throughout.[20]

*Structural aspects of the monocolon*
With respect to the stanza, a monocolon can come at the beginning, at the end and in the body of a stanza. If within a stanza, then more than one monocolon can occur. These remarks are significant in determining the functions of the monocolon (see below).

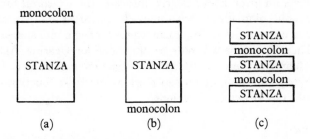

(a)  (b)  (c)

*Establishing monocola*
The presence of monocola within a poem can be established by one or more of the following ways. 1. By segmentation and elimination: once all the other strophic elements (bicola, tricola, etc.) have been recognised in the text, the remaining single-line strophes must be monocola. However, care must be taken not to include instances of the 'split couplet' where a parallel bicolon encloses other material.[21]

---

structure and functions are indissolubly interlaced with the near and distant verbal environment, and the task of linguistic analysis is to disclose the levers of this coaction. When seen from the inside of the parallelistic system, the supposed orphanhood, like any other componental status, turns into a network of multifarious compelling affinities.'

18. See R. Austerlitz, *Ob-Ugric Metrics* (Helsinki, 1958) 39 and 69-75.
19. Notably the so-called 'Kurzvers' of Fohrer; see *ZAW* 66 (1954) 199-236.
20. See de Moor: 1978, 198ff.
21. For example, the couplet comprising lines A and A' is a unit into which intrusive material has been inserted:

See below under 'couplet'. Also, Tsumura, *Proceedings 8th World Congress of Jewish Studies* (Jerusalem, 1982) 1-6.

2. From position: lines used to head or close a stanza may well be monocola (see diagram under 'Structural aspects of the monocolon'). 3. From recurrence: single cola appearing more than once within a segment of poetry are probably monocola, and may well be refrains. Unintended single lines must not be confused with the presence of deliberately chosen monocola. Such isolated lines are not monocola but 1. remnants of a bicolon, the first or second line of which is missing; 2. the third line of a tricolon (see under TRICOLON) or 3. extra-metrical prose or editorial comment.

*Functions of the monocolon*
The diagram given above clearly illustrates the *structural* functions of the monocolon: it can *open* a stanza (or poem) as in (a); it can *close* a stanza or poem, as in (b); it can *segment* a poem into stanzas as in (c). These functions will now be illustrated for Ugaritic, Akkadian and Hebrew. There is yet another function (which will also be illustrated): the monocolon can mark a *climax*—a function clearly related to its structural functions.

*Ugaritic*
Commonly, monocola are used to open stanzas, especially as an introduction to speech; see

    *tšu gh wtṣḥ*          She raised her voice and screeched.[22]

Climactic is, for instance,[23]

    *wlyšn pbl mlk*        And King Pbl could not sleep;

coming at the end of a series of causes for insomnia. Other examples occur.[24]

*Akkadian*
A single line can close a speech, for example (from the Erra Epic):[25]

    *išmešuma qurādu Erra*    Hero Erra heard him;

---

22. *CTA* 4 ii 21. Similarly, *CTA* 4 ii 12: 'On lifting her eyes she espied', and 'There vowed Noble Keret' in *CTA* 14 iv 197-202.
23. *CTA* 14 iii 119-120.
24. E.g. *CTA* 19 ii 89-91: 'Dead is Hero Aqhat'. See the comments of Saliba, *JAOS* 92 (1972) 109 n. 14 and Cross, *HTR* 67 (1974) 10-15.
25. *Erra* IV 128.

or can be climactic, as in the Flood Epic:[26]

> *bâ abūbi 7 mūšišu iqbīšu*    The coming of the flood on the 7th day
> it (fore)told him.

Other instances could also be adduced.[27]

*Hebrew*

In classical Hebrew poetry type and function virtually correspond with regard to the monocolon. The examples to be adduced will show this to be the case.

1. *Introductory monocolon*

For example, Song 6,10:

> מי־זאת הנשקפה כמו־שחר    Who is it looking out like the dawn
> [followed by:]
> fair as the moon,
> bright as the sun,
> awesome as with trophies?[28]

and Jgs 5,25:

> מים שאל    Water he requested;
> [followed by:]
> Milk she gave
> in a lordly bowl,
> she proffered curds.

Such introductory lines are particularly frequent with verbs of saying, e.g. Am 3,11; Nah 1,12; Job 35,3.10; etc. See, too, Dt 33,13; Nah 2,2; Song 2,10.

2. *Closing monocolon*

For example Jer 14,9 where the final line of vv. 2-9 is:

> אל תנחנו    Do not abandon us.

See also Isa 63,9d; Jer 12,11; etc.

3. *Climactic monocolon*

Though sometimes difficult to distinguish from mere closing monocola, the following seem to qualify for this function: Hos 9,12:

---

26. *Atr* III i 37; translation as in *CAD* M/2, 293.
27. See, in general, Hecker, *Epik*, 109 and note *BWL* 74:69 [introductory] and *Gilg* (Nin) VI 168-169.
28. See Pope, *Song*, 552, for translation.

כי גם אוי להם בשורי מהם   Woe to them indeed when I turn away from them!

and Hos 13,2; Ez 32,15; Mal 3,1; etc.

### 4. *Monocolon as refrain*

In effect such monocola segment a poem into smaller units, notably in Am 4 where 'This is Yahweh's oracle' (נאם יהוה) is used in conjunction with 'Yet you did not come back to me' (vv. 6.8.9.10.11). A similar combination of monocolon and refrain recurs in Ps 136 (notably vv. 25 and 26).[29] Further examples are Joel 2,20 and 21; 4,10 and 11.

*For study*
Isa 8,10; 40,9; 41,8; Pss 2,12b; 136,16.

### 'Triple synonyms' and the 'aba' chiastic monocolon

The next two sections deal with subtypes of the monocolon which have been touched on only in passing, namely the 'three synonym colon' and the 'aba chiastic monocolon'. The diagram given immediately below shows the relationship of these two subtypes to the 'standard' monocolon; the letters 'a', 'b', etc., denote semantic sub-units of the sentence.

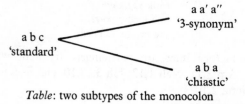

*Table*: two subtypes of the monocolon

### Triple synonyms

The 'triplet' or set of three synonyms (and near-synonyms) is a form of repetition. Examples could be quoted from most languages and the effectiveness of such sets is enhanced when they are alliterative, beginning or ending with the same consonant or consonantal sequence.

An example is Jer 4,2

ונשבעת חי יהוה   Then might you swear 'As Yahweh lives!'
באמת במשפט ובצדקה   truthfully, justly, rightly.[30]

---

29. Recognition by Auffret, *VT* 27 (1977) 4-5. See also Boadt, *CBQ* 25 (1973) 26-27; Kosmala, *VT* 14 (1964) 431-433; Gray, *Legacy*, 289-302, and others.

30. Following Bright, *Jeremiah*, 21. NEB prefers: 'If you swear by the life of the Lord/ in truth, in justice and uprightness . . .'

The initial alliteration in the second line (literally: '*in* truth, *in* justice, and *in* rectitude') gives the line its rhythmic flow and lends it the quality of a saying.[31] Such sequences are extensions of paired synonyms—and can themselves be extended further into catalogue-like lists or 'tours' (see TOURS). Before going on to discuss the various functions of this device, some examples from Ugaritic and Akkadian poetry will be given.

From the Baal Epic: (*CTA* 3C iii 15; etc.)

| | |
|---|---|
| *ḥšk 'ṣk 'bṣk* | Hurry yourself! Move yourself! Hasten yourself! |

the repeated final *-k* providing the line with both rhythm and urgency. Also, this time indicating a sequence of actions (*CTA* 3A i 4-5):

| | |
|---|---|
| *ndd y'šr wyšqynh* | He stood, made preparations and gave him drink. |

Other examples have been given elsewhere.[32] The Gilgamesh Epic attests the same device, for instance (OB II iii 31-32):

| | |
|---|---|
| *iptēqma inaṭṭal u ippallas* | He squinted, then was gaping and staring, |

with alliterative initial *i*-.[33]

*Functions*

The *functions* of triple synonyms seem to be as follows: to lend proverbial quality to a saying; to mark off a sequence of actions; to be exhaustive; to fill out a line and (less well attested) to lend a line rhythm. There is some overlap here with the 'law of increasing members' by which lengthier words tend to come at the end of a line.

1. To give a saying the character of a maxim or adage:

| | |
|---|---|
| | Go to the ant . . . |
| | she has no |
| קצין שטר ומשל | overseer, governor or ruler. (Prov 6,7) |

---

31. 'The triplet has its own special slot within repetition. Three words joined together and having the same initial (consonant) often take on the value of a maxim and serve to mark off (in every language, apparently) a progression'—Groupe μ, *Rhétorique de la poésie* (Brussels, 1977), 153-154 (my translation); see also 133. Also, Miller, *HTR* 73 (1980) 79-89.

32. Watson, *UF* 7 (1975) 483-484. And *CTA* 2:31.

33. Also *Atr* I iv 206; III iv 25; III vii 6; etc. (see previous note).

Also Qoh 2,21; Sir 11,11.

2. To portray a progression. Although referred to as 'synonyms', sometimes the three words (usually verbs in such cases) mark off stages in a sequence of actions. For example, Ps 95,6

| באו | Come! |
| נשתחוה ונכרעה נברכה | Let us worship, bow down, kneel! |

Similarly, Jer 25,16.27; Job 11,10 and 1 Sm 9,3 (prose). Particularly interesting is Hos 9,11 where the sequence given is the *reverse* of what happens in real life:

| מלדה ומבטן ומהריון | No birth, no pregnancy, no conception. |

3. To indicate exhaustive listing and so lend validity to a statement or simply denote totality. An example is Isa 37,28

| ושבתך וצאתך ובואך ידעתי | Your sitting down, your going out, your coming in I know. |

Further: Jer 4,2; Hos 2,10 (= Joel 2,19); Hos 4,13b; Joel 1,12.

4. Such triple synonyms can also function as expletives, filling out the line, as in Job 41,18b:

| משיגהו חרב בלי תקום | Who attacks, the sword avails not: |
| חנית מסע ושריה | nor spear, nor dart, nor javelin; |

where 'spear, dart, javelin' gloss 'sword' and make up the second line of the couplet. See, too, Jer 51,27; Ex 26,7.10.12; Hos 2,13; Joel 1,12; Pss 48,6; 98,4; Prov 26,18.

### 7.4 *The abc // b'c' Couplet*

The couplet, of course, is the commonest form of the strophe in Hebrew (Ugaritic and Akkadian) poetry—see under PARALLELISM. Here only one particular type of couplet will be considered.

*The abc // b'c' couplet*

The *abc // b'c'*-patterned couplet is essentially a bicolon in synonymous parallelism which has no counterpart in the second line to the very first word of the first line. In 2 Kgs 19,23 (// Isa 37,24c), for example, there is nothing corresponding to 'I felled' in the second colon:

| ואכרת קומת ארזיו | *I felled* its tallest cedars, |
| מבחר ברשיו | its choicest cypresses. |

In other words, there is *ellipsis of the initial verb* (אכרת). There can be ellipsis of a *non-verbal* element, too:

לפניו רגזה ארץ      *Before him*, the earth trembles,
רעשו שמים      the heavens quake. (Joel 2,10a)

In both cases, the structural (semantic) pattern is abc // b'c':

(a)ואכרת (b) קומת (c)ארזיו     (a)לפניו (b) רגזה (c) ארץ
מבחר (b') ברשיו (c')     רעשו (b') שמים (c')

Other couplets with verbal ellipsis are: Nb 21,29; Dt 33,10.10.18b; 1 Sm 18,7b; 2 Kgs 19,26.28; Hos 5,8; 7,1; 10,8; 12,1; Joel 1,2; 2,16c; 4,10; Am 2,9b; Mic 2,2.2; 3,8.10; 4,3b; 5,4b-5a; 7,1; Nah 3,4b.5c; Zech 9,10; Job 12,17; 38,9; Prov 30,14; Song 1,10; 8,2b.3b.

Other couplets with non-verbal ellipsis: Hos 6,10; 9,7d; 10,2; Joel 1,7; Mic 7,9; Job 34,10; Song 2,1.17; 3,8.

The same pattern is found in both Ugaritic and Akkadian, and, as in Hebrew, there can be ellipsis of either a verbal or a non-verbal element.

| | |
|---|---|
| *qḥ ks bdy*<br>*qb't bymny* | Take the cup from my hand,<br>the goblet from my right hand.<br>(*CTA* 19 iv 215-216[34]) |
| *ṯr ḫbr rbt*<br>*ḫbr ṯrrt* | The 'dukes' of great Hubur,<br>of lesser Hubur. (*CTA* 15 iv 19-20) |
| *aššu kaššāptu ukaššipanni*<br>*elēnītum ubbiranni* | For a witch has bewitched me,<br>a deceitful woman has accused me.[35] |

The pattern has been termed 'Canaanite'[36] but its occurrence in East Semitic and in later Hebrew seems to belie this name. In fact, the literature from Qumran provides several examples, such as:

להודות לאל צדקו     To praise El for his justice,
ולעליון תפארתו     And Elyon for his majesty. (1QS XI 15[37])

---

34. Also *CTA* 14 iv 214-217; 23:34-35; quasi-verbal in 14 iv 201-202.
35. *Maqlu* I 4-5 (also 18); cf. *CAD* E, 83; or 'encompassed me', cf. *AHw*, 4 and 198.
36. On verb-deletion in the second colon Greenstein, *JANES* 6 (1974) 91, notes: 'It is clear that in Canaanite poetry, when the two lines are syntactically parallel, the main verb may be deleted in the second line provided the grammatical subject and object of the second line correspond to the subject and object of the first line'.
37. Also 1QH II 22; IV 9-10.16.25.34-35; V 26; VII 8.20-21; 1QS XI 4-5.31-32; Ps 151,1b; Plea: 2-3.

The significance of the abc // b'c'-patterned couplet is not clear. It evidently shares the characteristics and functions of ellipsis (see ELLIPSIS. It also tends to occur in clusters—twice successively in Prov 30,14 for instance:

| דור חרבות שניו | A group whose teeth are swords, |
| ומאכלות מתלעתיו | whose jaws are cutters, |
| לאכל עניים מארץ | to eat the wretched out of land, |
| ואביונים מאדם | and the needy out of territory.[38] |

The couplet can also form a self-contained poem or poetic unit:

| הכה שאול באלפיו | Annihilation was by the thousand for Saul, |
| ודוד ברבבתיו | but by the myriad for David. (1 Sm 18,7b [etc.]) |

With regard to metre and structure, at least for Hebrew, the following points deserve mention:

—the metre seems to be 3 + 2 stresses, or 'qinah' metre, a rhythm used in laments. Silent stress is *not* operative since it would occur in the first beat of the second line (3:0+2).

—the overall length of the second line is usually equivalent to that of the first (the isocolic principle in operation), indicating that a word has been omitted for metrical reasons.

—the inverted form of the abc // b'c' couplet, is of course

a b c

c' b'

or partial chiasmus (see CHIASMUS). Examples are Dt 33,26b, Nah 3,8; Zech 9,7; Hab 1,3.5; Pss 35,17; 92,3; Job 33,22.

—the form is often used in conjunction with gender parallelism, as in Joel 2,16.

*For study*
See list of passages given above and the Qumran texts in note 37.

*Cross-references*
ANACRUSIS, ELLIPSIS.

BIBLIOGRAPHY

Gray, *Forms*, 75 discusses this form of couplet briefly; he terms it 'incomplete parallelism without compensation'. The pattern is referred to many times in Dahood, *Psalms I, II* and *III*. For discussion in the light of

---

38. A Ugaritic example is *CTA* 14 iv 214-217.

modern linguistic theory (psycholinguistics) cf. Greenstein, *JANES* 6
(1974) 87-105.

## 7.5 The Tricolon

*The tricolon*
As its name implies, the tricolon is a strophic unit composed of three
consecutive cola, generally in parallelism, but not infrequently
bonded only structurally.

| | |
|---|---|
| אף ערשנו רעננה | Our very couch is luxuriant, |
| קרות בתינו ארזים | the beams of our bowers, cedars, |
| רחיטנו ברותים | our rafters: cypresses. (Song 1,16-17[39]) |

The example forms a unit for a number of reasons: the three lines are
in parallel; they are linked by subject matter since they describe the
forest as a natural love-arbour; the suffix ־נו, 'our', occurs in every
line; the strophe differs sharply from the verses which precede and
follow. When examining a particular poem or section of poetry for
tricola, care of a similar kind must be taken to determine whether a
set of three lines does form a strophic unit and cannot be explained
away on other grounds. This is because the normal strophic unit in
Hebrew, as in Ugaritic and Akkadian, is the couplet.[40] However, it is
precisely because the tricolon is attested in both Ugaritic and
Akkadian[41] that its occurrence in Hebrew should occasion no
surprise.

Once a three-line segment has been isolated within a poem—
meaning that the strophes which come before and after it can
definitely be accounted for—whether it is a tricolon or not can be
determined by posing the following questions: Is the first line really
an introductory monocolon, so that the posited segment is in fact
made up of monocolon + bicolon (as in Isa 21,1; Ps 79,1)? Is one of
the cola an explanatory gloss or secondary insertion (e.g. Jer 1,10), or
suspect in certain textual traditions (Jer 2,31)? Can the lines be
segmented in some other way, by redivision of the cola or by
including the posited tricolon within a larger strophic unit?[42] And,

39. Adapting slightly Pope's translation in *Song*, 292 [and see 359-362].
40. Explaining the scepticism of Loretz and the over-scepticism of Mowinckel
(though Mowinckel largely ignored the Ugaritic material).
41. And in Phoenician.
42. See *CTA* 3B ii 39-40a, which forms part of the hexacolon 38-41.

finally, should the strophe turn out to be a tricolon, what is its function? (See below on functions.)

*Typology of the tricolon*

A further help in determining whether a three-line unit is a tricolon is to match it with known types. The typology itself is interesting for comparing the different poetic traditions. Of course, some tricola fall outside the types described here and there is some degree of overlap, but it is hoped that the differentiation suggested below will prove useful.

1. *The staccato tricolon.* Staccato-style tricola have two beats per line and tend to be effective by dint of brevity. Some tricola have a final line which is longer than the others though retaining only two beats.[43]

| | |
|---|---|
| *ynghn krumm* | They gored like wild oxen: |
| *mt 'z* | Mot was winning,[44] |
| *b'l 'z* | Baal was winning. |
| | (*CTA* 6 vi 18-19[45]) |

| | |
|---|---|
| ופרצים תצאנה | Through the gaps you'll go, |
| אשה נגדה | each woman (going) ahead, |
| והשלכתנה ההרמונה | ejected into the Harmon. (Am 4,3[46]) |

2. *Parallel patterns.* The following parallel patterns occur (using capitals to indicate cola):

A / A' / A''
A / A' / B —which, reversed, becomes
A / B / B'

The two other possible forms (A/B/A and A/B/C) are discussed in the next paragraph. The essential factor common to these patterns is

---

43. See under METRE. An Akk. example may be *Gilg* XI 131: 'The sea calmed, and the hurricane abated; stop did the flood'. Tricola with a longer final line include Agušaya Hymn B 24'-26'; *CTA* 4 iii 18-21; 3B ii 39-40; 5 vi 12-14; Dt 32,4; 33,6; Hos 7,15; 9,16; 10,13; Pss 59,10; 107,26.37; Prov 10,26; 28,11.28; Song 1,11; 7,7. For tricola with a longer initial line see *CTA* 2 i 23-24; 17 v 9-10; 19 iii 120-121. See Watson, *UF* 7 (1975) 485.

44. Lit. 'was strong'.

45. Also lines 16-17 and 19-20.

46. And Dt 32,24.29; Jgs 4,18; Hos 10,4; Nah 3,2; Pss 59,11; 80,10; 106,4; 107,3; 119,33; 124,6; Job 17,1.11; Song 2,16; 3,10; 6,3.

*parallelism*, sometimes reinforced by repetition of the same word, root or particle. *A/A'/A''*. Examples in Akkadian are rare.[47] The pattern is very common in Ugaritic and Hebrew verse.

| | |
|---|---|
| *aḥdy dymlk 'l ilm* | Only I am king over the gods, |
| *lymru ilm wnšm* | who truly fattens up gods and men, |
| *dyšb' hmlt arṣ* | who sates earth's hordes. |

(*CTA* 4 vii 49-52[48])

| | |
|---|---|
| שמעו־זאת הכהנים | Hear this, O priests! |
| והקשיבו בית ישראל | Pay attention, House of Israel! |
| ובית המלך האזינו | And royal house: bend an ear! (Hos 5,1[49]) |

Other OT texts: Dt 32,4; Hos 4,3b; Nah 3,2; Ps 124,4; Job 3,5.9; 10,17; 15,28; 24,24; 33,15; Jer 51,15.

As indicated, quite frequently a word, particle or root[50] is repeated throughout, acting as a linking device.

*lubki ana eṭlūti ša ēzibū ḫī[rēti]*
*lubki ana ardāti ša ultu sūn ḫā'irišina [šallupāni]*
*ana šerri lakê lubki ša ina lā ūmišu ṭar[du]*

*Should I bewail* the men who left their wives behind?
*Should I bewail* the girls torn from their husbands' embrace?
*Should I bewail* the suckling-child dismissed before its time?
(Descent of Ishtar[51])

| | |
|---|---|
| *yd pdry bt ar* | The love of Pidray *daughter of* light, |
| *ahbt ṭly bt rb* | the affection of Tallay *daughter of* rain, |
| *dd arṣy bt y'bdr* | the amours of Arsay *daughter of* Y'bdr. |

(*CTA* 3C iii 3-5[52])

| | |
|---|---|
| וכל־פסילה יכתו | *All her* images shall be beaten to pieces, |
| וכל־אתנניה ישרפו באש | *all her* 'snakes' burned with fire, |
| וכל־עצביה אשים שממה | *all her* idols I will lay waste. (Mic 1,7[53]) |

47. See, perhaps, *BWL* 229:22-23 and 219:11b-12.
48. Also *CTA* 4 iv 10; 3B ii 20-22.36-37.
49. Considered to form a question with the following line by Loewenstamm, *Gordon FS*, 127.
50. See particularly Gevirtz, *Or* 42 (1973) 169-170.
51. Conveniently in R. Borger, *Babylonisch-assyrisch Lesestücke*, II (Rome, 1963), 88-89, lines 34-36 (Nineveh recension).
52. Also *CTA* 3F vi 7-9 ('*br*, 'cross over'); 4 viii 1-4 ('*m*, 'towards'); iii 18-21 (*dbḥ*, 'sacrifice'); 6 vi 27-29 (*l*, 'indeed').
53. 'Snakes': a form of תנין with prophetic *aleph*, evocative of Ugar 5 7:73-74. See my 'Allusion, Irony and Wordplay in Micah 1,7', in *Bib* 65 (1984) 103-105.

Note, too, Gen 1,27 (ברא, 'created'); 1 Sm 2,2 (אין, 'there is none');
Jer 51,15 (ב, 'by'); Ez 26,8 (עליך, 'against you'); Hos 4,1 (אין, 'there is
no'); Prov 24,33 (מעט, 'a little'). Evidently there is some overlap with
triple repetition.[54] Another sub-group employs the 'word-triplet', as
in

| | |
|---|---|
| כי יבש חציר | For the grass is withered, |
| כלה דשא | the new growth fails, |
| ירק לא היה | there is no verdure. (Isa 15,6[55]) |

To this group, too, belong triple rhetorical questions (see RHETORICAL
QUESTIONS) and triple similes (see SIMILE). Also, number parallelism.

*A/A'/B.* Although tricola of this type, which do not exhibit
consecutive parallelism, might justifiably be classed as 'bicolon +
monocolon', they are considered as strophic units because there is
usually a link bonding the three lines. In nearly all cases, the link is
one of meaning or content.

| | |
|---|---|
| *eli ajjābīni* KUR *li'abit* | Onto our enemies, let the land/mountain collapse. |
| *eli lemnīni dūru ša iqūpu limqut* | Onto our adversaries let the teetering wall fall. |
| *erṣet nakri lirtessi ina gim[rīša]* | Let the alien country in its entirety be 'spellbound'. (*BWL* 228:15-16[56]) |
| *širh ltikl 'ṣrm* | His flesh the birds did eat, |
| *mnth ltkly nprm* | His limbs the sparrows did devour, |
| *šir lšir yṣḥ* | Flesh to flesh called aloud. (*CTA* 6 ii 35-37) |

In the two examples (from Akkadian and Ugaritic), the first two lines
almost form a parallel couplet—yet there is a very strong link with
the final, summary line which rounds off the strophe. Note the
repetition of *šir*, 'flesh', in the first and final line of the Ugaritic
example, and the clever use of what looks superficially like the same
construction in each line.

In Hebrew:

---

54. Discussed above.
55. The triplet was first noted by Greenfield, *AcOr* 29 (1965) 5.
56. The Akkadian component of this bilingual proverb is almost completely
preserved (text: *BWL* 228:15-16). For translations see *BWL* 232 and *CAD* L 124a
(lexical section), and for the difficult verb *russû* cf. *BWL* 232 and *AHw* 996. The
equivalent of KUR in line 15 may be either *mātu*, 'land' (so Lambert) or *šadû*,
'mountain' (so *CAD*).

| | |
|---|---|
| נפת תטפנה שפתותיך כלה | Nectar do your lips distil, O bride, |
| דבש וחלב תחת לשונך | honey and milk are under your tongue, |
| וריח שמלתיך כריח לבנון | and the scent of your garments is like Lebanon-scent. (Song 4,11) |

Also Job 24,12; 31,34.

*A/B/B'*. Much commoner is the tricolon where strong parallelism occurs over the last two lines. Ugaritic: *CTA* 23:62-63;[57] 24:17-19; *KTU* 1.93:1-3.[58] Hebrew:

| | |
|---|---|
| הכה אפרים | Stricken is Ephraim: |
| שרשם יבש | their root withered, |
| פרי בלי יעשון | no fruit shall it bear. (Hos 9,16) |

The link is formed both by content and by the wordplay: אפרים and פרי. Other texts: Gen 49,27; Hos 12,7; Nah 1,9; Ps 122,5; Job 10,1; 18,4; 19,12; 20,23; 24,13; 28,4; 38,41.

There is a special form of both the A/A'/B and A/B/B' tricola where the non-parallel line contains an element of each of the other lines, so that the bonding is more powerful than usual. So, in Song 1,5, the components 'black' and 'lovely', mentioned in the first line, are developed in the second and third lines respectively:

| | |
|---|---|
| שחורה אני ונאוה בנות ירושלם | Black am I and lovely, daughters of Jerusalem: |
| כאהלי קדר | (BLACK) like the tents of Qedar,[59] |
| כיריעות שלמה | (LOVELY) as Solomon's carpet. |

Also: Job 19,29; 28,3.[60] Good examples in Ugaritic are *CTA* 3C iii 23-25 and 4 iv 35-37.

3. *Other patterns*. The two main patterns to be considered now are the chiastic tricolon (ABA) and the structural tricolon (ABC).

*ABA*. Since chiasmus is treated in a separate section (see CHIASMUS), only the topic of three-line chiastic strophes need be dealt with. In general, tricola of this sort can be described as two parallel cola (AA) separated by an isolated line (B)[61] and forming a unit. The two outer cola may be identical (ABA) or not (ABA'). Examples follow.[62]

---

57. Unless part of a larger strophe (see above).
58. For translation cf. Dahood, *Bib* 50 (1969) 349.
59. The word 'Qedar' means 'black'. See Kugel, *Idea*, 40.
60. The reverse pattern obtains in *BWL* 70:9-11 (Theodicy).
61. R. Austerlitz, *Ob-Ugric Metrics* (Helsinki, 1958), 47. Note that the ABA' pattern is often confused with the pivot-patterned bicolon.
62. Less likely: *JNES* 33 (1974) 276 (= I lines 49-50); also, ibid., 274 (= I lines 12-13); *BWL* 218:53-54; *Erra* I 4-5. Note that all are written on two lines.

| *ypth̬ ḥln bbhtm* | A | Let a window be opened in the mansion, |
| *urbt bqrb hklm* | B | a lattice within the palace, |
| *wypth̬ bdqt ʿrpt* | A' | and let a fissure be opened in the clouds. (*CTA* 4 vii 17-19[63]) |

| הנה משמני הארץ | A | See, from the fat of the earth |
| יהיה מושבך | B | shall your dwelling be, |
| ומטל השמים מעל | A' | and from the dew of heaven above. |
| | | (Gen 27,39[63a]) |

Other Hebrew texts: Gen 40,16-17; 49,8; 1 Sm 2,2; Isa 5,25; 14,8; 25,7; 30,31; 51,3b; 56,9; Jer 10,25; 11,19; 14,17; Ez 34,6; Hos 10,4; Joel 2,1; Am 1,3 (etc.); Jon 2,6; Mic 5,4-5; Nah 2,4; 3,15.17; Hab 2,6; Pss 4,2; 6,11; 9,15; 29,3; 55,15; 56,5; 57,5; 64,11; 86,12; 88,6; 89,17; 92,12; 98,2; 101,2; 104,15; 109,14; 121,6.7; Job 3,1-2; 10,1; 10,22; 12,4; 15,30; 34,37; Prov 5,22; 7,18; 10,29; 17,25; Song 1,11; Lam 3,7; 3,10; 3,47; Sir 11,28ab.

Note the form with identical outer cola (ABA):

| ימין יהוה עשה חיל | A | Yahweh's right hand did valiantly! |
| ימין יהוה רוממה | B | Yahweh's right hand is exalted. |
| ימין יהוה עשה חיל | A | Yahweh's right hand did valiantly! |
| | | (Ps 118,15-16) |

Also Ps 27,14.

*ABC.* The structural tricolon is a set of three lines which exhibit no parallelism, strictly speaking, but are linked in some way; for instance, they can depict a succession of connected actions.

| *yprq lṣb wyṣh̬q* | He uncreases his forehead and laughs; |
| *pʿnh lhdm ytpd* | taps his feet on the stool; |
| *wykrkr uṣbʿth* | and twiddles his fingers. |
| | (*CTA* 4 iv 28-30[64]) |

Also *CTA* 5 vi 12-14; 6 i 14-16—both describing a progressive set of actions. Note

| בדי שפר יאמר האח | At trumpet sound he says 'Ho'; |
| ומרחוק יריח מלחמה | from afar he smells battle, |
| רעם שרים ותרועה | clamour of captains and shouting. (Job 39,25) |

---

63. The occurrence of a parallel tricolon in 25-28 shows the line 'according to the words of Kothar-wa-Ḥasis' in the first text to be a monocolon.
63a. Cf. Dahood, *Bib* 55 (1974) 79.
64. For the meaning 'forehead' of *lṣb* cf. Xella, *OrAnt* 17 (1978) 126-127.

and Hos 10,13; Ps 107,37; Job 10,3; 14,14. See also Ps 99,9.[65]

*Functions of the tricolon*
Tricola often occur quite randomly in sections of poetry where couplets are the norm—as in Job 6,4—for no obvious reason. In the main, though, the tricolon does have the function of *demarcating stanzas* (or segments of poetry), coming either at the beginning or at the end, and sometimes in both places. It can also mark a climax.[66] A secondary function is to express merismus. These functions will be briefly illustrated from Hebrew.

1. *Stanza-marker: opening.* The poem of Jer 10,12-16 (and 51,15-19) is a unit, which begins:

| | |
|---|---|
| עשה ארץ בכחו | Who made the earth by his power, |
| מכין תבל בחכמתו | set up the world by his sagacity, |
| ובתבונתו נטה שמים | by his skill extended the sky. |

Similarly: Gen 27,39; 49,8; Hos 5,1 (double tricolon); Am 1-2; Nah 1,9; Hab 2,6; Pss 4,2; 32,8; Job 3,1-2; 10,1.[67]

2. *Stanza-marker: close.* The long poem of Gen 49 ends with a tricolon (which is not a climax):

| | |
|---|---|
| בנימין זאב יטרף | Benjamin is a ravenous wolf: |
| בבקר יאכל עד | in the morning devouring prey |
| ולערב יחלק שלל | and at night dividing the spoil. (Gen 49,27) |

Note, further, Ez 34,6; Hos 12,7; Pss 27,14; 124,4; Job 10,22; 34,37; 39,25; Prov 3,18.[68] Hannah's song in 1 Sm 2 opens and closes with a tricolon (vv. 2 and 10).

3. *Climax marker.* Psalm 6 ends with a climactic strophe of confidence:

| | |
|---|---|
| יבשו ויבהלו מאד | Greatly ashamed and confused |
| כל איבי | will all my enemies be; |
| ישבו יבשו רגע | they will return shamefaced in a moment. |
| | (Ps 6,11) |

Other texts are Isa 51,3 and Ps 9,15.[69]

---

65. Kugel, *Idea*, 52.
66. First recognised by Gordon, *UT*, 133.
67. See *CTA* 3D iii 33-35; 4 iv 40 [both open a speech].
68. Also *CTA* 6 vi 50-52 [close of whole episode].
69. Gordon, *UT*, 133 cites *CTA* 6 ii 28-30.

4. *To denote merismus*.[70] Some passages already mentioned use a
tricolon for this function: Gen 49,27 (cited above); Ps 6,11 (also
cited); 9,15; Job 10,22; 34,37; also Pss 89,17; 109,14; 121,6.7; Isa 25,7
and

| | |
|---|---|
| כל חיתו שדי | All (you) beasts of the field, |
| אתיו לאכל | come to eat, |
| כל חיתו ביער | all (you) beasts of the forest. (Isa 56,9) |

the clue often being (as here) the use of כל, 'all, every'.

*Related topics*

The present section on the tricolon has been a rather dry catalogue of
different types. The classification given, however, is by no means
complete: there are many tricola which do not come under any of the
headings provided so far. A list of these passages can serve as
material for further study.[71]

To offset the rather arid presentation so far, a complete poem will
be analysed as a concrete example of the strophic form in question; it
is Isa 23,16.

*The trill of the trollop*[72]

| | | |
|---|---|---|
| קחי כנור | I | Lift your lyre, |
| סבי עיר | | circle the city, |
| זונה נשכחה | | worn-out whore. |
| היטיבי נגן | II | Sweetly strum, |
| הרבי־שיר | | sing many a song, |
| למען תזכרי | | and so be remembered. |

The poem is made up of two tricola only,[73] each line having a
staccato two-stress metre. There is little in the way of parallelism
('Lift[74] your lyre // circle the city', but these are really progressive
actions; 'Sweetly strum // sing many a song', concomitant actions, in
fact). The main linking feature throughout is *end-rhyme*: five words
end in *-î*, two in *-îr* (עיר, שיר) and there is assonance in both זונה נשכחה
and נגן—למען. Complex wordplay, too, is used: נשכחה can mean

---

70. See section on MERISMUS.
71. Set out below.
72. The alliterative title is an attempt at evoking the use in Hebrew of שירה, the
feminine form of שיר (both = 'song') in Isa 23,15 to match the obvious gender of זונה. For
a study of the poem cf. Lipiński, *ErIs* 14 (1978) 87* and *VT* 20 (1970) 39-40.
73. An opening and a closing tricolon comprise the entire song.
74. Lit. 'seize'.

'worn out; passionate[75] or forgotten'—זכר, 'to remember', evokes the term for 'male'[76]—in combination with irony.

*For study*
Isa 16,11; Jer 29,23; Joel 4,19; Pss 31,13; 32,8; 98,9; Job 24,14; Sir 51,2; Song 6,9.

*Cross-references*
CHIASMUS, RHETORICAL QUESTIONS, SIMILE, STAIRCASE PARALLELISM, WORD-PAIRS.

BIBLIOGRAPHY

Mowinckel, S. *Real and Apparent Tricola in Hebrew Psalm Poetry* (Oslo, 1957)—a rather negative work but the only book specifically on the topic.
Willis, J.T. 'The Juxtaposition of Synonymous and Chiastic Parallelism in Tricola in Old Testament Hebrew Psalm Poetry', *VT* 29 (1979) 465-480.
Also: Gray, *Legacy*, 295-296 [for Ugaritic examples]; Gordon, *UT*, 132-133; Hecker, *Epik*, 115-137; Revell, *VT* 31 (1981) 186-189.

## 7.6 *Strophic Patterns: the Quatrain*

The quatrain is a four-line strophe forming an independent unit within a stanza or poem. It should not be confused with two couplets (bicola) in succession or with a tricolon preceded or followed by a monocolon. It is often difficult to decide whether a set of four consecutive lines really is a quatrain and the following considerations are intended to be of some help in this respect.

The easiest type of quatrain to single out is the *ABBA quatrain*, where the keywords of each of the first two lines are repeated, in inverse order, in lines three and four. For example,

| | | |
|---|---|---|
| לא אמות כי־אחיה | A | I am not DEAD but living, |
| ואספר מעשי יה | B | and I recount the deeds of YAH; |
| יסר יסרני יה | B | though YAH fiercely punished me, |
| ולמות לא נתנני | A | to DEATH he did not give me up. |

(Ps 118,17-18)

---

75. See Rin, *BZ* 7 (1963) 23-24, who comments explicitly on the 'ingenious pun'. For a similar connection of this verb with singing, again in the form of a pun, see Ps 137.
76. Though unattested in Hebrew, *zkr* is common Semitic for male. Rin proposes 'be lain with', citing Arabic and Mishnaic Hebrew cognates.

where the verbal roots (keywords) which form the basis of the
pattern are מות יה מות. Related to this type of tetracolon is the
semantic ABBA quatrain, where the repeated words are not in
identical pairs but *semantically* parallel, as in

| | | |
|---|---|---|
| צדק מלאה ימינך | A | Your right hand is full of generosity, |
| ישמח הר ציון | B | let Mount Zion rejoice, |
| תגלנה בנות יהודה | B' | the daughters of Judah be glad, |
| למען משפטיך | A' | because of your justice. (Ps 48,11-12[77]) |

Also based on the repetition of certain keywords is the *ABCB*
*quatrain*. First noted by Gevirtz,[78] the pattern seems to be an
extension of the word pair and involves single words (usually, but not
always, verbs) in synonymous parallelism. In four successive lines,
the first colon uses a word (A) for which a parallel word (B) occurs in
the next colon. In the third colon the A word is not repeated; instead,
another synonym is used (C) and finally word B is repeated in the
last line. The pattern seems to be a variation on a simple ABAB
sequence, the use of C introducing an element of surprise or defeated
expectancy. An example is Isa 42,15

| | | | |
|---|---|---|---|
| אחריב הרים וגבעות | חרב | A | I will DRY UP mountains and hills |
| וכל־עשבם אוביש | יבש | B | and all their greenery I'll SHRIVEL; |
| ל ושמתי נהרות לאיים | שים | C | I will MAKE rivers into islands,[79] |
| ואגמים אוביש | יבש | B | and pools I'll SHRIVEL. |

Other examples include:

| | |
|---|---|
| Nb 23,7c-8a | ארר זעם קבב זעם |
| Isa 5,5 | סור היה פרץ היה |
| Isa 30,10 | ראה חזה דבר חזה |
| Isa 45,7 | יצר ברא עשה ברא |
| Jer 5,3 | חלה מאן חזק מאן |
| Jer 40,9 | ירא עבד ישב עבד |
| Gen 27,29a | עבד חשתחוו גביר חשתחוו |

The strophic pattern shows the last two examples to be poetry, not
prose.[80]

---

77. For other examples of both types see chapter on CHIASMUS. Note that the
quatrain is extremely common as a strophic form in Akkadian poetry.
78. Gevirtz, *Patterns*, 43-44. See also B. Porten—U. Rappaport, 'Poetic Structure in
Genesis IX 7', *VT* 21 (1971) 363-369—and Freedman, ibid. 368, n. 1; also, Kselman,
*BASOR* 220 (1975) 79, on Ps 72,5-8.
79. The meaning here is disputed.
80. See also Isa 28,23; Jer 50,2 [expanded sequence] and Isa 44,7.

Almost any *repeated component* can be used to build up a quatrain; sheer repetition of a basic syntactic sequence (Jer 15,2); gender patterns (Jer 5,17); keywords (ABAC in Gen 49,7) and so on. Occasionally it is difficult to distinguish between a true quatrain and a monocolon followed by a tricolon; for example, Jgs 5,25 (most probably an introductory line followed by an ABA' chiastic tricolon). The following strophe, though apparently formed from two parallel couplets, clearly forms a single unit:

| | |
|---|---|
| כי נפת תטפנה שפתי זרה | For the prostitute's lips drip with honey, |
| וחלק משמן חכה | and her palate is smoother than oil, |
| ואחריתה מרה כלענה | but her destiny is bitter as wormwood, |
| חדה כחרב פיות | sharp as an edged sword.  (Prov 5,3-4) |

*For study*
Gen 49,10.

*Cross-references*
CHIASMUS.

### 7.7 Strophic Patterns: the Pentacolon

The five-line strophe can be divided into two broad classes: those with a chiastic or concentric structure and those without. These will be considered in turn. The concentric pattern can be symbolised as ABCB'A'—for example, Isa 55,8-9:[81]

| | | |
|---|---|---|
| כי | | For |
| לא מחשבותי מחשבותיכם | A | my thoughts are not your thoughts, |
| ולא דרכיכם דרכי | B | nor your ways my ways; |
| כי־גבהו שמים מארץ | C | for as the sky is higher than the earth, |
| כן גבהו דרכי מדרכיכם | B' | so are my ways than your ways, |
| ומחשבתי ממחשבתיכם | A' | and my thoughts than your thoughts. |

Similarly, Isa 28,12; Jer 2,27-28; 30,16[82], Am 5,5[83]; Ps 104,29-30; and Prov 23,13-14. Related is the chiastic sequence AABCC as in Hos 14,10:

---

81. Omitting נאם יהוה as editorial.
82. Unless part of the larger sequence Jer 30,16-18; cf. J.R. Lundbom, *Jeremiah: A Study in Ancient Hebrew Rhetoric* (SBL Dissertation Series 18; Missoula, 1975) 150 n. 90.
83. Unless a hexacolon (including the colon immediately before these lines).

| | | |
|---|---|---|
| מי חכם ויבן אלה | A | Whoever is wise should understand these things, |
| נבון וידעם | A' | (whoever) can understand should know them; |
| כי־ישרים דרכי יהוה | B | for Yahweh's roads are straight: |
| וצדקים ילכו בם | C | upright men walk on them |
| ופשעים יכשלו בם | C' | but rebels stumble in them. |

Pentacola without a chiastic pattern are rarer and consequently cannot be grouped. Examples are Obd 11 and Ps 146,7b-9a:

| | |
|---|---|
| יהוה מתיר אסורים | Yahweh sets prisoners free, |
| יהוה פקח עורים | Yahweh 'gives sight to the blind',[84] |
| יהוה זקף כפופים | Yahweh straightens the bowed, |
| יהוה אהב צדיקים | Yahweh loves upright men, |
| יהוה שמר את־גרים | Yahweh guards visitors. |

See, further, Am 5,8 and Ps 146,6-7a. Also, Isa 51,11.

## 7.8 *Higher Strophic Units*

The lengthier a strophic pattern the fewer examples occur, so that this section will do little more than list texts.

*Six-line strophes* (hexacola, sestets or sixains) include those with chiasmus (ABCCBA: Isa 6,10; 65,18; Am 5,4-5; Zech 2,12-13; and Job 33,20-22) or its variants (ABCCBD: Jer 4,29; ABA: Jer 4,11-12a; Lam 2,4; cf. Isa 5,20; Am 2,11-12). Non-chiastic are Mal 1,6; Job 13,20-22; etc.

The *seven-line strophe* includes Am 5,4-5 (unless a hexacolon, see above) and Ps 12,4-5 (which is chiastic):

| | | |
|---|---|---|
| יכרת יהוה | A | Amputate may *Yahweh* |
| כל שפתי חלקות | B | all smooth LIPS, |
| לשון מדברת גדלות | C | every TONGUE speaking twistedly; |
| אשר אמרו | D | those saying: |
| ללשננו נגביר | C' | 'By our TONGUE are we great, |
| שפתינו אתנו | B' | our LIPS: our weapon; |
| מי אדון לנו | A' | who more *master* than us?'[85] |

*Octave strophes* (octocola) are Nb 12,6-8 and Jer 4,14-16 (both chiastic); Ruth 1,8-9 (if poetry), and, of course, the twenty-two stanzas that make up Ps 119.

---

84. An idiom for 'freeing captives'; cf. Paul, *JAOS* 88 (1968) 182 and n. 21, following Stummer, *JBL* 26 (1945) 180.

85. For details cf. Watson, 'Chiastic Patterns', 131.

Strophes of *ten lines* may be Ez 26,17-18 and Prov 6,16-19. Eleven-line units are discussed below, under ACROSTICS.

A particularly good example is Joel 3,1-2a (EVV 2,28-29) where the gender-pattern makes the 5-line structure (not including the introductory monocolon) self-evident:

|  |  |  |
|---|---|---|
|  |  | (Thereafter, the day shall come when) |
| אשפוך את רוחי על כל בשר | f + m | I will pour out my spirit (f.) on all flesh (m.): |
| ונבאו בניכם ובנותיכם | m + f | and your sons (m.) and your daughters (f.) will prophesy, |
| זקניכם חלמות יחלמון | m + f | your ancients (m.) will dream dreams (f.), |
| בחוריכם חזינות יראו | m + f | your youths (m.) see visions (f.)— |
| וגם על העברים ועל השפחות | m + f | even on slaves (m.) and handmaidens (f.). |

An example of a complete poem set out in quatrain stanzas is Ps 114; it is worth looking at because it will help establish the distinction between strophe and stanza even though here the two labels coincide.

| | |
|---|---|
| בצאת ישראל ממצרים | I |
| בית יעקב מעם לעז | |
| היתה יהודה לקדשו | |
| ישראל ממשלותו | |
| | |
| הים ראה וינם | II |
| הירדן יסב לאחור | |
| ההרים רקדו כאילים | |
| גבעות כבני־צאן | |
| | |
| מה־לך הים כי תנוס | III |
| הירדן תסב לאחור | |
| ההרים תרקדו כאילים | |
| גבעות כבני־צאן | |
| | |
| מלפני אדון חולי ארץ | IV |
| מלפני אלוה יעקב | |
| ההפכי הצור אגם־מים | |
| חלמיש למעינו־מים | |

| | | |
|---|---|---|
| I | 1 | When Israel went out of Egypt, |
| | | House Jacob from unintelligible people, |
| | 2 | Judah became his sanctuary, |
| | | Israel his dominion. |

II   3       The sea looked and fled,
             the Jordan turned back,
     4       the mountains gambolled like rams,
             the hills like young sheep.

III  5       What ailed you, Sea, that you fled?
             O Jordan, that you turned back?
     6       O Mountains that you gambolled like rams?
             O hills, like young sheep?

IV   7       In the Lord's presence, dance, Earth!
             in the presence of Jacob's deity,
     8       who converted rock into a water-pool,
             granite into water-springs.

Although within each stanza there seems to be some grouping into
couplets, particularly in view of the word-pairs ('Israel // Jacob',
'mountains // hills', etc.), the sense and the forward thrust indicate
units of 4-lines. The resulting symmetry is rare, but it does show that
balanced stanzas were by no means excluded. There is, too, an
element of chiasmus, stanzas I and IV corresponding, and II being
echoed even more closely by III.[86]

*For study*
A particularly clear example is Hos 13,7.

### 7.9 *Acrostics and Related Patterns*

*The alphabetic acrostic*
In an acrostic poem, the first letter[87] of each line follows a certain
sequence. Usually, this sequence is alphabetic, so that each line
begins with a successive letter of the alphabet. So, in Ps 111

| | | |
|---|---|---|
| אודה יהוה בכל לבב | א | 1 I will praise Yahweh with all my heart, |
| בסוד ישרים ועדה | ב | in the council of the upright and the assembly. |
| גדלים מעשי יהוה | ג | 2 Great are Yahweh's works, |
| דרושים לכל חפציהם | ד | to be pondered by all who enjoy them. |
| הוד והדר פעלו | ה | 3 Majestic splendour his deed, |
| וצדקתו עמדת לעד | ו | his honest-dealing lasts for ever. |

---

86. Van der Lugt, *Strofische Structuren*, 388-389, also acknowledges the symmetry
here, but combines stanzas II and III into a single unit.
87. Or, in Babylonian cuneiform, the first sign (see below).

| | | |
|---|---|---|
| זכר עשה לנפלאתיו | ז | 4 A record he achieved by his wonders, |
| חנון ורחום יהוה | ח | mercifully compassionate Yahweh. |
| טרף נתן ליראיו | ט | 5 Food gave he to his followers, |
| יזכר לעולם בריתו | י | he remembered his ancient covenant. |
| כח מעשיו הגיד לעמו | כ | 6 Power, by his works, he showed his people, |
| לתת להם נחלת גוים | ל | giving them the inheritance of nations. |
| מעשי ידיו אמת ומשפט | מ | 7 His handiwork is true justice, |
| נאמנים כל פקודיו | נ | dependable all his precepts, |
| סמוכים לעד לעולם | ס | 8 Upheld for utter eternity, |
| עשוים באמת וישר | ע | made by upright truth. |
| פדות שלח לעמו | פ | 9 Deliverance he sent his people, |
| צוה לעולם בריתו | צ | ordaining for ever his covenant. |
| קדוש ונורא שמו | ק | Fearsomely holy is his Name. |
| ראשית חכמה יראת יהוה | ר | 10 The inception of wisdom is fear of Yahweh, |
| שכל טוב לכל עשיהם | ש | good understanding to those who acquire it. |
| תהלתו עמדת לעד | ת | His praise lasts for ever.[88] |

Each colon begins with a different letter, the letters being in alphabetic order. Two aspects of the device are immediately apparent: the highly *artificial* nature of such a scheme and its *non-oral* character, these poems being intended to appeal to the eye rather than the ear. The basic pattern underwent various modifications, such as the arrangement of eight couplets each beginning with the same letter, as part of a long acrostic (Ps 119, see below), but the essential idea remained the same.

Acrostics and alphabetic acrostics are also known outside Hebrew literature. Although none has turned up in the Ugaritic texts,[89] *sentence-acrostics* or *name-acrostics* are to be found in Akkadian. The Babylonian 'Theodicy', for example, is a long poem of 27 stanzas. Each stanza has 11 lines, and within a stanza, every line begins with the same cuneiform sign. In this way the sentence *a-na-ku sa-ag-gi-il-ki-[i-na-am-u]b-bi-ib ma-áš-ma-šu ka-ri-bu ša i-li ú šar-ri* is spelt

---

88. The translation partly follows Dahood, *Psalms III*, 121ff., with some modifications.
89. Practice alphabets have been found on what must have been exercise tablets; see *KTU* 5.1-5.22. Note 5.1, with fifteen words beginning with *y* and 5.8, a list of five PN's starting with *il-*.

out.[90] Another acrostic simply spells $^d$*na-bu-u*, 'the god Nabû'.[91] Attempts have been made to detect sentence- or name-acrostics of this kind in Hebrew, but the results are not convincing.[92]

## Alphabetic acrostics in Hebrew

The following alphabetic acrostics occur in Hebrew: Nah 1,2-8; Pss 9; 10; 25; 34; 37; 111; 112; 119; 145; Prov 31,10-31; Lam 1-4; Sir 51,13-20. Note, too, Ps 155. Before any conclusions can be drawn it is worthwhile looking briefly at each of these poems.

*Nah 1,2-8.* Most recently studied by Christensen,[93] the poem constitutes only half an acrostic (on partial acrostics, see below), covering the letters א to י. The distribution is: א 7 cola; for each of the other letters, 2 cola, totalling 24 lines. However, the text is in some disorder: in v. 4 אמלל replaces a ד-word (דאב?); v. 6 reads לפני זעמו for an expected זעמו לפני; the exact stichometry of vv. 7-8 is uncertain. These displacements argue against the mnemonic value of acrostics.

*Pss 9-10.* These two psalms were originally two semi-acrostics, Ps 9 running from א to ר, and Ps 10 from ל to ת. However, certain acrostic-letters are missing, notably ד in v. 7, Ps 9,7; מ in Ps 10,3 and the letters ס צ. Various attempts at reconstruction have been made,[94] some more drastic than others, but the alphabetic sequence in Ps 10 is by no means clear.

Ps 9 allots 4 cola to א (and each begins with א), and to most of the other letters, and 6 each to ג, ה and ר (ignoring the final monocolon); י only has 2. The resulting total is 44 (+ final line), which is what could be expected if each letter were assigned four cola (11 × 4 = 44). In other words, the poem comprises 22 bicola. Further, the envelope figure created by vv. 6-7 and v. 19 indicates the poem is a complete unity. Ps 10 is too obscure for further evaluation.

90. Meaning 'I, Saggil-kinām-ubbib the incantation-priest, am adorant of god and king'; for details cf. *BWL*, 63.

91. A prayer to Nābû; both the first and last syllables of every line belong to the same acrostic. For this and other acrostic poems cf. *BWL*, 67, and the translations in Seux, *Hymnes*, 115-128. Note that no acrostic antedates 1000 BC.

92. Surveyed by Driver, *Semitic Writing*, 207-209 (and 276); to his bibliography add B. Lindars, 'Is Psalm II an acrostic poem?', *VT* 17 (1967) 60-67, and Bergler, *VT* 29 (1979) 257-288 (on Lam 5). In later Hebrew such acrostics were used extensively; cf. Marcus: 1947. For a possible acrostic in Song, cf. Webster, *JSOT* 22 (1982) 85-86. An extreme example is proposed by Schedl, *BZ* 26 (1982) 249-251.

93. D.L. Christensen, 'The Acrostic of Nahum Reconsidered', *ZAW* 87 (1975) 17-30, with bibliography.

94. See Driver, *Semitic Writing*, 200-207 (and 275-276).

*Ps 25.* A full acrostic, with a final ף-verse instead of a ו-verse (in addition to the ף-verse within the poem).[95] The distribution of cola to letters is again uneven, but the sum total is 44 lines (22 × 2). Keywords repeated throughout show the psalm to be a unity and not simply a conglomeration.

*Ps 34.* Here again a final ף-verse replaces the ו-line. Certain keywords are used, notably יהוה (× 15) and כל, 'all' (× 7).[96] The tricolon in v. 7

| | |
|---|---|
| זה עני קרא | This poor man called, |
| ויהוה שמע | and Yahweh heard, |
| ומכל צרותיו הושיעו | and from all his anguish saved him. |

is compressed to a bicolon in v. 18 and has echoes in vv. 5 and 20. This combination of recurring pattern and keywords gives the psalm its unity.

*Ps 37.* A wisdom poem divided up into almost independent stanzas, mostly of 4 lines each. There are four examples of 6-liners (ז ח ב) and 5-liners (ש ת נ ס), the exceptional 7-liner being ה. Normal alphabetic sequence is followed, slightly obscure at vv. 28b and 39. There is strong alliteration in v. 20 (final stanza of first half), and in vv. 34-35 as well as in the penultimate stanza, but no clear pattern emerges. Explanatory כי, 'for', is used some nine times.

*Ps 111.* The text has been set out above. Curiously, although each single colon is assigned a separate letter of the alphabet, the poem is written in couplets.

*Ps 112.* The full alphabet is used, again for single cola, and the stanza-division cuts across this pattern. The poem opens and closes with a tricolon. Much of the vocabulary from Ps 111 is used, and even some expressions ('and his honest-dealing lasts for ever', vv. 3b, 9b; 'mercifully compassionate', v. 4b).[97]

*Ps 145.* Apart from the ו-verse[98] the normal alphabet is used. 44 cola (+ a final monocolon) make up the poem without the missing verse, suggesting its omission was intentional. Noteworthy are the use of keywords[99] and the ingenious partial acrostic based on מלך, 'king', at the centre of the poem.

95. A phenomenon discussed below.
96. See Liebreich, *HUCA* 27 (1956) 181ff., and contrast Kugel, *Idea*, 47-48.
97. P. Auffret, 'Essai sur la structure littéraire des psaumes CXI et CXII', *VT* 30 (1980) 257-279.
98. Found in 11QPs^a and some of the versions.
99. See Liebreich, *HUCA* 27 (1956) 181ff.

*Ps 119*. The full 22-letter alphabet is used, the poem comprising 22 eight-line stanzas. The remarkable thing about the psalm is that within a stanza every line begins with the letter of that stanza. The result is a sustained acrostic of 8 × 22 lines or 176 verses. However, some are tricola.

In spite of the opportunity the poet had of demonstrating his skill with vocabulary, the choice of words for verse-initial is, in general, very poor. For instance five of the ט-words are טוב, 'good'; nearly all the מ-words simply begin with the preposition מן, 'from'. And, within the poem, the range of vocabulary is very poor. This is offset by the skilled use of many poetic patterns (notably the pivot pattern)[100] and devices.

*Prov 31,10-31*. This poem of praise for the good housewife[101] can be divided into two halves א—ר (vv. 10-20) and ל—ת (vv. 21-31). The standard alphabet is used, resulting in 23 + 23 (i.e. 46) cola. The first half is a series of couplets broken only by a tricolon at v. 15 (ו), its mathematical centre. The last two verses (19-20) form a chiastic quatrain. The second half (vv. 21-31) is also in couplets, with a tricolon at v. 30.

Use of alliteration is sparing (mainly vv. 11 ב and 21 ל). Interesting is the play on *yod/yad* and *kap* in vv. 20-21, combined with the chiastic arrangement כף יד יד כף.[102]

*Lam 1-4*. Chapters 1 and 2 are alphabetic acrostics only for the first word of each stanza (= verse); 3 and 4 follow the pattern of Ps 119, except that for each chapter only 3 verses are assigned to a letter.

*Sir 51,13-30*. A 50-line acrostic, mainly in couplets (tricola at vv. 15, 22, 25 and 27) largely arranged in quatrains. An additional ף-verse comes at the end (v. 30). Skehan maintains that 'there is here a degree of continuity not always to be found in Hebrew acrostics' and proposes a threefold division on the basis of the 3 m.s. suffix at vv. 17, 22 and 29-30.[103] The poem is akin, as Skehan notes, to Sir 6,18-37 (discussed below).

---

101. Besides the commentaries cf. M.B. Cook, 'The Marriageable Maiden of Prov. 31:10-31', *JNES* 13 (1954) 137-140.
102. On such ABBA quatrains cf. Watson, 'Chiastic Patterns'. The same play on the names of the alphabet-letters is apparent in Ps 119,73a; note the play on *samek* in Pss 37,12.24; 112,8; 119,116; 145,14.
103. P.W. Skehan, 'The Acrostic Poem in Sirach 51:13-30', *HTR* 64 (1971) 387-400; see also Sanders in *Dupont-Sommer FS*, 1971, 429-438. And Muraoka, *JSJ* 10 (1979) 168-178.

*Apostrophe to Zion*. Found in the Qumran texts, the 'Apostrophe to Zion' is an acrostic of 16 couplets framed by an opening and a final tricolon (or: 22 lines).[104] Significant is the use of the keyword 'Zion' which occurs 6[105] times, each time at the end of an initial colon (vv. 1,2,10,13,18).

## Ugaritic

Although no actual alphabetic acrostics have been found, it is remarkable that so many strophes and stanzas in Ugaritic tend to begin with an identical letter. This is often achieved simply by repetition of the same initial word or particle, but the effect remains the same. Some examples will show this. First, non-repetitive instances:

| | |
|---|---|
| *atr tn tn hlk* | After two, two went; |
| *atr tlt klhm* | after three, all of them. |
| *ahd bth ysgr* | The single man closed his house, |
| *almnt škr tškr* | the widow hired herself out. |

(*CTA* 14 iv 182-185 [initial *a*])

Also: *CTA* 14 iii 159-160 (*lqh, lla*); 17 ii 27-30 (a clear tricolon: *apnk, ap.hn, alp*); 19 iii 154-155 (and parallels: *'nt, 'nt, 'db*); however, even in these texts repetition is hardly ever avoided. Sheer repetition is much the more frequent:

| | |
|---|---|
| *mtb il mẓll bnh* | The dwelling of El is his son's shelter, |
| *mtb rbt atrt ym* | the dwelling of Lady 'Treader-on-the-Sea' |
| *mtb klt knyt* | is the dwelling of the noble brides, |
| *mtb pdry bt ar* | the dwelling of Pidray, mist-daughter, |
| *mẓll tly bt rb* | the shelter of Tallay daughter of showers, |
| *mtb arṣy bt y'bdr* | the dwelling of Arsay, daughter of Y'bdr. |

(*CTA* 4 iv 52-57 [and parallels])

Also *CTA* 4 v 113-116 (four lines beginning *ḥš*); vi 47-54 (8 lines beginning *špq*); 6 v 11-19 (7 × initial *'lk*) and so on.[106] This can have implications for stichometry; for instance in *CTA* 16 i 25-27, *bn*, 'O

---

104. See P. Auffret, 'Structure littéraire de l'Hymne à Sion de 11QPs[a] XXII,1-15', *RevQ* 38 (1980) 203-211. Also, Muraoka, *JSJ* 10 (1979) 167.

105. Or seven times, following 4QPs[f] (v. 15).

106. It is conceivable that the initial letters in *CTA* 19 iii 115ff. may play on the root *bky*, 'to weep', but it is not certain.

son', is clearly anacrusis since the next three lines begin *al* ('do not').[107]

*Features of the acrostic*
The repertoire of words and phrases found in these acrostics is very limited. For example, much of Ps 111 is echoed in Ps 112. Outside the psalms, however, vocabulary tends to be less stereotyped. There is a tendency towards the use of *keywords*, e.g. צדיק, רשע, כרת, סמך, יהוה in Ps 37; כל in Pss 34 and 145; synonyms for 'law' in Ps 119.

Perhaps the most notable characteristic is the use of strong *alliteration*, but usually with no consistent patterns. The following types can be singled out:
—identical initial letter for consecutive cola:

אל תתחר במרעים
אל תקנא בעשי עולה    (Ps 37,1[108]) = א

—identical, consecutive letters:

מלכותך מלכות כל עלמים    (Ps 145,13[109]) = מ

—same initial letter for first and last word of colon (or strophe):

טוב עשית עם עבדך יהוה כדברך טוב    (Ps 119,65[110]) = ט

Alliteration is evident in Nah 1,2-3a; Lam 2,16 and particularly in Ps 145,11-13.[111]

Another feature of acrostics is frequent *hendiadys*, perhaps to compensate for the bitty effect of the alphabetic sequence imposed on these poems. So, in Nah 1,3d בסופה ובשערה דרכו is probably to be translated: 'In the tempestuous whirlwind his road'. Likewise, Ps 37,2b ('green grass'); 111,4b ('mercifully gracious' = 112,4b); and 111,9b; 25,8.10.21.

---

107. See W.G.E. Watson, 'Quasi-Acrostics in Ugaritic Poetry', *UF* 12 (1980) 445-447, and add *KTU* 1.96 which has line-initial *'n* five times. Also, *CTA* 4 vii 49-52 (with anacrusis).
108. Also Pss 37,6-7; 119,103.174.58b.48c.64c.
109. Ps 119,124.131.138.142.154.156.157.170; Ps 37,3.18.23; Ps 145,1.10.12.
110. And Pss 119,130.134.139; 37,18-19.20. This is also a feature of the Babylonian acrostic to the god Nābû.
111. For details, cf. W.G.E. Watson, 'Reversed Rootplay in Ps 145', *Bib* 62 (1981) 101-102.

*Strophe, stanza and the acrostic*
The alphabetic sequence is only an approximate guide to the demarcation of a poem into strophes and stanzas. Letter-distribution results in the following table:

*One letter*

| | |
|---|---|
| per colon | Pss 111; 112; Sir 51. |
| per bicolon | Pss 25, 34, 145; Prov 31; Ps 119. |
| per 4 cola | Ps 37; Lam 4. |
| per 6 cola | Lam 1-3. |

However, closer inspection shows this distribution to be occasionally inexact; for instance, Lam 2,9 really comprises seven cola,[112] Lam 1,7 has eight. Also in Ps 119 some of the strophes are tricola (vv. 48.62.64.75.145.176). Accordingly, the presence of an alphabetic marker is not an automatic guide to strophic division. In one case, though, it is particularly helpful; and that is the 'pivot'-patterned bicolon (particularly frequent in Ps 119). When this pattern occurs in combination with colon-initial alliteration, the stichometry is remarkably clear. In v. 174 (a ת-verse),

| | |
|---|---|
| תאבתי לישועתך יהוה | I yearn for your salvation, Yahweh, |
| ( )תורתך שעשעי | your law is my delight, |

each colon begins with ת (ignoring the ubiquitous ו as secondary). See also v. 103. The same colon-initial marking occurs outside of the pivot pattern, as in

| | |
|---|---|
| חליתי פניך בכל לב | I entreat your favour with my whole heart, |
| חנני כאמרתך | pity me in accordance with your utterances. |
| | (Ps 119,58) |

In v. 64 the ABA structure is confirmed.

As regards stanza, the demarcation is much clearer: each of the 22 stanzas in Ps 119 is indicated by the repeated use of one letter; the same applies to Lam 1-4; with the other poems the stanza-structure ignores the acrostic device, so that other criteria have to be used. Perhaps Nah 1,2-8 has its unequal stanzas marked off by the alphabet.

*Functions of the acrostic*
Several proposals have been made to explain why certain poems

112. As do Lam 1,12.16.18.20.21; etc.

should be in acrostic form.[113] One commonly suggested is that with verses following the sequence of the alphabet, memorising was made easier.[114] However, this does not quite square with the apparently imperfect state of some texts or with disrupted sequences such as Nah 1,2-8 (ff.?), inversions (פ before ע in Lam 3 and 4), missing letters (ן in Ps 145; ד in Nah 1,4) and the difficulties of Ps 10.[115] Also, it is not quite certain who was intended to memorise such poems, which in any case were intended for reading rather than recitation.[116] It could be that the alphabet was taught in this way, but it seems unlikely.[117]

Two main functions can be singled out, either or both of which may have been operative for a particular poem: to convey the idea of completeness, and to display the author's skill.

—*Completeness*. By using every letter of the alphabet the poet was trying to ensure that his treatment of a particular topic was complete. At the same time, the reader gained the impression that the poem he was reading covered every angle. The use of keywords such as כל, 'all', would appear to confirm this view. Gottwald argues that Lam 1-4(5) 'offered a literary form corresponding to the completeness of grief, responsibility and hope which he [= the author] wished to communicate'.[118] A slightly different aspect of the same idea is conveyed by the frequent use of 'eternity', 'for all generations' and the like which occur so often in these poems.

—*To display skill*. By composing within the set framework of the alphabet, the poet was providing himself with a structure. He also had the first letters of at least 22 lines. At the same time, the acrostic pattern set a restriction on his free-ranging talent, forcing him to use his skill in a particular way. (The occasional deviations from the standard alphabetic sequence may have been due to the poet's creative talent overriding his self-imposed limits.) It is well known that Babylonian scribes delighted in virtuoso performances of their writing skills, especially when spelling their own names. Evidence for

---

113. See N. Gottwald, *Studies in the Book of Lamentations* (London, 1954), 23-32.
114. This is the general view. But see Gottwald.
115. Note, too, the missing ק in Ps 25, although this is compensated for by the repeated ר ש ר ש pattern in 18-19.
116. Marcus: 1947 thinks that instruction was conveyed in this way so it could be memorised easily and mentions Prov 31; Sir 51.
117. So Munch: 1936, 703-710.
118. N. Gottwald, *Studies in the Book of Lamentations* (London, 1954) 32.

this is provided by the acrostics mentioned above, one of which was based on the scribe's own name.

*Quasi-acrostics and partial acrostics*

Some of the acrostic poems use only half the alphabet; Nah 1,2-8 goes from א to מ ?; Ps 9 covers the first half of the alphabet, Ps 10 (it would seem) the second. Various explanations have been offered.[119] Partial acrostics also occur, for example Ps 145,11-13 (within a complete acrostic) and Song 4,9-11.[120] Such partial acrostics were perhaps extensions of initial alliteration.[121] Also Psalm 155.

*11-line and 22-line poems.* Poems of these lengths were obviously modelled on alphabetic acrostics, the restrictive feature of alphabetic sequence being lifted. Lam 5 consists of 22 couplets and is a freer form of the patterns used in Lam 1-4. The 22-verse structure, in fact, seems to characterise laments, notably Ps 38;[122] however, note Isa 10,27c-34.[123] Eleven line poems are: Job 9,25-35;[124] Jer 5,4-5; Hos 12,3-6. It is probably coincidence that the Babylonian 'Theodicy', an acrostic, is written in 11-line stanzas.

*Standard and non-standard alphabets*

Some of the acrostics, as has been noted, omit certain letters[125] or transpose some.[126] Particularly significant is the omission of ו in both Ps 25 and Ps 34, which is compensated for by an extra פ after the ת-verse. While Sir 51 has both the ו-verse and an additional פ-verse, Ps 155 has neither. It has been argued that at some stage in the development of the Hebrew alphabet, the פ replaced the ו.[127] If such

---

119. See Christensen, *ZAW* 87 (1975) 17-30.
120. For Ps 145 see above; on Song 4,9-11 cf. Paul, *IDBS*, 600.
121. See Skehan, *CBQ* 33 (1971) 137, and Auffret, *ZAW* 92 (1980) 369 n. 11.
122. So Dahood, *Psalms I*, 234; previously, Löhr: 1905, 197 (following Bickell).
123. D.L. Christensen, 'The March of Conquest in Isaiah X 27c-34', *VT* 26 (1976) 385-399.
124. See Skehan, *CBQ* 13 (1951) 125-142.
125. Ps 25 omits ק; Ps 37 an ע, Ps 145 a ו.
126. ע comes before פ in Lam 2,16-17; 3,46-51 and perhaps in Prov 31,25-26 and Ps 34,16-17.
127. Johnstone: 1978, 165-166 says: 'Because there are very few words which begin with *w*, writers of acrostic poems were faced with a problem when they reached the sixth letter of the alphabet. In Psalm 25 (though the occurrence of almost consecutive tricola in vv. 5 and 7 in place of the prevailing bicola suggests that the text may be disordered), and in Psalm 34, no verse beginning with *waw* occurs. Instead, a second verse beginning with *pe* is added at the end of both Psalms. That is, on occasion Hebrew omits consonantal *waw* from sixth position in the alphabet and replaces it at the end of the alphabet with *taw* with a related bilabial consonant'.

should prove to be the case then (i) there is no need to 'correct' the text of these poems, and (ii), perhaps a relative chronology for acrostics can be proposed. If so, Sir 51 would be earlier than both Pss 25 and 34.

*For study*

Prov 7,6-23; Ps 94; Jer 2,5-9; Nb 23,18-24; Ez 27,25b-32a; Sir 6,18-37; Sir 24; Job 8,2-22. Alliteration in texts such as Sir 51,13b-14a (ב); Ps 25,17 (צ); Nah 1,4b (למן); Lam 1,20 (ר); 2,5 (ב); 2,8 (ח); 3,52 (צ); Ps 119,143 (צ); etc.
Isa 51,11 ('joy').

## BIBLIOGRAPHY

Driver, *Semitic Writing*, 181.207-209.269ff.

Freedman, D.N. 'Acrostics and Metrics in Hebrew Poetry', *HTR* 65 (1972) 367-392.

Hillers, D.R. *Lamentations* (*AB* 7A; Garden City, 1972) xxiv-xxvii.

Johnstone, W. 'Cursive Phoenician and the Archaic Greek Alphabet', *Kadmos* 17 (1978) 151-166.

Löhr, M. 'Alphabetische und alphabetisierende Lieder im Alten Testament', *ZAW* 25 (1905) 173-198.

Marcus, R. 'Alphabetic Acrostics in the Hellenistic and Roman Periods', *JNES* 6 (1947) 109-115.

Munch, P.A. 'Die alphabetische Akrostichie in der jüdischen Psalmendichtung', *ZDMG* 90 (1936) 703-710.

Paul, S.M. 'Mnemonic Devices', *IDBS*, 600-602.

Piatti, T. 'I carmi alpfabetici della Bibbia chiave della metrica ebraica?', *Bib* 31 (1950) 281-315; 427-458 (281, n. 1).

Sweet, R.F.G. 'A pair of Double Acrostics in Akkadian', *Or* 38 (1969) 459-460.

Watson, W.G.E. 'Quasi-Acrostics in Ugaritic Poetry', *UF* 12 (1980) 445-447.

# 8

## VERSE-PATTERNS

### 8.1 *Introduction*

This section lists and describes various verse-patterns to be found in ancient Semitic poetry. The selection is by no means exhaustive nor can every example be set out or listed. It might well be asked what purpose such a list and the corresponding descriptions could serve. Can anything be gained from recognition of such patterns? The answer, given simply, is that the topic of verse-patterns is very profitable. First of all there is some confusion, even among scholars, concerning which patterns are which. The outline given here will help dispel some of the confusion that prevails. Further, each pattern has been used (by the poets) for a particular purpose; to appreciate the poetry better it is well worthwhile being able to determine which pattern is being used, and why. Also, as mentioned at the outset, not all the verse-patterns have been isolated and described. Study of those so far known will lead to the discovery of yet more verse structures as well as to more precise definition of known verse-patterns. Recognition of deviations from established patterns may also lead to a better understanding of the purpose and functions of the patterns. (Note that this Chapter overlaps, to some extent, with Chapter 7, STROPHE AND STANZA.)

### 8.2 *Chiasmus and Chiastic Patterns*

*Chiasmus*
By chiasmus is meant a series (a, b, c, ... ) and its inversion ( ... c, b, a) taken together as a combined unit. In Hebrew poetry such a unit is generally a parallel couplet, so that the combined (chiastic) unit would be a,b,c // c,b,a. The components of such a series are usually sub-units of the sentence, considered semantically or grammatically.

For example, Isa 40,12a:

מי מדד בשעלו מים   Who has measured the waters in his palm,
ושמים בזרת תכן   or set limits to the sky with a span?

where the semantic pattern is a-b-c // c'-b'-a'. Grammatical chiasmus
is present in Jer 4,5a:

הגידו ביהודה   Broadcast in Judah     (V—NP₂)
ובירושלם השמיעו   and in Jerusalem proclaim!   (NP₂—V).

When the components (a, b, c, etc.) are not parts of the sentence but
complete lines, then larger chiastic patterns emerge, as will be seen.
(Such components are usually designated by capitals: A, B, C, etc.)

Chiasmus is present in many literatures,[1] being by no means
confined to Hebrew poetry. Both Akkadian and Ugaritic use chiasmus,
but in neither language is it so developed as in Hebrew. Some
examples will be enough by way of illustration.

### Chiasmus in Ugaritic and Akkadian

Since this topic has been examined elsewhere[2] there is little need to
provide a string of examples. In *CTA* 17 ii 24-25 there is partial
chiasmus (NP₁ M V // V NP₁ M):

*dnil bth ymǵyn*     Daniel to his house did move,
*yštql dnil lhklh*     proceed did Daniel to his palace.

The Babylonian Epic of Erra uses chiasmus frequently, for instance
(I 144):

*zīmū'a tubbûma*     My countenance expressed haughtiness,
*galit niṭlī*     fury, my glance.

### Typology of chiasmus in Hebrew

Our chief concern here will be with the couplet, although chiasmus
(chiastic patterns) can extend over much longer sequences.

---

1. Notably in Italian; cf. A. Riva, 'La figura del chiasmo in un sonetto di Jacopo da
Lentini', *REI* 25 (1979) 145-160. On the theoretical background to chiastic parallelism
see above on SYMMETRY, ASYMMETRY and PARALLELISM, particularly under 'chiasmus
or mirror symmetry (reflexive congruence)'.

2. In Ugaritic cf. J.W. Welch, 'Chiasmus in Ugaritic' in Welch, *Chiasmus*, 36-49. A
notable example is *KTU* 1.96 where the sequence *bty + btt* ('flatterer, flatteress')—*mhr*
('assembly')—*phr* ('potter')—*tgr* ('gatekeeper') is inverted to become *tgr, phr, mhr, bty*
+ *btt*; cf. de Moor, *UF* 11 (1979) 647-648. In Akkadian cf. R.F. Smith, 'Chiasmus in
Sumero-Akkadian', in Welch, *Chiasmus*, 17-35. See, also, Shea, *ZAW* 92 (1980) 380.

1. *Mirror chiasmus* is very rare indeed; the second line repeats the components of the first in reverse sequence, as in Isa 22,22:

וּפָתַח וְאֵין סֹגֵר   He shall open and no one will shut,

וְסָגַר וְאֵין פֹּתֵחַ   he shall shut, and no one will open.

2. *Complete chiasmus*: all the elements comprising the second colon are set out in the reverse order of the first. Two main types belong here: ab // b'a' and abc // c'b'a'. Taking the second type to start with, an example is Job 20,6:

אִם־יַעֲלֶה לַשָּׁמַיִם שִׂיאוֹ   Even if his height reaches the sky,

וְרֹאשׁוֹ לָעָב יַגִּיעַ   and his head touches the clouds.

See, too, (as abc // c'b'a') Isa 14,30; 29,17; 42,4; Pss 7,17; 147,4; Job 20,1; 32,14; Prov 13,6. The other pattern (ab // b'a') is evident in Jer 2,19:

תְּיַסְּרֵךְ רָעָתֵךְ   You will be punished by your wickedness,

וּמְשֻׁבוֹתַיִךְ תּוֹכִחֻךְ   your defections will convict you;

and in Dt 32,16; Isa 32,6; Ez 19,7; Hos 2,2; Ps 139,1; Lam 5,21; etc.

3. *Split-member chiasmus* is a further variation of complete chiasmus, where the /a/ and /b/ components are themselves split into yet smaller elements. So, in Prov 7,21 (a-bc // b'c'-a')

הִטַּתּוּ בְּרֹב לִקְחָהּ   *She led him on* with her many persuasions,

בְּחֵלֶק שְׂפָתֶיהָ תַּדִּיחֶנּוּ   by her smooth talk *she pressed him*,

chiasmus is effected simply by the alteration in position of the underlined sequences. Likewise: Isa 11,1; Ps 22,13; Job 13,12; Lam 3,22. Other variations include ab-c // c'-a'b' (Hos 4,9; Job 10,15); ab-cd // c'd'-a'b' (Isa 33,4; Job 3,6; Prov 4,14).

4. *Partial chiasmus* comprises a set of patterns in which the position of one element remains unchanged and can be considered as standing outside the chiasmus. These patterns include abc // c'b' (with the element a unaffected); ab-c // b'a'-c (c unaffected) and a-bc // a-cb. The abc // c'b'a' pattern belongs here, too. In abc // c'b', the unchanged element is at the beginning, for example, 'who rides' in Dt 33,26b:

רֹכֵב שָׁמַיִם בְּעֶזְרֶךָ   *Who rides* through the sky to your help,

וּבְגַאֲוָתוֹ שְׁחָקִים   and in his majesty, the heavens.

Also Isa 49,18; Hab 1,3; Song 1,4.

With a /c/ element outside the pattern (ab-c // b'a'-c') see Isa 27,5;
49,22; Pss 21,9; 143,1. For an unchanged /a/ element: Nb 24,18; Isa
59,3b; Prov 2,2.

### Chiasmus and line-forms

Grammatical analysis (rather than semantic analysis, as above)
provides the following correlation between chiasmus and line-forms:[3]

| | | |
|---|---|---|
| Type II A i | 2 = NP₁ V // V NP₁ | e.g. Isa 2,11; 24,18; Jer 12,1. |
| | 3 = V NP₁ // NP₁ V | e.g. Isa 28,18; 32,3.10; 35,5; Jer 48,41; Hos 4,13.[4] |
| Type II B ii | 2 = V M // M V | e.g. Isa 6,10; 10,4; 48,1; 65,4; Jer 4,5; 6,15; 48,11; Ez 19,12; Am 4,7; 8,12. |
| | 3 = M V // V M | e.g. Isa 16,8; Jer 2,36; 23,12; Hab 2,1; and Jer 17,8; Ez 26,16; Hos 7,14. |
| Type II C ii | 2 = V NP₂ // NP₂ V | e.g. Isa 3,15; 5,24; 10,1; 13,11 and many more. |
| | 3 = NP₂ V // V NP₂ | e.g. Isa 41,22; 47,3; Am 5,11. |

### Other types of chiasmus

The couplet is the standard unit for chiasmus. There are also chiastic
(aba') *monocola* (see MONOCOLON) and *tricola* (also treated under
TRICOLON). Briefly, the chiastic tricolon is of two kinds:

1. ABA strophes, where the two outer lines are identical; such
tricola are very rare—examples being confined to Ps 27,14 and
Ps 118,15-16 (set out as follows):

| | |
|---|---|
| ימין יהוה עשה חיל | (A) Yahweh's right hand achieved victory. |
| ימין יהוה רוממה | (B) Yahweh's right hand was exalted. |
| ימין יהוה עשה חיל | (A) Yahweh's right hand achieved victory.[5] |

2. ABA' strophes, the outermost lines being in parallelism, for
example, Prov 17,25:

| | |
|---|---|
| כעס לאביו | (A) A worry to his father |
| בן כסיל | (B) is a foolish son |
| וממר ליולדתו | (A') and bitterness to 'her who bore him'. |

By far the commoner, ABA' tricola include Isa 30,31; Am 1,3; Nah
3,17; Ps 86,12; Song 1,11.

---

3. See Collins, *Line-forms*, 94-95.106-107.114-115.
4. And the 'semantic set' given by Collins, *Line-forms*, 95.
5. Translation: Dahood, *Psalms III*, 154.

Longer chiastic units include the ABB'A' quatrain, chiastic pentacola, hexacola, heptacola, etc.—all dealt with more fully in the
chapter on strophe and stanza.

*The functions of chiasmus*

By and large, the basic function of chiasmus is to relieve the
monotony of persistent parallelism. At a more specific level, chiastic
patterns can be either structural in function, or expressive. Structural
chiastic patterns, as the name indicates, contribute to the overall
shape of a poem or poetic sub-unit. Expressive chiasmus, on the
other hand, describes chiasmus as it is used to express a variety of
modes, ranging from merismus to antithesis.

1. *Structural functions.* Fairly often a chiastic couplet is used *to
open a stanza or poem*, e.g. Hab 2,1:

| | |
|---|---|
| על־משמרתי אעמדה | At my post will I stand, |
| ואתיצבה על־מצור | I will position myself on the watch-tower. |

Also Nb 23,7; Isa 32,3; Jer 20,14; Ps 92,2; Job 26,5. The same
function can be attributed to chiastic tricola (Gen 27,39; Hab 2,6;
Ps 32,8; Job 10,1).

Similarly, a chiastic couplet can *close a poem or stanza*—as in
Job 30,31:

| | |
|---|---|
| ויהי לאבל כנרי | Turned to mourning has my lyre, |
| ועגבי לקול בכים | and my flute to weepers' voices. |

Further: Isa 14,20-21; Jer 8,8-9; Song 1,11. Again, the same applies to
chiastic tricola: Isa 51,3; Ez 34,6; Ps 9,15; Prov 5,22.

Chiasmus can *link* the components of a strophe (e.g. Nah 1,2) as
well as *indicating the midpoint* of a poem (examples: Jer 2,27-28;
Prov 1,26-27).

2. *Expressive functions.* A very common way of expressing *merismus*
or a totality is to use chiasmus: Isa 40,26b (with reference to the
stars):

| | |
|---|---|
| המוציא במספר צבאם | He who led out by numbers their host, |
| לכלם בשם יקרא | all of them called by name. |

Also: Jer 6,7; Ez 17,23; Hab 3,3; Job 7,18; Sir 3,1. Merismus can also
be expressed by a chiastic tricolon,

| | |
|---|---|
| כל חיתו שדי | (A) All you beasts of the field |
| אתיו לאכל | (B) come to eat, |
| כל־חיתו ביער | (A') all you beasts of the forest (Isa 56,9), |

the clue to merismus being the use of 'all'. Also Isa 25,7; Ps 9,15; Job 34,37.

Chiasmus also expresses *reversal* of existing state, as in Zeph 3,19:

| | |
|---|---|
| והושעתי את־הצלעה | I will rescue the lost, |
| והנדחה אקבץ | and the dispersed I will gather. |

Also Isa 13,10b; Ez 17,4b; Mic 4,6; Mal 3,24a; Song 1,6; etc.

Emphatic *negation* or *prohibition* is effectively underscored by this poetic device, too. For example Prov 25,6:

| | |
|---|---|
| אל־תתהדר לפני־מלך | Do not put yourself forward in the king's presence, |
| ובמקום גדלים אל־תעמד | and in high places do not take your seat. |

Further: Jer 6,25; Sir 7,5; 11,8. Simple negation: Isa 27,11b; emphatic denial: Ps 101,7; etc.

Finally, chiasmus can express *antithesis* or contrast and is fairly frequent in the Book of Proverbs; for example Prov 10,3:

| | |
|---|---|
| לא־ירעיב יהוה נפש צדיק | Yahweh does not make the upright go hungry with respect to appetite, |
| והות רשעים יהדף | but he disappoints the craving of wicked men. |

And Prov 10,4.12; 12,20; 13,24; 14,4; etc. as well as Ps 38,8; Job 10,5; Sir 10,10.

## Chiasmus in long passages

As has already been noted, chiasmus is by no means confined to the couplet. Chiastic patterns can be found in the following:[6]

| | |
|---|---|
| Jgs 9,8-15 | —gender chiasmus (m., f., f., m.) combined with a refrain-like structure; |
| 2 Sm 1,19-27 | —a combination of refrain and chiasmus; |
| Isa 1,21-26 | —the chiastic pattern is ABCDED'C'B'A'; |
| Isa 28,15-18 | —an ABCC'B'A' pattern; |
| Jer 2,5-9 | —chiasmus of content, repeated words and catchphrases; |
| Hos 12,3-6[7]; | |
| Am 9,1-4[8]; | |
| Ps 136,10-15[9]; | |

6. For Song cf. W.H. Shea, 'The Chiastic Structure of the Song of Songs', *ZAW* 92 (1980) 378-396; Webster, *JSOT* 22 (1982) 73-93.

7. Holladay, *VT* 16 (1966) 53-64.

8. N.W. Lund, *Chiasmus in the New Testament* (Chapel Hill, 1942) 86-87.

9. Auffret, *VT* 27 (1977) 1-12.

Job 32,6-10 —chiastic arrangement of repeated words;
Qoh 3,2-8 —complex chiastic pattern of positive and negative assertions (and many more).[10]

*For study*
Ps 95,1-7; Isa 16,6-12; 29,1-3; 51,1-11; Jer 5,1-8; 50,2-46; Hos 8,9-13; Pss 7; 15; 29; 30; 51; 59; 72; 105,1-11; 137; 139; Prov 30,1-4.

*Cross-references*
PARALLELISM, STANZA, STROPHE.

BIBLIOGRAPHY

Alden, R.L. 'Chiastic Psalms (I): A Study in the Mechanics of Semitic Poetry in Psalms 1-50', *JETS* 17 (1974) 11-28.
—'Chiastic Psalms (II): A Study in the Mechanics of Semitic Poetry in Psalms 51-100', *JETS* 19 (1976) 191-200.
Boadt, L. 'The A:B:B:A chiasm of identical roots in Ezekiel', *VT* 25 (1975) 693-99.
Ceresko, A.R. 'The A:B:B:A Word Pattern in Hebrew and Northwest Semitic, with Special Reference to the Book of Job', *UF* 7 (1975) 73-88.
—'The Chiastic Word Pattern in Hebrew', *CBQ* 38 (1976) 303-11.
—'The Function of Chiasmus in Hebrew Poetry', *CBQ* 40 (1978) 1-10.
Dahood, M.J. 'Chiasmus in Job: A Text-Critical and Philological Criterion', *Myers FS*, 119-30.
—'The Chiastic Breakup in Isaiah 58,7', *Bib* 57 (1976) 105.
Holladay, W.L.'Chiasmus, the Key to Hosea XII 3-6', *VT* 16 (1966) 53-64.
Holmgren, F. 'Chiastic structure in Isaiah LI 1-11', *VT* 19 (1969) 196-201.
Kselman, J.S. 'Semantic-Sonant Chiasmus in Biblical Poetry', *Bib* 58 (1977) 219-23.
—'The ABCB Pattern: further Examples', *VT* 32 (1982) 224-29.
Lichtenstein, M.H. 'Chiasm and Symmetry in Proverbs 31', *CBQ* 44 (1982) 202-11.
Lundbom, J. *Jeremiah: A Study in Ancient Hebrew Rhetoric* (SBL Dissertation Series 18; Missoula, 1975).
Marco, A. di 'Der Chiasmus in der Bibel. 1. Teil. Ein Beitrag zur strukturellen Stilistik', *LB* 36 (1975) 21-97.
—*Il Chiasmo nella bibbia. Contributi di stilistica strutturale* (Turin, 1980).
Porten, B.—Rappaport, U. 'Poetic Structure in Genesis IX 7', *VT* 21 (1971) 363-69.
Riding, C.B. 'Psalm 95 1-7c as a Large Chiasm', *ZAW* 88 (1976) 418.
Watson, W.G.E. 'Chiastic Patterns'.
—'Further Examples of Semantic-Sonant Chiasmus', *CBQ* 46 (1984) 31-33.
—'Strophic Chiasmus in Ugaritic Poetry', *UF* 15 (1983) 259-70.

10. For example Isa 2,6-22; Ps 58; Lam 2,1-22; see under 'For study'.

Welch *Chiasmus*.

Wenham, G.J. 'The coherence of the flood narrative', *VT* 28 (1978) 336-48.

Yee, G.A. 'An Analysis of Prov 8 22-31 According to Style and Structure',
    *ZAW* 94 (1982) 58-66.

See the references given in Welch, *Chiasmus*.

### 8.3 *The Terrace Pattern (Anadiplosis) and Sorites*

*The terrace pattern and related patterns*

The terrace pattern[11] is simply a form of repetition where the last
part of a line is repeated as the beginning of the next line.

| | |
|---|---|
| אמרתי | I said: |
| לא־אראה יה | I'll never see *Yah* |
| יה בארץ החיים | *Yah* in the land of the living. (Isa 38,11[12]) |

This can be represented graphically as:

and there should be no confusion with either staircase parallelism[13]
or the pivot-patterned couplet. The similarity with staircase parallelism lies in the common element: both expand one line of poetry into
two, and their functions overlap slightly. Further, in Ugaritic, they
tend to occur together.

The terrace pattern is well attested in both Ugaritic and Akkadian,
as the examples given below will show. The pattern is known, too, to
later poetry.[14] Its artificiality can be demonstrated by comparing
two almost parallel passages in Hebrew:

| | |
|---|---|
| אז ירננו עצי היער | Then the trees of the forest will rejoice |
| מלפני יהוה כי־בא | in the presence of Yahweh, *for he comes,* |
| לשפט את־הארץ | to judge the earth (1 Chr 16,33) |

| | |
|---|---|
| אז ירננו כל־עצי־יער | Then all the trees of the forest will rejoice |
| לפני יהוה כי בא | in the presence of Yahweh, *for he comes,* |
| כי בא לשפט הארץ | *for he comes* to judge the earth. (Ps 96,12b-13) |

---

11. A term coined by Austerlitz.

12. Some MSS read יהוה for יה, suggesting that even in antiquity the terrace
pattern was not always recognised.

13. As does Avishur, *UF* 4 (1972) 9-10.

14. As, variously, anadiplosis, epanadiplosis and epanastrophe. See Leech, *Guide*,
81; *PEPP*, 33-34; Elkhadem, *Dictionary*, 8.

The repetition of כי בא is omitted in the Chronicles passage, but the Psalm is better poetry (note the stress pattern 2 + 2 + 3).[15]

*Functions of the terrace pattern*
Before going on to consider variations of the pattern, it is better to take a look at the functions of the terrace in its simplest form. (Here examples from Ugaritic and Akkadian will be included.) Since the verse-form is basically repetition of a kind, it will share the functions of iteration, namely to link the components of a strophe or stanza and for dramatic effect. In addition, the terrace serves to create tension, to denote duration in time, to express inevitability and to help the poet improvise verse.

1. *Cohesive function.* As with repetition in general, the terrace pattern serves to link up components within a poem. For example:

| | |
|---|---|
| פצחו ורננו וזמרו | Burst forth in joyous song and *sing*, |
| זמרו ליהוה בכנור | *sing* to Yahweh *with the lyre* |
| בכנור וקול זמרה | *with the lyre* and the sound of song. (Ps 98,4-5) |

Also Ez 30,3. The cohesive function is more developed in the extended forms of the terrace, discussed below.

2. *To create tension.* Occasionally the poet will break off halfway through a sentence, then repeat the last words spoken and complete the sentence.[16] This creates tension and increases the attentiveness of the audience. Examples are available in Akkadian,[17] and, more clearly, in Ugaritic.

| | |
|---|---|
| *hlm ilm tphhm* | See! The gods *espied them*, |
| *tphn mlak ym* | *espied* the envoys of Yam, |
| *t'dt ṭpṭ nhr* | the embassy of Judge Nahar. |

(*CTA* 2 i 21-22[18])

| | |
|---|---|
| ואתה בן־אדם התשפט | And you, son of man, *will you judge*, |
| התשפט את־עיר הדמים | *will you judge* the bloodstained city? (Ez 22,2) |

Also Jgs 5,23; Isa 38,11; Pss 38,40; 115,12; 135,12 (136,21.22).
3. *To denote duration.* A function perhaps peculiar to the pattern in

---

15. Cf. de Moor, *UF* 10 (1978) 208.
16. The true meaning of 'expanded colon'.
17. See *Atr* I ii 189-190 and examples given by Kinnier Wilson, *JSS* 13 (1967) 99-102.
18. See Gibson, *CML* 41 n. 5 for the verb forms; another instance is *CTA* 23:37-38.

question, it can refer to the past, present or impending future. There is some overlap with the expression of inevitability.[19]

| | |
|---|---|
| *lymm lyrḥm* | From days to months, |
| *lyrḥm lšnt* | from months to years. |

(*CTA* 19 iv 175-176)

| | |
|---|---|
| יסף יהוה עליכם | May Yahweh give increase *to you*, |
| עליכם ועל־בניכם | *to you* and to your children. (Ps 115,14) |

4. *To create poetry*. From the composing poet's point of view the use of repetition in the form of the terrace enables him to improvise by the adding style technique. This is apparent from the following examples: the short respite provided by repetition is enough to allow the poet to reflect.

| | |
|---|---|
| *[ina qaq] qari eṣir u[ṣurtu]* | On the ground draw *the design* |
| *[uṣur] tu lumurma* | *the design* for me to see (so) |
| *eleppa [lupuš]* | I may build the boat. (*Atr* W 14-15) |

| | |
|---|---|
| *ymǵ lqrt ablm* | He came to 'Mourners'-City', |
| *ablm qrt zbl yrḥ* | Abilim, city of prince Moon. |

(*CTA* 19 iv 163[20])

The Ugaritic text shows why this type of repetition is sometimes called 'epithetic'.

| | |
|---|---|
| אנה יהוה כי־אני עבדך | O Yahweh: truly *am I your servant*, |
| אני־עבדך בן־אמתך | *I am your servant*, your handmaid's son. |

(Ps 116,16)

Also: Jer 2,13; Joel 2,27; Prov 30,1; Song 2,15. Note the frequent use of the pattern in Ps 122.

5. *Other functions*. The repeated use of this pattern in *CTA* 23 seems to suggest a *magical* function (but this is truer of the extended forms), or perhaps it was a device to ensure no word of an important ritual was left out. Against this is the evident omission of a complete line from the couplet

| | |
|---|---|
| *hn špthm mtqtm* | Lo, their lips *are sweet* |
| *mtqtm klrmnt* | *sweet* as pomegranates (line 50), |

—the second line is not repeated in line 55.

19. An example in prose comes from a Neo-Assyrian letter: 'It is four whole months, four whole months, since my lord went away'; see Kinnier Wilson, *JSS* 13 (1967) 102 for comment.
20. Also *CTA* 22B:16-17; 23:35-36.42.45-46.

*Variations of the terrace pattern*
Two principal variants of the pattern merit discussion here: the
chiastic terrace and the extended terrace. They are, in fact, diametrically opposed with respect to structure: the chiastic pattern is a
closed unit, whereas the extended terrace can be continued indefinitely.
   a. *The chiastic terrace.* When chiasmus and the terrace pattern are
combined, the result is what could be termed a 'cyclic couplet', the
outer elements being parallel and the inner elements being identical:

| | |
|---|---|
| *mt uḫryt mh yqḥ* | Man, as his destiny, what does he get? |
| *mh yqḥ mt aṯryt* | What does he get, a man, as his fate? |
| | (*CTA* 17 vi 35-36) |

Its function is, chiefly, to increase the listeners' tension by delaying
the denouement to the third line (in this case: 'Glaze will be poured
on my head, quicklime into my crown; and the death of everyman
will I die, and I, of a certainty, will die'). The combination is very
frequent in Ugaritic.[21] It occurs, too, in Hebrew, notably:

| | |
|---|---|
| אל תצטדק לפני מלך | Do not justify yourself *in a king's presence* |
| ופני מלך אל תתבונן | *and in a king's presence* do not display your wisdom. (Sir 7,5) |

Also: Isa 29,17; Ez 22,2; Nah 1,2; Am 4,7b. The chiastic terrace is, by
contrast, very rare in Akkadian.[22] A secondary function is to convey
a sense of inevitability.
   b. *The extended terrace.* The terrace pattern has the property of
being extended over several cola, each colon repeating the final
elements of the previous colon; schematically:

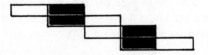

Very clear examples are to hand in both Ugaritic and Akkadian.[23]
One is the prologue to the Akkadian incantation 'The Worm and the
Toothache':

---

21. Also *CTA* 4 vii 38-39; 12 ii 51-52; 17 v 10-11; 19 iii (passim, e.g. 132-133).
22. E.g. Gilg (Nin) X i 15-16: 'The ale-wife saw him / and locked her door (*ētedil bābša*) / her door she locked (*bābša ētedil*) / she locked its bolt'. Note, further, *Atr* S v 18-21; rev. vi 7-10.
23. See Watson, *UF* 7 (1975) 485-489.

| | |
|---|---|
| *ultu Anum [ibnû šamê]* | After Anu had created sky, |
| *šamû ibnû [erṣetam]* | sky had created earth, |
| *erṣetum ibnû nārāti* | earth had created rivers, |
| *nārāti ibnâ atappāti* | rivers had created canals, |
| *atappāti ibnâ rušumta* | canals had created mire, |
| *rušumta ibnû tūltu* | mire had created Worm, |
| *illik tūltu . . .* | Worm went . . .[24] |

Another example, from the Erra Epic (IV 76-82), runs to a total of six couplets, each linked to the other.

From Ugaritic (again in a magical incantation):

| | |
|---|---|
| *šmk at aymr* | Your very own name is 'Expeller'; |
| *aymr mr ym* | Expeller, expel Sea, |
| *mr ym lksih* | expel Sea from his throne, |
| *nhr lkḥṭ drkth* | River from his dominating seat. |

(*CTA* 2 iv 18-20[25])

The Hebrew examples include Hos 2,23-24; Joel 1,3.4 and Isa 24,18 (also Jer 48,43-44):

| | |
|---|---|
| והיה | Surely, |
| הנם מקול הפחד | anyone fleeing the yap of the *pack* |
| יפל אל הפחת | will fall into the *gap* |
| והעולה מתוך הפחת | and anyone climbing out of the *gap* |
| ילכד בפח | will be caught in the *trap*.[26] |

The main function, apparent both in the Akkadian example[27] and in Isa 24,18 (and Jer 48,43-44), is to depict *inevitability*: there is no escape. A lesser function is to represent a chain of transmission, as in the 'Worm and Toothache' and ergot incantations, and in Joel 1,3.

*Other variants* of the terrace pattern include the 'parallel' terrace of Gen 49,9 and 24; Mic 4,8 where synonymous expressions replace the simple repetition of the terrace.

### Sorites

Strictly defined the sorites (also, sorite) is 'a set of statements which proceed, step by step, through the force of logic or reliance upon a

24. Text: *CT* 17, plate 50:1-7; translation: *ANET*, 100.
25. In lines 11-13 the weapon is named 'Chaser' (*ygrš*) and told to 'chase Sea' (*grš ym*).
26. The equivalents 'pack, gap, trap' have been adopted in an attempt to echo the assonance in Hebrew—these lines being an expansion of Isa 24,17 (= Jer 48,43) 'pack and gap (lit. hole or pitfall), and trap'. For the meaning 'pack' for Heb. פחד cf. Dahood, *Ugaritic-Hebrew Philology* (Rome, 1965) 69, and Akkadian *illatu*.
27. *Erra* IV 76-82, cited in *UF* 7 (1975) 487.

succession of indisputable facts, to a climactic conclusion, each statement picking up the last key word (or key phrase) of the preceding one'.[28] There is some overlap with the extended terrace (discussed above) which is not so strictly logical as sorites. The various types of sorites include the transmissional (e.g. Joel 1,3), the catastrophic (Erra IV 76-82), the numerical[29] and others.[30] A good illustration of sorites used in evocative imagery is Ps 133,2-3a:[31]

> Like the sweet oil on the head,
> flowing down on the beard,
> (the sweet oil) on Aaron's beard,
> flowing down on the collar of his robes;
> like the dew on Mount Hermon,
> flowing down on Zion's mountains.

Tsumura notes: 'v. 2 describes vividly the continual graceful movement of "the sweet oil", first poured on "the head", which flows down to "the beard", and then from "the beard (of Aaron)" to "the collar (of his robes)"'. Related is pseudo-sorites, common in Hos.[32]

*For study*
Hab 1,8; Pss 96,13; 78,3-8; 116,16; Am 5,19. Also, Jgs 19,23; 2 Sm 13,12.25; 2 Kgs 4,16.

*Cross-references*
KEYWORDS, REPETITION, STAIRCASE PARALLELISM.

### BIBLIOGRAPHY

Fischel, H.A. 'The Use of Sorites (*Climax, Gradatio*) in the Tannaitic Period', *HUCA* 44 (1973) 119-151.
Mirsky, A. '[The origin of anadiplosis in Hebrew literature]', *Tarbiz* 28 (1958-59) 171-180 [in Hebrew].
Tsumura, D.T. 'Sorites in Psalm 133,2-3a', *Bib* 61 (1980) 416-417.

---

28. Fischel: 1973, 119.
29. For example, *CTA* 4 vi 9-12: 'Sixty-six cities he took, seventy-seven towns, eighty Baal smote, ninety Baal expelled'; here inevitability is expressed.
30. Listed by Fischel: 1973; see, too, Watson, *UF* 7 (1975) 485-489.
31. Tsumura: 1980.
32. Discussed by Andersen-Freedman, *Hosea* (see index).

### 8.4 *The Pivot Pattern*

*The pivot pattern: definition and theory*
Basically, the 'pivot pattern' is a couplet where the expected final
word is not expressed as it is implied by the last word (or words) of
the first line. So, in

| רץ לקראת רץ ירוץ | Runner to meet runner, *does run*, |
| ומגיד לקראת מגיד | messenger to meet messenger. (Jer 51,31) |

the second line means 'Messenger to meet messenger does run', with
ellipsis or gapping of the verb (ירוץ). Since the same verb affects both
cola, it has been termed a 'double duty modifier';[33] alternatively, the
verb can be considered as central to the whole couplet, hence the
name 'pivot'.

Quite often the 'pivotal' word is a noun in the vocative, 'suspended'[34]
almost, between the two lines:

| מלפני אדון חולי ארץ | In the presence of the Lord, writhe, O Land, |
| מלפני אלוה יעקב | in the presence of Jacob's God. (Ps 114,7) |

In terms of *metre* the pivot pattern can be defined as *a couplet with
final silent stress*. Hebrew verse, being accentual, is made up of
patterns of stress, usually in balanced couplets (see METRE). When an
expected stress-word is missing from a line, the effect is to produce
silent stress.[35] For example, in

| ולא תדלחם רגל־אדם עוד | Disturb them shall foot of man no more, |
| ופרסות בהמה לא תדלחם | nor cattle-hooves disturb them (Ez 32,13[36]), |

the stress-pattern is

$$/ \ / \ / \ /$$
$$/ \ / \ / \ 0$$

the expected עוד (as part of the construction לא ... עוד, 'no longer')
not being expressed, leaving the second line short by one stress-unit.

---

33. So Dahood: 1967, 574.
34. 'The double-duty modifier is a phrase, sometimes just a divine name or title in
the vocative case, suspended between the first and third cola of a verse and
simultaneously modifying both of them' (Dahood: 1967, 574). Note that Dahood's
'third colon' is really the *second* since the pattern is basically a couplet; the pivotal
word belongs to the first colon.
35. On silent stress, see D. Abercrombie, 'A Phonetician's View of Verse Structure',
*Ling* 6 (1964) 5-13.
36. Note, incidentally, the use of both chiasmus and gender-matched synonyms.

Accordingly, the full name of the strophic unit should be 'pivot-patterned bicolon with silent (final) stress'; here, the expression 'pivot pattern' is used for convenience.

*The pivot pattern and related patterns*
The pivot pattern is akin to both the aba-monocolon and ABA (or ABA′) tricolon—which, of course, are forms of chiasmus; it is also like staircase parallelism. Since these four strophic patterns are often confused[37] a special paragraph has been devoted to differentiation between them. The patterns in question have been defined elsewhere, so there is no need for repetition here. Instead, a complete poem exhibiting at least three of the strophic forms will be briefly set out analytically as a concrete example. The example chosen is *Psalm 57* because it uses three, if not four of the strophic patterns[38] and because it has been discussed very recently by Auffret with the pivot pattern in mind (see below). Also, it is relatively short. The pivot pattern occurs, in fact, no less than five times (vv. 5.6.8.10.12), twice as a refrain.[39] The psalm opens with an aba (chiastic) monocolon and there is an example of staircase parallelism in v. 9. Several readings of the poem may be necessary before it becomes clear that the patterns in question, though related, are really distinct.

*Distinguishing related patterns: Ps 57*

| | | |
|---|---|---|
| חנני אלהים חנני | 2 | *aba (chiastic) monocolon* |
| כי בך חסיה נפשי | | |
| ובצל־כנפיך אחסה | | |
| עד יעבר הוות | | |
| אקרא לאלהים עליון | 3 | |
| לאל גמר עלי | | |
| ישלח משמים ויושיעני חרף שאפי | 4 | |
| ישלח אלהים חסדו ואמתו | | |
| נפשי בתוך לבאים אשכבה | 5 | *couplet with silent stress* |
| להטים בני־אדם | | *('pivot')* |
| שניהם חנית וחצים | | |
| ולשונם חרב חדה | | |
| רומה על־השמים אלהים | 6 | *couplet with silent stress* |
| על כל־הארץ כבודך | | *('pivot') as refrain* |

---

37. Borderline cases do occur but these have to be judged in the wider context of undisputed examples.
38. The ABA-pattern may be present in v. 4.
39. The same use of a pivot pattern may be operative in Ps 67.

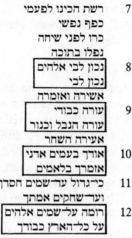

רשת הכינו לפעמי    7
כפף נפשי
כרו לפני שיחה
נפלו בתוכה

נכון לבי אלהים    8    *couplet with silent stress*
נכון לבי              *('pivot')*

אשירה ואזמרה
עורה כבודי    9    *staircase parallelism*
עורה הנבל וכנור

אעירה השחר
אודך בעמים אדני    10    *couplet with silent stress*
אזמרך בלאמים          *('pivot')*

כי־גדול עד־שמים חסדך    11
ועד־שחקים אמתך

רומה על־שמים אלהים    12    *couplet with silent stress*
על כל־הארץ כבודך          *('pivot') as refrain*

### Translation of Ps 57[40]

2  Mercy on me, God, mercy on me,          *aba monocolon*
   for in you does trust my soul,
   and in the shadow of your wings I trust
   until the 'word' passes on.

3  I will cry to God, the Highest,
   To the avenger El, the High.

4  May he send down from heaven and save me
   from shivering and fear (??);
   May God send down his grace and fidelity.

5  Myself amid lions do I lie,          *pivot pattern*
   swallowers of mankind;
   their teeth: spear and arrows,
   and their tongue: a sharp sword.

6  High above the heavens, God,          *pivot pattern* (refrain)
   above the whole earth is your 'self'.

7  A net they prepared for my feet,
   a snare for my neck;
   they dug, for my face, a pit
   and fell into it!

40. For philological details see Dahood, *Psalms II*, 49-55. For the structure, P. Auffret, 'Note sur la structure du *Psaume LVII*', *Semitica* 27 (1977) 59-73. The minor differences from Ps 108 have been ignored. V. 4 is notoriously difficult; cf. perhaps Akk. *ḫurbāšu*, 'shivers of fear'. In v. 5 לחם is considered equivalent to Akk. *la'ātu*, 'to swallow'. See also Gevirtz, *HUCA* 52 (1981) 101-110, on *kābôd* = 'self'.

8 Firm is my resolve, God,       *pivot pattern*
  firm is my resolve;
  I will sing songs,

9 Awake, my 'self',       *staircase parallelism*
  awake harp and lyre;
  I will awake the Dawn.

10 I will praise you among the peoples, Lord,
   I will sing to you among the nations.    *pivot pattern*

11 For, great till the heavens is your mercy,
   till the sky your fidelity.

12 High above the heavens, God,     *pivot pattern* (refrain)
   above the whole earth is your 'self'.

*Akkadian and Ugaritic examples*
Although, it would seem, Akkadian and Ugaritic poetry is not based
on stress, the pivot pattern is used in one if not both traditions;[41]
some examples will be discussed here.

| | |
|---|---|
| *ša igigi ṭēnšunu tīdêma* | The decision of the Igigi, *you know*, |
| *ša anunnaki milikšun* | the counsel of the Anunnaki. |

(*Erra* IIIc 40)

The verb 'you know' is to be understood in the second line. Also:

| | |
|---|---|
| *epiš taqbî ēpuš Ištar* | I have done what you ordered me |
| | to do, Ishtar, |
| (*Ištar*) *lū kaššāpī lū kaššapti* | my sorcerer or my sorceress . . . , |

where 'Ishtar' closes one line and simultaneously opens the next.[42]
The pattern is very frequent in Ugaritic, for instance:

| | |
|---|---|
| *ṯnh ksp atn* | Twice (her weight) in silver, *will I give* |
| *wṯlṯh ḫrṣm* | thrice, even, in gold. |

(*CTA* 14 iv 205-206)

41. See my 'Pivot Pattern'.
42. Text and translation as in W. Farber, *Beschwörungsrituale an Ištar und Dumuzi*
(Wiesbaden, 1977) B 16'-17'; Farber comments (253): 'Beachte den Doppelbezug des
dIštar das in der vierhebigen Zeile . . . auch thematisch deutlich einen Abschluss der
Selbstbeschreibung des Zustands des Kranken markiert, gleichzeitig jedoch als
emphatischer Beginn der dreihebigen (fast auftaktartigen) Zeile . . . den völlig anders
gearteten auch rhythmisch bewegteren anklagenden Passus einleitet'.

Over a score more examples are known,[43] some of which will be
cited under 'function' and 'type'.

## Types

Broadly speaking, and without going into minute detail, four factors
determine the typology of the pattern: whether or not the non-
repeated word (the 'pivotal word') is an essential part of the syntax[44]
and whether the constitutive lines are repetitive or in parallelism.
Simple repetition is at the core of such couplets as

> *ul aqabbaku ibrī*         I cannot tell you, *my friend*,
> *ul aqabbaku*             I cannot tell you. (Gilg XII 89)

and others in Akkadian,[45] and Ps 57,8 (see above). By contrast,
strophes like

> *hlk aḫth b'l y'n*       The coming of his sister, Baal *does see*,
> *tdrq bt abh*           the approach so swift of his father's
>                            daughter. (*CTA* 3D iv 83-84[46])

are essentially two parallel lines.

The same two examples illustrate the other component: the non-
repeated word can be simply additional, almost—'my friend' in the
text from Gilgamesh—or form an integral part of the sentence: 'does
see' (from the Baal Epic).

The pivot pattern is not confined to poetry, as indicated by texts
such as

> הנה שמע מזבח טוב      See, to obey *is better* than sacrifice,
> להקשיב מחלב אילים     to hearken, than rams' fat. (1 Sm 15,22b)

and Ruth 2,19.[47]

Extended forms of the pattern occur; these are discussed below.

## Functions

Quite frequently the pivot-pattern comes at the beginning or end of a
stanza, speech or poem. Its function, then, would appear to be the

---

43. *CTA* 3B ii 3-5; 3D iv 83-84; 3E v 27-28; 4 vii 12-14; 5 i 14-16, vi 17-18 (= 6 i 2-3);
6 ii 26-27; 14 i 12-13.35-37.41-43; ii 94-95; iii 150-151; 15 iii 23-25; 16 i 36-38; vi 11-
12.29-31 (//43-44).57-58; 17 vi 41; 18 iv 31-33; 19 i 18-19; iii 75 (etc.), etc.

44. See Auffret, *VT* 27 (1977) 62 n. 5.

45. E.g. *BWL* 146:50.

46. Both this and the alternative emendation *ybmt limm* (cf. *CTA* 4 ii 4-6) are
proposed and discussed in detail by Pardee, *BO* 37 (1980) 279.

47. LXX adds an extra 'today', but this would appear unnecessary.

demarcation of poetic units. Occasionally, the final pivot marks a climax. For the composing poet, use of a repetitive pattern such as the pivot enables him to mark time (so to speak) and think up the next part of his improvised poem; the pivot pattern, therefore, can function as a filler.[48] On the part of the listening audience such repetition allows them to follow the course of the poem by the twin process of reinforcement (reiteration of what has been said already) and rest (concentration is lessened). The extended forms of the pattern are indicative of its expletive function.

Here, a few examples of the stanza-marking function will be presented, with very brief discussion and texts for private study. In many cases, the function of the pattern cannot, as yet, be determined.

a. *To open a stanza, speech or poem*. The famous 'battle scene' of the goddess Anath begins (after a description of her toilet):

| | |
|---|---|
| *ḳlat ṯǵrt bht 'nt* | Shut the mansion gates, did *Anath*, |
| *wtqry ǵlmm bšt ǵr* | and meet the pageboys at the foot of the rock, (*CTA* 3B ii 3-5[49]) |

and there are a few other passages.[50] The pattern is very much more used in Hebrew in this function; Psalm 72, for instance, begins:

| | |
|---|---|
| אלהים משפטיך למלך תן | O God, your judgment to the king, *give* |
| וצדקתך לבן מלך | your justice to the son of a king.[51] |

Also: Isa 28,24; Jer 4,15; Mic 7,14; Pss 5,2; 59,2; 75,3; 114,7; 119,169; 132,11b; Prov 1,21; Job 18,11; 19,23; 32,6.

b. *To close a sentence, speech or poem*. One clear example from Ugaritic is at the close of El's speech to Keret:

| | |
|---|---|
| *mlk ṯr abh yarš* | The kingship of his father, the Bull, *he wants* |
| *hm drkt kab adm* | or (perhaps) dominion like the father of mankind? (*CTA* 14 i 41-43) |

Of the many passages in Hebrew (2 Sm 23,3; Isa 15,9; 24,3; 28,29; Jer 4,2; 51,10; Joel 1,7.16; Nah 2,5; Pss 7,3; 90,17b; 119,144.160), Sir 40,11 is probably sufficient for illustration. It closes the section vv. 8-11:

48. See sections on ORAL POETRY and REPETITION.
49. Following Gibson, *CML*, 47; but note Pardee's dissent in *BO* 37 (1981) 275.
50. *CTA* 14 i 12-13; 17 vi 4-5.
51. The first word ('God') may be a later liturgical addition (courtesy Loretz), but this does not affect the pattern in question. (Note the epithetic word-pair 'king // son of a king'.)

כל מארץ אל ארץ ישוב    And all that is from the earth, to the earth *will return*,

ואשר ממרום אל מרום    and what is from the sky to the sky.[52]

c. *As a climax*. A prayer to Gula ends:

*ina qibīt Baba ušarbi šumuša*    At B.'s command I will exalt her name,

*ana kal nišē [azakkar]*    to all the peoples will I tell (it).[53]

The use of a pivot to climax a section is common enough in Ugaritic, as witness

*wbklhn šph yitbd*    In its totality the clan perished

*wbphryh yrt*    in its entirety the heirs.

              (*CTA* 14 i 24-25[54])

Hebrew supplies further instances; from Habakkuk:

העל כן יריק חרמו ותמיד    Is he therefore to empty his net *always*,[55]

להרג גוים לא יחמול    to kill nations mercilessly? (Hab 1,17)

and: Jer 51,12; Nah 1,5.

Very occasionally the pivot pattern serves both to open and close a segment of poetry—when it is akin in function to the envelope figure. In the Keret Tale, for example, the dream sequence (*CTA* 14 i 35-43) begins with a pivot pattern and also ends with one. An example in Hebrew is Mic 5,9 and 13.

### Combination with other devices

The texts discussed show that the pivot pattern does not occur in isolation but is used in combination with other poetic devices. Such combinations have been pointed out, but some additional examples will provide further illustration.

Quite often the pattern is used together with gender-patterns: in the stock formula

---

52. Contrast the Greek version.

53. Text and translation: Nougayrol, *RA* 36 (1939) 30:10; Seux, *Hymnes*, 463.

54. Following the reading in *KTU*; cf. Dietrich—Loretz—Sanmartín, *UF* 7 (1975) 598 and Pardee, *BO* 37 (1980) 285.

55. Note emphatic *waw*.

| | |
|---|---|
| *bph rgm lyṣa* | From his mouth his word *had hardly* |
| | *issued*, |
| *bšpth ḥwth* | from his lips his speech, |

the gender of both *p* and *rgm* in the first line is m. and that of *špt* and *ḥwt*, f. Similar parallelism is operative in *CTA* 15 iii 23-25, while the genders are reversed in 5 vi 17-18 and 6 i 2-3. Hebrew provides even more texts, including Isa 34,19; Ez 32,13 (cited); Hos 13,12; Ps 109,14; Job 28,14; Prov 18,20; Sir 40,11 (cited); with reversal: Ps 119,105 and

| | |
|---|---|
| ציון במשפט תפדה | Zion (f.) by justice (m.) *shall be redeemed* |
| ושביה בצדקה | and those (m.) of her who repent, by right (f.). |
| | (Isa 1,27) |

Chiasmus and the pivot intermesh in

| | |
|---|---|
| בית גאים יסח יהוה | The house of the proud is torn down by *Yahweh* |
| ויצב גבול אלמנה | but he maintains the widow's boundary. |
| | (Prov 15,25[56]) |

*For study*
What function does the pattern described above have in Prov 24,3; Jer 4,1-2; Nah 2,5? What combination of patterns can be recognised in Job 28,14 and Isa 34,10? What can be deduced from tabulating the distribution of this pattern in Hebrew poetry?

*Cross-references*
CHIASMUS, ELLIPSIS, METRE, STAIRCASE PARALLELISM, STANZA.

BIBLIOGRAPHY

Althann, R. 'Jeremiah IV 11-12: Stichometry, Parallelism and Translation', *VT* 28 (1978) 385-391.

Auffret, P. "'Pivot Pattern'": Nouveaux exemples (Jon ii 10; Ps xxxi 13; Is xxiii 7)', *VT* 28 (1978) 103-110.

Dahood, M.J. 'A New Metrical Pattern in Biblical Poetry', *CBQ* 29 (1967) 574-582.

Watson, W.G.E. 'The Pivot Pattern in Hebrew, Ugaritic and Akkadian Poetry', *ZAW* 88 (1976) 239-252.

Also Dahood, *Psalms III*, 439-444; Watson, *UF* 7 (1975) 489-491 and *Chiastic Patterns*, 152.

---

56. The passive is used in English to help the pattern stand out.

# 9

## SOUND IN HEBREW POETRY

### 9.1 *General*

When considering poetic devices involving sound—assonance, alliteration, rhyme, onomatopoeia and wordplay—the pronunciation of a language is very much to the fore. This applies to classical Hebrew as well as to Ugaritic and Akkadian. There is no need to repeat here what is set out in the standard grammars, although there is no complete consensus of opinion. Two points have to be borne in mind. Firstly, there is no such thing as *the* pronunciation of Hebrew (or of Ugaritic and Akkadian). Like any other language, Hebrew developed and evolved, so that its pronunciation changed over the centuries. Also, Hebrew had its share of dialects and idiolects both regional (particularly North and South) and social. Secondly, in spite of a certain levelling effect brought about by the collection of Hebrew poetry into the canon, relics of these language variations remain. And, in the absence of other guides, the Masoretic vocalization is very reliable—any alterations must be vouched for.[1] With these provisos, the study of sound patterns in Hebrew poetry is rewarding and interesting.[2]

### 9.2 *Assonance*

*Theory*

If alliteration can be defined in terms of repeated consonants,

---

1. See particularly J.C.L. Gibson, 'The Massoretes as Linguists', *OTS* 19 (1974) 86-96; also Revell, *JSS* 25 (1980) 165-79.
2. Culler, *Poetics*, 65, remarks: 'We have only the crudest ideas of what makes a line euphonious or successful and of how phonological modulations from one line to another contribute to the effects of a poem'. Useful is A.A. Hill, 'A Phonological Description of Poetic Ornaments', *LS* 2 (1969) 99-123.

assonance is a form of *vowel* repetition. It occurs when there is a
series of words containing a distinctive vowel-sound[3] or certain
vowel-sounds in a specific sequence. However, since the borderline
between vowels and consonants is not irrevocably defined, there is
some overlap between alliteration (of consonants) and assonance (of
vowels). This is inevitable since poets are not phoneticians and deal
with words, not abstract entities. For convenience, though, alliteration
has been dealt with separately. Yet another section will deal with combinations of alliteration and assonance. Here, the topic is assonance.

*Typology of assonance*
The simplest form of assonance is based on the repetition or
dominance of a single vowel sound. In Jer 49,1 the distinctive 'A'-
sound is evidently to be heard throughout the couplet:[4]

| | |
|---|---|
| *madû[a'] yāraš malkām 'et-gād* | Why has their king[5] inherited Gad |
| *w[e]'ammô b[e]'ārāyw yāšāb* | and his people settled in his cities? |

Also in Ps 48,7a. In Jer 49,8 it is 'E', in Ps 113,8 'I', in Isa 58,12d and
Job 5,21 'O' and in Lam 4,15 'U'.
Assonance becomes more complex when based on certain vowel
sequences; for example, in Job 9,16b:

| | |
|---|---|
| *lo' 'a[u]mîn kî ya[u]zîn qôlî* | I do not believe he would listen to my voice. |

3. Here, cases have not been limited to either final-vowel assonance (called 'vocalic
rhyme') or stressed-vowel assonance. 'Assonance occurs when two words have the
same vowels but different consonants' (Elkhadem, *Dictionary*, 14). According to
Adams: 1973, 8, assonance is 'the repetition of a stressed vowel, but not of a following
consonant or consonant cluster, in syllables near enough to each other for the echo to
be discernible to the ear'; and it is 'a conscious musical device in poetry of all
countries' (ibid. 9).
4. In this section the Hebrew is given in transliteration so that the sound is
immediately evident. For obvious reasons, Ugaritic has not been discussed, and to
avoid imbalance, nor has Akkadian although we know how it was spoken. For Akk.
examples see Hecker, *Epik*, 139-40. For instance, in

| | |
|---|---|
| *inanna alkī attī* | Now you go, |
| *atkašī tā'iššā* | rush to her chamber |
| | (Agušaya Hymn A vi 34'-35'), |

only the vowels 'A' and 'I' are used; in Gilg M iii 3, the vowel sequence is 'I-U-A'. See
Kinnier Wilson: 1968 for the deliberate avoidance of assonance in Akkadian.
5. Or 'Milkom'—see the versions.

where the -a-a-i- pattern recurs twice; similarly, -u-a comes twice in 2 Sm 23,5. This kind of assonantal sequence is more frequent in assonantal alliterative word-pairs such as *lintôš wᵉlintôṣ*, 'to destroy and demolish' (Jer 1,10) discussed below. Such patterns often occur as colon-initial sets like

| | |
|---|---|
| *qošrēm 'al* ... | Tie them upon ... |
| *'ondēm 'al* ... | bind them ... (Prov 6,21) |

Also: Jer 12,2cd; Ps 89,13.15; Job 8,11; Prov 9,5; Song 6,2b; Lam 1,1—and with three consecutive lines, Jer 12,7.

Somewhat rare are sequences such as

| | |
|---|---|
| *yôm mᵉhûmâ umᵉbûsâ umᵉbûkâ* | A day of tumult, undertreading and hubbub. (Isa 22,5) |

Also Isa 24,17. There is evident overlap with onomatopoeia. *Chiastic assonance* expressing reciprocity, occurs in

| | | |
|---|---|---|
| *ᵃnî lᵉdôdî* | I–O–I | I'm my lover's |
| *wᵉdôdî lî* | O-I–I | and my lover's mine. |
| | | (Song 6,3⁶) |

*Functions of assonance*
The chief purpose of using assonance within a poem is in order to *link* its component parts together, whether at the level of single words (in word-pairs), at the level of single phrases, or over longer segments of verse. In

| | |
|---|---|
| *dāmîtî* ... | I was like a desert-owl, |
| *hāyîtî* ... | I was like a hooting-bird of the ruins |
| | (Ps 102,7⁷) |

the couplet is bound closer together by the repetitive opening sound-pattern. See, too, Isa 34,3-4; Jer 51,30a; Hos 7,13a; etc. As a corollary to this function, it is easy to determine where a colon begins (stichometry). Assonance can also be used for *emphasis*. As already mentioned, assonance helps link sound with meaning, as in onomatopoeia, e.g. *qôl qôrē'*, 'A loud shout' (Isa 40,3—lit. 'a voice which cries [out]').

---

6. Also Isa 1,18; Job 40,10; etc.
7. Or 'I am like an owl in the desert ...'—note the onomatopoeic words *qa'at*, 'owl(?)' and *kos* (ditto).

*For study*
Hos 4,16; 10,1; 12,12; Prov 3,35; Mic 2,4a; 7,1b. Last two words of
Ps 29,1; of Ps 109,13a; of Lam 2,5.

BIBLIOGRAPHY
(a) *General*
Adams, P.G. 'The Historical Importance of Assonance to Poets', *PMLA* 88
(1973) 8-18.
(b) *Semitic*
Glück, J.J. 'Assonance in Ancient Hebrew Poetry', *Selms FS*, 69-84.
Kinnier Wilson, J.V. '"Desonance" in Akkadian', *JSS* 13 (1968) 93-103.
Saydon, P.P. 'Assonance in Hebrew as a means of Expressing Emphasis',
*Bib* 39 (1955) 36-50.287-384.
Westhuizen, J.P. van der 'Assonance in Biblical and Babylonian Hymns of
Praise', *Semitics* 7 (1980) 81-101.
Also Kinnier Wilson, *Iraq* 18 (1956) 146; *ZA* 54 (1961) 74-77; Alonso
Schökel, *Estudios*, 90. Also, O'Connor, *Structure*, 143.

## 9.3 *Alliteration*
*Notes on theory*
Alliteration is the effect produced when the same consonant recurs
within a unit of verse. It is, in fact, a form of repetition, the repeated
element being a consonant (see REPETITION). The following features
of alliteration need to be borne in mind:
—Alliteration refers to *consonants*, not vowels; the same kind of
repetition of vowel-sounds is termed assonance (see ASSONANCE). Of
course the two kinds of sound repetition are related, and indeed often
occur in combination. For clarity of presentation, though, they are
here considered separately.[8]
—Alliteration is here understood in its wider sense of consonant
repetition and is *not* confined to word-initial alliteration.
—*Near-alliteration* has also to be taken into account. By this is meant
that similar-sounding consonants are considered to be equivalent.
For example, /t, d and ṭ/ can be grouped together, as can the sets
/g,k,q/, /s,z,ṣ/ and so on. The degree of alliteration involved, though,
is lesser than that of identical consonants.[9]

8. The terms 'consonant alliteration' and 'vowel alliteration' are used by some
scholars, e.g. Chatman in Sebeok, *Style*, 152.
9. For Hebrew a list is given by I. Casanowicz, *Paronomasia in the Old Testament*
(Boston, 1894), 28-29; these interchanging consonants are:
ה/כ, ש/ז, ס/ת, ש/שׂ, ט/ת, ר/ק, ק/ב, ג/נ, ף/ב, ע/א.
Margalit prefers the term 'partial alliteration' e.g. Ps 119,13.

—*Alliterative clusters* are of particular importance. Sets can be strictly repetitive (mb—mb; sk—sk etc.) or quasi-repetitive (gz—qs; pt—bd etc.) or even with jumbled consonant sequences (nsk—skn). Such clusters may occur within the same colon or extend over several lines.

In common with other poetic traditions where oral improvisation or recitation was the norm, alliteration was comparatively significant in ancient Semitic verse-forms.[10] It tended to determine the poet's choice of words, as Margalit has shown.[11]

### Alliteration in Ugaritic and Akkadian

Partial studies of this device are available for Ugaritic;[12] little has been done for Akkadian, though it is recognised as a feature of Akkadian poetry.[13] Rather than discuss these two poetic traditions separately, examples will be provided under the various types, which follow immediately.

### Typology of alliteration

Alliterative patterning can take the following forms (no separate discussion is provided for near-alliteration):

1. *Word-initial alliteration*. Though never so frequent as in English poetry, initial alliteration occurs surprisingly often.

Ug (*'a*)   *'at 'ah w'an 'a[htk]*     You are my brother and I, your sister.[14]

Akk (*š*)   *šikāram šiti šīmti māti*   Drink beer: it's the country custom.[15]

Heb (ב)     ברך בניך בקרבך     He blesses your sons within you.[16]

Hugger distinguishes between *simple* alliteration (repetition of one

---

10. 'Two natural harmonic principles, *parallelism* and *alliteration*, were perhaps the universal basis of songcraft' (Jakobson, *Lang* 42 [1966] 406, citing a Russian author).

11. Margalit distinguishes between constitutive and ornamental alliteration; the first type forms an essential part of the poetry, the second does not (Margalit: 1979).

12. Margalit: 1979; also *UF* 7 (1975) 310-13.

13. See Hecker, *Epik*, 139-40.139f; 'Die Alliteration (Stabreim) findet sich nicht selten': so von Soden, *ZA* 68 (1978) 53, and 78.

14. *CTA* 18 i 24; cf. 17 vi 32-33 (also *'a*); etc. For the use of the same initial letter to begin consecutive lines (couplets) see ACROSTICS.

15. Gilg P 94; other examples: Hecker, *Epik*, 139-40. Also *Erra* IIc 14 (*ša*).

16. Ps 147,13. See Dahood, *Psalms III* index [479] under 'alliteration'. Also: (א) Isa 24,6; Hos 5,14b-15a; Ps 56,4; Job 5,8; 10,2; 29,16; (ח) Ps 57,5; (ע) Ps 104,23; (ז') Lam 3,52; (ש) Pss 127,1; 122,6; 137,3.8; Song 7,1.

letter), as here, and *compound* alliteration, where the same cluster of letters recurs, as in

יהיו כאין וכאפס     They'll be like nowt, like nothing.[17]

## Functions of alliteration

Alliteration has been defined as 'a cohesive grouping of identical or similar sounds within a poetic text coordinated to produce an identifiable effect that has *a perceptible function* within the whole of that text'.[18] In other words, alliteration is only significant in terms of its function, a topic to which we now turn. The principal function of alliteration is *cohesive* in nature, binding together the components of line, strophe, stanza or poem. Such cohesion, in fact, is the effect of word-initial alliteration, which occurs relatively often, as we have seen, generally within the confines of a single *line*, as in

בעיר בשוקים וברחבות     In the city, in the streets and in the squares.
(Song 3,2)

Alliteration occurs chiefly within the *strophe*, for instance,

כציץ יצא וימל     Like a *blossom* he *blooms*, but withers;
ויברח כצל ולא יעמוד     he is fleet as a *shadow* and does not stay. (Job 14,2)

The linking feature is even more apparent over longer stretches of verse: in Joel 2,15-16a the letter *q* features eight times over eight cola:

| | |
|---|---|
| תקעו שופר בציון | Blow a trumpet in Sion, |
| קדשו צום | set aside a fast, |
| קראו עצרה | call for restraint, |
| אספו עם | assemble people, |
| קדשו קהל | set aside a group, |
| קבצו זקנים | gather elders, |
| אספו עוללים | assemble infants, |
| וינקי שדים | those sucking both breasts. |

—and there are other examples.[19]

---

17. Isa 41,12; see Isa 8,15 (4 × וג); also Ez 40,24; Ps 127,5; Song 2,14. Long sequences of alliterative verse are known as 'tumbling verse'—cf. J. Schipper: 1910, 89. The term 'echo-alliteration' describes the repetition of the consonants of the last word in a line at the beginning of the next line, helping them cohere—so Boadt, *CBQ* 35 (1973) 32ff on Isa 41; cf. Dahood, *Psalms III*, 222f, on Ps 127,1a and 5.

18. Wheelock: 1978, 403.

19. Inter-line linkage: Jer 30,15-16; Hos 7,3-4; 10,14; 12,3-4; Am 1,3 (etc.); Hab 1,10-11; 2,15; Zech 11,2b-3; Job 16,8; Prov 9,2-3; Song 2,14; 4,13.

Besides cohesion, alliteration has several other functions (identified by Wheelock) which will be considered briefly. They are the *mnemonic* function,[20] serving to assist memorization (Prov 11,15), the *enargaeic* function, 'to focus the reader's attention, vividly and suddenly on the physical details of an object, a person or an event'[21]—which often involves onomatopoeia (Isa 2,20; 7,19-20; 9,5a; Job 4,10). Thirdly, there is the *vocative* function, giving 'a sense of energetic imperative or request'[22] as in the passage cited (Joel 2,15-16)—and fourthly, the *endstop* function which brings a segment of poetry to a close (Job 12,25 for example).

As noted, alliteration is akin to onomatopoeia,[23] and shares, too, the functions of repetition. In addition, it is a form of rootplay and can help highlight the dominant word in a strophe or stanza—כשל in Isa 3,8 or חזק in Isa 41,6-7,[24] or even a whole poem.[25] On alliterative word-pairs, see below.

*Effects of alliteration*
Consonantal patterns tend to force a poet's hand, leading to the selection of particular words or word-forms which best fit the alliterative scheme. They dictate the choice between synonyms, tip the scales in favour of rare words and word-forms and can also lead to the avoidance of certain words as non-alliterative.[26]

*For study*
Isa 22,8-9; Hos 10,14.

---

20. Which 'involves the compact statement of a moral, theological or eschatological principle, embellished, or, rather, stressed by simultaneous sound repetition' (Wheelock: 1978, 379).

21. Wheelock: 1978, 379-89.

22. Wheelock: 1978, 390-96.

23. For example, Job 12,2 which has nine *mems* in the space of seven words, producing a humming sound 'which suggests Job's mocking sarcasm' (R. Gordis, *Job* [Chicago, 1965] 166-67).

24. Alonso Schökel, *Estudios*, 115.

25. Notably Ps 29, which Fitzgerald, *BASOR* 215 (1974) 61-63, has shown is built round the letters of the divine name *bʻl*; however, see the critique by O'Connor, *BASOR* 226 (1977) 16-17.

26. As a corollary, once a sound-pattern has been identified, textual corrections (where needed) can be made; see TEXTUAL CRITICISM.

BIBLIOGRAPHY

(a) *General*

Hymes, D.H. 'Phonological Aspects of Style: Some English Sonnets', in: Sebeok, *Style*, 109-31.

Lawrence, R.F. 'The Formulaic Theory and its Application to English Alliterative Poetry', Fowler, *Essays*, 166-83.

Leavitt, J.A. 'On the Measurement of Alliteration in Poetry', *CompHum* 10 (1976) 333-42.

Ryder, F.G. 'How Rhymed is a Poem?', *Word* 19 (1963) 310-23.

Schipper, J. *A History of English Versification* (Oxford, 1910) 13-36.46-55.85ff; and bibliography, 150.

Stoll, E.E. 'Poetic Alliteration', *MLN* 55 (1946) 388-90.

Wheelock, J.T.S. 'Alliterative Functions in the *Divina Commedia*', *LeS* 13 (1978) 373-404.

(b) *Semitic*

Gábor, I. *Der hebräische Urrhythmus* (*BZAW* 52; Berlin, 1929).

Hugger, P. 'Die Alliteration im Psalter', *Ziegler FS* 2, 81-90.

Jordahl, R.S. 'Alphabetic Alliteration in the Song of Deborah', Wisconsin Symposium, 1979 (unseen).

Ley, J. *Alliterierende Poesien der Hebräer* (Leipzig, 1865).

Margalit, B. 'Alliteration in Ugaritic Poetry: Its Role in Composition and Analysis', Part I: *UF* 11 (1979) 537-57; Part II: *JNSL* 8 (1979) 57-80.

Rankin, O.S. 'Alliteration in Hebrew Poetry', *JTS* 31 (1930) 285-91 = review of Gábor: 1929.

Zorell, F. 'Kunstvolle Verwendung des Reimes in Ps 29', *BZ* 7 (1909) 286-91.

Also Wyk, W.C. van, *ZDMG Supplement* I, 1969, 296-301.

## 9.4 *Rhyme*

*Rhyme and poetry*

A word rhymes with another (its rhyme-fellow) when the two words sound the same. This sound-identity can be of varying degrees, from almost perfect to merely approximate, so that the corresponding rhyme will be within the range of good to near-rhyme. There is no need here to itemise all the different types of rhyme since, unlike Indo-European, the Semitic languages provide rhymes only incidentally. One sub-type that does occur is feminine or two-syllable rhyme (pencil—stencil). There is some overlap with both repetition and assonance, and in Semitic particularly it is sometimes difficult to make sharp distinctions. The metrical and rhetorical functions of rhyme will be discussed separately; there is no need to speculate here on the origins of rhyme.[27]

27. On which see *PEPP*, 706.

## Rhyme in Semitic

It is generally agreed that rhyme does not play an important part in ancient Semitic poetry. The role it has in rhymed European verse (as distinct from blank verse) is taken over by parallelism in all its forms. Even so, rhyme does occur and is sometimes exploited. There is none of the finesse, though, found in non-Semitic poetry and quite often rhyme is really a form of repetition (particularly of suffixes).[28]

### Ugaritic

Since the exact pronunciation can only be guessed at, unequivocal examples cannot be given. But, since it is fairly probable that rhyme was used, one passage can be quoted [as reconstructed by Cross]:[29]

| | |
|---|---|
| *'abduka ba'lu ya-yammu-mi* | Baal is your slave, O Sea, |
| *'abduka ba'lu la-'ala-mi* | Baal is your slave forever |
| *bin dagani 'asiruka-mi* | Dagan's Son, your prisoner. |

### Akkadian

Again, there is no *systematic* use of rhyme, and examples are comparatively rare, but it does occur. An instance of sustained end-rhyme is a set of six lines from *Erra*:

| | |
|---|---|
| *tamtamma dalḫāta* | The oceans you convulse, |
| *šaddêma gamrāta* | the mountains you finish off. |
| *nišīma redâta* | Men you govern, |
| *būlamma re'âta* | the herds, you shepherd. |
| *ešarrama pānûkka* | E. is at your disposal, |
| *e'engurrama qātûkka* | E. is in your hands. |

and three lines further on comes a rhyming tricolon:

| | |
|---|---|
| *ilāni-ma palḫūka* | The gods fear you, |
| *igigi-ma šaḫtūka* | the Igigi shy away from you, |
| *anunnaki-ma galtūka* | the Anunnaki are in dread of you.[30] |

It is to be noted that these are cases of feminine and triple rhyme. An additional example of end-rhyme (also feminine) is to be found in a proverb about a pig:

28. Many examples of so-called rhyme adduced by Hecker, *Epik*, 197, are merely repetition.
29. 'The enclitic *-mi* provides perfect overall symmetry of line ... as well as rhyme' (Cross, *JThC* 5 [1968] 3, n. 8); the text is *CTA* 2 i 36-37. See also *CTA* 2 iv 10.
30. Texts: *Erra* IIID 5-7 and 9b-10 respectively.

| | |
|---|---|
| *šaḫû lā simāt ekurri* | The pig: unfit for the *shrine* |
| *lā amēl ṭēme* | is senseless, |
| *lā kābis agurri* | unused to tread *tile*.[31] |

Other examples, too, could be mentioned.[32] In Akkadian poetry, rhyme is non-metrical[33] but serves to mark strophic structure.[34]

### Rhyme in Hebrew poetry

The commonest form of rhyme in Hebrew is *end-rhyme*, usually achieved by the use of the same suffix or ending in successive cola.

| | |
|---|---|
| כי | For |
| יהוה שפטנו | Yahweh is our Judge, |
| יהוה מחקקנו | Yahweh is our Lawgiver, |
| יהוה מלכנו | Yahweh is our King, |
| הוא יושיענו | He alone can save us.[35] |

The fourfold final *-nû*, or rather *-ēnû*, in Isa 33,22 is a powerful rhyme which cannot be ignored, even though it may sound repetitive. Other passages using rhyme of this type are Job 21,14-15a (3 × *-nû*); 31,25 (5 × *-î*); 10,8b-12 (10 × *-î* = 4 × *-nî* + 4 × *-ēnî* + 2 × *-î*).[36]

Such end-rhymes can be formed into complex patterns when whole poems are involved. Examples are Isa 41,8-13, using both masculine and feminine rhyme in alternating, chiastic and sequential combinations;[37] and Isa 3,18-23

| | |
|---|---|
| ביום ההוא יסיר אדני את תפארת | |
| העכסים והשביסים והשהרנים | *-îm -îm -îm* |
| הנטיפות והשירות והרעלות | *-ôt -ôt -ôt* |
| | |
| הפארים והצעדות והקשרים | *-îm* |
| ובתי הנפש והלחשים | *-îm* |
| הטבעות ונזמי האף | |

---

31. Lambert, *BWL* 215:15; my translation, based on his, is an attempt to mirror the rhyme of the original; *ekurru* means 'temple' and *agurru*, '(kiln-fired) brick' and hence, 'pavement'.

32. E.g. the triple end-rhyme *bubūti, ilūti, šarrūti* of Gilg (Nin.) VI 26-28—see Hecker, *Epik*, 152.

33. Hecker, *Epik*, 120.

34. Hecker, *Epik*, 62.

35. Perhaps the parallel Ugaritic passage *CTA* 4 iv 43-44 [and 3 v 41-42]—a parallel recognised by Lipiński, *Bib* 44 (1963) 458-59—may exhibit rhyme too.

36. See Skehan, *CBQ* 23 (1961) 133 for this and other examples.

37. Boadt, *CBQ* 35 (1973) 24-34.

המחלצות והמעטפות והמטפחות    -ôt -ôt -ôt
והחריטים והגלינים והסרינים    -îm -îm -îm
והצניפות והרדידים    -îm[38]

*Rhyming word-pairs* of the type *tohu wabohu*, 'empty and void' (Isa 34,11; etc.) are more frequent than such complete rhymed poems, and provide little islands of pleasing sound-patterns in larger complexes. Other examples are *'aṭeret tip'eret*, 'glorious crown' (Isa 62,3);[39] *'ereṣ wᵉtebel*, '(the) earth and the world' (Ps 90,2);[40] *ṣiyyim 'et 'iyyim*, 'marmots with jackals' (Isa 34,14) and so on.

Such paratactic word-pairs can be extended, so that three or more words form a rhyming sequence:

| | |
|---|---|
| *kî yôm* | For it is a day |
| *mᵉhûmâ umᵉbûsâ umᵉbûkâ* | of tumult, trampling, turmoil. |
| | (Isa 22,5; cf. NEB) |

*Controls*

Although some cases of rhyme may be fortuitous, due to the limited number of word-endings available,[41] the following data do indicate that rhyme could be intentional.

1. *Abnormal word-order*. In Nah 2,1 for example, the word יהודה comes before חגיך in order to effect rhyme:

| | |
|---|---|
| *ḥoggî yᵉhûdâ ḥaggayik* | Feast, O Judah, your festivals. |
| *šallᵉmî nᵉdārāyik* | Fulfil your vows. |

Even more striking is the breaking of a construct chain in Isa 10,5:

| | |
|---|---|
| *hoy 'aššûr šēbeṭ 'appî* | Hoy, Assyria's my wrathful *wand.* |
| *ûmaṭṭê hû' bᵉyad-mi za'mî* | My rod of fury is he in my *hand.*[42] |

---

38. Recognised by Alonso Schökel, *Estudios*, 220-21. NEB translation: 'In that day the Lord will take away all finery: anklets, discs, crescents, pendants, bangles, coronets, head-bands, armlets, necklaces, lockets, charms, signets, nose-rings, fine dresses, mantles, cloaks, flounced skirts, scarves of gauze, kerchiefs of linen, turbans and flowing veils'.
39. Rhyme may explain the difficult form *ṣᵉnup*: it was used to rhyme with *mᵉlukâ*.
40. See Avishur, *Semantics* 2 (1971-72) 23, etc.
41. 'Grammatical repetition replaces rhyme' (Fowler in *Linguistics and Literary Style*, 1970, 357).
42. See D.N. Freedman, 'The Broken Construct Chain', *Bib* 53 (1972) 534-36. My translation is an attempt at reproducing the rhyme.

2. *Use of rare or invented words*. Sometimes the poet uses a rare word, or the rare form of a common word, to produce lines that rhyme. It is probable, too, that such rhyming formations were invented. Examples are the sequence in Isa 22,5 (cited above); *minni* in Isa 30,1.[43]

*Functions of rhyme*

The functions of rhyme can be classed, for convenience, into structural[44] and 'rhetorical'. The examples already set out show this. For instance, Isa 3,18-22 is not a shapeless list of women's finery, but a catalogue-poem with a definite pattern. Again, the repeated suffixes (*-nû*, *-î*, *-ka* and the like) serve to show *line-endings*, and mark the limits of the strophe. Also, rhyme helps to *link together* components of a poem.

On the other hand, sequences such as *mᵉhûmâ umᵉbûsâ umᵉbûkâ* (Isa 22,5, cited above) serve to produce a particular effect: here the hullaballoo of battle-slaughter. Similar is the set in Isa 24,17 (though assonance is more at play here than straight rhyme).

*For study*

Isa 21,12; Lam 1,21; Sir 44,1-14 cf. Skehan, *CBQ* 23 (1961) 133.

### BIBLIOGRAPHY

(a) *General*

Bolinger, D.L. 'Rime, assonance and morpheme analysis', *Word* 6 (1950) 117-36.

Luelsdorff, P.A. 'Repetition and Rime in Generative Phonology', *Ling* 44 (1968) 75-89.

Ryder, F.G. 'How Rhymed is a Poem?', *Word* 19 (1963) 310-23.

Also *PEPP* 705-10, with bibliography, 709-10.

(b) *Semitic*

Burney, C.F. 'Rhyme in the Song of Songs', *JTS* 10 (1908-09) 584-89.

Grimme, H. 'Durchgereimte Gedichte im AT', *BSt* 6 (1901) 39-56.

Prijs, L. 'Der Ursprung des Reimes in Neuhebräischen', *BZ* 7 (1963) 33-42.

Schmalzl, P. 'Der Reim im hebräischen Text des Ezechiel', *TTQ* 79 (1897) 127-32.

43. 'The less common form *minnî* supplies a good rhyme for *rûḥî*' (Irwin, *Isaiah 28-33*, 73).

44. As already noted, rhyme is also used in Akkadian to mark off strophes; see Hecker, *Epik*, 62. Thiering, *JSS* 8 (1963) 205, maintains that one of the innovations in the Qumran Hodayoth is 'the deliberate and sustained use of rhymes' and cites 1QH IX 29-36.11a-13a; X 6a-7b; XI 3b-4b.7b-8b.29b-31b.

Also Glück, *Selms FS*, 74ff; Skehan, *BASOR* 200 (1970) 69-70; Zorrell, *BZ* 7 (1909) 286-91.

## 9.5 Onomatopoeia

### Onomatopoeia and mimicry

It is important to distinguish onomatopoeia from mimicry. Mimicry is the imitation of sound by a human, and the greater the talent of an individual (irrespective of mother-tongue) the more effective his or her mimicry. Onomatopoeia, instead, can be defined as the imitation of a sound *within the rules of the language* concerned.[45] Unlike mimicry, an onomatope is language-dependent,[46] can be reduced to writing and becomes part of the lexicon.[47] This last characteristic means, in effect, that such words are subject to grammatical change. As much is evident from Isa 17,12:[48]

| | |
|---|---|
| הוי המון עמים רבים | Ah, the rumble of many peoples: |
| כהמות ימים יהמיון | like the rumble of the sea, they rumble; |
| ושאון לאמים | And the shout of nations: |
| כשאון מים כבירים ישאון | like the shout of heavy seas they shout. |

### Onomatopoeia in poetry

Exaggerated claims for the appropriateness and effect of certain sound-imitative words in poetry have led to a degree of caution in asserting the presence of onomatopoeia in verse. It is true that animal-like noises differ from language to language, for example, or that a verb like 'to hammer' has no universal form. But no claims need be made about the onomatopoeic origin of 'primitive' words for its proper appreciation in poetry. Every language has its own *sound-imitative words* which are felt as fitting by native speakers. Part of a poet's skill lies in exploiting this class of words (or even inventing his own), and while it is a mistake to see more such sound-imitation than is actually intended, it is equally incorrect to ignore its presence.

---

45.  Although laws of phonotactics (sounds coming together) can be broken.
46.  Compare English *to whisper*, German *flüstern*, French *chuchôter*, Italian *bisbigliare*, etc.
47.  For the distinction between onomatopoeia and mimicry see Bladon: 1977, 158-66, and Dubois, *Dictionnaire*, 346.
48.  Adduced by Alonso Schökel, *Estudios*, 113. Wilkinson: 1942 would divide onomatopoeia into seven types: imitation of sounds; sympathetic mouth-gesture; expressive mouth-gesture; significant euphony and cacophony; significant rhythm; metaphor from verse-technique and metaphor from word-form.

## *Onomatopoeia in Ugaritic and Akkadian*

Although difficult to detect in Ugaritic[49] sound-imitation is probably present in

| | |
|---|---|
| *hlk lalpm ḫdd* | Marching by the thousand like thunder |
| | (*CTA* 14 ii 92) |

and generally in the whole passage. Other examples are *yntkm kbtnm*, 'they ripped like reptiles' (*CTA* 6 vi 19); also 4 iv 28 (laughter); 6 ii 31-34 (winnowing, burning, etc.); 14 iii 120-123 (animal noises);[50] 3 iii 19-20 (whispering).

In Akkadian, the foaminess of beer is evoked by

| | |
|---|---|
| *šikār našpi duššupi* | Sweet light ale. (*Erra* I 58) |

Also: *imâ' mārtam*, 'he was belching bile' (lit. 'vomiting': *Atr* III ii 47); *arkīšunu ardud aḥmuṭ urriḫ*, 'after them I harried, I hurried, I hied' (*CuthLeg* 121).[51]

## *Onomatopoeia in Hebrew verse*

Since the use of sound-imitative words is largely random, there is little that can be done in the way of classification. Instead, a wide selection of examples will be set out, the sounds being mimicked set out in capitals. (Without forcing the English language too much some attempt will also be made to represent the onomatopoeia in translation.)

- BIRDS TWITTERING (Isa 10,14)

| | |
|---|---|
| ופצה פה ומצפצף | (None) opened its mouth or *chirruped*.[52] |

- HARP (Song 2,12)

| | |
|---|---|
| עת הזמיר הגיע | The time to zither is hither. |

- KISS (Song 1,2)

| | |
|---|---|
| ישקני מנשיקות פיהו | O for his mouth's smacking kiss![53] |

49. Since the exact pronunciation is unknown; see introductory section.
50. On Ug. *ġz, ġr, zġ* in this passage cf. Izre'el, *UF* 8 (1976) 447, n. 4.
51. See Watson, *UF* 9 (1977) 274, for the corresponding passage in Ug. [*CTA* 3C iii 15].
52. Note the chiastic use of *PṢ* and *ṢP(ṢP)*. For onomatopoeia in the names of birds in Heb. cf. Driver, *PEQ* (April 1955) 5; *ZAW* 65 (1953) 255.258; *JSS* 7 (1962) 15-16; these articles now need updating.
53. To offset the limited choice of words for 'to kiss' the poet simply repeated the root, producing the desired effect.

- GALLOPING HORSES (Jgs 5,22)

אז הלמו עקבי־סוס        Then hammered the horses' hooves,
מדהרות דהרות אביריו      with his steeds going gallopy-gallop.

- THUNDER (Isa 29,6)

ברעם וברעש וקול גדול      With thunder and earthquake and mighty boom.[54]

Other examples: a battle: Job 39,24-25; whip: Nah 3,2-3; straw burning: Isa 5,24; water: Song 4,16; the sea: Isa 5,30; serpents: Ps 140,4.[55]

*The function of onomatopoeia*
The main purpose in using sound-imitation is to heighten the imagery, lending substance to the bare words by making them sound like the event they describe. Such sound-effects can only be appreciated when onomatopoeic words are heard. It follows, therefore, that such poetry was intended to be listened to rather than read silently (see section on ORAL POETRY).

A secondary function is the linking of sound with meaning, as in assonance. Accordingly, where there was a choice of vocabulary or word-order, the poet would opt for the one which suited his purposes. So in

וכתתו חרבותם לאתים      They hammered their swords into 'shares,
וחניתותיהם למזמרות      their spears into sickles, (Isa 2,4[56])

the poet could have used לטש, which also means 'to hammer'—but he preferred a verb which had a repeated root (*kitt<sup>e</sup>tû*) in imitation of repeated hammer blows, and which sounded like *'ittîm*. There is similar reduplication in the second line.

*For study*
Ps 22,16ab; Jonah 2,6.

54. Possibly *wtn qlh b 'rpt šrh larṣ brqm*, 'he sent out his thunder from the clouds, his lightning flashed to the earth', *CTA* 4 v 70-71 [cf. Irwin, *Isaiah 28-33*, 53].
55. 'The psalmist succeeds in imitating the hissing sounds of serpents' (Dahood, *Psalms III*, 301). For a good selection of examples cf. Alonso Schökel, *Estudios*, 113-15.
56. Adduced by Alonso Schökel, *Estudios*, 115 (= Mic 4,3). In Joel 4,10 onomatopoeia has been sacrificed in favour of gender-matching (in reverse).

BIBLIOGRAPHY

(a) *General*
Bladon, R.A.W. 'Approaching Onomatopoeia', *AL* 8 (1977) 158-66.
Hymes, D. 'Phonological Aspects of Style: Some English Sonnets', in:
    Sebeok, *Style*, 109-31, esp. 111-14.
Wilkinson, L.P. 'Onomatopoeia and the Sceptics', *CQ* 36 (1942) 121-33.
Woodring, C.R. 'Onomatopoeia and Other Sounds in Poetry', *CE* 14 (1953).
Also Dubois, *Dictionnaire*, 346; Leech, *Guide*, 96-100; Nowottny, *Language*,
    2-4; *PEPP*, 590-91; Ullmann, *Semantics*, 82-92; *Language*, 69-71.

(b) *Semitic*
There is no major work on this aspect; cf. J. Barr, *Comparative Philology and
    the Text of the Old Testament* (Oxford, 1968) 273-76; Izre'el, *UF* 8
    (1976) 447; Alonso Schökel, *Estudios*, 113ff.

## 9.6 *Wordplay*

### 1. *Introductory notes on theory*

Wordplay is based on *lexical ambiguity*[57] which is simply a way of saying that words can be polyvalent (i.e. have multiple meanings). Lexical polyvalency is of two kinds: homonymy and polysemy. These will be explained in turn.

homonymy    When two (or more) words are identical in sound but have
            different meanings, they are homonyms.
                'can' = 'to be able (to)'
                'can' = 'metal container'.[58]

polysemy    Simply implies that one and the same word can have
            several meanings.
                '(to) do' = 'to perform, carry out, be sufficient,
                prosper, etc.'

The distinction between polysemy and homonymy is usually clear-cut (though there are exceptional cases) and it provides a convenient basis for classifying wordplay (see presently). Far from reducing language to unintelligibility, lexical ambiguity in the shape of polysemy prevents our memories being overburdened. In any case, polysemy is

---

57. Ambiguity can also be phonetic (within sentence structure) and grammatical. Most of this paragraph is derived from Ullmann, *Semantics*, 156-92.
58. Strictly speaking there is a further distinction between *homophones*, words which sound alike but mean different things ('bow', 'bough') and *homographs* or words with identical spelling but two or more meanings ('might' = 'power' and 'might' = verbal form of 'may'). For practical purposes, the difference can be ignored, especially as we are dealing with dead languages.

more widespread than homonymy, and for both types of ambiguity there are elements which lessen the possibility of misunderstanding. These elements, termed 'safeguards' by Ullmann,[59] include noun-gender, inflexion,[60] word-order, compound-forms[60] and modifications of form. In addition, homonyms can be differentiated by context, spelling and word-class.

The classification of puns or wordplay depends, of course, on the basis adopted for differentiation. Ullmann prefers the categories 'explicit' and 'implicit', valid for both homonymy and polysemy.[61] Yet other categories have been suggested[62] but I prefer to base my classification on the homonymy/polysemy distinction, with some modifications.

Scholars also tend to use a variety of names for the various types of wordplay; as far as possible, I will restrict myself to a single set.[63] The table setting out the different kinds of wordplay is also a guide to the presentation adopted in this section.

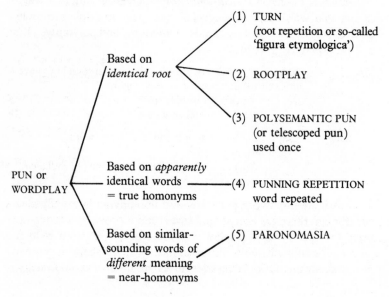

PUN or WORDPLAY

Based on *identical root*
- (1) TURN (root repetition or so-called 'figura etymologica')
- (2) ROOTPLAY
- (3) POLYSEMANTIC PUN (or telescoped pun) used once

Based on *apparently* identical words = true homonyms
- (4) PUNNING REPETITION word repeated

Based on similar-sounding words of *different* meaning = near-homonyms
- (5) PARONOMASIA

59. Ullmann, *Semantics*, 169ff and 180ff.
60. Not applicable to Hebrew.
61. Ullmann, *Semantics*, 188ff.
62. E.g. Wimsatt: 1950; Leech, *Guide*, 208-14; Brown: 1956.
63. See Diez Macho: 1948, 293-95 (including Hebrew terms) for traditional nomenclature.

## 2. Various forms of wordplay

1. *Turn*. Instead of 'figura etymologica' I prefer to adopt Wimsatt's designation, namely 'turn', for wordplays involving repetition of a root.[64] Wordplay of this kind is feeble, considered as ambiguity, but nonetheless effective by dint of its repetitive aspect. Examples are numberless, ranging from epithets such as Ugaritic

| | |
|---|---|
| *bny bnwt* | Creator of creatures.[65] |

to longer lines, as Akkadian

| | |
|---|---|
| *luzzirki izra rabâ* | I will curse you with a great curse. |
| *ḫantiš ḫarpiš izrū'a litḫûki kâši* | With great speed let my curses reach you.[66] |

The turn, in fact, is very largely a form of repetition (see REPETITION), shown clearly in

| | |
|---|---|
| רזי לי | A curse on me! |
| רזי לי | A curse on me! |
| אוי לי | Alas for me: |
| בגדים בגדו בגד | traitors were treacherous with treachery, |
| בוגדים בגדו | traitors were treacherous. (Isa 24,16[67]) |

The root בגד, 'to be treacherous', occurs no less than five times.

Other examples include Isa 17,12; Jer 3,22 and Prov 7,14. Generally speaking, such turns share the functions of repetition, but some do fulfil functions peculiar to wordplay (e.g. Ps 35,1 expresses poetic justice).

2. *Rootplay*. In rootplay the consonants of a key verbal root are used as the basis for alliterative transpositions. So in Ugaritic

| | |
|---|---|
| *tqḥ mlk 'lmk* | You'll take your sovereignty of eternity, |
| *drkt dt drdrk* | your power, for ever and ever. |

(CTA 2 iv 10-11)

---

64. According to Wimsatt: 1950, 14-15, the *turn* is 'when a *word* or *root* is repeated (or seems to be repeated) in various connections or with various modifications', and is a kind of polysemy.

65. *CTA* 17 i 15. See also *rd lmlk amlk*, 'Down from your ruler (-throne) so I may rule' (*CTA* 16 vi 37).

66. Gilg VII iii 8-9; text, translation and parallels in J. Tigay, *The Evolution of the Gilgamesh Epic* (Philadelphia, 1982) 171.

67. Alternatively, 'Traitors were treacherous with treachery / traitors were treacherous'. See, too, Isa 32,19.

there is play on the letters of *mlk* in the first line, and on *drkt* in the
second, both being highly significant words in the context.[68]

| | |
|---|---|
| *imbaru liqturma* | May fog *haze*, and |
| *urqīt [erṣetim] lippatqu* | earth's *grazing* be formed. |

This example from 'Nisaba and the Wheat'[69] is based on similarity
between *liqturma* (root *qtr*) and *urqīt* (root *wrq*).

Rootplay in Hebrew is extremely frequent, so that the texts listed
here represent only a modest sample. To begin with, a transparent
couplet from Second Isaiah:

| | |
|---|---|
| והיה העקב למישור | The *ugly*-heights will become a plain, |
| והרכסים לבקעה | the ranges, a *glen*. (Isa 40,4) |

Here the letters of עקב (found only here, so perhaps invented by the
poet for his purpose) are transposed to form בקעה, of opposite
meaning (and gender).

Other examples include: צרי רצין 'Rezin's enemies' (Isa 9,10); חרב
'steel'[70]—בחור 'elite' (Isa 31,8; Ez 30,17); פקדתי 'stuck am I'—קפדתי
'cut off have I' (Isa 38,10.11); מלא מאלה 'filled from these' (Jer 4,12);
קרבם '(their) inwards'—קבר 'grave' (Ps 5,10); רכב על כרוב 'he rode on
the cherubim' (Ps 18,11); ומשאניך נשאו ראש 'your haters, head high'
(Ps 83,3); שבת אחים גם יחד 'brothers living *together*' (Ps 133,1—cf. חיים
'life' in v. 3); ואשברה מתלעות עול 'I smashed the "heathen's" teeth'
(Job 29,17); יחלץ 'he rescues'—בלחץ 'by squeezing' (Job 36,15); לקח
'allure'—חלק 'smoothness'[71] (Prov 7,21; also Sir 14,9); woman is a
'well' (באר) who 'waylays' (ארב: Prov 23,27-28); דברי חכמים כדרבנות
'wise men's epigrams are goads' (Qoh 12,11); and elsewhere.[72]

Rootplay is, of course, related to *alliteration* (see ALLITERATION)
and it is sometimes difficult to determine which is operative or
whether one is dominant. Occasionally there is a parallel text which
acts as a *control*: both texts may exhibit similar rootplay, as in
Isa 42,3-4 and Ps 147,15.[73] Alternatively, there may be a strong
contrast; compare Ps 107,33,

---

68. Also *CTA* 2 i 32-33; iv 8-9; 3 C iii 15; 4 iv 41-43.

69. Text: *BWL* 169 obv. i 18, and 346. Also *BWL* 132:100.106.119; 192:20; *Erra*
IIIA 24; *Atr* x rev. ii 46.

70. Lit. 'sword'.

71. Note the combination with a polysemantic pun: חלק can also mean 'to destroy'.

72. Nb 24,8e; Isa 40,22; 30,17; Nah 1,10 (difficult text); Pss 18,4 and 7; 99,6-8; Prov
6,7-8; Sir 32,21ab.

73. See Dahood, *Psalms III*, 349.

ומצאי מים לצמאון     Water-springs to thirsty ground

with Isa 35,7:

וצמאון למבועי מים     Thirsty ground to bubbling water.[74]

3. *Polysemantic pun*. Though such plays are often termed 'double meaning' (or 'double entendre'), the term polysemantic pun is preferable since it denotes a word which can have two or more meanings. Such puns are the most effective kind because they demand quick-wittedness from both poet and audience since the operative word occurs once only. They exemplify the principle of thrift operative in oral poetry—though many polysemantic puns are strictly literary in nature.

Very few examples are to be found in *Ugaritic*; one is

*nšu riš ḥrṭm*     The ploughmen raised their heads.
                               (*CTA* 16 iii 12)

where the expression which means, literally 'to lift one's head' is also an idiom for 'to rejoice'.[75] The context (a severe drought) describes the man ploughing and suddenly looking up as the welcome rain falls. In *Akkadian* poetry polysemantic puns are equally rare, for example:

*iptêma ina īnāša puratta idiglat*     From her *eyes* he made the
                                           Euphrates and Tigris flow.
                                                 (*Ee* V 55)

the term *īnu* meaning both 'eye' and 'source, spring' (as in West Semitic).

*Hebrew* examples include Prov 28,23 ('Correct a man and you will ultimately obtain more thanks . . .')

ממחליק לשון     than someone slippery-tongued,

the verb חלק meaning both 'to be smooth' and 'to perish' (hiph. 'to destroy').[76] Also Jgs 14,14;[77] Isa 29,4 (and Qoh 12,4) שפל 'to be

---

74. Curiously, rootplay is also used in the prose text Dt 8,15 (almost exactly as in Ps 107), the only other text where צמאון occurs, suggesting that the word may have been specially invented.

75. For a good discussion of the same idiom in Hebrew see Speiser, *Genesis*, 308; note that the context in both Krt and the Joseph story is a prolonged drought.

76. Other texts include Prov 2,16; 7,21; 7,5; also Ps 5,10.

77. A much discussed text; see most recently de Moor, *UF* 7 (1975) 590-91.

quiet/lowly';[78] Isa 30,1 מסכה 'cover/idol';[79] Isa 57,6 יד 'hand/penis';[80] Job 7,6 תקוה 'hope/thread'; Song 8,1-2 אשקך 'I would kiss you/cause you to drink'; and others.[81] Evidently, true wordplay is not all that frequent; it took a skilled poet to exploit multiple meaning.

　　4. *Punning repetition*. In punning repetition what appears to be the same word occurs twice, often in succession. For example, the Ugaritic word *npš*, which can mean both 'living being' and 'appetite', occurs twice in a single line of poetry, first with one meaning, then with the other:

> *npš npš lbim thw*　　　　Live(-prey) the *appetite* of a lion craves.
> 　　　　　　　　　　　　　　　(*Ugar* 5 4 obv. 2-4)

An even better instance comes from Akkadian: it plays on the two meanings 'enemy' and 'friend' of *ahû*:

> *ana aḫî aḫī itūra*　　　　Into a *foe* my *friend* has turned.[82]

Unfortunately, the Hebrew passages in question, Jgs 15,16; Prov 5,19-20,[83] are obscure.

　　5. *Paronomasia*. In the absence of homonyms (words which sound alike, but mean different things) and polysemy (one word with several meanings), the next best solution for the poet wishing to play on words is to use paronomasia, which lies somewhere in between. It simply means the deliberate choice of two (or more) different words which sound nearly alike.

　　There are a few cases in Ugaritic, none of certain translation.[84] More prolific in this regard is Akkadian, as in

> *ša pīšu maṭû*　　　　No word his mouth gave?
> *aššassu amat*　　　　His wife's a slave.[85]

which plays on the similarity in sound of *maṭû*, and *amat* (3f.s. stative of *amtu*) meaning 'to diminish' and '(she is a) slave' respectively.

---

78. Irwin, *Isaiah 28-33*, 50-51.

79. Irwin, *Isaiah 28-33*, 73; also 90-91 (on Isa 30,21f); 97 (on Isa 30,28); 126 (on Isa 32,8).

80. Also in Song 5,4; Isa 57,8-10; cf. Ug. *yd* in *CTA* 23:46-47.

81. Lam 2,13; Isa 29,15; on the double meaning of רוח ('weapon/anger') see Cohen, *JANES* 7 (1975) 17 and n. 28.

82. *BWL* 34:84; note also *būrtu/burtu*, 'well/cow' in *BWL* 146:51.

83. See Irwin, *Isaiah 28-33*, 16 [שנה = 'to reel/go astray'].

84. Including *Ugar* 5 7:65-67 and *CTA* 6 i 49-65 [on which cf. Watson: 1980].

85. *BWL* 236, obv. 3-4; Lambert's translation: 'The wife of a man who cannot talk well [*CAD* M/1, 429 'who speaks humbly'] is a female slave'.

Another example is *bunnū zēr nullâta ibanni*, 'approval produces blasphemous offspring'.[86] There are other instances.[87]

Hebrew easily lends itself to paronomasia and there is no shortage of such puns, though it must be admitted that many of them are quite feeble. Here is a selection of them:

| | |
|---|---|
| לא־עשה לרעהו רעה | He did no *mischief* to his *mate*. (Ps 15,3) |
| אב אנכי לאביונים | A *father* am I to the *fatherless*. (Job 29,16a) |
| בער אשה השחתו רבים | On account of a *dame* many went to the pit, |
| וכן אהביה באש תלחט | and so her lovers by *flame* were consumed. |
| | (Sir 9,8) |

See, further, Isa 31,1.2; 33,4; 63,2; Ps 18,13; 28,5; 129,5-6; 148,3-5; Job 31,40a; Sir 4,11; also Song 1,3; Lam 3,1.

Akin to paronomasia is *assonantal paronomasia* or wordplay based on vowel-patterns. The similarity between the near-synonyms $p^e$ '*ullat*, 'reward, recompense' (in cstr. state) and $t^e bu$ '*at*, 'income' (also cstr.) is played on in

| | |
|---|---|
| פעלת צדיק לחיים | A just man's *recompense* is life, |
| תבואת רשע לחטאת | A bad man's *income* is guilt. (Prov 10,16) |

See also Isa 8,6; 13,12 ('*ôqîr*— '*ôpîr*: 'I will make scarcer—Ophir');[88] Ps 107,11 (*kî him^e rû 'imrē-'ēl*, 'for they demurred against El's words'); Prov 12,5 (*mišpaṭ—mirmâ*, 'lawful—awful') and many others.[89]

An example from Akkadian is perhaps

| | |
|---|---|
| *mīnsu ana ili u amēli lemuttu* | Why did you plot evil against man |
| *takpud* | and god?[90] |

Wordplay of this kind is difficult to establish in the unvocalised Ugaritic script, but a possible example is

| | |
|---|---|
| *ap ab kmtm tmtn* | Rather, father, like 'squires' you'll expire.[91] |

---

86. *BWL* 207:10 (Fable of the Fox); he translates 'kindness begets a blasphemous offspring' and on p. 308 suggests that *būnu (or bunnū)* is elliptical for 'smiling face, approval, consent'. *CAD* B, 89: 'Spoiling one's offspring creates worthless behaviour'.

87. *Maqlu* VI 5: *ubānātīja bīnu*, 'Are my fingers of the tamarisk?'; *Erra* IIIc 51: *imittašu miṭṭa iṣbat*, 'In his right he grasped the smiter'; and *māru lā ašru mūru*, 'A son not humble is a colt' [cited by Khanijan, *RSP* II, 378].

88. Alonso Schökel, *Estudios*, 117.

89. Including Isa 1,23; Mic 6,3-4; Mal 3,20; Pss 37,20; 64,5; Job 3,8; Qoh 10,6.

90. *Erra* IIIc 36; also *BWL* 86:251-252 (= Theodicy).

91. *CTA* 16 i 17; lit. 'Shall you die, then, father, like mortals/men?'—to be read, possibly, *\*ap abi kamutima tamutinna*.

244        *Classical Hebrew Poetry*

6. *Complex wordplay.* In certain passages several different kinds of wordplay are present and interact in a manner which is more effective than simple wordplay. In Isa 65,11-12 two kinds occur, one an etymological pun on the deity 'Meni' taken to mean 'destiny' and the other, rootplay on the verbs ערך, 'to arrange, set out' and כרע, 'to crouch'.

| | | |
|---|---|---|
| ואתם עזבי יהוה | 11a | But those of you abandoning Yahweh, |
| השכחים את הר קדשי | b | forgetting my Holy Hill, |
| הערכים לגד שלחן | c | who *set* the table for Gad, |
| והממלאים למני ממסך | d | and *m*easure out the *m*ixture for *M*eni, |
| ומניתי אתכם לחרב | 12a | I will *m*ean you for the sword, |
| וכלכם לטבח תכרעו | b | and you all shall *stoop* to be butchered. |

Another example is Hos 8,7

| | |
|---|---|
| קמה אין לו צמח | The standing-grain has no heads, |
| בלי יעשה קמח | it shall yield no meal, |

where קמח, 'flour, meal' combines the sounds of both קמה, 'standing grain' and צמח, 'sprout, growth'—neatly expressing in one portmanteau word the end-product (flour) of a long organic process. Other examples are Gen 49,16 (etymological pun + rootplay); Mic 1,10ff (paronomasia, etymological pun and rootplay); Ps 85,2 (rootplay + etymological pun); Prov 23,2 (rootplay + double entendre). Examples occur in Ugaritic[92] and Akkadian.[93]

7. *Wordplay on names.* Anyone conversant with Hebrew knows that puns on proper names of both places and people occur frequently. They can all be grouped under the classes discussed so far, and are largely of two kinds: puns based on the etymology (or what is thought to be the etymology) of a name; and paronomasia. Name wordplay can also form the basis for complete poems (as will be seen). Here it will be enough to look briefly at the two kinds of name wordplay just mentioned.

Correct etymology lies behind

יחזקיהו חזק עירו        Hezekiah fortified his city,

which opens the eulogy to Hezekiah (Sir 48,17-25), the root being חזק, 'to be strong'. The same applies to Hos 12,4 where עקב, 'to supplant' is the root of the personal name 'Jacob'. In sharp contrast,

92. *CTA* 2 iv 28-30; 6 iii/iv 46-48.
93. *mār mārīšu īmar*, 'his grandsons he'll see' (*YOS* 10, 44:70), which combines paronomasia with root repetition.

'Ephraim' is variously related to פרי, 'fruit' in Hos 9,16 and 14,9 but to פרא, 'wild ass' in 8,9 and 13,15. In Isa 63,1-2 'Edom' is connected with אדם, 'to be red'. Such etymologies were probably popular, even if inexact.

### 3. *Functions of wordplay*

Wordplay is largely a feature of oral poetry, since it depends on how words sound.[94] The following functions can be detected:

1. *To amuse and sustain interest*. The use of an ambiguous word would make listeners alert, ready to determine which particular meaning (or meanings) the poet intended. Puns on proper names, especially, must have been popular since they occur so frequently, and the ability to give a humorous twist to a name must have been well received.

2. *To assist composition*. Generally considered, a poet could peg his sayings on a series of wordplays based on selected lexical items. More particularly, sequences of proper names such as the twelve tribes of Israel obviously provided the framework for several poems, notably Gen 49, Dt 33 and parts of Jgs 5. Place-names, perhaps ancient itineraries, played a similar role in poems such as Isa 10,27-32[95] and Mic 1,10-16.

3. *To lend authenticity*. Wordplay in all its forms was evidence of a poet's mastery of language, and in the case of the prophets must have increased their authenticity.

4. *To link a poem or its parts*. In Isa 11,4 the similarity between ושפט, 'he will judge', שבט, 'rod' and שפתיו, '(his) lips', is a powerful link bonding the couplet together. Again, in Ps 148,3-5 the chopped-up effect of a detailed list is offset by the paronomasia which melds the cola together:

| | |
|---|---|
| הללוהו שמש וירח | Praise him, *sun* and moon; |
| הללוהו כל כוכבי אור | praise him all stars of light;[96] |
| הללוהו שמי השמים | praise him *uttermost skies*, |
| והמים אשר מעל השמים | and the *waters* which are above the *skies*. |

Also, Hab 2,16.[97]

---

94. Although some wordplay is based on written texts.

95. For translation: D.L. Christensen, 'The March of Conquest in Isaiah X 27c-34', *VT* 26 (1976) 385-99.

96. Or 'stars of morning': Dahood, *Psalms III*, 353 who cites Job 24,14; Neh 8,3 and Job 38,7.

97. For the context-linking effect of puns see Brown: 1956, 16 and 26.

5. *To denote reversal*. Reversal of fortune is often neatly expressed by wordplay, as in

| יבשו ויבהלו מאד | Utterly *confounded* and dismayed |
| כל איבי | shall be all my enemies, |
| ישבו יבשו רגע | *turning away* in sudden *confusion*. (Ps 6,11) |

with its play on בוש, 'to be ashamed' and שוב, 'to turn'. The chiastic ABA′ strophic pattern confirms this, since chiasmus also denotes inversion of an existing state. The well-known assonantal pun in Isa 5,7 is another example, this time confirmed by the simultaneous use of gender parallelism. See, too, Nb 24,8e; Isa 31,8; 38,10-11; 40,4; Ps 107,33 as well as Isa 9,10 and 65,11-12.

6. *To show appearance can be deceptive*. The inherent ambiguity of wordplay is eminently suited to depict deceptive appearances. A good example is Ps 5,10 with its contrast between the deviousness of the psalmist's enemies and their smooth talk:

| כי אין בפיהו נכונה | For there is nothing trusty in any mouth, |
| קרבם הוות | their *inwards* are words, |
| קבר פתוח גרונם | an open *grave* their throat, |
| לשונם יחליקון | their tongue is *glib*. |

Other examples are Prov 7,21 (cf. 2,16; Sir 14,9); 23,27-28.

7. *To equate two things*. Wordplay can equate two disparate things by playing on the similarity of their names, as in Sir 4,11 where בן 'son' and מבין '(he) who understands' are made out to be equivalent:

| חכמות למדה בניה | Wisdom teaches her *sons*, |
| ותעיד לכל מבינים בה | and cherishes all *who understand* her. |

A related function is to show like breeds like, as in the Akkadian proverb 'No word his mouth gave? His wife's a slave' (cited above), or Prov 13,20. See Prov 25,13.

8. *Other functions*. Since wordplay is very frequent in laments[98] it must evidently have been effective in distracting the mourners, momentarily turning their sorrow to laughter. Wordplay assisted the memory of both poet and audience, and was instructive at the same time: a poem such as Gen 49 provided the unlettered with a potted history of Israel.[99]

---

98. As noticed particularly by Dahood, *Psalms III*, 233.271; *Psalms II*, 45 and 78.
99. Schmidt, *BZ* 24 (1938) 7-13, discusses functions such as the *explanatory* as in plays on personal names, the *ornamental* (Prov 25,13; Hos 9,15) and the *allusive*. Gevirtz also remarks on the power geo-political puns have to create an allusion, citing Gen 31,47.49; 49,22 and 32,23-33 (*HUCA* 46 [1975] 33ff).

## 4. *Rediscovering Hebrew wordplay*

Our growing knowledge of languages cognate with Hebrew, particularly Ugaritic[100] and of languages with vast vocabularies, such as Akkadian, has helped us uncover hidden puns in Hebrew poetry. The double-meaning of 'lips' in Prov 5,3[101] is brought out by the Akkadian text:

> May my lips be lallaru-honey,
> may my hands be all charm,
> may the *lips of my pudenda* be lips of honey.[102]

## *Example for wordplay: Psalm 12*

A good example of sustained ambiguity in the form of several *polysemantic* (or telescoped) puns is Ps 12. The main theme of the poem is the contrast between the double talk of deceitful men, and the true, unambiguous content of God's words ('pure', 'refined seven times', v. 7). In spite of certain philological difficulties, the polysemy of the operative words is transparent. Before these can be considered, though, the text and translation have to be set out.

| | | |
|---|---|---|
| הושיעה יהוה | I(A) | 2a Help, O Yahweh, |
| כי גמר חסיד | | b for the loyal person is done for, |
| כי פסו אמונים מבני אדם | | d for *truth* is removed from mankind. |
| | | |
| שוא ידברו | II(B) | 3a Falsehood they speak, |
| איש את רעהו | | b each with his fellow, |
| שפת חלקות | | c with *glib* lips |
| בלב ולב ידברו | | d and two-faced mind they speak. |
| | | |
| יכרת יהוה | III(C) | 4a Yahweh should amputate |
| כל שפתי חלקות | | b all *glib* lips, |
| לשון מדברת גדלות | | c (every) tongue speaking *big*; |
| אשר אמרו | | 5a those who say: |
| ללשננו נגביר | | b 'By our tongue we are great, |
| שפתינו אתנו | | c our *weapon* is our lips, |
| מי אדון לנו | | d who more master than us?' |

100. Apparent homonyms in Hebrew can be distinguished when Ugaritic cognates are known since Ugaritic had not lost the distinction between *ḥ* and *ḫ* (= ח) and *ʿ—ġ* (= ע). For Akkadian cf. Held: 1970-1971.

101. Unnoticed by M. Dahood, 'Honey that Drips: Notes on Proverbs 5,2-3', *Bib* 54 (1973) 65-66.

102. Cited in *CAD* K, 396.

| | | |
|---|---|---|
| משד עניים IV(C′) | 6a | 'For the sobbing of the poor, |
| מאנקת אביונים | b | for the groans of the needy, |
| עתה אקום יאמר יהוה | c | I must make a stand (says Yahweh). |
| אשית בישעי יפח | d | I'll make a witness of my intervention!' |
| לו אמרות יהוה אמרות V(B′) | 7a | Surely Yahweh's sayings are pure sayings, |
| טהרות | | |
| כסף צרוף בעלי | b | silver refined in the crucible, |
| לארץ מזקק שבעתים | c | from earth purified sevenfold. |
| אתה יהוה תשמרם VI(A′) | 8a | Yahweh, you really keep them [= promises], |
| תצרנו מן הדור זו לעלם | b | you protect us from the deception-group, |
| סביב רשעים יתהלכו | 9a | (while) the wicked prowl around, |
| נכר מזלות לבני אדם | b | *calamity* overtaking mankind. |

Besides certain translation problems[103] and structural features,[104] the following points are relevant.

The ambiguity of at least three words is exploited:

| חלק | (3c, 4b) | = 'to be smooth' and 'to be divisive'[105] |
|---|---|---|
| גדל | (4c) | = 'to be great' and 'to be distorting'[106] |
| את | (5c) | = 'with' and 'weapon' |

103. 2c 'is removed': cf. Akk. *pasāsu*, 'to wipe out', used of oaths and contracts [*AHw*, 838]. 4a: Cutting out the tongue was punishment, in Mesopotamia, for breaking contracts, etc. [for texts see *CAD* L, 211]. Cf., too, Prov 10,31. 6a 'sobbing': cf. Dahood, *Psalms I*, 74 and Ug. *šd*, Aram. *šdâ*, 'to pour'. 6d 'witness': cf. Ug. *yph*, also 'witness', discussed by Pardee, *VT* 28 (1978) 204-13. P.D. Miller, 'Yāpîah in Psalm XII 6', *VT* 29 (1979) 495-501, translates this line 'I will place in safety the witness in his behalf'. 7b 'in the crucible': so Dahood, *Psalms I*, 74 who reads בעלי לאון assuming dittography of ל. 8b 'deception-group', lit. 'group which [זו] is of deception'; the root of the last noun is עלם, 'to conceal'; cf. Prov 26,4. 9b 'calamity'—reading the final ו of 9a as beginning 9b; an alternative meaning is 'deceit', cf. נכר in Prov 26,24 and Akk. *nakāru*, 'to lie'. 'Overtaking', reading מזלות, with the otherwise unattested root מזל, cognate to Ug. *mzl*, 'to run, overtake'. The two nouns נכר and מזלות are in apposition (so the gender discord is irrelevant).

104. Structural features include the *overall chiastic pattern* (ABCC′B′A′) showing the climactic line to be 6d, 'I'll make a witness of my intervention' (spoken by Yahweh), *chiasmus* in stanza III and the *envelope figure* in stanzas I and VI ('sons of man'). The verbs for speaking occur seven times (3 x דבר and 4 x אמר). See Watson, 'Chiastic Patterns', 131, and contrast the four-strophe division of van der Lugt, *Strofische Structuren*, 165.

105. A further meaning may be 'to be destructive'; cf. Ug. *hlq*, Akk. *halāqu*.

106. So Dahood, *Psalms I*, 73.

and possibly of

| | | |
|---|---|---|
| אמונים | (2c) | = 'truth' and 'true (men)' |
| נכר | (9b) | = 'calamity', 'deceit' and 'to be strange' |
| עלם | (8b) | = 'to conceal' and 'to be ignorant'. |

In 5c 'our lips are our weapon' could be rendered idiomatically as 'our lips are a two-edged sword', since the punishment for double-talk (breaking oaths, contracts, etc.) is amputation of the tongue.[107] Even in 2b, גמר 'to complete, finish' may also evoke the meaning 'to avenge'.[108] And there may be other double meanings which we are unable to recognise, though they were evident to native speakers of Hebrew.

*For study*

Jgs 14,14; Isa 22,2.17.18; 25,7; 27,7; 29,16; 32,1; 33,1; Jer 48,15; Pss 4,6; 11,7; 27,3; 35,1; Prov 25,27.
Nah 1,2-3; Ps 25,3; Lam 2,16.
Mic 7,11; Qoh 7,1.
Hos 8,7; Job 5,21.

## BIBLIOGRAPHY

(a) General
Brown, J. 'Eight Types of Puns', *PMLA* 71 (1956) 14-26.
Empson, W. *Seven Types of Ambiguity* (London, 1953, 3rd ed.).
Wimsatt, W.K. (Jr.) 'Verbal Style, Logical and Counterlogical', *PMLA* 65 (1950) 5-20.

(b) Semitic
Bohl, M.T. 'Wortspiele im AT', *JPOS* 6 (1926) 196-212.
Casanowicz, I.M. 'Paronomasia in the Old Testament', *JBL* 12 (1893) 105-67.
—*Paronomasia in the Old Testament* (Boston, 1894).
Glück, J.J. 'Paronomasia in Biblical Literature', *Semitics* 1 (1970) 50-78.
Guillaume, A. 'Paronomasia in the Old Testament', *JSS* 9 (1964) 282-90.
Peeters, L. 'Pour une interprétation du jeu de mots', *Semitics* 2 (1971-72) 127-42.
Payne, D.F. 'Characteristic Word-Play in "Second Isaiah": A Reappraisal', *JSS* 12 (1967) 207-29.

107. As prescribed in the Code of Hammurapi, §192.
108. For this meaning cf. M.J. Dahood, 'The Root גמר in the Psalms', *TS* 14 (1953) 595-97; M. Tsevat, *A Study of the Language of the Biblical Psalms* (Philadelphia, 1955) 80 n. 34; Gibson, *CML* 144 (Ug. *gmr*). For a similar study cf. P.D. Miller, 'Poetic Ambiguity and Balance in Psalm XV', *VT* 29 (1979) 416-24.

Sasson, J.M. 'Wordplay in the OT', *IDBS* (1976) 968-70, with bibliography.

Watson, W.G.E. 'An Example of Multiple Wordplay in Ugaritic', *UF* 12 (1980) 443-44.

(c) On homonymy

Barr, J. 'Did Isaiah know about Hebrew "root-meaning"?', *ExpT* 75 (1964) 242.

—*Comparative Philology and the Text of the Old Testament* (Oxford, 1968) 151-55 and index, 349.

Delcor, M. 'Homonymie et Interprétation dans l'ancien Testament', *JSS* 18 (1973) 40-54.

Díez Macho, A. 'La homonimia o paronomasia = al-muyānasa = lašon nofel 'al lašon', *Sef* 8 (1948) 203-321; 9 (1948) 269-309.

Held, M. 'Studies in Biblical Homonyms in the Light of Akkadian', *JANES* 3 (1970-71) 46-55.

Sawyer, J.F.A. 'Root-meanings in Hebrew', *JSS* 12 (1967) 37-50.

# 10

## IMAGERY

### 10.1 *Imagery*

At the technical level poetry is at its best when composed with *thrift*, that is to say, when the poet expresses as much as he can in a few words as possible. To use an analogy, this would correspond to an artist drawing a sketch with a minimum of pencil strokes (Matisse, Picasso).

Of course poetry is not just economy of expression for, at the very least it would tend to be rather dry if not extremely dull. Like the painter, a poet has to infuse his word pictures with life and movement and make them appeal to the senses. The artist can use a whole range of colours while the poet has to resort to *imagery*, to evoking pictures with figurative language.

In the larger sense, poetry is imagery, but here we are more directly concerned with technique which boils down to the use of simile and metaphor. And before we can turn to these topics we must first examine the nature of the image and imagery.[1]

An *image* is 'a figure of speech expressing some similarity or analogy' and most images are metaphorical.[2] The converse is not necessarily true, though: not all metaphors or comparisons are images. Imagery must be:

1. concrete and sense-related, not based on abstract concepts:[3]

---

1. Much of the following is dependent on Ullmann's chapter 'The Nature of Imagery' in *Language*, 174-201.
2. Ullmann, *Language*, 177.
3. 'There can be no question of an image unless the resemblance it expresses has a concrete and sensuous quality' (Ullmann, *Language*, 178).

You tear men's skin away from them,[4]
and their flesh away from their bones,
eating my people's flesh,
flaying their skin from them,
crunching their bones,
breaking (them) as if for the pot,
or like meat within a cauldron. (Mic 3,2-3[5])

2. Further, an image should contain an element of surprise[6] as in the oracle against Jehoiakin:

They'll not bewail him with
'My poor brother,
my poor "fraternity"'.

They'll not bewail him with
'Poor Master,
Poor "His Majesty"'.

He'll be buried with an ass's burial:
dragged along and ejected
way outside Jerusalem's gates. (Jer 22,19[7])

3. And, finally, imagery is more effective if new or at least relatively unknown,[8] or at least if an old image is given a new twist; in Joel 1,6-7 the well-worn image of devouring locusts is combined with the equally hackneyed metaphor of devouring lions to give:

Their teeth are lion's teeth,
their jaws a lioness's,
making havoc of my vine,
defoliating my figs ...[9]

Original imagery, such as that of the tomb-robber in Job 3,20-23,[10] is exceptional.

Images can be ornamental, but the expert poet will use imagery for particular functions.[11] They can express a significant theme within a corpus—the covenant-theme, for instance, in Hos 14,9:

4. There are some difficulties in the Hebrew, but the sense is clear enough.
5. See, too, Jer 50,17 for more concrete imagery.
6. Ullmann, *Language*, 178, uses the adjectives 'striking and unexpected'.
7. Also Jer 9,21; 17,11.
8. Ullmann, *Language*, 179.
9. See Mic 2,12-13.
10. As pointed out by Gibson, *SJT* 28 (1975) 264; he also mentions the sirocco imagery in Job 4,9 (265).
11. Ullmann, *Language*, 193-201.

אני כברוש רענן   I am like a leafy pine-tree.[12]

'Some images and image-patterns carry strong emotional overtones and convey implicit value-judgments'[13]—often in the form of animal imagery which can be positive, as in the metaphorical use of such names for officials (see below), or negative as in Am 4,1:

> Listen to this matter,
> cows of Bashan.

One image can sum up a writer's philosophy—'wind' in Qoh—or form part of a portrait—Egypt as a 'heifer' in Jer 46,20.[14] The otherwise inexpressible can be conveyed by an apt image or set of images; an example is Job 28 which successfully puts across the concept of God's unfathomable wisdom.[15] Recognition of the correct image can have text-critical and philological repercussions.[16] An illustration is provided in the section WORKED EXAMPLES, on Ps 47.

*For study*
Ez 19,1-9; Job 32,18ff; 6,2-3.

BIBLIOGRAPHY

(a) *General*
Antoine, G. 'Pour une methode d'analyse stylistique des images', *Langue et littérature* (Liège, 1961) 154ff.
Hornstein, L.H. 'Analysis of Imagery: a Critique of Literary Method', *PMLA* 57 (1942) 638-53.
Lewis, C.D. *The Poetic Image* (London, 1947).
Richards, I.A. *The Philosophy of Rhetoric* (London, 1936).
Also *PEPP*, 363-70, with bibliography.

(b) *Semitic*
Brown, S.J. *Image and Truth: Studies in the Imagery of the Bible* (Rome, 1955).
Bruggemann, W. 'From Dust to Kingship', *ZAW* 84 (1972) 1-18.
Caird, G.B. *The Language and Imagery of the Bible* (London, 1980).
Collins, T. 'The Physiology of Tears in the Old Testament', *CBQ* 33 (1971) 18-38.185-97.

---

12. Note, incidentally, the allusion to ברית in the name of the tree.
13. Ullmann, *Language*, 195; also 147-49.
14. Also, Ez 27.
15. Craigie: 1978, mentions two further functions: the dramatic and the religious. For structuring functions of imagery, cf. Lack: 1973.
16. See Paul: 1978 for a good illustration.

Craigie, P.C. 'Deborah and Anat: A Study of Poetic Imagery (Judges 5)', *ZAW* 90 (1978) 374-81.

Curtis, A.H.W. '"The Subjugation of the Waters" Motif in the Psalms; Imagery or Polemic?', *JSS* 23 (1978) 245-56.

Emerton, J.A. 'The Origin of the Son of Man Imagery', *JTS* 9 (1958) 225-42.

Fisch, H. 'The Analogy of Nature. A Note on the Structure of the OT Imagery', *JTS* 6 (1955) 161-73.

Joines, K.R. *Serpent Symbolism in the OT* (Haddonfield, 1974).

Kelly, S. 'Psalm 46: A Study in Imagery', *JBL* 89 (1970) 305-12.

Lack, R. *La symbolique du Livre d'Isaïe. Essai sur l'image littéraire comme élément de structuration* (*AnBib* 59: Rome, 1973).

Lichtenstein, M.H. 'The Poetry of Poetic Justice: A Comparative Study in Biblical Imagery', *JANES* 5 (1973) 255-65.

Margalit (Margulis), B. 'Psalm 24: A Study in Imagery', *JBL* 89 (1970) 292-304.

Paul, S. 'The Image of the Oven and the Cake in Hosea VII 4-10', *VT* 18 (1968) 114-20.

—'Fishing Imagery in Amos 4:2', *JBL* 97 (1978) 183-90.

Reymond, P. *L'eau, sa vie, et sa signification dans l'ancien Testament* (*VTS* 6; Leiden, 1958).

Rimbach, J.A. 'Animal Imagery in the O.T.: Some Aspects of Hebrew Poetics' (Dissertation Johns Hopkins 1972); cf. *Diss Abs* 33 (1972-73) 1825A.

Tsumura, D.T. 'Twofold Image of Wine in Psalm 46:4-5', *JQR* 71 (1981) 167-75.

Wakeman, M. *God's Battle with the Monster: A Study in Biblical Imagery* (Leiden, 1973).

Wittstruck, T. 'The Influence of Treaty Curse Imagery on the Beast Imagery of Daniel 7', *JBL* 97 (1978) 100-02.

The lengthy list provided here shows imagery to be a much-studied topic in Hebrew poetry, though very little seems to have been done in the area of Mesopotamian studies and only a few titles refer directly to Ugaritic. A good model for the study of Hebrew imagery is Alonso Schökel, *Estudios*, 269-307, where he examines the imagery of water, mountains, fire, other nations as the instrument of divine punishment and the stumbling block, chiefly in connection with Isaiah.

## 10.2 *Simile*

*The simile in general*

Simile and metaphor overlap, to a certain extent: they express the same thing but in different ways. Broadly speaking, the simile is more obvious than metaphor. This is either because it is more *explicit*, or because the *ground of comparison* is actually stated. By contrast, metaphor is more concise and at the same time, more vague.[17] So, in

> Like heads of grain they wither (Job 24,24)

everything is expressed and there is no room for divergent interpretations. (However, as will be seen, similes favour the use of ellipsis.)

## Similes and oral poetry

In his study of the Homeric simile, Scott concluded that 'the simile is an independent entity entering the narrative either at the beginning of the line or else beginning at one of the traditional caesurae of the line'.[18] This applies, in a limited way, to ancient Near Eastern poetry too, indicating that poets had a stock of similes which they could use at various points in their improvisation. In general, such similes (whether borrowed or invented) served a twofold purpose; one audience-oriented, the other to the poet's own advantage. Ready-made similes were suitable to sustain interest, highlight certain characters or particular aspects and to demarcate or link up the several sections of the composition. At the same time, a memorised stock of similes provided the components for improvised verse.

## Types of simile

There seems little point in classifying simile according to animals, trees, precious objects and the like.[19] Such data may be of interest in determining the cultural or geographic milieu of both poet and audience; it is not directly of concern to studying poetic technique. Of its nature, the simile tends to diffuseness and extension (in contrast to the conciseness of metaphor, as mentioned briefly above). Accordingly the simile will be repeated, cumulative or extended, often occurring in series or clusters. However, similes (especially those originating in metaphor) can be brief.[20]

## The simile in Akkadian

Babylonian and Assyrian literature is rich in simile, some expressions having an exact match in Hebrew,[21] other comparisons being more original. For example:

17. Leech, *Guide*, 156-57. Note especially his definition: 'Simile is an overt, and metaphor a covert comparison'.
18. Scott: 1974.
19. A catalogue of this nature is D. Marcus, 'Animal Similes in Assyrian Royal Inscriptions', *Or* 46 (1977) 86-106.
20. Other types: omissible or essential; stylised; inverted, cf. Payne: 1970.
21. E.g. 'like water' on which cf. Gevirtz, *JNES* 30 (1971) 94-95.

| | |
|---|---|
| *ašnan šumma daddariš ala'ut* | Grain I swallow as if it were like stinkweed.[22] |

From an examination of this literary figure in Akkadian, two points emerge: first, there is *clustering* of similes (as in Ugaritic and Hebrew);[23] and, more importantly, there is a marked tendency for *extending* a simile quite beyond bounds acceptable to Western ears. In the following excerpt from *Šurpu*, for instance, the simile has been developed to such a degree that a resumptive noun phrase is necessary, which repeats the point of comparison (here: 'just like this tuft of wool'):

> As this tuft of wool is plucked and thrown into the fire, where the flames consume it so thoroughly that it does not return onto its sheep nor does it serve as ceremonial clothing, so may invocation, oath (etc.) be plucked—just like this tuft of wool—and may the flames consume it thoroughly on this very day; may it depart, that I may see the light.[24]

### The simile in Ugaritic
The parallelistic nature of Ugaritic poetry creates a tendency for similes in pairs.

| | |
|---|---|
| *kirby tškn šd* | Like locusts, let them settle in the field, |
| *km ḥsn pat mdbr* | like hoppers on the desert fringe. |
| | (*CTA* 14 ii/iii 103-105 and parallels) |

This, of course, is not unexpected. Less frequent, but again not surprisingly, similes also come in threes (corresponding to the tricolon).

| | |
|---|---|
| *tṣi km rḥ npš* | Out will go, *like a wind*, his breath, |
| *km iṯl brlth* | *like spittle* his life, |
| *km qṭr baph* | *like incense* from his nose. |
| | (*CTA* 18 iv 24-26[25]) |

---

22. Text: *BWL* 44:88 (= Ludlul II). Cf. 'like a thief; furtively', in *Atr* 74:19; 76:33. Note that in addition to particles such as *kīma*, 'like' there is the terminative formation with *-iš*, meaning much the same, e.g. *išātiš*, 'like fire', *ḫašikkiš*, 'like a mute', and *edāniš*, 'like a recluse' (all Ludlul I 68.71.79).

23. See Buccellati: 1976, 65-66 and the threefold simile, *BWL*, 40:42-44.

24. *Šurpu* V/VI 93-100, cited by Buccellati: 1976, 61. It follows, then, that to prune down such lengthy similes to their bare bones and to designate the remainder as 'gloss' is a procedure to be used with extreme caution. (Contrast O. Loretz, 'Vergleich und Kommentar in Amos 3,12', *BZ* 20 [1976] 121-25.)

25. The additional line, *bap mhrh*, 'from his warriors' noses' (so Gibson, *CML*, 112 and n. 9) does not appear in the parallel section, lines 36-37. Other triple similes: *CTA* 3 ii(B) 9-11; *CTA* 12 i 9-11 (as reconstructed in *TO*, 334f); *Ugar* 5 3 i 1ff.

More characteristic is the clustering of similes in these texts. The lines just quoted form part of a set of five, grouped into 2 + 3. Note, too, four similes in *CTA* 5 i 14-17.

As noted by Buccellati for Akkadian,[26] *ellipsis* (or gapping) is often a feature of the simile; not only can the comparative particle be omitted, but this can happen even in the first line:

| *hlk lalpm ḥdd* | Marching by the thousand (like) thunder, |
| *wlrbt kmyr* | and by the myriad like rain. |
| | (*CTA* 14 ii 92-93 etc.) |

There are other examples of this use of 'double-duty' *k*.[27]

The peculiar construction *k//k//km* will be examined below for both Hebrew and Ugaritic.[28]

Certain similes of Hebrew verse already find counterparts in Ugaritic: 'to bite like a serpent' occurs as *ynṭkn kbṭnm*, 'they bit like serpents' (*CTA* 6 vi 19), corresponding to 'at the last it bites like a serpent' (Prov 23,32).[29]

Note the *extended simile* in *CTA* 17 vi 30-33:

| *kb'l kyḥwy* | Like Baal, when he is revived— |
| *y'šr ḥwy* | the reviver prepares, |
| *y'šr wyšqynh* | he prepares to give him to drink, |
| *ybd wyšr 'lh* | he improvises and sings before him, |
| *n'm [dy]'nynn* | the minstrel who serves him— |
| *ap ank aḥwy aqht ġzr* | I too can revive the youth Aqhat![30] |

*Hebrew similes*

The simile in Hebrew shares features of both Akkadian and Ugaritic poetry, but in rather more developed form. There is ellipsis, extension of the simile and similes in even longer series than those known from Ugaritic. Little is new, though, except perhaps in content and function.

Note that the particles used to introduce simile (though not always present) are *kᵉ* (and its variants, *kᵉmô* etc.), *māšal*, 'to be like', *'im,*

26. Buccellati: 1976, 59ff.
27. *CTA* 15 i 5-7; 22B 16ff.
28. See the section on triple parallelism. Called by Gray the cumulative simile 'a variation of the simple simile developed under the exigency of parallelism', *Legacy*, 298f.
29. Cassuto, *Anath*, 24; cf. above on METHOD.
30. As translated by Dijkstra—De Moor, *UF* 7 (1975) 187. For a slightly different version: Gibson, *CML*, 109.

in its specialised meaning of 'like'[31] and sequences such as $k^e$ . . . $k\bar{e}n$, 'like . . . so (is)'.

1. *Simple similes*. All kinds of simile are to be found in Hebrew, only a sample of which can be mentioned here. Some of the more striking are: 'pour wrath like water' (Hos 5,10); 'I will press you down in your place as a cart full of sheaves presses down' (Am 2,13); 'lament like a virgin girded with sackcloth for the bridegroom of her youth' (Joel 1,8); 'I eat ashes like bread' (Ps 102,9); 'make yourselves as bald as the vulture' (Mic 1,16). Also: 'she makes a sound like a serpent gliding away' (Jer 46,22).

2. *Paired similes*. Since so much of Hebrew verse is in parallelism, many similes come in sets of two:

> If you seek it out *like silver*,
> And *like hidden treasures* you search for it. (Prov 2,4)

> So I am *like a moth* to Ephraim
> And *like dry rot* to the house of Judah. (Hos 5,12[32])

Such paired similes can be combined with other verse-forms such as chiasmus, e.g. Hos 4,16; 2 Sm 23,4.

3. *Triple similes*. Since the tricolon is an established pattern in both Ugaritic and Hebrew poetry, sets of three similes do occur, though not very often.

> Left is Daughter Zion
> > *like* a hut in a vineyard
> > *like* a lodge in a cucumber field
> > *like* a defended city. (Isa 1,8[33])

Other examples are 2 Sm 23,4,[34] Joel 2,5 (within a set of 2 + 3 + 0 + 2 in vv. 4-9), and Job 7,1b-2.

4. *Cumulative similes*. Similes cast in this form tend to heighten the suspense slightly by delaying the final line. It occurs in Ugaritic:

| | |
|---|---|
| *klb arḫ l'glh* | Like the heart of a cow for her calf, |
| *klb ṭat limrh* | Like the heart of a ewe for her lamb, |
| *km lb 'nt aṭr b'l* | So is the heart of Anath towards Baal. |

(*CTA* 6 ii 6-9//28-30)

---

31. For bibliography on Ug. *'m* = Heb. *'îm*, 'like' cf. Paul, *JNES* 31 (1972) 351, n. 2.

32. Also Isa 13,14; Am 5,24; Mic 1,4; Joel 2,7; Song 1,5cd.

33. Or perhaps 'besieged city'. Note the complete congruence of gender (all feminine), which reinforces the similes.

34. Mettinger, *SEA* 41-42 (1976-77) 152-53.

Also: (with ellipsis) *CTA* 15 i 5-7.[35] In Hebrew, the corresponding pattern uses the particles $k^e$ ... // $k^e$ ... // *kēn*.

אנוש כחציר ימיו    Man, *like* grass his days,
כציץ השרה        *like* a wild weed
כן יציץ          *so* he grows. (Ps 103,15[36])

Similarly: Pss 83,15-16; 123,2 and perhaps Isa 51,6.[37]

The cumulative simile is very probably a development of what might be termed the explicit simile:

> *As* a lily among brambles,
> *so* is my love among maidens. (Song 2,2ab)

Other examples: 2,3ab; Isa 25,5b.

5. *Similes in series.* As in Ugaritic, similes in Hebrew poetry often come in sets of four and more.

> May my teaching drop *as the rain*,
> My speech distil *as the dew*,
> *As the gentle rain* upon the tender grass,
> And *as the showers* upon the herb. (Dt 32,2-3)

Other sets of four are Isa 32,2; Joel 2,4-5; Hos 13,3. In Hos 13,7-8 there are five ('like a lion, like a leopard, like a bear robbed of her cubs, like a lion, as a wild beast'), but the sequence is interrupted; the same applies to Hos 14,5-7.

Particularly interesting is the series of eleven similes in Sir 50,6-10:

> *Like* the morning-star from between the clouds,
> And *like* the full moon between the festival days,
> And *like* the sun shining on the King's temple,
> And *like* the (rain)bow appearing in the cloud,
> *Like* a rose on its branches on festival days,
> And *like* a lily beside streams of water,
> *Like* a green shoot of Lebanon (-cedar?) in summer days,
> And *like* burning incense on the offering,
> *Like* a vessel of hammered(?) gold upon which precious stones
>      are mounted,
> *Like* a flourishing olive full of berries,
> And *like* a cypress-tree, towering into the clouds.

---

35. See M.J. Dahood, 'Proverbs 28,12 and Ugaritic *bt ḫpṯ*', *PradoFS*, 163-66, for this difficult strophe.

36. So Dahood, *Psalms II*, 29.

37. Except for the text from Isaiah, cf. *RSP* I, 225 for bibliography.

6. *The extended simile*. As remarked on already, similes in ancient Near Eastern literature are liable to be drawn out to almost unbearable lengths. This is indicative, perhaps, of a certain degree of improvisation: once the simile had been established, the poet could exercise his imagination fairly freely, without the constraint of a particular verse-form. In Jer 17,7-8 the following comparison is made about the man who trusts in God:

> He is like a tree planted by the water:
> > that sends out its roots by the stream,
> > and does not fear when the heat comes,
> > for its leaves remain green,
> > and it is not anxious in the year of drought
> > for it does not cease to bear fruit.

Even so, perhaps out of habit, the presence of alternating parallelism is unmistakable. See, too, Dt 32,11 (eagle); Hos 7,4.6.11 (baking); Joel 2,2 (gloomy day); and especially the long comparison in Ez 31,2-9 (cedar of Lebanon). Rather briefer is Song 3,6 (rising smoke).

Mixed forms also occur. In Song 4,1e-5c there is a set of six consecutive similes, each in extended form. In 6,5c-7b there are three, in 5,12-13b, only two.

Mixing of metaphor and simile is also to be found (e.g. Song 8,14) while in Song 7,2c-10 there is a series of similes and metaphors. However, since the prime concern of this book is to set out clear principles, such mixtures need not be considered.[38]

*Ellipsis*
Ellipsis in Akkadian similes has been explored by Buccellati,[39] following Schott, and its presence in Ugaritic has already been discussed. The most significant form of ellipsis in Hebrew simile is omission of the comparative particle. There is no real problem when it occurs in the first line but not in the second, as in

| צדקתך כהררי־אל | Your justice is like the towering mountains, |
| משפטך תהום רבה | Your judgment (like) the vast abyss. (Ps 36,7[40]) |

---

38. On inverted similes, where the thing being compared comes before the comparison, cf. H.W. Wolff, *Hosea* (Philadelphia, 1974), 83, and Andersen—Freedman, *Hosea*, 360.

39. Buccellati: 1976, 59ff.

40. Dahood, *Psalms III*, 436 where Pss 48,7b-8a; 58,9; 90,4; 102,8 and 125,1-2 are also listed.

But often enough, the preposition is not used till the second or even third line:

חצי גבור שנונים    (Like) sharpened arrows of a warrior,
עם גחלי רתמים    Like glowing coals of broom. (Ps 120,4[41])

An example of an omitted $k^e$ in the last two lines of a tricolon is 2 Sm 23,4.

*Functions of the simile*
The functions can be divided into two broad categories: structural and non-structural. These will be considered in turn.

1. *Structural functions of the simile*. The simile can be used to open a section or stanza (usually a speech) or to end one; it can also function as a link between sections of a poem.

  *opening similes*

> Your mother was like a vine in a vineyard,
> transplanted by the water,
> fruitful and full of branches ... (Ez 19,10-14)

Also Isa 54,9; Jer 22,6; 46,7-8; 50,11; Ez 31,2; Ps 11,1.[42]

  *closing similes*

> Pain as of a woman in travail. (Jer 22,20-23)

And Isa 51,23; Jer 15,18; 18,17; 23,14b; 25,38; Ez 21,10b; Joel 2,9; Am 5,24; Hab 3,19; Job 5,26; 24,24.[43]

  *to both open and close*

> Therefore,
> as the tongue of fire devours the stubble,
> . . . . . .
> . . . . . .
> . . . . . .
> Their roaring is like a lion,
> like young lions they roar. (Isa 5,24-29[44])

And Jer 50,42-43; 51,38-40.

---

41. So Dahood, *Psalms III*, 437 and 196-97.
42. In Ugaritic: *Ugar 5* 3 i ff.
43. Ugaritic examples: to close a speech: *CTA* 6 i 10; 12 i 9-11.30-31; to end a description: *CTA* 4 ii 42-44 (goblet); 5 vi 20-22 (mourning rite); 14 vi 291-92 (Keret's wife-to-be).
44. However, v. 30 actually ends the poem. Note that it is difficult to tell whether the locust similes in *CTA* 14 ii 92-93 (and par.) close the foregoing section or comprise the start of a new one.

*linking similes*

> They are all adulterers,
> they are *like a heated oven*,
> . . . . . .
> . . . . . .
> For, *like an oven*
> . . . . . .
> . . . . . . *like a blazing fire*
> All of them are *hot as an oven*. (Hos 7,4-7[45])

2. *Non-structuring functions of simile.* The simile serves to sustain interest, emphasise a motif and express vividness or emotive intent. It can also be informative or merely ornamental and provides relief, or provokes suspense.

*For study*
Sir 15,2; Prov 7,22. Compare Ps 133 and 1 Sm 21,4.

*Cross-references*
HYPERBOLE, METAPHOR, ORAL POETRY, STANZA.

BIBLIOGRAPHY

(a) *General*
Scott, W.C. *The Oral Nature of the Homeric Simile* (Supplements to Mnemosyne xxviii; Leiden, 1974).

(b) *Semitic*
Buccellati, G. 'Towards a Formal Typology of Akkadian Similes', *Kramer FS*, 59-70.
Exum, J.C. 'Of Broken Pots, Fluttering Birds, and Visions in the Night: Extended Simile and Poetic Technique in Isaiah', *CBQ* 43 (1981) 331-352.
Labuschagne, C.J. 'The Similes in the Book of Hosea', *OTWSA* 7-8 (1964-65) 64-76.
Payne, D.F. 'A Perspective on the Use of Simile in the OT', *Semitics* 1 (1970) 111-25.
Rosner, D. 'The Simile and its Use in the OT', *Semitics* 4 (1974) 37-46.
Schott, A. *Die Vergleiche in den akkadischen Königsinschriften* (*MVAG* 30/2; Leipzig, 1926).
Super, A.S. 'Figures of Comparison in the Book of Amos', *Semitics* 3 (1973) 67-80.
Also Cassuto, *Anath*, 24-25 and Gray, *Legacy*, 298-99 (on Ugaritic).

---

45. In *CTA* 6 i 10 *tšt kyn udm't*, 'she (= Anath) drank tears like wine', forms a link between two speeches.

### 10.3 *Metaphor*

*The theory of metaphor and poetry*

Metaphor belongs to the stuff of poetry, so that to understand poetry involves coming to grips with metaphor and metaphorical expressions. Accordingly, some account of metaphor is required here as in any book on poetry. However, since figurative expression forms part of the language of poetry rather than being a matter of technique (metaphor does not seem to have any structuring function, for instance) discussion need only be brief and succinct. It can also be pointed out that the theory of metaphor is still being debated in the field of modern linguistics, so that it would be premature to offer a summary of the findings so far. For a deeper analysis the reader is referred to the bibliography.

The present paragraph will present (1) two possible ways of analysing metaphor and (2) two attempts at classifying metaphor. In this way some idea of the problems involved can be gained.

1. *Analysis of metaphor: two approaches*. Metaphor is generally presented analytically as follows:

> *X is like Y in respect of Z*
> where
> X: tenor
> Y: vehicle
> Z: ground.

For example, 'I was eyes to the blind' (Job 29,15). Here *Job* (tenor) is like *eyes* (vehicle) in respect of *seeing* (ground).

Without attempting a deep theoretical analysis[46] a metaphor can also be represented as the overlap of two word-meanings. So, in the metaphor 'Why, then, has Israel become a prey?' (Jer 2,14), the overlapping aspect of the two concepts '(the nation) Israel' and 'prey' is 'vulnerability':

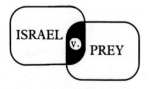 (v.: vulnerability)

46. For which see J. Dubois et al., *Allgemeine Rhetorik* (Heidelberg, 1974 [original: *Rhétorique génerale*, Brussels, 1970]) 176-84.

2. *Classifying metaphor*. Two main types of metaphor can be distinguished: the referential and the conceptual (or semantic).[47]

i.   *referential metaphor*: such metaphors are based on what the poet can actually see or visualise. E.g.

> Many shepherds have destroyed my vineyard. (Jer 12,10)

where the picture evoked is concrete. Also, 22,28; 23,19.

ii.  *conceptual metaphor*: metaphors of this class are based on abstract rather than concrete imagery.

Three grades of metaphor can be established: lexicalised, conventionalised and creative.[48]

i.   *lexicalised metaphor*: words (or expressions) that originally were metaphorical, but have since passed into everyday language, as 'blood of trees', meaning 'wine' (Gen 49,11).[49]

ii.  *conventionalised metaphors* or clichés which may not belong to ordinary language[50] but are not new coinage. An example is the use of 'cup' to denote allotted portion or destiny (Ez 23,32-34; Ps 75,9; etc.). See also the shepherd/flock imagery to express the relationship between God and Israel, or the 'harlot' imagery for a negative version of the same relationship (Mic 1,7; etc.).

iii. *creative metaphors* are the inventions of first-class poets. An example from many is

> you who turn justice to wormwood (Am 5,7 [cf. 6,12])

A sub-set of the creative metaphor is when a worn-out expression is provided with a new twist. So, in Am 1,2 the stock representation of God as a lion becomes:[51]

> Yahweh roars from Zion,
> and shouts out from Jerusalem:

47. Dubois, *Allgemeine Rhetorik*, 181.
48. G. Kurz—T. Pelster, *Metapher. Theorie und Unterrichtsmodell* (Düsseldorf, 1976) 63.
49. See also Dt 32,14 and Ez 19,10(?). The same expression is used in Ugaritic: *dm 'ṣm*, *CTA* 4 iv 38 (//iii 44, restored). Note also *dm zt*, 'blood of olives' (= olive oil), *Ugar* 5 1 rev. 6.
50. Also termed 'frozen metaphors'.
51. For a similar passage in Mesopotamian literature see *BWL*, 334.

the shepherds' pastures wither,
Carmel's peak dries up.

Of course, a metaphor cannot be pinned down as belonging exclusively to one or other of these categories: the scale is a sliding one. What may be a totally new metaphor for a particular group of people (due to their language, social class or geographic location) may be a worn-out cliché for another.

*Metaphor and the poet*
Metaphor 'is a special use of words which foregrounds[52] one or more of the underlying semantic parameters by either of two devices: (1) by parametric reinforcement, or (2) by parametric neutralization'.[53] Examples will make this evident:
1. *Reinforcement of parameters.*

> Yahweh is my *rock* and my fortress,
> my God is my haven,
> my mountain where I take refuge;
> my shield and my saving horn,
> my stronghold, worthy of praise. (Ps 18,3[54])

Here the immediate context[55] shows that the positive side of this series of metaphors is intended: they reinforce the semantic parameters 'firm, solid, immovable, protective' underlying 'rock'.
2. *Neutralisation of parameters.*

> Let us destroy the *tree* with its fruit,
> let us cut him off from the land of the living,
> that his name be remembered no more. (Jer 11,19b)

Evidently the positive aspects only of a tree are in question; the concept of a tree as an object of worship (hence, to be condemned) is neutralised. Similarly, Jer 2,13 (water as beneficial, not as destructive, e.g. a flood).

Corresponding to the selection by the poet of a particular metaphor there is the correct interpretation by the listener (or reader). He can

52. Foregrounding is a technical term (coined by Mukarovsky) for the exploitation of grammatical deviation in poetry (see Leech, *Guide*, 56-72).
53. L.G. Heller—J. Macris, *Parametric Linguistics* (The Hague, 1967) 70-71.
54. Largely following the version in Dahood, *Psalms I*, 101.
55. According to Weinrich, metaphor is 'a word in a co-determining context' and is 'never a simple word, but always a piece of text, even if small'. Metaphor is not simply word-substitution, but has always to be considered in context (Weinrich: 1967).

either select those properties of the expression in focus which are relevant to the context (e.g. a lamp as light-producing in Job 21,17) or he can establish the relationship between the two concepts involved.[56]

### Metaphor in Akkadian poetry

In common with most poetry, both metaphor and metaphorical expressions are to be found. As in other cultures, divine epithets tend to be metaphorical: Nergal is addressed as 'dragon', 'terrible flood' and 'furious fire', Marduk is termed 'radiant sun' and 'brilliant flame' and so on. Many expressions also occur in Ugaritic or Hebrew; curiously, the phrase 'to drink tears' is common to all three cultures.[57] Note, too, 'at the mention of your (= Ishtar's) name, the earth and sky tremble'[58] and the series of metaphors denoting peril in a prayer to Nābû:[59]

> He lies in the mass of high water and the flood bears down on him.
> The shore is far off, distant is terra firma.
>
> He has perished in a web of tricks, which cannot be cut.
> He has lain in the marsh, is held by the bog.

However, a detailed catalogue and analysis of the metaphors used in Akkadian poetry would serve no purpose here. The significance of being familiar with the figurative language used is in elucidating imagery found in Hebrew that would otherwise be obscure. The sentence

> At my terrible bellow the mountains and river dry up

corresponds to Am 1,2.[60] More significant is the veiled reference to Lamashtu in Jer 9,20:

| | |
|---|---|
| כי־עלה מות בחלונינו | For Death has come up into our windows, |
| בא בארמנותינו | has entered our palatial apartments, |
| להכרית עולל מחוץ | to cut off infants from (ever being on) the street, |
| בחורים מרחבות | and young men from (ever being on) the squares. |

Not only is the metaphor identifiable once it is known that according to Mesopotamian belief the baby-snatching demon called Lamashtu

56. Reinhart: 1976.
57. Cf. *tšt kyn udm't*, 'she drank tears like wine' *CTA* 14 i 30 and Pss 42,4; 80,6; 102,10 (strictly speaking, hyperbolic simile in Ugaritic).
58. Seux, *Hymnes*, 189.
59. Seux, *Hymnes*, 182.
60. Text: *BWL* 192:18; see Lambert's remarks, 334.

was thought to enter houses by the window[61]—it also becomes richer when the allusion to a passage in the Baal Cycle is recognised.[62] This brings us conveniently to the next paragraph: figurative language in the texts from Ras Shamra.

## Metaphor in Ugaritic poetry

Again, there is no lack of metaphor in the literary texts from Ras Shamra. Examples are *rgm 'ṣ*, 'tale of trees' (*CTA* 3C iii 23-24); *tkmm ḥmt*, 'shoulders of the wall' (i.e. parapet, *CTA* 14 ii 75; *šnt tluan*, 'sleep overpowered him' (personification, *CTA* 14 i 33; cf. 4 v 66); and the couplet (after two similes)

| | |
|---|---|
| *d 'qh ib iqni* | Whose eyeballs are lapis lazuli, |
| *'p 'ph sp ṭrml* | her eyelids, alabaster bowls. |

(*CTA* 14 iii 147-8)

And, as already mentioned, many metaphors have exact counterparts in Hebrew:[63] cf. *CTA* 6 iii 6-7 (heavens raining oil, ravines running with honey) and Gen 27,28; Ex 3,8; Job 20,17; Ez 32,14 and Joel 4,18. For instance,

| | |
|---|---|
| *km aḫt 'rš mdw* | Because you have become brother to a sick-bed, |
| *anšt 'rš zbln* | companion to an invalid-bed. |

(*CTA* 16 vi 35-36)

and

| | |
|---|---|
| לשחת קראתי אבי אתה | (If I) say to the pit: You are my father; |
| אמי ואחתי לרמה | to the maggot: My mother and my sister. |

(Job 17,14[64])

## Identifying metaphors

The points to be examined here show how important it is to identify whether metaphor is present in a text, and if so, which metaphor.

61. S. Paul, 'Cuneiform Light on Jer 9,20', *Bib* 49 (1968) 373-76. See, too, 'There is no compassion when Death seizes an infant' in line 31 of Combination II of the Deir 'Alla Plaster Inscriptions, as translated by Levine, *JAOS* 101 (1981) 200.

62. Namely, *CTA* 4 vi 8-9 etc. (so Cassuto, *Anath*, 22 but contrast Gibson, *CML*, 62, n. 3 and Paul's article in note 61).

63. Animal names as metaphors are discussed below. For a convenient survey see Cassuto, *Anath*, 21-23, though not all his examples are correct.

64. Cf. Prov 7,4. Also *'nq sm dlbnn*, 'the purple necklace of Lebanon' (*CTA* 22B 19-20) and Hos 14,6-8—on which cf. J.C. de Moor, *New Year with Israelites and Canaanites* (Kampen, 1972) II, 13.

Further, the metaphor or metaphors must be interpreted in the light of the larger context in which they are used.[65]

1. *Animal names as metaphors*. 'Frequently animal names were used metaphorically as designations or titles for leaders or nobles of some sort or for warriors'[66] in both Hebrew and Ugaritic. So, in

| | |
|---|---|
| ṣḥ šb'm ṯry | Call my seventy bulls, |
| tmnym ẓbyy | my eighty gazelles, |
| ṯr ḥbr rbt | the bulls of greater Hubur |
| ḥbr ṯrrt | of lesser Hubur. |

(*CTA* 15 iv 6-9 [restored from 17-20])

the terms 'bull' and 'gazelle' in reality designate Keret's high officials. Accordingly, they have to be translated 'dukes' and 'barons' or the like.[67] The same usage in Hebrew supplies a long list (here given alphabetically):

| | |
|---|---|
| אביר | 'bull, stallion' (1 Sm 21,8; Ps 68,31; Job 24,22; etc.) |
| איל | 'ram' (Ex 15,15; 2 Kgs 24,15; Jer 4,22; Ez 30,13; Ps 58,2; etc.) |
| כפיר | 'young lion' (Ez 38,13; Nah 2,14) |
| עתוד | 'he-goat' (Isa 14,9; Zech 10,3) |
| צבי | 'gazelle' (1 Sm 1,19; Isa 23,7;[68] Ug. ẓby) |
| שור | 'bull' (Gen 49,6; Ug ṯr).[69] |

Unless such animal names are identified as metaphorical for people of rank, certain Hebrew texts remain unintelligible. For instance, in

| | |
|---|---|
| על הרעים חרה אפי | My anger is hot against the shepherds, |
| ועל העתודים אפקוד | And I will punish the *he-goats*. (Zech 10,3) |

the term *'attûdîm* evidently denotes 'leaders'.

2. *Recognising the metaphor*. To establish which metaphor is present is to find the key to a text. The metaphor of *writing* makes sense of Job 22,22. Isa 23,7 becomes understandable once the metaphor of *paying tribute* has been identified:

65. There will be some overlap between the various sections, but (one hopes) this will not detract from clarity. On this topic cf. Loewenberg: 1975.

66. Miller: 1970, 177.

67. First recognised by H.L. Ginsberg, *The Legend of King Keret: A Canaanite Epic of the Bronze Age* (New Haven, 1946) 42. See *CTA* 14 iii 118-123 for the literal meaning of such terms.

68. See Dahood, *Bib* 50 (1959) 161-62; *Or* 44 (1975) 439-41.

69. Further examples are given by Miller: 1970, 177ff.

> Can this be your joyful city?
> From ancient times
> her tribute they brought to her
> at her feet
> from a distance made to reverence.[70]

Further: 'wine' as figurative for 'love' (Song 1,2; 2,4; etc.). In the same vein, personification, once recognised, is often the clue to an obscure passage.[71]

3. *Congruity of metaphor*. Although mixed metaphors do occur, generally speaking Hebrew poets were consistent in their use of figurative language. Or, to put it the other way round, metaphors must be presumed as congruous unless the contrary cannot be ruled out.[72] So, in Isa 28,20-21, the couplet

כי קצר המצע מהשתרע    For the bed is too short to stretch out on,
והמסכה צרה כהתכנס    and the cover too narrow to wrap up in.

is not a disconnected proverbial saying, but introduces the 'bed in the Underworld' motif.[73]

## Other kinds of metaphor

Under this heading come extended metaphor, metaphors in series, hyperbolic metaphor and personification. Still other forms could be discussed (e.g. metonymy) but do not need to be since they are not specific to Hebrew poetry.

1. *Extended metaphor*. Relatively often in Hebrew literature a metaphor is fully fleshed out in minute detail, the effect being to drive home a particular message. So, in Mic 3,2-3 the metaphor of cannibalism is exploited to the full with reference to the way Israel's leaders treated their subjects:

> Tearing their skin from upon them,
> and their flesh from their very bones,
> who eat the flesh of my people,
> and their skin flay off them
> and break up their bones,

---

70. See W.G.E. Watson, 'Tribute to Tyre (Is XXIII 7)', *VT* 26 (1976) 371-74, and the corrective remarks by Auffret, *VT* 28 (1978) 106-08.
71. See below, 270.
72. M.J. Dahood, 'Congruity of Metaphors', *VTS* 16 (1967) 40-49.
73. So Irwin, *Isaiah 28-33*, 34; see 29 on Isa 2,10 and 28,15.

> and chop them up as in a cauldron,
> and like meat within a cooking-pot.[74]

Also: Isa 47,1-3.5 (mourning); Ez 23,32-34 (cup); 27,25-36 (Tyre: treated as a ship); 29,3-5 (Egypt as a crocodile); Ps 76 (God as a lion); (on Gen 49 see next section).

2. *Metaphors in series*. Like the simile, metaphors can come in groups. In the difficult poem Gen 49 (and to a lesser extent Dt 33) Judah is metaphorically a lion, Zebulun a harbour, Dan a serpent, Naphtali a hind, Joseph a well(?), Issachar a donkey, Benjamin a wolf, etc.[75]

3. *Hyperbolic metaphor*. Somewhat rare in Hebrew, e.g.

> Like one rent and riven in the nether world
> my bones are strewn at the mouth of Sheol. (Ps 141,7[76])

4. *Personification*. The metaphors of Ugaritic verse imply inanimate objects as acting like persons. To the examples given above can be added *šbt dqnk ltsrk*, 'the grey hairs of your beard instruct you' (*CTA* 4 v 66); *tbkyk ab ģr b'l*, 'weep for you, father, do the rocks of Baal' (*CTA* 16 i 6); and so on.[77] It is difficult to decide whether these are examples of animistic belief, high-flown poetic imagery or a mixture of both. According to current scholarship 'personifications replace mythical figures when rational attitudes supersede the primitive imagination'.[78] In the case of Hebrew poetry, it was largely a matter of demythologising ancient Canaanite borrowings. Not every reference of this kind was expunged; to mention Sheol is enough proof.[79]

### Functions of metaphor

Two main functions can be discerned in the poetical use of metaphor. They are

1. *Representational*. The poet uses metaphor to transfer something familiar to what is less well known, though of more importance. For example,

---

74. For the term *qallaḥat* see Cathcart, *RSO* 47 (1973) 57-58. In the preceding line *ka'ašer* is usually emended to *keše'ar*, 'like flesh'.

75. For excellent studies of Gen 49 see the articles by Gevirtz.

76. Dahood, *Psalms III*, 313 notes the overall figure of simile. 'Metaphorical hyperbole is the language of joy': so Soulen: 1967, 190.

77. Also *lḥšt abn*, 'whisper of stone' (*CTA* 3C iii 20); *tant šmm 'm arṣ*, 'sigh of sky to earth' (ibid 21; cf. 22). Note Dnil cursing town, spring and tree in *CTA* 18, or embracing and kissing stalks in *CTA* 19 ii 61ff.

78. *PEPP*, 612.

79. Isa 5,14; etc.

> Your lips drip honey, bride,
> honey and milk under your tongue. (Song 4,11[80])

2. *Presentational*. Here the poet simply describes something which is, in a way, made present; at the same time he mentions the main subject. What is *not* mentioned is the sensation both produce. For example,

> Your eyes are pools in Heshbon (Song 7,5)

implies that the eyes of the woman have the same effect on her lover as do the cool, deep, inviting waters of Heshbon. This *juxtaposition* technique is particularly frequent in Song 4 and 7[81] and there is a certain element of overlap with simile.[82]

*For study*

Isa 28,15-17; Job 10,17; Sir 50,15; Isa 55,12; Prov 8; Pss 77,16; 96,11-12.

### BIBLIOGRAPHY

(a) *General*

Bickerton, D. 'Prolegomena to a Linguistic Theory of Metaphor', *FL* 5 (1969) 34-52.

Campbell, B. 'Metaphor, Metonymy and Literalness', *GL* 9, no. 9 (1969) 149-66.

Loewenberg, I. 'Identifying Metaphors', *FL* 12 (1975) 315-38.

Rose, C.B. *A Grammar of Metaphor* (London, 1958).

Shibles, W.A. *Metaphor: An Annotated Bibliography and History* (Wisconsin, 1971).

Also Nowottny, *Language*, 49-98 and Weinrich, *Poetica* 2 (1968) 100-30.

(b) *Semitic*

Dahood, M.J. 'Congruity of Metaphors', *VTS* 16 (1967) 40-49.

Dhorme, E. *L'emploi métaphorique des noms de parties du corps en hébreu et en akkadien* (Paris, 1923).

Dick, M.B. 'The Legal Metaphor in Job 31', *CBQ* 41 (1979) 37-50.

Good, E.M. 'Ezekiel's Ship: Some Extended Metaphors in the Old Testament', *Semitics* 7 (1970) 79-103.

Görg, M. 'Eine formelhafte Metapher bei Joel und Nahum', *BN* 6 (1978) 12-14.

---

80. As translated by Pope, *Song*, 453.
81. See the discussion by Soulen: 1967, 183-90.
82. For these two functions of metaphor, termed epiphor and diaphor respectively, see P. Wheelwright, *Metaphor and Reality* (Indiana, 1962) 70-91.

Gray, J. 'A Metaphor from Building in Zephaniah II 1', *VT* 3 (1953) 404-07.
Miller, P.D. 'Animal Names as Designations in Ugaritic and Hebrew', *UF* 2 (1970) 172-86.
Roberts, J.J.M. 'Job's Summons to Yahweh: The Exploitation of a Legal Metaphor', *ResQ* 16 (1973) 159-65.
Soulen, R.N. 'The Waṣfs of the Song of Songs and Hermeneutic', *JBL* 86 (1967) 183-90.
Watson, W.G.E. 'The Metaphor in Job 10,17', *Bib* 63 (1982) 255-57.

# 11

## POETIC DEVICES

### 11.01 *The Interplay of Poetic Devices*

In a way this chapter collects together and examines all the poetic devices not already discussed and analysed. However, it is intended to be more than that. In the first section structuring devices are considered and it is evident that they are interrelated. The second part deals with non-structural topics such as simile and metaphor; abstract nouns with concrete meaning and so on. Two points, though, need to be made.

First, the distinction between structural and non-structural devices cannot be clinical; it is used largely for clarity of presentation. A simile, to take only one instance, can act as a structuring device. Again, rhetorical questions, similes, metaphors tend to come in series; evidently this is a form of repetition. Demarcation, therefore, is often artificial. Note, too, that mixed forms also occur, for example, mixed similes and metaphors; hyperbolic metaphor and the like.

The other point, as the sub-heading indicates, is that poetic devices do not occur in isolation but within the context of a poem. They therefore relate to each other and can often only be understood within the setting of another device or of the poem in whole or in part. Such intermeshing is best shown by the full analysis of a complete poem, and the reader is referred to the appendix of worked examples for ample illustration.

The chapter is divided into two main parts: structural devices and non-structural devices. The sequence within each part is to a certain extent arbitrary and the table accompanying the section on repetition is intended to offset this.

## 11.02 *Repetition*

### a. *forms of repetition*

SOUND REPETITION ⟶ —rhyme
  —alliteration
  —assonance
  (— wordplay)

PURE REPETITION
—repetition-initial    a————
            a————

—end-repetition      ————b
            ————b

—immediate repetition   a  a
            ab  ab

—identical word-pairs   a // a

### b. *devices using repetition*

—refrain

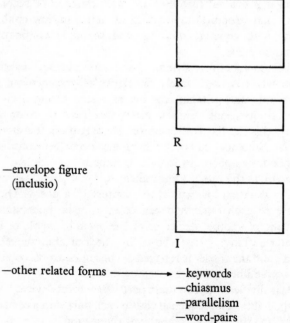

R

R

—envelope figure      I
  (inclusio)

I

—other related forms ⟶ —keywords
  —chiasmus
  —parallelism
  —word-pairs

*TABLE: Forms and devices of repetition*

*Repetition and poetry*

'Repetition is the verbal device under which the technical devices of poetry can all be subsumed'.[1] Although somewhat exaggerated, this claim does hold true to a limited extent. For instance, alliteration is simply repetition of the same consonants according to particular patterns; other devices, too, could be reduced to forms of repetition. These kinds of repetitive pattern will be outlined in paragraph 1. The main topic of the present section, though, is pure repetition, to be examined more closely in paragraph 2. A later section is devoted to the ways in which repetition can be avoided. See TABLE.

1. *Poetic form as repetition.* Where *sound-units* are repeated, the result can be alliteration (= repetition of certain consonants), assonance (= exploitation of similar vowel-sounds), rhyme in all its forms, and finally, word-play. All these topics are discussed in Chapter 9 ('SOUND IN HEBREW POETRY'), but, as mentioned in the introduction, could equally well have been set out here.[2]

The repetition of *single words* within a poetic unit (strophe, stanza, poem) is characteristic of key-words, chiasmus in all its forms and of word-pairs (i.e. identical word-pairs).[3] Again, these are dealt with elsewhere.

Lastly, the iteration of either *phrases* or *complete lines* ('cola') results in structural patterns such as the refrain, the antiphonal response and the envelope figure.[4]

2. *Pure repetition.* Traditionally, a whole set of technical terms exists which denote the various forms and sub-forms of repetition. As Leech has aptly observed, though, there is no need to learn such labels: it is much more important to be able to recognise repetition-patterns and to determine why they are being used.[5]

*Types of repetition*

Three main types of repetition can be distinguished:

---

1. F.W. Bateson, *English Poetry and the English Language* (Oxford, 1973) 18, n. 29. There he outlines 'a sort of elementary poetic grammar' as follows:

   (a)   repetitions of sound (rhythm, metre, rhyme, assonance, alliteration);
   (b)   repetitions of sense (refrains, puns, ambiguities, metaphor, irony);
   (c)   repetitions of context (quotations, the use of proper names or specialised words from a particular literary tradition);
   (d)   deliberate variations of the prose order (hypallages, inversions, zeugma).

2. Such indeed is the layout in Bühlmann—Scherer, *Stilfiguren*, 15-42.
3. See especially Dahood, *RSP* I, 75-77.
4. Quotation, too, could be included here; see note 1, above.
5. Leech, *Guide*, 4.77.

1. *Repetition-initial* where a series of two or more consecutive lines begin with the same word or phrase.[6]

| Akk. | *ē taplaḥā ilīkun* | Do *not* reverence your gods. |
| | *ē tusalliā ištarkun* | Do *not* pray to your goddesses.[7] |

| Ug. | *klnyn qšh nbln* | *Both of us* his goblet would bear, |
| | *klnyn nbl ksh* | *both of us* would bear his cup.[8] |

| Heb. | מי עלה שמים וירד | *Who* has ascended to the heavens and come down? |
| | מי אסף רוח בחפניו | *Who* has gathered the wind in his garments? |
| | מי צרר מים בשמלה | *Who* has wrapped up the waters in his robe? |
| | מי הקים כל אפסי ארץ | *Who* has established all the ends of the earth? |

(Prov 30,4[9])

The number of consecutive lines is usually two (Jer 23,10; Mic 1,9; Nah 2,10; 3,2; Zeph 1,14; 3,1; Job 19,23; Prov 30,4c; Qoh 1,4; Lam 2,5) or three (Jer 15,5; Obd 18; Mic 7,11-12; Qoh 1,8); more rarely four (Mic 5,9-13; Prov 30,11-14), seven (Zeph 1,15-16) or even nine (Jer 51,20-23).

2. *End repetition*: the repeated element coming at the close of successive lines.[10]

| Ug. | *mrǵb yd mṯkt* | The hungry *by the hand she grasped.* |
| | *mẓma yd mṯkt* | The thirsty *by the hand she grasped.*[11] |

| Heb. | וזרח השמש | Rise does *the sun.* |
| | ובא השמש | Set does *the sun.* (Qoh 1,5a[12]) |

6. Technically: anaphora; see under ACROSTICS.

7. *Atr* II ii 9-10; also III ii 46 (*ul*); S v 20-21 (*zibānīt*); *Erra* I 158-59 (etc., *ali*); IIIA 20B-21 (*eṭla*); note the eleven-line set in IV 76-86 (*ša*). Also, *Erra* IV 7-10 (*ša*).

8. *CTA* 4 iv 45-46; and i 31-32 (*kt il*); ii 21-24 (*ik*); viii 2-4 (threefold *'m*); 15-18 (*al*); 5 vi 23-24 (= 6 i 6-7 *my*); 6 ii 17-19 (*npš*); ii 31-35 (fivefold *b-*); v 11-19 (sevenfold *'lk*); 14 iii 182-83 (*atr*); iii 120 (threefold *l-*); 16 i 25-27 (threefold *al*); iii 13-16 (threefold *kly*).

9. For translation cf. K. Cathcart, 'Proverbs 30,4 and Ugaritic *ḥpn*, "garment"', *CBQ* 32 (1970) 418-20.

10. Termed epistrophe. For Akkadian see the refrain-like *tuštamīt*, 'you will kill', in *Erra* IV 104-111 (eightfold).

11. *CTA* 15 i 1-2 (restored); also 5 v 14-16 (*arṣ*); 6 i 54-55 (*'ttr 'rẓ*).

12. Also Nah 3,15b.

Evidently end-repetition is comparatively rare and not much used. It is not surprising, therefore, that combinations of repetition-initial and end-repetition are equally rare.[13] Examples are *CTA* 17 vi 38

| | |
|---|---|
| *wmt kl amt* | And the death of everyman *will I die*. |
| *wan mtm amt* | And I myself, certainly *will I die*. |

and Mic 5,9.12.

3. *Immediate repetition* is the third category of iteration: a word or phrase is used, and then repeated immediately afterwards, without a break. Examples are few.

| Akk. | *kikkiš kikkiš* | O reed-wall, reed-wall |
|---|---|---|
| | *igār igār* | Wall! Wall! |
| | *kikkišu šimema* | Reed-wall, listen. |
| | *igāru ḫissas* | Wall, pay attention.[14] |
| | | |
| Ug. | *yngr ngr ptḥ* | O watchman, watchman! Open.[15] |
| Heb. | סורו סורו אל תגעו | Away! Away! Keep off! |
| | | (Lam 4,15) |

In nearly all these texts immediate repetition is used to convey a sense of *urgency*; note, further, Jgs 5,12 'Up, up!'; Isa 52,1 'Awake, awake!'.[16]

Pure repetition can be used to construct *complete stanzas* or *poems*. The best example (although the text is difficult) is Isa 28,10 (= 13):[17]

| | |
|---|---|
| כי | For |
| צו לצו | Go out, let him go out. |
| צו לצו | Go out, let him go out. |
| קו לקו | Wait, let him wait. |
| קו לקו | Wait, let him wait. |
| זעיר שמ(ע) | Servant, listen. |
| זעיר שמ(ע) | Servant, listen. |

13. Known as symploce.

14. Gilg XI 21-22: contrast the non-use of repetition in *Atr* III i 21. See, too, *Atr* V obv. 5-6; I 195-96; I v 257-58; Etana cC 93ff.

15. *CTA* 23:69-70; and 16 ii 87-88 *wqbr ṯṣr, qbr ṯṣr*, 'And a grave you must fashion, a grave you must fashion'.

16. Contrast Zeph 1,2 and Qoh 1,6. Of a different order is the repetition-series in *Erra* IV 131-135 ('the sea the sea [will destroy], the Subartean the Subartean . . . ), its function being to depict total and reciprocal destruction.

17. For this convincing translation cf. A. van Selms, 'Isaiah 28:9-13: An Attempt to Give a New Interpretation', *ZAW* 85 (1973) 332-39.

Another is Jer 15,2:[18]

| | |
|---|---|
| אשר למות למות | Who belongs to Death: To Death. |
| ואשר לחרב לחרב | Who belongs to the Sword: To the Sword. |
| ואשר לרעב לרעב | Who belongs to Famine: To Famine. |
| ואשר לשבי לשבי | Who belongs to Captivity: To Captivity. |

Less clear are Qoh 1,9 and 11. Examples from Ugaritic and Akkadian compare well with the passage from Jeremiah.

| | |
|---|---|
| 'n ṯgr ltġr ṯṯb | Let the gate-keeper's eye return to the gatekeeper. |
| 'n pḫr lpḫr ṯṯb | Let the potter's eye return to the potter. |
| 'n mhr lmhr ṯṯb | Let the rival's eye return to the rival. |
| 'n bty lbty ṯṯb | Let the flatterer's eye return to the flatterer. |
| 'n bṯṯ lbṯṯ ṯṯb | Let the flatteress' eye return to the flatteress. (*KTU* 1.96[19]) |

| | |
|---|---|
| šuṣašši 1 šūši m[urṣī . . . ] Ištar | Release against her the sixty miseries, against Ishtar: |
| muruṣ īnī [ana īnī] -ša | misery of the eyes against her eyes; |
| muruṣ aḫī a[na aḫī] -ša | misery of the sides against her sides; |
| muruṣ šēpī a[na šēpī] -ša | misery of the feet against her feet; |
| muruṣ libbi a [na libbīša] | misery of the heart[20] against her heart; |
| muruṣ qaqqadi [ . . . ] | misery of the head . . . |
| ana šâša gabbīšama ana [ . . . ] | Against her, against all of her, against . . .[21] |

## Functions

The *functions* of repetition can be considered first, in a general way and then with respect to specific patterns.

Generally speaking, and with particular reference to the oral aspect of poetry, repetition enables the audience to re-hear a verse which they may have missed through inattention or on account of

---

18. Note, incidentally, the gender-pattern m+m // f+f // m+m // f+f and contrast Jer 43,11.

19. Translation: De Moor, *UF* 11 (1979) 648. See, too, the repetition of *tld pġt* in *CTA* 15 iii 5-12.

20. One meaning of *muruṣ libbi* is 'worry, preoccupation'; *murṣu* can also mean 'illness'; cf. *CAD* M/2, 224.

21. Text: *CT* 15, 46:69-75 = Descent of Ishtar. Note, incidentally, that this list has both an initial and a final total. Other sequences are *Erra* IV 40-41 and *Atr* I i 10-13.

interference ('noise'). Repetition also reduces the need for a poet to invent new material: it helps 'fill up' a poem.

Repetition also reinforces the *structure* of a poem, and helps link its components. This obtains for such texts as Nah 3,15; Prov 30,4. The non-structuring (rhetorical) functions are more numerous. *Dramatic effect* is achieved by immediate repetition (see above) and texts like Zeph 1,15-16; *CTA* 6 i 54-55. Repetition expresses *completeness*, too: notably in Jer 15,2; Qoh 3,2-8; Zeph 1,2.[22] *Emphasis* is more to the fore in Prov 30,4d and *CTA* 16 i 25-27. *Emphatic negation* is the effect in Prov 3,25-32 and *CTA* 19 i 44-46.

Note that staircase parallelism could be considered a form of repetition, but is treated elsewhere (cf. the alternative description: 'incremental repetition').

*Devices to avoid repetition*
The foregoing discussion of the forms and functions of repetitive verse patterns shows that the poets were well able to exploit repetition. Too much of the same word or phrase, though, can lead to monotony and therefore become boring. As will be seen, various manoeuvres were to hand to prevent this happening. These can be described as the avoidance of repetitive parallelism, the breaking up of sustained sequences and the telescoping of set patterns. Numerical parallelism is a special case.

1. *Avoidance of repetitive parallelism.* Since not every word in Hebrew (or the other related languages) has its apposite synonym it was often inevitable that the same word (or verbal root) had to be used in both lines of a parallel couplet.[23] To offset this lack of variation the poet could alter the tense, the voice or mood or even the conjugation.

—*variation of tense (yqtl // qtl and qtl // yqtl)*
Since its recognition in Ugaritic by Cassuto[24] what Gevirtz terms 'parallelization of selfsame verbs' in 'conjugational variation'[25] is now accepted as part of Hebrew verse as well. The examples given immediately will show this:

---

22. Also *CTA* 14 iii 182-83; 15 i 1-2; 16 iii 13-16. Note the probable incantatory function of *CTA* 15 iii 5-12.
23. An extreme example is Job 31 where at least ten identical word-pairs are used (vv. 9.10.11.14.16.17.25.31.35.40).
24. Cassuto in *Or* 7 (1938) 288-89.
25. See the title of Gevirtz's article in *JNES* 32 (1973) 99ff.

(a) *yqtl // qtl*

*ṭl šmm tskh*                     Dew the heavens *poured upon her*.
*[rb]b nskh kbkbm*               Showers the stars *did pour upon her*.[26]

אהבי ורעי מנגד נגעי יעמדו   My friends and companions *stand* aloof from my
                                plague,
וקרובי מרחק עמדו          even my confidants *stand* far off. (Ps 38,12)

Also Am 7,4 and perhaps Dt 33,12.

(b) *qtl // yqtl*

No certain example is attested in Ugaritic.[27]

וינקת חלב גוים       And *you shall suck* the milk of nations,
ושד מלכים תינקי     and the breast of kings *shall you suck*. (Isa 60,16)

And Prov 11,7.[28]

—*variation of 'voice'*. By 'voice' is meant a change from active to
passive, simple ('qal') to causative, and the like. By far the most
frequent is the active/passive form, called by scholars the 'action and
result formula'. [29] E.g. *CTA* 4 v 113-116:

*[h]š bhtm [bn]*            Swiftly: (Build) houses,
*hš rmm hk[lm]*           Swiftly: Erect palaces.
*hš bhtm tbn[n]*           Swiftly: Let houses be built,
*hš trmmn hk[lm]*         Swiftly: Let palaces be erected.[30]

שאו שערים ראשיכב     *Raise up*, O gates, your heads,
והנשאו פתחי עולם      and *be raised up*, O eternal portals. (Ps 24,7)

Also Jer 31,4; Hos 5,5; Ps 69,15.

The parallelism of causative-simple occurs in *CTA* 17 vi 28-29.[31]

2. *Interruption of sustained sequences*. A sustained series can be
altered in three ways: by omitting an item, by providing a synonym
or by changing the word order. So, in the passage *CTA* 5 v 8-11,

---

26. *CTA* 3B ii 40-41; also 4 vi 38-40; 19 iii 114-15.

27. A possible case, adduced by Held, is *CTA* 4 iii 14-16, but contrast Gibson, *CML*, 58.

28. For Akkadian examples of both types see Gevirtz: 1973, 102-04.

29. Apparently coined by Held and accepted by Gordis and others.

30. Cited by Held. Less clear is *CTA* 4 vi 34-35 (*sb*, 'turns' // *nsb*, 'is turned'). A parallel in Akk. is from the Adapa Legend (EA 356:5-6).

31. See also the list in Dahood, *Psalms III*, 414. The 'plea and response' formula is the use of the same verb within a single colon, e.g. 'Heal me, O Lord, and I shall be healed' (Jer 17,14a); cf. 17,14b; 31,17c; Lam 5,21.

| | |
|---|---|
| *'mk šb 't ğlmk* | (Take) *with you* your seven lads, |
| *ṭmn ḥnzrk* | your eight commanders,[32] |
| *'mk pdry bt ar* | *with you* Pidray, Mist-girl, |
| *'mk ṭly bt rb* | *with you* Tallay, Rain-girl, |

the expression *'mk* has simply been left out of the second line. In *CTA* 4 i 13-19 (and parallels) the term *mẓll*, 'shelter' is substituted for *mṯb*, 'dwelling' which occurs five times. This corresponds to the use of והשחתי, 'I destroy', in an otherwise unbroken series of ונפצתי, 'I hammer', (nine times over ten lines) in Jer 51,20c. Similarly, Mic 5,9b-13. Changed word-order is operative in *CTA* 17 vi 20-23.[33]

Note that Jer 2,6 combines substitution of synonym ('desert' for 'land' in the second line) and omission of repeated word (final line):

| | |
|---|---|
| המעלה אתנו מארץ מצרים | Who brought us from the *land*, Egypt, |
| המוליך אתנו במדבר | steered us through the *desert*, |
| בארץ ערבה ושוחה | through the *land* of steppe and chasm, |
| בארץ ציה וצלמות | through the *land* both hot and dark, |
| בארץ לא עבר בה איש | through the *land* no one crosses, |
| ולא ישב אדם שם | where no one lives. |

This amounts, in effect to substitution of two different kinds: of a synonym and of zero.[34]

3. *Telescoping*. Rigid repetitive series, which occur fairly often in Akkadian poetry,[35] are sometimes made more bearable for the listener both in Akkadian itself[36] and in Ugaritic.[37] Since no clear examples are to hand from Hebrew poetry (though some prose instances can be mentioned)[38] it need not be discussed here.[39]

---

32. The word literally means 'boar' and is here used metaphorically; see below under METAPHOR.

33. Contrast Sanmartin in *UF* 9 (1977) 371-73, who attempts to restore the 'original' word-order.

34. See also *CTA* 4 i 26-29.

35. See Hecker, *Epik*, 152, n. 1, and add Gilg XI 141-46.

36. For instance, Gilg (Nin) X iv 4-8, cited by Hecker, *Epik*, 153. See, too, Cooper: 1977.

37. See especially S.E. Loewenstamm, 'The Seven Day-Unit in Ugaritic Epic Literature', *JSS* 15 (1965) 121-33. He mentions (123) the 'marked tendency both to avoid the archaic style of the scheme and avoid excessive verbatim repetitions of the descriptive formula', citing *CTA* 17 ii 30-40 as an example of full repetition and *CTA* 4 vi 22-23; 14 iii 103-109.114-120 and 17 i 1-17 as telescoped variations.

38. Ex 24,16 and Jos 6, cited by Loewenstamm.

39. Note A. van Selms, 'Telescoped discussion as a literary device in Jeremiah', *VT* 26 (1976) 99-112.

4. *Numerical parallelism.* 'Since there are no synonyms for the numerals, yet repetition of the same word is to be avoided, the Canaanite poets invented the progressive numerical formula n // n + 1'.[40] This sequence is probably much older than Held suggests (it is attested in Sumerian) and is discussed in the section on PARALLELISM. The topic has been mentioned here for the sake of completeness and perspective.

*For Study*
Ps 78,8; Jgs 5,6.7.12.20.21.23.24.27.30.

*Cross-References*
See TABLE, above.

BIBLIOGRAPHY

(a) *General*
Gonda, J. *Stylistic Repetition in the Veda* (Amsterdam, 1959).
Also, Leech, *Guide*, 73-100; *PEPP*, 699-701.

(b) *Semitic*
Cooper, J.S. 'Symmetry and Repetition in Akkadian Narrative', *JAOS* 97 (1977) 508-12.
Gevirtz, S. 'Evidence of Conjugational Variation in the Parallelization of Selfsame Verbs in the Amarna Letters', *JNES* 32 (1973) 99-104.
Goldingay, J. 'Repetition and Variation in the Psalms', *JQR* 68 (1978) 146-51.
Held, M. 'The *yqtl-qtl* (*qtl-yqtl*) Sequence of Identical Verbs in Biblical Hebrew and Ugaritic', *Neuman FS*, 281-90.
— 'The Action-Result (Factitive-Passive) Sequence of Identical Verbs in Biblical Hebrew and Ugaritic', *JBL* 84 (1965) 272-82.
Muilenburg, J. 'A Study in Hebrew Rhetoric: Repetition and Style', *VTS* 1 (1953) 97-111.
Thompson, J.A. 'The Use of Repetition in the Prophecy of Joel', *Nida FS*, 101-10.
Also, O'Connor, *Structure*, 109-11.361-70; Hecker, *Epik*, 143.

### 11.03 *Envelope Figure*

*The envelope figure*
Envelope figure (a term coined by Moulton who first recognised it) is the repetition of the same phrase or sentence at the beginning and

---

40. Held: 1965, 275.

end of a stanza or poem. In effect, the poem is *framed* between the repeated phrases. For example, the first and last verse of Ps 103:

ברכי נפשי את יהוה    Bless Yahweh, O my soul.[41]

The envelope figure, broadly speaking, is related to other forms of repetition such as keywords or the refrain and structures a poem in the same way as chiasmus (see below on functions). However, there are differences. Akin though it is to the refrain, the envelope figure[42] occurs not more than twice. Similarly, the envelope figure could be described as 'incomplete chiasmus', only the extremes corresponding (schematically: A ... A). Finally, both envelope figure and distant parallelism have the same structure. In sum, then, envelope figure differs from its related forms (not including distant parallelism) on the numerical level: unlike them it is repeated only *once*.

### Ugaritic and Akkadian examples
Curiously, exact repetition of framing lines in Ugaritic poetry is rare; perhaps this is an indication of oral composition. One of the clearest examples is Anath's speech to Aqhat (whose bow she craves: *CTA* 17 vi 26-33). It begins:

> *irš ḥym laqht ǵzr*          Ask for life, O hero Aqhat,

and ends

> *ap ank aḥwy aqht ǵzr*          so will even I give life to hero Aqhat,

marking off a stanza of ten lines. There are other examples.[43]

A good illustration in Akkadian poetry is *Erra* I 40b-44:

> Let them march at your side:
> > When the hubbub from the citizens becomes too much for you,
> > and your heart is inclined to destroy—
> > to kill human beings,
> > to fell wild animals,
> > let these be your fierce weapons:
> Let them march at your side.

---

41. Or: 'O my throat'; the same figure recurs in Ps 104, indicating, perhaps, liturgical origin.

42. Also termed 'inclusio'.

43. *CTA* 6 ii 35-37 (strophic inclusio); 19 iv 173-78; 16 vi 1-2 and 13-14. See, too, *CTA* 4 i 19 and 44; 23:61-63; also 3D iii 33—iv 48.

The line *lillikū idâka* frames Anum's speech, marking its opening and its close.[44]

## Types of envelope figure

The type of envelope figure considered so far affects a complete stanza or a whole poem. Other examples are Ps 8,2 and 10:

> Yahweh, our Master,
> how great is your name
> in all the world.

101,2b-3 and 7; 118,1 and 29; and 'Praise Yah' at both the beginning and end of Pss 145-150.

Instead of a whole phrase or sentence, the repeated element is very often only a word (or the repeated words may simply have a common root). With identical single words: Ps 1,1.6 'wicked'; 17,1.15 'vindication'; 29,1.11 'power'; 73,1.28 'good'; 96,1.13 'the earth'; Isa 29,3.5 'shame'; 29,6.7 'beast'; 30,27-33 'fire'; Lam 2,12 'their mothers'.

With the same root: Ps 20,2.10 'to reply'; 52,3.11 'to be kind'; 59,2.8 'to be a bulwark(?)'; 71,1.24 'to be ashamed'; 82,1.8 'to judge'; 97,1.12 'to rejoice'; 134,1.3 'to bless'; etc.

Ranking between the complete phrase and the single word are such short phrases as 'sons of men' (Ps 12,2.9), 'house of Yahweh' (Ps 122,1.9) or clusters such as 'in your triumph' (Ps 21,2.14).

A table of these types can now be set out:

*envelope figure* (poem/stanza)
—complete (repeated element not less than colon)
—partial ('echo inclusio')
—repeated phrase
—repeated word
—repeated (common) root

There is yet another set, to be considered below, where the stretch of poem involved is a single strophe (occasionally two).

## Function of envelope figure: delimitation

The use of identical words at the beginning and end of a poem serves to *delimit it*. The function of envelope figure, then, is much the same

---

44. Also: *Ee* VI 35-38; *Erra* I 181-89 (Erra's speech); *BWL* 134:140-42; 220:23-25; Lines 1 and 40 of Ashurbanipal's coronation hymn (cf. Seux, *Hymnes*, 110ff).

45. Also: Song 2,8.14 'voice'; 5,2.8 'I'; 5,10.16 'my beloved'; Ruth 1,11.13 'my daughters'.

as that of the refrain. In the case of the Psalms little is gained (even if some or all of the inclusios are not liturgical in origin), but in other books of the OT the extent of an individual poem can be determined unequivocally, whenever the envelope figure can be identified.[46]

### Strophic inclusio

Very often the unit of poetry framed by the repeated element is not a complete poem or stanza but a single strophe,[47] for example:

| | |
|---|---|
| טוב עשית עם עבדך | (With) GOOD did you act towards your servant, |
| יהוה כדברך טוב | Yahweh, according to your word (which is) GOOD. |

(Ps 119,65-66a[48])

In most cases the frame-words are not identical, as in the example just set out, but either synonymous or from the same root. *Synonymous* frame-words occur in

| | |
|---|---|
| אלהים אל דמי לך | O DEITY, do not keep yourself silent, |
| אל תחרש | be not silent |
| ואל תשקט אל | and be not still, O GOD. (Ps 83,2[49]) |

with two words for 'God'. Similar is Ps 77,14. Frame-words from the *same root* are used in

| | |
|---|---|
| שכרו ולא יין | INTOXICATED (as) you are, but not with wine, |
| נעו ולא שכר | staggering, but not with INTOXICANT. |

(Isa 29,9[50])

where the common root is שכר. See, too, Isa 29,3b (צרה),[51] Jer 5,21 (שמע) and 8,4-5 (שוב).

Other kinds of envelope figure within the compass of a strophe involve assonance (Isa 29,10; Jer 22,22-23; Ps 119,13) or are at the level of grammar (Pss 100,1 'he . . . we'; 103,3). The value of recognising such frame-words is that the limits of a strophe can be established. For example, Ps 119,65-66a (see above) where the initial טוב of v. 66 really belongs to v. 65, as its final word.

---

46. Kessler: 1978, describes the functions of envelope figure as follows: to frame a unit; to stabilise the material enclosed; to emphasise by repetition and to establish rhetorical connection of the intervening material.

47. First recognised by Dahood.

48. As established by Dahood, *Psalms III*, 181 (my translation brings out the inclusio).

49. See Dahood, *Psalms III*, 273 for a slightly different version.

50. Recognised by Irwin, *Isaiah 28-33*, 56.

51. Also Irwin, *Isaiah 28-33*, 56.

*Other aspects*

Here the relationship of envelope figure to other poetic devices will be briefly explored.

1. *Break-up and word-pairs.* In Ps 58,2 and 12 the same word-pair (*ṣdq // mšpṭ*) occurs. Both times this provides an effect similar to the envelope figure.

In Isa 29 the first words of v. 2

> Then will I lay siege to Ariel

provide the components for a corresponding couplet in v. 7:

> The mob from every nation warring against ARIEL
> In fact, all warring against her, besieging her and LAYING SIEGE TO HER.

Similarly Pss 105,8 and 42; 107,1 and 43.

2. *Distant parallelism.* As has been seen, sometimes the framewords are not identical but synonymous (i.e. in parallelism). A clear example where distant parallelism of this kind functions as inclusio is Ps 127,1b and 5

> If Yahweh does not guard the CITY
> . . .
> . . .
> Rather than being humiliated
> he'll drive the enemy from the GATE.[52]

See, further, Ps 73,23.26; 74,3.22.

3. *Refrain.* Although there is a difference between the envelope figure and the refrain, occasionally the distinction is blurred as in Isa 29,5.16; Ps 107,4.7; 126,1.4.

*For study*

1 Sm 2,1.10; Jer 4,22; 22,6-7.20-23; Zeph 3,14a-15b; Job 3,4-5; Pss 20; 82; 135,1.26.

*Cross-references*

CHIASMUS, CLOSURE, KEYWORDS, REFRAIN, REPETITION, STANZA.

---

52. Dahood's understanding of this verse [*Psalms III*, 225] is now confirmed by the Ugaritic Prayer for a Beleaguered City (set out in Chapter 13.2).

BIBLIOGRAPHY

(a) *General*
Häublein, *Stanza*, 72-77.

(b) *Semitic*
Kessler, M. 'Inclusio in the Hebrew Bible', *Semitics* 6 (1978) 44-49.
Liebreich, J. 'Psalms 34 and 145 in the Light of Their Key Words', *HUCA* 27 (1956) 181-92 (esp. 183, n. 7 and 190-92).
Lundbom, J.R. *Jeremiah: A Study in Ancient Hebrew Historic* (SBL Dissertation Series 18; Missoula, 1975) 23-60.
Moulton, R.G. *The Literary Study of the Bible* (London, 1896) 53-54, 70, 77ff. 150-51.
Also Boling, *JSS* 14 (1969) 122; Campbell, *Ruth* (passim); Exum, *ZAW* 86 (1973) 58; Liebreich, *JQR* 46 (1956-57) 127-28; Muilenburg, *JBL* 59 (1940) 356; Barré, *CBQ* 45 (1983) 195-200.

## 11.04 *Keywords*

*The Keyword and its sub-types*
Some poems contain a certain number of repeated words which by their sound,[53] position within the poem and meaning function as keywords. Obviously, the presence of keywords is a form of repetition and so shares its characteristics. The difficulty for students is to determine whether there are keywords within a poem (or within its component stanzas) and this a question of judgment, not a statistical computation. The most frequent words are not necessarily the most significant.

The term 'keyword' can be understood in three different, if related, ways:[54]

1. *Dominant word.* Here keyword is taken to mean that lexical item which provides a basis for understanding a stanza or poem; an example is 'cauldron' in Ez 24,3-13 where the imagery is based on a pot of stew over a fire. This sense is excluded from our discussion here.

2. *Repeated word.* When a word recurs with insistent frequency within a poem—as does 'voice' in Ps 29—then it is very probably a keyword. Similar are 'to raise' in Ps 24; 'to guard', Ps 121 and 'to

---

53. For such 'summative' words cf. Hymes: 1960, 109-31.
54. Lack: 1973, 85, n. 20, distinguishes between *keywords* which relate to structure and *theme-words* which relate to content. Some words can function as both simultaneously. He notes, further, that words which occur first in a poem tend to be the most significant.

honour', Sir 3,6-11. Of course a poem (or stanza) may have several interacting keywords.

3. *Thematic words*. A poem may use a series of synonyms on a dominant theme—for example, Ps 129 includes words for 'to say, speak': קול קרא דבר קוה used six times.

Again, the thematic words of Ps 90 all concern TIME: דר בטרם מעולם עד עולם שנה יום אתמול לילה בקר ערב עד מתי אשמורה some two dozen occurrences in all).

## Method

The most comprehensive method of determining the presence or keywords is to tabulate all the repeated words in a poem and so establish their comparative frequency and relative positions. Such a procedure is time-consuming and so has only been applied to very few poems;[55] it has, though, the merit of providing objective data. It is important to realise that not only nouns and verbs but even prepositions, particles, adverbs and the like can be relevant. For example, the particle כל, 'all', recurs no less than 17 times in Ps 145 and is evidently related to the universalist theme of the poem.

## Functions

The main function of keywords is *to express the principal theme* of a poem. A poem 'provides its own interpretation by repetition of what is essential to its understanding'.[56] A secondary function is *to indicate the structure* of a poem (see presently). Finally, such words may function *as catchwords* linking separate verses or stanzas. Examples are Isa 30,13-14 and 30,26—linked by שבר; and Isa 33,5.16.24, all linked by the same word שכן.[57]

## Ugaritic and Akkadian

The thematic keyword *rgm*, 'word' (and synonyms), recurs in a stock stanza of Ugaritic narrative verse, namely *CTA* 3D iv 57-62 (etc.):

| | |
|---|---|
| dm rgm iṯ ly wargmk | For I have a TALE I would TELL you, |
| hwt waṯnyk | a WORD I would repeat to you, |
| rgm ʿṣ | a TALE of trees, |
| wlḫšt abn | and a WHISPER of stone, |

55. See Magne: 1958 for Pss 1, 29, 51, 91, 123, 126 and 137.
56. Buber: 1953, 52.
57. So Irwin, *Isaiah 28-33*, 96 and 161.

| | |
|---|---|
| *rgm ltd' nšm* | a TALE mankind cannot know, |
| *wltbn hmlt arṣ* | the earth's crowds cannot understand, |
| *tant šmm 'm arṣ* | the SIGHING[58] of heavens to earth, |
| *thmt 'mn kbkbm* | of deeps to stars. |

Fortuitously, perhaps, the keyword appears seven times and is evidently the focus of attention. See, similarly, five synonyms for '(wine-) vessel' in *CTA* 3A i 10-17 (*ks, krpn, bk, dn, kd*).

At the beginning of tablet II of 'The Righteous Sufferer' the negative particle *ul* is reiterated seven times in as many lines, a thematic keyword of transparent meaning:[59]

My ill-luck has increased, and I have NOT found prosperity.
I called to my god, but he did NOT show his face.
I prayed to my (personal) goddess, but she did NOT raise her head.
The diviner, through divination, has NOT investigated (my) situation.
The dream-interpreter, through libanomancy, has NOT elucidated my case.
I prayed to the z.-ghost, but it gave me NO instructions.
The exorcist with his ritual could NOT dissolve the divine wrath (against) me.

Similarly, *lā*, 'not', is used four times in three lines from the same text (lines 12-14) and an equal number of times in a quatrain from a fragment of epic.[60] Fourfold, too, is the keyword 'to cross' in Gilg X ii 21-23.[61] The keyword 'to heal' has been identified in lines 79-87 of a Hymn to Gula.[62]

### Keywords and structure

As has been noted, recognition of keywords can help in determining the structural pattern(s) of a poem. Among the few scholars to use this method, Pierre Auffret has been most assiduous (see bibliography). Only two examples will be set out here: one is Ps 142, which will be considered only briefly; the other is Ps 82, which will be discussed at length.

Whatever the literary category to which this poem belongs,[63] it seems at first glance to comprise an unbroken unit. If the keywords

---

58. The thematic keyword excludes the meaning 'meeting' for *tant*, here.
59. Text: *BWL* 38:3-9. Translation: *BWL*, 30 and *CAD* M/2, 279 and 381.
60. Text: Kinnier Wilson, *Iraq* 31 (1969) 9:12-15 (Etana Myth?).
61. See Millard, *Iraq* 26 (1964) 101, for the text.
62. Recognised by Barré, *Or* 50 (1981) 243-44.
63. See Loretz, *Psalmen*, 355-59 for discussion.

עיק, 'to cry, call for help', and נפש, 'life', are highlighted, it is evident that they each occur twice and *in the same sequence*.[64] They serve to mark off the two halves of the psalm (vv. 2-5 and vv. 6-8) corresponding to I: description of plight, and II: appeal for help.

### Ps 142

| I | v. 2 | With my voice to Yahweh DO I CALL OUT (אזעק) |
|---|------|---------------------------------------------|
|   | v. 5d | no one inquires about MY LIFE (נפש) |

---

| II | v. 6 | I CALLED OUT (זעקתי) to you, Yahweh, |
|----|------|--------------------------------------|
|    | v. 8 | Lead out MY LIFE (נפש) from prison. |

*Ps 82.* This poem has been chosen to illustrate the use of keywords because it is short (and therefore manageable) and because it exhibits a fairly clear structure. The first step (once lineation has been established) is to list and tabulate the repeated words.

The next procedure is to arrange the table to show those words which are repeated throughout the poem and those only occurring in part of it. The result can be set out in two columns:

---

64. For this device, known as 'panel writing', cf. S.E. McEvenue, *The Narrative Style of the Priestly Writer* (Rome, 1971), 13ff and 158ff. For an application to Gen 6,5-7 see Wenham, *VT* 28 (1978) 340-41.

|  | throughout psalm | | | only occurring in part of psalm | | | | | |
|---|---|---|---|---|---|---|---|---|---|
| 1a | אלהים | (נצב) | ב | | | | | | |
| b | אלהים | שפט | ב | | | | | | |
| 2a | | שפט | | | | | | (עול) | |
| b | | | | | | | | רשע | |
| 3a | | שפט | | | | | | | דל |
| b | | | | | | | | | |
| 4a | | | | | | | | | דל |
| b | | | | | | | | רשע | |
| 5a | | | | | | לא | | | |
| b | | | | | | לא | | | |
| c | | | ב | | | | | | |
| d | | | | כל | ארץ | | | | |
| 6a | אלהים | | | | | | | | |
| b | | | | כל | | | | | |
| c | | | | כל | | | | | |
| 7a | | | | | | | כ | | |
| b | | | | | | | כ | | |
| 8a | אלהים | | | | | | | | |
| b | | שפט | | | ארץ | | | | |
| c | | (נחל) | ב | כל | | | | | |

### Ps 82

| | | |
|---|---|---|
| אלהים נצב בעדת־אל | 1a | A |
| בקרב אלהים ישפט | b | |
| עד־מתי תשפטו־עול | 2a | B |
| ופני רשעים תשאו (־סלה) | b | |
| שפטו־דל ויתום | 3a | |
| עני ורש הצדיקו | b | |
| פלטו־דל ואביון | 4a | |
| מיד רשעים הצילו | b | |
| לא ידעו | 5a | C |
| ולא יבינו | b | |
| בחשכה יתהלכו | c | |
| ימוטו כל־מוסדי ארץ | d | |
| אני־אמרתי | 6a | |
| אלהים אתם | b | |
| ובני עליון כלכם | c | |
| אכן כאדם תמותון | 7a | |
| וכאחד השרים תפלו | b | |
| קומה אלהים | 8a | A' |
| שפטה הארץ | b | |
| כי־אתה תנחל בכל־הגוים | c | |

Evidently the most repeated words are אלהים, שפט and ב—and they recur throughout the psalm. The first two also reflect the keynote: God as just judge.

The other repeated words act as structural markers: רשע דל דל רשע form a frame (vv. 2b-4b) and together with עול (v. 2a) mark off a sub-unit in the first half. This sub-unit (vv. 2a-4b) is also a sense-unit.

The psalm divides into two main parts (vv. 1-4 and 5-8) and the second part is bound together by repetitions of ארץ and כל.

Finally, v. 1 and v. 8 provide a frame based on the words שפט נצב נחל שפט in chiastic sequence, and both verses are addressed directly to God.

Considerations of this order, though based on keywords, are not purely mechanical and have to intermesh with other observations concerning change of person and of theme.

The consecutive repetitions כ (v. 7) and לא (v. 5) are merely connective in function, linking together components of the strophe.

The Psalm can now be set out as follows: (words occurring throughout: CAPITALS, others: *italics*) [65]

A      1 GOD presides IN the divine council,
            IN among the *gods* does he JUDGE.

B      2 How long will you JUDGE (favouring) evil men,
            and towards *wicked* men be biased?

          3 *Judge* the feeble and fatherless,
            the troubled and *poor*: vindicate.
          4 Rescue the feeble and *poor*,
            from the hand of the *wicked* save (them).

C      5 *Not* knowing,
            *not* understanding,
            IN dark (ignorance) they wander,

            shaken are *all* the foundations of the *earth*.

          6 I thought:
            GODS you are,
            and sons of the Mightiest, *all* of you.

          7 But, *like* men will you die,
            and *like* any prince, fall.

A′     8 Up, GOD,
            JUDGE the *earth*.
            Truly you should govern *all* nations.

Further examples: Ps 12; Prov 1,20-33. For Isa 19,1-4 see Chapter 13.4.

*For study*
An interesting passage for investigation is Zeph 1-3 where certain keywords recur in intricate patterns. The most frequent lexical items

---

65. Van der Lugt, *Strofische Structuren*, 340-43, prefers the division: I vv. 1-4; II vv. 5-7; v. 8: a prayer. See, too, M. Tsevat, 'God and the Gods in Assembly, an Interpretation of Psalm 82', *HUCA* 40/41 (1969-70) 123-37.

are יום, 'day'–21 times—and קרוב 'near'–10 times.[66] Curiously, the second word does not appear at all in Zeph 2. Other common words are

> אסף — 5× (to gather)
> קבץ — 3× (to assemble)
> פקד — 5× (to punish)
> כרת — 5× (to cut)
> שפט — 4× (to judge).

Another group relates to the sea:

> ים — 3× (sea)
> דג — 2× (fish/fisher).
>
> cf. איים נהר

Note, too,

> שם — 5× (name)
> ארץ — 5× (earth/underworld).

## BIBLIOGRAPHY

(a) *General*

Hymes, D. 'Phonological Aspects of Style: Some English Sonnets', Sebeok, *Style*, 109-31.

(b) *Semitic*

Auffret, P. 'Structure littéraire et interprétation du Psaume 155 de la Grotte XI de Qumran', *RevQ* 35 (1978) 323-56.

—'Structure littéraire et interprétation du Psaume 154 de la Grotte XI de Qumran', *RevQ* 36 (1978) 513-45.

—'Essai sur la structure littéraire des Psaumes CXI et CXII', *VT* 30 (1980) 257-79.

Fretheim, T.E. 'Psalm 132: A Form-Critical Study', *JBL* 86 (1967) 289-300.

—twenty keywords used two or more times.

Lack, R. *La symbolique du Livre d'Isaïe. Essaie sur l'image littéraire comme élément de structuration* (Rome, 1973).

Liebreich, J. 'Psalms 34 and 145 in the Light of Their Key Words', *HUCA* 27 (1956) 181-92.

- in spite of the title, concentrates on envelope figure.

Magne, J. 'Répétition de mots et exégèse dans quelques Psaumes et le Pater', *Bib* 39 (1958) 177-97.

—by far the best study on keywords.

---

66. Also in the form 'to approach'; as with keyword study generally, attention is paid chiefly to word root.

Ward, J.M. 'The literary form and liturgical background of Psalm LXXXIX', *VT* 11 (1961) 321-39
Also van der Lugt, *Strofische Structuren*, 213-18 and O'Connor, *BASOR* 226 (1977) 15-29.

## 11.05 *The Refrain*

*The refrain and its subtypes*

A refrain is a block of verse which recurs more than once within a poem. Such a block can comprise a single word, a line of poetry or even a complete strophe. The refrain, of course, is simply a form of repetition, but its distinguishing feature is its structuring function (discussed below). It differs from inclusio in occurring not only at the opening and close of a poem but within it as well. In fact, generally speaking, a refrain rarely begins a poem (but see Ps 129). Subtypes of the refrain are the strict refrain, the variant refrain and the chorus. These will be considered in turn, with examples.

1. *The strict refrain*. The wording of the strict refrain remains *unchanged*, no matter how many times it is repeated. For example in Am 4 the refrain

> Yet you did not return to me,
> Yahweh's oracle

occurs five times (vv. 6.8.9.10.11), with exactly the same words each time. Similarly Ps 67,4.6. Also Song 2,7 (=3,5; 5,8); Isa 9,11 (= 16.20; 10,4); cf. Mal 1,11.

2. *The variant refrain*. Much more frequently (for reasons to be proposed below) subsequent repetitions of the refrain are not verbatim. Variations—often quite minor—though not enough to completely alter the refrain, do result in a changed refrain. For example, in Ps 80 the basic refrain is

> God, return to us,
> show favour and we will be saved (v. 4.[67])

In vv. 8 and 20 insertions and/or additions modify this basic pattern; e.g. v. 20

> *Yahweh*, God *of the Armies*, return to us
> show favour and we will be saved,

---

67. Lit. 'make your face shine'.

the additions being 'Yahweh' and '(of the) Armies'. In v. 15 the
second line is dropped:

> God *of the Armies*, return *please*,

the last word now being an imperative. Other variant refrains are
Ex 15,6.11.16; 2 Sm 1,19.25 and 27; Am 1-2; Pss 99,3.5.9; 107,6.13
= 19.28; 114,4.6; 144,7-8.10c-11.

In some of these examples the refrain provides a kind of grid into
which can be slotted words appropriate to the stanza accompanying
the refrain. The best-known instance is Am 1-2 with the pattern:

> Thus speaks Yahweh:
> Because of three
> sins of (PLACE NAME)
> and because of four,
> I'll not revoke it,

(vv. 3-5.6-8.9-10.11-12.13-15; 2,1-3.4-5.6-8). A place-name is to be
fitted into the slot.[68]

Interesting is Ps 107 which uses both the identical and the variant
refrain (strict: vv. 8.15.21.31; variant: 6.13.19.28).

The refrain of Song 2,16

> My beloved is mine,
> and I am his

is inverted in 6,3 (and abbreviated in 7,11).

3. *The chorus*. The basic difference between the chorus and the
refrain is frequency of repetition: the chorus is repeated after every
line. This is most manifest in Ps 136, where the antiphonal response
is

> For eternal is his kindness.

Evidently such responses formed part of the liturgy and indicate
strong audience-participation. Quite possibly this was the practice,
too, in non-liturgical poetry.

*Functions of the refrain*

The refrain (and here its subtypes are also included) shares the
functions of repetition (see REPETITION). Here only two major

---

68. In each of the stanzas there are other refrain-like elements.

functions will be looked at: the structuring effect and the involvement of the audience, already briefly alluded to.

1. *The refrain and poem-structure.* As mentioned elsewhere (see STROPHE & STANZA) one of the problems in analysing ancient Hebrew poetry is the determination of stanza-divisions. Evidently refrains segment a poem into smaller units and generally these can be identified as stanzas. However, the refrain is only one of several possible indications of such divisions and these must be considered too, before certainty can be reached. This is especially true of Song.[69] Clear cases of stanza-division are Ps 67 and Ps 46—the two refrains coming at (roughly) the middle and end of each psalm. In a poem such as 2 Sm 1,19ff (David's lament), although the four refrains divide it into three parts, the parts are very unequal. Further subdivision may be required, using other criteria.

Often (though not a general rule) the final refrain is longer than the others—forming a climax, e.g. Isa 2,17-18 (cf. 11);[70] Ps 99,9 'For holy is Yahweh our God' (vv. 3 and 5: 'holy is he').[71]

2. *The refrain and oral poetry.* The purpose of a constant refrain must surely have been to enable people listening (whether as audience or congregation) to join in. This is particularly true of the chorus (as defined above). In fact evidence is available from Chron. On the occasion of the ark of the covenant being transferred to the newly-built temple,

> All the levitical singers, Asaph, Heman and Jeduthun and their sons and brothers, linen-clad, were standing on the east side of the altar, with cymbals, harps and zithers; with them stood 120 priests blowing trumpets. Such was the harmony between trumpeters and singers that only one melody was audible when they praised and thanked Yahweh. Then the music began, accompanied by trumpets, cymbals, song-instruments, to render:
>
> > Praise Yahweh greatly,
> > for eternal is his kindness.[71]

An invitation to join may be present in Ps 129,1-2:

---

69. See Exum, *ZAW* 85 (1975) 51ff; Gordon, *UT*, 291, n. 3.

70. R.G. Moulton, *The Literary Study of the Bible* (London, 1896), 158, terms this *augmenting the refrain* and refers to 2 Sm 1,19ff.

71. 2 Chr 5,13-14; for the refrain, cf. Ps 136. For this translation cf. J.L. Kugel, 'The Adverbial Use of *kî ṭôb*', *JBL* 99 (1980) 433-39.

> 'Much have they oppressed me since my youth'
> —Let Israel now say:
> 'Much have they oppressed me since my youth'.[72]

Further proof is forthcoming from the variant refrains: not only were they modified for the sake of variety, the constantly changing form prevented the audience joining in.[73]

### The refrain in Akkadian and Ugaritic

The refrain was particularly common in Assyrian and Babylonian hymns and prayers. In fact, being a standard component, the copyist scribes tended to abbreviate as much as possible, or use a ditto sign.[74] A single example will suffice; it is from a prayer to the divine judge. It begins:

> I (shall go) to the judge, I (shall go) to the judge.

and continues:

> I (shall go) to the Lord of Erabriri—I (shall go) to the judge.
> I (shall go) to the Lord of Egalmah—I (shall go) to the judge.

and so on for 13 more lines.[75]

In Ugaritic, one of the few prayers to come to light uses refrain-like repetition.[76] The account of the contest between Baal and Mot also uses what amounts to a refrain:

| | |
|---|---|
| *mt 'z* | Mot was strong, |
| *b'l 'z* | Baal was strong, (*CTA* 6 vi 16-19) |

with the final refrain, since it is climactic, a variant:

| | |
|---|---|
| *mt ql* | Mot fell |
| *b'l ql* | Baal fell. (lines 21-22[77]) |

The episode is thereby structured into four scenes.

More liturgical are the chorus-like repetitions, or antiphons:

---

72. Although not all scholars agree that this is a refrain.
73. These variants also attest the fluidity of oral poetic tradition.
74. Very largely to save both space and labour, significant factors when writing on clay.
75. See conveniently Seux, *Hymnes*, 155-56; also the prayers on 139-52.237.253, etc.
76. See *KTU* 1.119, set out in section 13.2 in the chapter WORKED EXAMPLES.
77. See De Moor, *UF* 10 (1978) 194, n. 7.

| | |
|---|---|
| *špq ilm krm yn* | He supplied the gods with rams, wine. |
| *špq ilht ḫprt [yn]* | He supplied the goddesses with ewes, [wine]. |
| *špq ilm alpm y[n]* | He supplied the gods with oxen, wi[ne]. |
| *špq ilht arḫt [yn]* | He supplied the goddesses with cows, [wine]. |
| *špq ilm kḫtm yn* | He supplied the gods with seats, wine. |
| *špq ilht ksat [yn]* | He supplied the goddesses with chairs, [wine]. |
| *špq ilm rḥbt yn* | He supplied the gods with barrels of wine. |
| *špq ilht drkt [(yn)]*[78] | He supplied the goddesses with hogsheads of [wine]. (*CTA* 4 vi 47-54) |

Similarly, *CTA* 1 iv 23-24 = 25 = 27 = 29; 6 v 11-19; *Ugar* 5 8 13-19.

## For study
It would be interesting to compare MT with the Dead Sea Scrolls where there is a tendency to insert or add refrains—for example, Ps 145 and 11QPs 145.

## Cross-references
ENVELOPE FIGURE, REPETITION, STANZA (also KEYWORD).

### BIBLIOGRAPHY

Freedman, D.N. 'The Refrain in David's Lament over Saul and Jonathan', *Widengren FS*, 115-26.
— 'Strophe and Meter in Exodus 15', *Myers FS*, 163-203, esp. 163-66.
Fullerton, K. 'The Original Form of the Refrain in Is. 2:6-21', *JBL* 38 (1919) 64-76.
Kuhl, C. 'Die "Wiederaufnahme"—ein literarkritisches Prinzip?', *ZAW* 23 (1952) 1-11.
Also, Exum, *ZAW* 85 (1973) 51ff; O'Connor, *Structure*, 466-82 (on poems with 'burdens').

## 11.06 *Allusion*

### Theory
Allusion is the reference (usually not explicit) within one body of literature to the culture and letters of another body. To quote from a standard work of reference:

---

78. Last word omitted from tablet by mistake. Gibson, *CML*, 63, n. 4: 'Alternatively "he did supply the ram gods with wine etc."'. See my discussion, *JBL* 99 (1980) 338.

The technique of allusion assumes: (1) an established literary tradition as a source of value; (2) an audience sharing the tradition with the poet; (3) an echo of sufficiently familiar yet distinctive elements; and (4) a fusion of the echo with the elements in the new context ... It usually requires a close poet-audience relationship, a social emphasis in literature, a community of knowledge, and a prizing of literary tradition.[79]

## Allusion in the OT

The conditions outlined above apply to Hebrew literature where both audience and poet share a common tradition (the OT writings in first their oral and then their written stages) and the echoes to this tradition have varying degrees of overtness. With the discovery of literary traditions outwith the OT (the *belles-lettres* of the ancient Near East, in effect) some account, too, has to be taken of allusion to extra-biblical texts. The point about 'social emphasis in literature' is particularly true of the prophetic writings and of much in the wisdom tradition.

## Different kinds of allusion

From what has been said it is clear that allusion can fall into one of two classes: inner-biblical and extra-biblical. Discussion of either would take us far afield so here only what is significant to poetic technique will be mentioned. A third class comprises the allusion to a theme or topic which is never expressly mentioned, or 'repressed reference'.

1. *Inner-biblical allusion.* Many allusions are made, in Hebrew poetry, to historical events (and here creation would be included); for example, Hos 12,3-6 refers to the Jacob and Esau stories (Gen 32,20; 33,4; 35,15).[80] Isa 55,13 alludes to the flood stories,[81] as do Isa 51,10[82] and Jer 4,23-26.[83] Zeph 1,3 alludes to Gen 1,26 and, in general, to the creation stories.[84]

2. *Extra-biblical allusion.* Only the cognoscenti would have recognised these allusions, unless their frequency attests widespread

79. *PEPP*, 18.
80. Cf. Gertner, M. *VT* 10 (1960) 241-84; Ginsberg, *JBL* 80 (1961) 339-47; Ackroyd, *VT* 13 (1963) 245-59; Holladay, *VT* 16 (1966) 53-64; Good, *VT* 16 (1966) 137-51; Coote, *VT* 21 (1971) 389-402.
81. Gunn: 1975, 503-08.
82. Gunn: 1975, 495-97.
83. Muilenburg, *JBL* 59 (1940) 363; Holladay, *JBL* 85 (1966) 496.
84. Roche: 1980.

knowledge by the populace. For instance,

השמים כסאי    The sky is my throne,
והארץ הדם רגלי    and earth a footstool for my feet. (Isa 66,1)

alludes to Yahweh's enormous size and evokes a passage in the Ugaritic texts where Athtar, attempting to usurp Mightiest Baal's position, is described as hopelessly inadequate:

| | |
|---|---|
| *ytb lkḥt aliyn bʻl* | He sat on the throne of Mightiest Baal, |
| *pʻnh ltmǵyn hdm* | his feet did not reach the footstool, |
| *riš lymǵy apsh* | his head did not reach its edge. |

(*CTA* 6 i 58-61)

It is also significant that in Mesopotamian tradition the footstool was distinctive of kings. Other allusions of this kind include Isa 19,1, 'See Yahweh riding on a swift cloud', and Baal's epithet, *rkb ʻrpt*, 'Cloud-Rider';[85] Isa 28,16 '(Yahweh) does not act hastily' in the context of building, and the fourfold anaphoric *ḥš*, 'Hurry!', in the account of the construction of Baal's palace (*CTA* 4 v 113-116). Additional allusions to Ugaritic literature and mythology can be mentioned. One is Song 8,6 כי עזה כמות אהבה, 'For strong as death is love'. Rather than the superlative[86] 'it appears more likely that the allusion is to the god Mot, Death personified'[87] in view of the refrain *mt ʻz*, 'Mot (= Death) is strong' (cited under REFRAIN, above).[88] Another is Hos 6,4 (= 13,3) which plays on Pughatu's stock epithet.[89]

There are also numerous allusions to Mesopotamian literature. In Isa 40,15-17.22, the land is said to appear small, reminiscent, perhaps, of the Etana Legend, where an eagle is described as carrying the hero on his back up into the sky. Told to look down, Etana first sees the sea looking like a tub; further on in the flight the land appears to be a garden plot and the sea a breadbasket and eventually even these are lost to sight. The restoration of old buildings mentioned in Isa 58,12 is a common theme in Assyrian royal texts.[90] Weeping

85. 'The description of the cloud as swift hardly makes sense unless the cloud is a vehicle' (Moran, *Bib* 43 [1962] 324).
86. So Winton Thomas, *VT* 3 (1953) 221.
87. Pope, *Song*, 668.
88. The correct translation of Song 8,6 may be 'truly Love is stronger than Death'.
89. See Watson, *UF* 8 (1976) 378, n. 56 for details.
90. Sample passage: 'For his life and the well-being of his city the wall of the Step Gate—it had become delapidated—I restored and deposited my clay cone' (Inscription of Puzur-Ashur III; see conveniently A.K. Grayson, *Assyrian Royal Inscriptions*, [Wiesbaden, 1972] I 35 and elsewhere).

on the housetop (Isa 15,3; 22,1) may be a reference to an Assyrian custom in view of the passage from Sargon's Annals where the people of Musasir 'went up on the roofs of their houses and wept bitterly'.[91] Lastly, Isa 55,13, 'Instead of camel-thorn, pine-trees shall shoot up; and instead of briars, myrtles shall shoot up', recalls the tree-contest fables of Babylonian sapiential texts.[92]

3. *Repressed reference*. For various reasons (considered below) a topic or even a main theme is never expressly mentioned in certain poems. Ps 67, for instance, is a prayer for rain set as a blessing on a plough,[93] but words such as גשם יורה מטר (all terms for 'rain')[94] or even דשן, 'fertility' are not used. Similarly, the location for the poem Isa 34 is only referred to indirectly;[95] 'wisdom' does not occur in Sir 51,13-20,[96] and in Ps 82, although God is referred to in terms evidently related to the sun ('arise', 'darkness', 'justice'—the Sun is the god of justice in Mesopotamia), the word שמש is not used.

*Functions of allusion*

Generally speaking, such allusions (chiefly in the context of oral poetry) cater for the more learned sections of the audience, help maintain interest and at the same time, enable the poet to display his knowledge. There is also the economy factor: a word or two evokes more than could be expressed by the poet and indirectly adds to the richness of his language. So for instance in Ex 15,7,

| וברב גאונך תהרס קמיך | Through your great majesty you destroyed your foes. |
| תשלח חרנך יאכלמו כקש | You sent out your anger, it devoured them like stubble. |

'the association of anger with fire, and of both with the sword, is so

91. Ginsberg, *JAOS* 88 (1968) 47 and n. 6.
92. See the fables collected in *BWL*, 150-67. For a parallel to Isa 60,13 cf. Lipiński, *ZAW* 85 (1973) 358-59. On Isa 45,15 as a satirical allusion to the Babylonian 'absence of divinity' theme, see Heintz, *RHPR* 59 (1949) 436.
93. See Watson, 'Chiastic Patterns', 157-58.
94. So Dahood, *Psalms II*, 127.
95. 'One of the most marked features of the second part of the poem is the repressed reference to the land, or the desert, or whatever the place described may be. It is referred to again and again by a pronoun or adverb' (Muilenberg, *JBL* 59 [1940] 354).
96. 'Wisdom is the obvious theme; yet, by an artifice no doubt intended, the word *ḥkmh* occurs nowhere in the poem' (Skehan, *HTR* 64 [1971] 390).

standardized that the poet needs only to hint at the combination in his allusive statement to evoke all three images'.[97]

A significant function of such hidden references was the *avoidance of taboo topics or themes*. This explains the non-mention of the sun in Ps 82 since it would automatically have been equated with the Sun-god. The same applies to Ps 67 and its veiled reference to Baal.

*Exploitation of poetic technique*
The poets drew on their craft to keep these allusions from being too obvious, yet at the same time providing indications of their presence. In Ps 29, for example, the alliterative pattern which appears to be based on the letters *b*, *l* and ', points to the deity Baal.[98] The expression קו תהו ואבני בהו, 'Chaos-line and void-plummet', of Isa 34,11 not only evokes the account of creation but breaks up the well-known phrase תהו ובהו of Gen 1,2 to form a word-pair.[99]

*For study*
Mic 7,3 and Jgs 9; Nah 3,18 and Song 2,8; Ps 65,9-14 (see above on Ps 67); Isa 10,33-34; Isa 28,15 and the Akk. expression *irat erṣetim*, 'bosom of the Underworld'. Compare Jer 3,25; Isa 14,11; Job 7,5; 21,16 with Gilg XII 94.

BIBLIOGRAPHY

(a) *General*
Ben-Porat, Z. 'The Poetics of Literary Allusion', *PTL* 1 (1976) 105-28.

(b) *Semitic*
Delcor, M. 'Allusions à la déesse Ishtar en Nahum 2,8?', *Bib* 58 (1977) 73-83.
Gunn, D.M. 'Deutero-Isaiah and the Flood', *JBL* 94 (1975) 493-508.
Roche, M. De 'Zephaniah I 2-3: the "sweeping of creation"', *VT* 30 (1980) 104-09.

## 11.07 *Ellipsis*

*Definitions*
Ellipsis is the omission of a particle, word or group of words within a

---

97. Freedman, *Myers FS*, 181.

98. So Fitzgerald, *BASOR* 215 (1974) 61-63; but see the critique by O'Connor, *BASOR* 226 (1977) 15-29.

99. For the allusion, cf. Muilenburg, *JBL* 59 (1940) 339-65, though he did not notice the break-up of a stock phrase. See, too, Jer 2,20 and Gen 49,14-15 (as translated by Gevirtz, *ErIs* 12 [1975] 104*-12*).

poetic or grammatical unit, where its presence is expected. In other words, ellipsis is the suppression of an element demanded by the context.[100] For example, in Hos 5,8,

תקעו שופר בגבעה    Blow the trumpet in Gibeah,
הצצרה ברמה    the horn in Ramah,

the verb 'blow' is to be understood in the second colon (corresponding to 'blow the trumpet in Gibeah' of the first line). Ellipsis, of course, belongs to ordinary language as well as to poetry—but the problem with ellipsis in poetry (our main concern here) is that an obscure passage or an ambiguous context can make its recognition difficult.

Apart from meaning and context, the main clue to determining elliptical expressions is structure. An example illustrating this is Ps 100 (see presently). Examples of different types of ellipsis have been collected elsewhere[101] and include double-duty pronouns, double-duty suffixes, double-duty nouns, verbs and prepositions, double-duty particles and other expressions.

## Ps 100

This psalm has been chosen as an excellent example of ellipsis on a large scale (i.e. not merely within a single strophe). There are problems with regard to stichometry, but fortunately none with regard to translation. In what follows, some notes will be set out showing how ellipsis is to be recognised. (For convenience *consonantal transliteration* has been used.)

1. *Structural patterns*. There are four patterns in the psalm: one main set (comprising two subsets) and three other patterns. The first pattern comprises an imperative (here designated I) followed by certain specifications:

---

100. Greenfield: 1971, 140 includes the definition: 'An omission of a form or forms in a clause or sentence the presence of which is demanded or suggested by existing forms and context in order to make sense—and in poetry, to make the most or richest sense—of the message'. He distinguishes phonological from syntactic ellipsis.
101. Dahood, *Psalms III*, 429-44. See also Kugel, *Idea*, 22.90-94, etc.

| 1(i) | = I(Y) | impv (2 pl.) | + | object | + | adverb | Ps 100: |
|---|---|---|---|---|---|---|---|
| | | *hrydʿw (kl-hʾrṣ)* | | *lyhwh* | | ø | v. 1 |
| | | *ʿbdw* | | *ʾt-yhwh* | | *bśmḥh* | 2a |
| | | *hwdw* | | *lw* | | ø | 4c |
| | | *brkw* | | *šmw* | | ø | 4d |

| 1(ii) | = I(P) | impv (2 pl.) | + | place | + | adverb | |
|---|---|---|---|---|---|---|---|
| | | *bʾw* | | *lpnyw* | | *brnnh* | 2b |
| | | *bʾw* | | *šʿryw* | | *btwdh* | 4a |
| | | ø | | *ḥṣrwtyw* | | *bthlh* | 4b |

In pattern 1(i,ii), Y denotes actions honouring Yahweh, P, actions where the People move. The other three sets are statements: 2: about Yahweh, S(Y); 3: about the people, S(P); 4: about Yahweh's attributes, S(A).

| 2 | = S(Y) | noun | + | copula | + | complement | |
|---|---|---|---|---|---|---|---|
| | | *yhwh* | | *hwʾ* | | *ʾlhym* | 3a |
| | | ø | | *hwʾ* | | *ʿśnw* | 3b |
| | | (*ṭwb yhwh* for *yhwh hwʾ ṭwb* | | | | 5a) | |

| 3 | = S(P) | complement | + | | | pronoun | |
|---|---|---|---|---|---|---|---|
| | | *lʾ* | | | | *ʾnḥnw* | 3b |
| | | *ʿmw wṣʾn mrʿytw* | | | | ø | 3c |

| 4 | = S(A) | adverb | + | | | noun | |
|---|---|---|---|---|---|---|---|
| | | *lʿlm (wʿd)* | | | | *ḥsdw* | 5b |
| | | *dr wdr* | | | | *ʾmntw* | 5c |

2. *Comment*. If we look at set 1, it is evident that with a single exception (v. 2a), the adverb is missing in 1(i) or I(Y). There is 'trumpet to Yahweh', etc., but only once 'worship Yahweh *with joy*'. In the next set 1(ii) or I(P), although the adverb is always present, there is ellipsis of 'enter' in v. 4b. It can be argued that, since the adverb is omitted in the very first verse, no expectancy has been set up, so there is no ellipsis, the line בשמחה עבדו את יהוה (v. 2a) simply foreshadowing what is a standard pattern in I(P).

The analysis of the statements is less clear, particularly for 3 = S(P) and 4 = S(A), so that less certainty is possible. There is ellipsis in v. 3b: 'he made us' for an expected *'Yahweh, he it was made us'. In v. 3c, ellipsis may also be operative.

3. *Deviation*. Examples of deviation from the set patterns include טב יהוה for יהוה הוא טב (v. 5a), identical in meaning; and לעלם חסדו ועד

for an expected לעלם ועד חסדו, perhaps to provide a semi-chiastic strophe as a climax.[102]

*For study*
Hos 1,6; Jer 22,10; 3,2; Nb 23,19a; Mic 7,1b; Isa 38,18—on all these texts cf. Andersen—Freedman, *Hosea*, 188-90. This section has not dealt with ellipsis in Ugaritic and Akkadian poetry since too much syntactical discussion would be involved, but these areas certainly need to be studied. See Greenstein: 1974 for Ugaritic and O'Connor, *Structure*, 125-26 on *Erra* IV 131-35. Another and longer 'gap' in Akkadian is *Šurpu* IV 4-59.

*Cross-references*
PROSE OR POETRY: SIMILE.

### BIBLIOGRAPHY

(a) *General*
Greenfield, S.B. 'Ellipsis and Meaning in Poetry', *TSLL* 13 (1971) 137-47.

(b) *Semitic*
Greenstein, E.L. 'Two Variations of Grammatical Parallelism in Canaanite Poetry and their Psycholinguistic Background', *JANES* 6 (1974) 87-105.
O'Connor, *Structure*, 401-04 ('The Line-level Trope of Gapping and Related Phenomena'); also 122-29.—This is perhaps the most comprehensive (and controversial) survey of ellipsis (or gapping) in Semitic verse and provides some bibliographical references. Note his statement that in Hebrew 'verb gapping only occurs in poetry' (124), a view discussed above under PROSE OR POETRY and contested by Kugel, *Idea*, 322.

## 11.08 *Irony*

*Introductory*
Failure to recognise irony—whether in everyday language or in a poem—can lead to complete misunderstanding. Much as in metaphor and idiom, it is not always enough to determine the *literal* meaning of a sentence or phrase since the overt sense is not always what is intended. In fact, in an ironical statement the literal significance is

---

102. Note, incidentally, that line-form analysis does not uncover ellipsis: v. 1 V NP$_2$ (or M); 2 V NP$_2$ M—V M; 3 nom.—nom.—nom. 4 V M—M—V M; 5 nom.— nom.—nom. For a convenient translation see Dahood, *Psalms II*. According to Loretz, *Psalmen II*, 77-80, the psalm is late and v. 3 was inserted even later.

precisely the opposite of what must be understood. Nor can irony be ignored since it occurs in all languages and has even been termed a universal of language.[103] The main problem as far as sight reading of written poetry is concerned (and the same would apply to prose) is the lack of extralinguistic markers such as body gestures,[104] and the *absence of intonation* which would otherwise provide a clue to ironical intent. This is true, evidently, of ancient Hebrew, Ugaritic and Akkadian. *Context* is probably the best guide to the presence of irony, as in Am 4,4-5:

| | |
|---|---|
| באו בית אל ופשעו | Come to Bethel and rebel! |
| הגלגל הרבו לפשע | to Gilgal, and rebel the more! |
| והביאו לבקר זבחיכם | Bring your sacrifices for the morning, |
| לשלשת ימים מעשרתיכם | your tithes within three days. |
| וקטר מחמץ תודה | Burn a thank-offering without leaven, |
| וקראו נדבות השמיעו | announce, proclaim free-offerings, |
| כי כן אהבתם בני ישראל | for you love what is proper, Israelites! |

Contrast the direct insult in Am 4,1:

שמעו הדבר הזה פרות הבשן      Listen to this, you cows of Bashan.

In theoretical terms, irony is present when the literal meaning is nonsensical and it has to be replaced by a derived meaning, usually in direct opposition to the superficial sense.[105] In the example set out above (Am 4,4-5) 'rebel' contradicts the meaning of 'bring sacrifices', etc., and 'for you love what is proper'. The literal meaning 'proper' (Hebrew כן) is unacceptable, and the derived meaning 'outward conformity' or the like is evidently intended.

There are, occasionally, indications that irony is present. In Jer 30,7, for instance, reversal of the normal word-order in the last line is the clue, as וממנה יושע ('he shall come through it safely') occurs instead of expected ממנה אך יושע or ויושע ממנה. Vv. 5-7, then, constitute an oracle of judgement and not one of hope.[106] Another pointer is

---

103. So I. Robinson, *The New Grammarian's Funeral* (Cambridge, 1975), 49.

104. See M.I. Gruber, *Aspects of Nonverbal Communication in the Ancient Near East* (StPohl 12; Rome, 1980) I and II; 'Ten Dance-Derived Expressions in the Hebrew Bible', *Bib* 62 (1981) 328-46.

105. Irony should not be confused with oxymoron. In oxymoron (e.g. 'profound shallowness') the literal sense of *both* words is intended, but in telescoped form. In irony, the literal meaning becomes subordinate to the derived meaning.

106. See Holladay, *JBL* 81 (1962) 53-54, for extensive discussion.

evident in Jer 9,16-17 where 'make haste' is expressed in long words so that there is incongruity between meaning and sound.[107]

The main effect of irony is to *increase the distance* between speaker and listener, the classic example being 1 Kgs 22,15 where Micaiah is consulted by the king about the forthcoming battle. 'Attack and win the day, Yahweh will deliver it into your hands', he says, in apparent conformity with Zedekiah and the rest of the false prophets.

Note, finally, that irony can be *verbal* (as can be seen from the examples given) or *situational* ('dramatic irony')—though the two forms are related.[108] Examples will be given below.

From the point of view of the audience (or reader), there are those who are 'in the know' and can appreciate irony, and there are the others, who miss the poet's point. For example, in Jer 14,6,

| | |
|---|---|
| ופראים עמדו על שפים | While the wild asses stand on the *hills* |
| שאפו רוח כתנים | panting for air like jackals, |
| כלו עיניהם | their eyes all glazed |
| כי אין עשב | for want of fodder, |

the term 'hills' (literally, 'bare heights') is used. In Jer 3,2.21.23 it occurs, too in the context of (forbidden) fertility rites. The language is ironic: 'where fertility is sought, there fertility is least';[109] and those unfamiliar with Jeremiah's word usage would simply see the first line as descriptive. As Scholes puts it:

> Often irony is a matter of delicate interaction between code and context. It may draw upon the private language or the special experience of an intimate group. One of its primary qualities is that it divides its audience into an elite group who 'get' the irony and a subordinate group who miss it.[110]

Irony 'has the power to make any given set of representations represent something else than it does in normal usage'.[111] So much is evident from the following couplet in Ugaritic: (*CTA* 5 vi 28-30)

---

107. Holladay, *JBL* 85 (1966) 411.

108. On this point see Muecke: 1978, 481-82, who comments on how situational and verbal irony influence each other mutually.

109. Holladay, *JBL* 81 (1962) 52.

110. Scholes: 1974, 36-37; he notes that the ability to recognise irony distinguishes the good (native/adult) reader from the bad (foreigner/child).

111. Riffaterre, *Semiotics*, 65. He remarks: 'Irony, or its verbal mechanism, is but one special case of marker permutation'.

| | |
|---|---|
| *tmǵ ln'my arṣ dbr* | She reached 'Pleasure' land of pasture, |
| *ysmt šd šḥl mmt* | 'Delight', the fields by the shore of Death's realm. |

The immediate context converts the euphemisms 'Pleasure' and 'Delight' into their opposites, both belonging to the 'code' of death. In other words she reached the underworld. This is the main *function* of irony, then, namely the generation of a special code.[112] The code has to be known before the significance of the lines under scrutiny can be understood. Whether in this particular case (which appears to be a stock phrase since it occurs more than once) the avoidance of taboo words was a factor is irrelevant, since the code is ironic and not, say, descriptive (for example 'house of dust').

The important point is that a text can be misunderstood entirely if it is taken at its literal meaning and not as ironic in intent. A wisdom passage in Babylonian shows this clearly:

> When the rutting stallion mounts the she-ass
> like a rider he whispers in her ear:
> 'Let the foal you bear be a racer like me;
> do not make it like an ass which carries loads'.

The point is that a jenny-ass is sterile and will have no offspring, so the lot of asses will not change. The proverb, therefore, is probably an acid comment on unchanging social conditions (slaves remain slaves). Without the knowledge that the jenny-ass is sterile these four lines are utterly meaningless.[113]

*Recognition of irony from ANE parallels*
Before looking at some examples of irony in Hebrew it is well worth demonstrating how comparison with Akkadian and Ugaritic texts can make one aware of ironic intent. The full irony of much in Isa 14 can only be appreciated from a knowledge of the Gilgamesh Epic. In particular, Isa 14,12, which can be read and translated:

| | |
|---|---|
| איך נפלת משמים הילל בן שחר | How you have fallen from heaven, Helel Son of Dawn! |
| נגדעת לארץ חולש על גוי(ם) | (How) you've been cut down to the ground, *helpless on your back*! |

---

112.  In Riffaterre's words the function of irony is 'the generation of idiolectic codes'.
113.  Text: *BWL* 219:15-18. Cf. *CAD* A/2, 482. Another example from Mesopotamian tradition is *Erra* III 41 (and 54-56) where the Fire-god (Išum), who is accused of ignorance, is ironically addressed with the words 'you grant wisdom'.

is an ironic allusion to Utnapishtim, who although immortal, merely 'lives the life of a retired and tired old man'. On seeing him, Gilgamesh exclaims:

> My heart had imagined you as resolved to do battle,
> yet you lie indolent on your back![114]

Also, in Mic 7,1 the expression אללי, 'Woe is me!' (or the like), is used to open a passage strong in agricultural imagery. It is an ironic reference to Akkadian *alali*, an exclamation of joy or a refrain of a work song, often used in connection with the harvest.[115] In both these examples, intelligibility is not impaired if the irony goes unnoticed, but for those acquainted with Mesopotamian tradition the passages acquire added sharpness and depth.

To these illustrations from Akkadian can be added at least one from Ugaritic. It is Isa 28,8:

| כי כל שלחנות מלאו קיא | Yes, every table is laden with vomit, |
| צאה בלי מקום | filth, without clear space. |

Irwin comments: 'The fine irony . . . can be appreciated when the nuance of *ml'* in a text such as UT,51:I:39-40 is compared'.[116] The text (*CTA* 4 i 39-40) runs

| *ṭlḥn il dmla mnm* | A huge table full of inlays, |
| *dbbm dmsdt arṣ* | the effusion of earth's foundations, |

as translated by Margalit.[117]

*Examples in classical Hebrew*
In Ez 19,1-9, Israel's 'mother' is depicted as a lioness whose offspring is taken off to Egypt and then Assyria. The irony here is that Judah is often represented metaphorically as a lion (e.g. Gen 49,9), yet is defeated by the Lion of Assyria. (See, in equivalent terms, vv. 10-14: Israel the vine.)

Another example is Mic 2,6:[118]

---

114. For fuller details see R.C. van Leeuwen, 'Isa 14:12, *ḥôlēš 'al gwym* and Gilgamesh XI,6', *JBL* 99 (1980) 173-84 (esp. 182).
115. *CAD* A/1, 328-29; *AHw*, 34. See, also, A. Livingstone, 'A Fragment of a Work Song', *ZA* 70 (1981) 55-57.
116. Irwin, *Isaiah 28-33*, 20.
117. Margalit, *AMOLAD*, 13 and 20-22.
118. Unfortunately the text is extremely difficult here.

אל תטפו יטיפון  'Do not spout'—they spout,

where those complaining about Micah prophesying are guilty of
exactly the same fault—a point driven home both by the use of נטף
('to drip, distil, spout, preach') and by v. 11:

| | |
|---|---|
| לו איש הלך | Surely, (if) someone went round |
| רוח ושקר כזב | falsely and deceitfully inspired, (saying), |
| אטף לך ליין ולשכר | 'I spout to you of wine and beer'— |
| והיה מטיף העם הזה | that would be this people's spouter; |

where again the term נטף is used (twice).

Irony is common in idol polemic, e.g. Dt 32,37-38; Isa 46,1-2; Jer
2,27; Zeph 1,18. See further Nah 2,6,[119] Zeph 3,3 (metaphorical use
of animal names for leaders used negatively; cf. Isa 34,6-7); Ps 114,5-
6 (cf. 3-4); Job 26,2-3; Am 3,12;[120] Isa 28,14;[121] 28,22;[122] Joel 2,20;
4,4 (EVV 3,4);[123] and the passages collected by Good[124] and
Gordis.[125]

*Dramatic irony*
In dramatic or situational irony, the audience is aware of a situation
of which the actor(s) is(are) ignorant. So, in Jgs 5,30 Sisera's people
are expecting him back victorious (see vv. 28-29) and explain his
delay in the following proleptic terms:

| | |
|---|---|
| הלא ימצאו יחלקו שלל | They must be finding and dividing spoil, |
| רחם רחמתים לראש גבר | one girl—two girls per warrior head; |
| שלל צבעים לסיסרא שלל צבעים | booty of dyed stuff for Sisera, booty of dyed stuff; |
| רקמה צבע רקמתים לצוארי שלל | striped dyed stuff—two lengths, for the plunderer's neck. |

Yet Sisera has had his brain crushed in by Jael and he lies,
conquered, at her feet. The effect of irony here is to heighten the
defeat of the enemy, Sisera, by providing a strong contrast with his
expectation of victory. Another example is Jer 14,16 (see above).

---

119. K.J. Cathcart, *Nahum in the Light of Northwest Semitic* (Rome, 1973), 75.92-95.
120. Rabinowitz: 1961.
121. Holladay, *VT* 20 (1970) 167, n. 4.
122. Irwin, *Isaiah 28-33*, 37.
123. Thompson, *Nida FS*, 107.
124. Good: 1965.
125. Gordis, *HUCA* 22 (1949) 157-219; also Blank: 1970.

*For study*
Hos 10,1; 12,12.

*Cross-references*
HYPERBOLE, IMAGERY, LITOTES, OXYMORON, RHETORICAL
QUESTIONS.

BIBLIOGRAPHY

(a) *General*
Kerbrat-Orecchioni, C. 'L'ironie comme trope', *Poétique* 14 (1980) 108-27.
Muecke, D. *The Compass of Irony* (London, 1969).
Schaefer, A. (ed.) *Ironie und Dichtung* (Munich, 1970).
Sedgewick, G.G. *Of Irony, Especially in Drama* (Toronto, 1948).
Thomson, J.A.K. *Irony: An Historical Introduction* (Harvard, 1927).
(These last three are unseen by me.)
Also Leech, *Guide*, 171-78; Nowottny, *Language*, 26-48; Ullmann, *Language*,
    111-16. Volume 36 (1978) of *Poétique* is devoted to 'irony'.

(b) *Semitic*
Blank, S.H. 'Irony by Way of Attribution', *Semitics* 1 (1970) 1-6.
Good, E.W. *Irony in the Old Testament* (London, 1965; reissue Sheffield,
    1981).
Holladay, W.L. 'Style, Irony and Authenticity in Jeremiah', *JBL* 81 (1962)
    44-54.
Rabinowitz, I. 'The Crux in Amos III 12', *VT* 11 (1961) 228-31.
Williams, J.G. 'Irony and Lament: Clues to Prophetic Consciousness',
    *Semeia* 8 (1977) 51-74.

## 11.09 *Oxymoron*

Oxymoron is 'the yoking together of two expressions which are
semantically incompatible, so that in combination they can have no
conceivable literal reference to reality'.[126] Examples are 'female
grandfather', 'dry water' and the like, the pattern generally being
ADJECTIVE + NOUN. When two such contradictory words are
combined—as in 'dry water'—'dry' negates the aspect WET of water,
and not, say, its life-supporting property, its coolness or its fish
content. Oxymoron, therefore, *picks out one aspect of a thing and
negates it.*[127]

An example in Hebrew is Jer 22,19: Jehoiakim, when dead, will not
be lamented; in fact

126. Leech, *Guide*, 132. See 135.140ff.147.198.
127. Dubois, *Dictionnaire*, 199-201.

קבורת חמור יקבר    They will give him a *donkey's funeral*.

In other words, he won't even be buried, as the next couplet explains:
'Hauled out and dumped—outside the gates of Jerusalem'. The
expression 'a donkey's funeral' (the Hebrew equivalent of an adjective
+ noun construction) is oxymoron since the two words are contradictory. Note that *only the aspect* 'unburiable' of 'donkey' is negated
here; no comment is implied on the donkey's obstinacy, capacity for
carrying loads, sexual prowess, etc.

An example in Akkadian comes from the Gilgamesh Epic, where
the hero's conflicting impulses are alluded to when he is referred to
as *ḫadī-ū'a-amēlu*, 'Happy-gloom-man'.[128]

In general, the *effect* of oxymoron is to drive a point home with
vigour; what has been termed 'intellectual shock technique'.[129] For
example, Prov 28,19:

עבד אדמתו ישבע לחם    One who works his soil will be sated with food,
ומרדף ריקים ישבע ריש   but one with empty pursuits *will be sated with
poverty*.

Lack, of course, cannot be satisfying, so that joining these two
concepts together jars the listener into awareness and makes the
message very vivid. In Prov 25,15 oxymoron shows that the truth is
not always self-evident:

בארך אפים יפתה קצין   By patience, a ruler is seduced;
ולשון רכה תשבר גרם   and a soft tongue can crush bone.

Oxymoron is related to irony (see there) and merismus.[130]

*For study*
Prov 17,26. Also, Hos 10,1; 12,12.

*Cross-references*
IRONY, MERISMUS.

BIBLIOGRAPHY

McCann, E. 'Oxymoron in Spanish Mystics and English Metaphysical
Writers', *CompL* 13 (1961) 16-32.

128. Gilg I v 14; cf. *CAD* Ḫ, 24: 'joy-woe-man'. Another is 'His name is "An old
man will become young again"' (Gilg [Nin] XI 281).
129. See McCann: 1961.
130. *PEPP*, 596.

## 11.10 *Abstract for Concrete*

*Theory*
Strictly speaking, 'abstract noun with concrete meaning' should be
discussed under the heading of figurative language, or metaphor.
However, the significance of recognising an abstract noun as having
a concrete meaning is not at issue here. What is of more interest in
the context of this book is the contribution made by this device to
parallelism in general, and to certain forms of parallelism (e.g. gender
parallelism) in particular.

*Abstract nouns intended to be understood concretely*
The classic example is provided by Ugaritic, where *t'dt* (Heb. *t^e'ûdâ*)
must mean 'embassy' in view of the parallel concrete noun *mlak*,
'messenger':

| | |
|---|---|
| *tphn mlak ym* | They perceived Yam's messengers, |
| *t'dt ṭpṭ nhr* | the *embassy* of 'Judge' Nahar. |
| | (*CTA* 2 i 22 [cf. 26][131]) |

From Hebrew:

| | |
|---|---|
| מתיך בחרב יפלו | Your men by the sword will fall, |
| וגבורתך במלחמה | and your warriors, in war. (Isa 3,25) |

where *g^ebûrâ* literally means 'strength'.

*Functions*
Rather than provide a classification for this device, it is simpler to
look immediately at its functions. Broadly speaking, they can be
divided into two classes: functions related to parallelism and other
functions. The first group includes the balancing of a masculine by a
feminine noun, the preservation of singular-plural combinations and
the heightening of antithesis. Then come the creation (or preservation)
of assonance, preservation of a poetic pattern and word-play on a
fixed pair. These will be considered in turn.

1. *Balancing m. and f. terms*. This is evidently related to Gender-
matching of synonyms (see that section). An unequivocal example is
Ps 36,12:

| | |
|---|---|
| אל תבואני רגל גאוה | Let not the foot of the *presumptuous* overtake me, |
| ויד רשעים אל תנדני | nor the arm of the wicked fling me down. |

---

131. Gibson, *CML*, 159, notes 'abstract for concrete' and adduces the Heb. word.

The word here translated 'presumptuous' is an abstract: 'presumption', but the poet has preferred using a feminine noun to balance masculine $r^e \check{s} \bar{a} \check{\ } \hat{i}m$.[132]

Similarly: Pss 40,18b; 68,33; 102,23; 107,42; 109,2; 111,8; 119,150.

### 2. *Singular-plural parallelism*

| | |
|---|---|
| כי יהוה אהב משפט | For Yahweh loves *a just man*, |
| ולא־יעזב את־חסידיו | nor does he neglect his devoted ones. (Ps 37,28[133]) |

Here *mišpaṭ*, balanced by plural 'those devoted to him', has a concrete meaning.

### 3. *Antithesis.*

It seems that an abstract noun is occasionally used to deepen the contrast between parallel cola, as in

| | |
|---|---|
| עיני יהוה נצרו דעת | Yahweh's eyes keep watch on (his) *acquaintance*, |
| ויסלף דברי בגד | but he overthrows the words of traitors. |
| | (Prov 22,12) |

And: 11,14; 13,8; Ps 119,139.150.

### 4. *For assonance.*

Alliterative assonance dictated the choice of *ṣrt* in the Ugaritic line *ht tṣmt ṣrtk*, 'Now must you vanquish your enemies' (*CTA* 2 iv 9).[134] The same consideration applies to texts such as Prov 7,4; 13,23; Isa 33,18 and

| | |
|---|---|
| בא זדון ויבא קלון | Struts a fop: there's a flop, |
| ואת־צנועים חכמה | but with the humble there's wisdom; |
| | (Prov 11,2[135]) |

here, too, an element of antithesis is present. See also Isa 29,7 (below).

### 5. *To preserve verse pattern.*

At times an abstract noun is used in order to maintain a poetic pattern. So, in Isa 29,7 the law of increasing members is operative:

| | |
|---|---|
| וכל־צביה ומצדתה והמציקים | Yes, all who are making war on her, *besieging* |
| לה | her and laying siege to her. |

'The alliterative trio *ṣbyh*, *mṣdth* and *hmṣyqym lh* are arranged according to the "Law of Increasing Members".'[136]

---

132. See Dahood, *Psalms I*, 224.
133. See Dahood, *Psalms I*, 231.
134. See Van der Weiden: 1965; *CML*, 43: 'enemies'.
135. Van der Weiden: 1965, 51, n. 4, notes the assonance and adds: 'Perhaps this is the reason why the sacred author used the word *zadon* as abstract for concrete'.
136. Irwin, *Isaiah 28-33*, 54.

Another example is Isa 60,17 where the dominant function of portraying reversal has entailed both chiasmus and reversed gender-matching. This, in turn has necessitated the use of abstract *pᵉquddâ* (balancing *ṣᵉdāqâ*, both fem.) as the counterpart of concrete *nōgeš*.

ושמתי פקדתך שלום    I will make your *overseers* peace,
ונגשיך צדקה    and your taskmasters justice.

See, too, Isa 28,9.[137]

6. *For word-play on a fixed pair.* In Isa 30,12 the expression עשק ונלוז, 'a most perverse tyrant', means, literally, 'tyranny most perverse'. Irwin comments: 'It may be that the poet, aware of the fixed pair, intended to play upon it with his own creation *ʿšq wnlwz*'[138]—the pair in question being נלוז // עקש in Prov 2,15.

*Final comments*
Generally speaking it can be seen that the use of an abstract noun to balance a concrete term is not simply poetic fancy but demanded by various factors. To those mentioned can be added merismus (e.g. the examples in section 1, above) and allusion (e.g. Ps 136,8-9 evokes the language of Genesis).

*For study*
Prov 2,8. Hos 5,12 (cf. Andersen—Freedman, *Hosea*, 412).

*Cross-references*
PARALLELISM, PERSONIFICATION: WORD-PAIRS.

BIBLIOGRAPHY

Van der Weiden, W.A. '"Abstractum pro concreto", phaenomenon stilisticum', *VD* 44 (1966) 43-52.
Also Dahood, *Psalms III*, 411-12; *Bib* 63 (1982) 60 and n. 4; Driver, *JRAS* 1948, 164-76; Greenberg, *JAOS* 90 (1970) 598; Pardee, *UF* 5 (1973) 232.

## 11.11 *Hyperbole*

*The theory of hyperbole*
Hyperbole is a way of expressing exaggeration of some kind (regarding size, numbers, danger, prowess, fertility and the like) using common

137. Irwin, *Isaiah 28-33*, 21: *dēʿâ* = 'message'.
138. Irwin, *Isaiah 28-33*, 84.

language. By this means the idea stands out. It is a rhetorical device common to most literatures, but in the ancient Near East where it was standard practice to depict royalty and important personages as larger than life on wall-paintings, reliefs and in sculpture, hyperbole was practically part of everyday language.[139] In essence, hyperbole belongs to economy of expression, which is the hallmark of good poetry and can therefore be related to the principle of thrift operative in oral composition (see ORAL POETRY). As will be seen, there is some overlap between hyperbole and both simile and metaphor. Litotes or understatement—the antithesis of hyperbole—is not much used in Hebrew poetry.[140]

## Ugaritic and Akkadian poetry

Hyperbole is chiefly used in Ugaritic *belles-lettres* to express numerical exaggeration. For instance, in place of the normal week of mourning, seven years are observed for both Aqhat and Baal,

| | |
|---|---|
| *'d šb't šnt ybk laqht ġzr* | Seven years they wept for Hero Aqhat. (*CTA* 19 iv 176-78) |

Again, numerical word-pairs feature in descriptions of Baal mating ('seventy // eighty', *CTA* 5 v 19-20), of the building of his palace ('silver by the thousand // gold by the myriad', *CTA* 4 i 26-28) and in the stereotype expression *balp šd // rbt kmn*, 'over a thousand fields, a myriad acres'.[141] Also in this bracket is Yatpanu's boast: 'The hand that felled Aqhat will strike down enemies by the thousand' (*CTA* 19 iv 220-21).[142]

Akkadian poetry in its turn exhibits the use of hyperbole. In the Hymn to the Ezida Temple, for instance, the building is described as rooted in the underworld with its roof reaching the clouds—a

139. 'In the imagination of the peoples of the ancient Near East great gods were taller than lesser deities, gods were taller than men, great men like famous kings were taller than mortals' (De Moor, *ZAW* 88 [1976] 330).

140. On both litotes and hyperbole, as well as their relationship to each other, see Leech, *Guide*, 167-71. G.B. Caird, *The Language and Imagery of the Bible* (London, 1980) 134, comments: 'The Hebrew people never discovered the emphatic use of understatement' and cites Gen 18,4, 'a drop of water', as one of the rare instances. Another example may be Isa 10,7.

141. Note the interesting grammatical deviation: area is used to express distance.

142. Further: the greed of the newly-born gods: 'One lip to the sky, the other to the ground', *CTA* 23: 61-64. For the allusion to Baal's tremendous size and for an example of extended hyperbole, see below.

commonplace image.[143] Another example, from the Gilgamesh
Epic, is the divine epithet

| | |
|---|---|
| *[a]gû ezzu mu'abbit dūr-abnī* | The furious flood-wave who destroys even stone walls.[143a] |

### Hyperbole, simile and metaphor

The hyperbolic *simile* is very frequent in Hebrew (it also occurs in
Ugaritic).[144] The stock simile 'like (or as numerous as) the sands of
the sea' was probably too well-worn to make much impression (texts:
Isa 48,19; Hab 1,9; Hos 1,10 etc.). Comparable is the comparison 'like
dust' (Zech 9,3 of silver; likewise Job 27,16; Ps 78,27 of quails). More
interesting is Jer 9,21:

| | |
|---|---|
| ונפלה נבלת האדם כדמן על־פני השדה | The corpses of men shall fall like dung in the fields, |
| וכעמיר מאחרי הקצר ואין מאסף | like swathes behind the reaper, but no one shall gather them. |

See too Hos 12,11 ('altars common as heaps of stones beside a
ploughed field'); Lam 2,13 ('vast as the sea is your ruin'); Ps 79,3
('blood shed like water'). Clearly all are expressive of quantity; cf.
Ps 81,4.

An example from Ugaritic of hyperbolic *metaphor* is

| | |
|---|---|
| *šmm šmn tmṭrn* | The skies will rain oil, |
| *nḥlm tlk nbtm* | the wadis will run with honey, |
| | (CTA 6 iii 6-7) |

where the idea of fierce fertility is conveyed by a combination of
figurative language and exaggeration. For similar expressions cf. Joel
4,18; Mic 6,7; Job 20,17; 29,6. More arresting is Ps 5,10:

| | |
|---|---|
| קבר פתוח גרונם | A wide-open grave is their throat; |

and, of Job's heart:

| | |
|---|---|
| ויתר ממקומו | It leaps out of its place. (Job 37,1) |

---

143. Text: Köcher, *ZA* 53 (1964) 238 lines 5-6. See, too, *qarnāšu šamê nakpâ*, 'its (=
a tree's) tip poked the sky', cited *AHw*, 718, and compare Gen 11,4. Cf. *BWL*, 327.
143a. Text and translation: Wiseman, *Iraq* 37 (1975) 160:32; see his comment, 163.
144. E.g. *kirby tškn šd, km ḥsn pat mdbr*, 'like locusts they occupy the fields, like
crickets the desert fringe', *CTA* 14 ii 103—iii 105. Also *tirkm yd il kym, wyd il kmdb*,
'May El's "hand" be as long as the sea, and the "hand" of El like the flood', *CTA*
23:33-35, etc.

A combination of both simile and metaphor can make up a hyperbolic expression, as in:

| | |
|---|---|
| כמו פלח ובקע בארץ | Like one rent and riven in the netherworld, |
| נפזרו עצמינו לפי שאול | my bones are strewn at the mouth of Sheol. |

(Ps 141,7[145])

*Types of hyperbole*

As indicated above, quite the most common hyperbole is *numerical*. In Isa 4,1,

| | |
|---|---|
| והחזיקו שבע נשים באיש אחד | Seven women will take hold of one man, etc. |

the disastrous effect of war (cf. 3,25) is depicted with awful clarity. See, too, Job 1,3,[146] Am 5,3 and Isa 30,7.

Another type of hyperbole is the *extended* form. It is attested in both Ugaritic and Akkadian.[147] Hebrew examples include Jer 5,16-17; 15,7-9; Nah 3,15b-17 (locusts); Job 3,4-9 (birth-curse); Pss 69,2-3 and 15b-16; 22,16-18; see also Job 1; 8,14-18. Akin is the series of hyperbolic expressions in Am 9,2ff. Cf. Mic 6,6-7. See, as well, Joel 2 (extended hyperbolic metaphor).

As regards content, the hyperbole is very often of a military nature, Hab 1,6-11; Ez 24,6 being cases in point.[148]

*The function of hyperbole*

Hyperbole is another word for 'exaggeration' with the additional implication that the poet is striving after vividness of imagery. Hyperbole is common to the poetry of almost every language, eventually becoming part of normal speech, so that there is always the danger of over-used hyperboles turning into meaningless clichés. The main function of hyperbole, in fact, is to *replace over-worked adjectives* (such as 'marvellous', 'enormous', 'colossal') with a word or phrase which conveys the same meaning more effectively.[149] Both Jeremiah and Ezekiel employ the commonplace to great effect in the well-known proverb: 'The fathers have eaten sour grapes but

---

145. Recognized by Dahood, *Psalms III*, 313.

146. Though Pope, *Job*, 7-8, remarks that this list of Job's vast property is not necessarily excessive.

147. See Watson: 1979. Note, too, the 'reaction to bad news' cliché in *CTA* 3D 29-32, etc., and Anath's massacre in *CTA* 3B ii.

148. Besides *CTA* 3B ii, note 4 vii 7-12 where Baal is described as conquering 90 towns, and 6 ii 31-37 (and v 11-19): Anath's 'massacre' of Mot.

149. This is particularly true of Hebrew which has only few adjectives.

their children's teeth are set on edge' (Jer 31,29; Ez 18,2). The hyperbole is effective precisely because simple language is used. Again, what could be more banal than a reference to human hair? Yet

| רבו משערות ראשי שנאי חנם | More numerous than the hairs on my head are those hating me for no reason. |
| עצמו מצמיתי איבי שקר | Many more than my locks are my lying foes. |
|  | (Ps 69,5) |

is powerful hyperbole. The really outstanding poet can give even the jaded simile 'as many as the sands of the sea' a new twist:

> Could my anguish but be weighed,
> my misery heaped on the balances,
> 'twere heavier than the sands of the sea. (Job 6,2-3)

Besides abundance, hyperbole is used to express negative events such as destruction, war and danger: Am 9,2-3; Ez 30,12; 35,8; Isa 34,3-4; Jer 26,18. Perhaps this is of a piece with the broader function of reversal (see FUNCTION: reversal) exemplified by

| ונתתי נערים שריהם | I will make the lads their princes, |
| ותעלולים ימשלו־בם | and suckling-babes will govern them. |
|  | (Isa 3,4 [see 5cd]) |

*Further on theory*
Hyperbole can be related to the word-pair and to the origin of the construct state. According to Avishur numerical word-pairs of the type אלף // רבבה, 'a thousand // ten thousand' were formed into single units ('thousands of myriads') due to the exigencies of poetry. 'The tendency to create poetic hyperbole apparently led to the use of pairs of words in the construct state, and the phenomenon gave rise to instances of poetic hyperbole which are scarcely intelligible.'[150]

*For study*
Song 1,4b.8b; 3,6-7; 5,15-16; 6,8; 8,11. Additionally: Isa 48,19; Job 25,5; Pss 6,7; 10,8.10; 14,1 (= 53,1); 21,5-6; 27,3-4; 38,3-14; 69,2-3; 73,7-10; Prov 27,3.

Note the numerical hyperbole in Gen 4,24 (discussed by Kugel, *Idea*, 31-32; compare Gevirtz, *Patterns*, 25-34). Also, Isa 5,10; Ps 119,164; Prov 24,16; Am 6,9; Qoh 6,6; 7,19 and 8,12 (stylistic trait?); Song 5,10-11.

---

150. Avishur, *Semitics* 2 (1971-72) 81.

*Cross-references*
BREAK-UP, METAPHOR, ORAL POETRY, SIMILE, WORD-PAIR.

BIBLIOGRAPHY

Eybers, I.H. 'Some Examples of Hyperbole in Biblical Hebrew', *Semitics* 1 (1970) 38-49.
Stuart, D. 'The Sovereign's Day of Conquest', *BASOR* 221 (1976) 159-64.
Watson, W.G.E. 'An Unrecognized Hyperbole in *Krt*', *Or* 47 (1979) 112-17.

## 11.12 *Merismus*

*Introductory*
When a totality is expressed in abbreviated form, we are dealing with merismus. The expression 'body and soul' (Isa 10,18), for example, stands for (and means) 'the whole person'. The significant point is that in merismus, of whatever form, it is not the individual elements themselves that matter but what they amount to *together*, as a unit. In

| מכף רגל ועד ראש | From sole to crown |
| אין בו מתם | nothing was healthy. (Isa 1,6) |

the whole body is implied and not just the anatomical parts actually mentioned ('sole, head'), an interpretation confirmed by 'nothing was healthy' in the second colon. Merismus, then, belongs to metonymy (the part for the whole) and is a form of ellipsis, akin to hendiadys. In hendiadys, expressions of the type בקול־רנה ותודה do not mean 'loud shouts AND thanksgiving' but 'loud shouts OF thanksgiving' (Ps 42,5). It is the total concept that is important; the components are not significant in isolation. Merismus, then, is an abbreviated way of expressing a totality.

*Types of merismus*
Merismus can take several forms. The most abridged form is the use of *polar word-pairs* (e.g. 'sky // earth'). *Selective listing* is another convenient form of merismus. Two further types are *chiastic parallelism* and the related device, *gender-matched parallelism*. In each of these forms, an expression for totality (such as כל) may be present; this is explicit merismus; or it may have to be understood (in implicit merismus).
Here Honeyman's words can be cited:

Merismus ... consists in detailing the individual members, or
some of them—usually the first and last, or the more prominent—
of a series, and thereby indicating either the genus of which those
members are species or the abstract quality which characterises the
genus and which the species have in common. Symbolically
expressed, merismus is the brachylogous use of A + Y or A + B + Y
in place of the complete series A + B + C ... X + Y to represent
the collective Z of which the individuals A to Y are members or the
abstract *z* which is their common characteristic, and the terms
selected for mention are commonly joined to each other by the
copula. A particular type of merismus is that in which the two
named species exhaust the whole genus, and the merismus assumes
the form of a polar expression; in this case, if Z = A + Y, Z may
also be expressed by A + non-A.[151]

1. *Meristic list* (A + B + C ... + M + N = Z or *z*). The use of a list
to denote a totality is only a partial abbreviation, and the longer the
list the less of an abbreviation it becomes. Of course, few such lists
could be completely exhaustive so that one could say that almost
every list is meristic (excluding detailed inventories or catalogues).
What then marks off the meristic list is not only that it is generally
short and that a total is either expressed or implied, but that the
items enumerated belong to the same level. For example, the
common element to the list in Isa 3,18ff is that they all denote
cosmetics. Three subtypes of the meristic list can be distinguished,
therefore. There is the meristic list *headed by a total*: Isa 3,18-23;
2,12-16; Hos 4,3; Pss 146,6-9; 148,7-12. Second is the list with a total
*at the end*: Isa 41,19; Pss 76,4.8; Sir 39,26-27. Lastly is the meristic
list with an *implied total*: Gen 12,6; Hos 4,1; Ps 81,3. (See further
details under LIST, 12.2 below.)

2. *Polar word-pairs*. Since the topic of word-pairs is dealt with
elsewhere (see WORD-PAIRS) it will be discussed here only so far as is
relevant to merismus. The nature of Hebrew poetry which is
predominantly made up of parallel couplets, lends itself to expressing
merismus by means of polar word-pairs of the type

בקר // לילה   morning // night.[152]

Krasoveč has provided a comprehensive listing of such pairs so only a
few examples need be given here:[153]

---

151. Honeyman: 1952, 13-14; 'brachylogous' simply means 'elliptical'.
152. Isa 21,12; Am 5,8; Ps 92,3 = always.
153. Krasoveč: 1977 (though not all his examples are meristic).

| | |
|---|---|
| יבשת // ים | sea // dry land, Ps 95,5 = the universe; |
| בשר // דם | flesh // blood, Ps 50,13 = sacrificed animals; |
| נער // ישיש | young // aged, Job 29,8 = everybody; |
| מדבר // כרמל | desert // Carmel, Isa 32,16 = everywhere. |

Not every polar word-pair is meristic in function; in different contexts the same word-pair may express antithesis instead. So, the pair 'to give // to take' is antithetical in Hos 13,11:

| | |
|---|---|
| אתן לך מלך באפי | I GAVE you a king in my fury, |
| ואקח בעברתי | but I TOOK (him away) in my anger. |

In Ps 15,5 on the other hand it expresses merismus (total innocence):[154]

| | |
|---|---|
| כספו לא נתן בנשך | He does not GIVE money with interest, |
| ושחד על נקי לא לקח | nor does he TAKE bribe against an innocent person. |

Merismus is also expressed by 3. chiastic parallelism and 4. gender-matched (antithetic) parallelism which are discussed in the chapter on PARALLELISM. Examples include Isa 10,4a; 11,4b; Jer 2,9; Ez 17,27; Nah 3,1; Hab 3,3 and Prov 21,7 (chiastic) as well as Isa 41,4; Jer 14,8; Pss 98,5-6; 135,6 and Prov 22,17 (gender parallelism).

### Merismus in Ugaritic and Akkadian
In Ugaritic, meristic lists include *CTA* 3B ii 38-41 and 16 vi 45-50. Note the meristic pair in *CTA* 6 ii 16 (etc.):

| | |
|---|---|
| *kl ġr lkbd arṣ* | Every ROCK to the earth's core, |
| *kl gb' lkbd šdm* | every HILL to the core of the fields. |

where merismus is indicated by the use of *kl*; see also *CTA* 6 i 31-32.59-61 and 6 v 2-3. The opening lines of the Creation Myth (*Ee* I 1-2) provide excellent illustration for Akkadian:

| | |
|---|---|
| *enūma eliš lā nabû šamāmi* | When the SKY above was not named, |
| *šapliš ammatum šuma lā zakrat* | the EARTH below was not given a name. |

For other examples see under LIST.

### Further notes on theory
One of the functions of the devices mentioned—polar word-pairs,

---

154. Also Job 1,21 and 35,7—cited by Dahood, *RSP I*, 218.

lists, chiastic parallelism and gender-matched parallelism—is to express merismus, as has been illustrated. In its turn, merismus is governed by the principle of economy or thrift which is operative in both oral and written poetry. The dramatic effect of a segment of poetry can be heightened when a whole universe is denoted by merely two items. Also, the unifying nature of merismus counters the polarizing effect of its components. Although, for example, 'going' and 'coming' are opposite in meaning, paradoxically, mention of one arouses expectancy of the other and at the same time the two terms are considered a unit meaning 'whatever you do'.

*For Study*
Prov 14,20; contrast the identical pair in Sir 7,13 and Prov 14,27. Jgs 5,17. Job 2,7.

*Cross-references*
CHIASMUS, ELLIPSIS, GENDER-MATCHED PARALLELISM, HENDIADYS, LIST, OXYMORON, WORD-PAIRS.

BIBLIOGRAPHY

(a) *General*
Hofman, J.B. 'Zum Wesen der sogenannten polaren Ausdrucksweise', *Glotta* 15 (1927) 45-53.

(b) *Semitic*
Boccaccio, P. 'Termini contrari come espressione della totalità in ebraico', *Bib* 33 (1952) 173-90.
Brongers, H.A. 'Merismus, Synekdoche und Hendiadys in der bibel-hebräischen Sprache', *OTS* 14 (1965) 100-14.
Hartmann, B. *Die nominalen Aufreihungen im Alten Testament* (Zurich, 1953).
Honeyman, A.M. 'Merismus in Biblical Hebrew', *JBL* 71 (1952) 11-18.
Krasovec, J. *Der Merismus im biblisch-Hebräischen und Nordwestsemitischen* (Rome, 1977).
—'Die polare Ausdrucksweise im Psalm 139', *BZ* 18 (1974) 224-48.
Also O'Connor, *Structure*, 114.377-78.388-89.

## 11.13 *Hendiadys*

*Definitions*
Hendiadys is the expression of one single but complex concept by using two separate words, usually nouns. Wright[155] defines it as 'the

155. Wright: 1981.

use of two substantives, joined by a conjunction, to express a single but complex idea'. The two words may be collocated, be joined by a copula or be in apposition. Hendiadys is used very often in Hebrew — (Weiss claims that 'it has been established that hendiadys is in more frequent use in biblical Hebrew than in any other language'[156]) and the reader should always be on the look-out for its occurrences in a text. The important aspect of hendiadys is that its components are no longer considered separately but as a single unit in combination. So, בזנותיך וברעתך (Jer 3,2) does not mean 'your harlotry *and* your evil' as if the wife, symbolising Judah, had committed crimes on top of being unfaithful. Instead, the expression means 'your vile harlotry', her continuing infidelity condemned as evil.

*Ugaritic and Akkadian*
Examples include the following: from Ugaritic verse:

| | |
|---|---|
| b ̔l ytlk wyṣd | Baal went a-hunting (*CTA* 12 i 34). |
| tbkynh wtqbrnh | Weeping she buried him (*CTA* 6 i 16-17, lit. she wept for him and buried him — but the two actions are simultaneous). |

And from Akkadian:

| | |
|---|---|
| epir u kubbit | Provide honourably for (*BWL* 102:62, lit. provide for and honour).[157] |

*Recognition of hendiadys*
The presence of the poetic device in question can be determined from the following indications.[158]

(a) *Parallelism with a simple semantic unit*. In Hab 2,6

Shall not all these utter *a taunt* against him in *scoffing derision* of him?

the expression מליצה חידות, lit. 'scorn, riddles', is matched by the single term משל, 'taunt'. We can therefore understand the two terms in the second line as hendiadys (as the translation shows). Similar are Ex 15,2 and Ps 55,6.

---

156. Weiss: 1967.
157. See Lambert's comments, *BWL*, 314. Also, in *Atr*, 156.
158. See also T.O. Lambdin, *Introduction to Biblical Hebrew* (London, 1973) 238-40.

(b) *Non-repetition of (common) regent.* As in Ps 42,5

בקול־רנה ותודה    With a shout of joyful thanks,

literally, 'with a voice of joy and of thanks', the missing repetition of בקול showing the phrase to be a single unit. Also, Ps 43,1b and Jer 30,13.

(c) *Common grammatical element in the singular.* The singular verb in Ps 55,6a indicates that the first two words are in hendiadys:

יראה ורעד יבא בי    Trembling fear came upon me,

confirmation for which comes from the parallel term, 'horror', which is also in the singular (cf. *a*, above). See, too, Ex 15,16.[159]

(d) *Lack of expected copula.* As in Ps 50,20, lit. 'you sit, against your brother you gossip':

תשב באחיך תדבר    You sit gossipping against your brother.

Cf. Ex 15,14a.

(e) *Successive parallelism of components.* By far the commonest type of hendiadys comes in the form of two verbs or two nouns in immediate succession. If verbs, as in Ps 42,3, the actions described may be simultaneous or successive:

מתי אבוא ואראה    When shall I come and see?.

Also Ps 42,5 ('remembering I pour out'), etc. If nouns, then the two substantives are considered as one (see on Isa 51,19 and Job 13,20-22, below).

Other indicators of hendiadys include the use of יחד, 'together' (as in Ps 40,15), and word-pairs (see below).

Perhaps the clearest indication that two words can combine to form a single unit, namely hendiadys, comes from Isa 51,19.[160] There, the prophet refers to *two* events, but in fact mentions *four*—or, rather, two sets of words in tandem:

| | |
|---|---|
| שתים הנה קראתיך | These *two* disasters have overtaken you |
| מי ינוד לך | —Who can console you? |
| השד והשבר | Destructive desolation,— |
| והרעב והחרב | stabbing starvation |
| מי ינחמך | —Who can comfort you?—[161] |

Rather less clear is Job 13,20-22.

159. Unless the verb is repointed as factitive.
160. Adduced by D. Spiegel apud Kaddari: 1973, 169, n. 14.
161. Note, incidentally, the chiastic pattern here.

*The development of hendiadys*

Some examples of hendiadys comprise two words in the bound state; others, two words in appositional hendiadys. It would seem that certain cases of appositional hendiadys are closely related to word-pairs (see WORD-PAIRS, BREAK-UP), though which way the development proceeded is far from certain. Avishur comments: 'Pairs of synonymous words appear together in appositional hendiadys. In this form the word and its apposition appear together without any connective waw and both words behave as a semantic unity'.[162]

For example the word-pair צדק // תמם, 'just // blameless' (Job 9,20) appears in the form

צדיק תמים    blamelessly just

in Job 12,4.

Other examples can be quoted:

'dream // vision' (Isa 29,7) becomes 'in a dream, in a vision of the night' (Job 33,15);
'mourns // languishes' (Hos 4,3) becomes 'the land languishingly mourns' (Isa 33,9);
'to instruct // to strengthen' (Job 4,3) becomes 'I strengthened their arms by training' (Hos 7,15).[163]

Wright[164] argues that true hendiadys is not formulaic and predictable (of the type 'nice and warm' and so on). Instead, it should contain an 'element of surprise, of improvisation, and of eccentric coordination'. Perhaps an example in Hebrew is Ps 42,11:

ברצח בעצמותי    With a death-wound in my bones.

*Functions of hendiadys*

The two main functions of hendiadys can be paraphrased as 'extending the existing vocabulary'; they are when hendiadys is used in place of an adverb, and as hyperbole (see HYPERBOLE). Other functions are more general.

(a) *As surrogate for adverb*

וינסו וימרו את אלהים    But they defiantly tempted God,

162. Avishur: 1971-72, 66.
163. See further, Avishur: 1971-1972, 66-74; Held, *BASOR* 200 (1970) 37-38.
164. Wright: 1981, 171. Westhuizen: 1978, 57, suggests that hendiadys developed into parallelism.

Ps 78,56; lit. 'they tempted and defied'. Also Pss 69,18; 106,13; 112,9; 129,5.

(b) *As hyperbole*

ספו תמו מן בלהות          Utterly swept away

Ps 73,19; cf. Pss 71,13; 83,18; Hab 3,11. There is some overlap with function (a).

(c) *Other functions*. To evoke a word-pair: Pss 32,5; 132,9; for assonance: Isa 29,9; Song 2,3; to produce rhyme: Lam 3,56; to preserve rhythm: Ps 106,13; for parallelism: Ps 85,9b.

*For Study*

Isa 2,10 and 2,19; 28,23 (contrast Hos 5,1); Pss 60,8; 62,3. Note that Pss 42-43 uses at least eight instances of hendiadys (42,3.5.8.11; 43,1b.3.4); what are the indications for the presence of hendiadys and what functions do they have; why is Ps 42,3 problematic? Note that Ps 71 has at least three examples: vv. 13.18 and 21. See, too, Pss 8,3a; Isa 38,12.16 and Ez 15,16a.

*Cross-references*

BREAK-UP, HYPERBOLE, MERISMUS, PARALLELISM, WORD-PAIRS.

BIBLIOGRAPHY

(a) *General*

Hahn, E.A. 'Hendiadys: is there such a thing?', *CW* 15 (1921-22).
Wright, G.T. 'Hendiadys and *Hamlet*', *PMLA* 96 (1981) 168-93.

(b) *Semitic*

Avishur, Y. 'Pairs of Synonymous Words in the Construct State (and in Appositional Hendiadys) in Biblical Hebrew', *Semitics* 2 (1971-72) 17-81, esp. 66-74.
Brongers, H.A. 'Merismus, Synekdoche und Hendiadys in der bibel-hebräischen Sprache', *OTS* 14 (1965) 100-14.
Westhuizen, J.P. van der, 'Hendiadys in Biblical Hymns of Praise', *Semitics* 6 (1978) 50-57.
Also Dahood, *Psalms I-III*; Weiss, *JBL* 86 (1967) 416-23.

## 11.14 *The 'Break-up' of a Composite Phrase*

*Definitions*

By the term 'break-up' is meant the re-distribution of components of a phrase over two parallel lines. For example, the phrase 'innocent blood', which occurs at least 18 times in Hebrew[165] becomes:

נארבה לדם      Let us lie in wait for BLOOD,
נצפנה לנקי חנם    let us ambush the INNOCENT for no reason,

in Prov 1,11.[166] The device is used in Ugaritic poetry, too. The expression *'bd 'lm*, 'permanent slave', of *CTA* 14 iii 127, becomes

*'bdk an*      Your SLAVE am I,
*wd'lmk*      yours permanently,

in *CTA* 5 ii 19-20.[167] It may also occur in Akkadian verse.[168] Whitley is correct in reducing the number of alleged occurrences in Hebrew and in rejecting the expression 'stereotype phrase', since quite often such phrases are only attested once.[169] All the same, break-up is common enough and, as will be seen, it does have recognisable rhetorical functions.

*Relationship to hendiadys, etc.*
There is evidently an interrelationship between parallel word-pairs, hendiadys, merismus and even with the development of the construct state.[170] Unfortunately, the exact lines of development are difficult to trace. Presumably, set phrases became word-pairs by the device under study, though this is by no means the origin of all word-pairs. Since the development of technique in Hebrew poetry is not considered here,[171] little more need be said. Possibly, break-up is a transitional device between the formula and the word-pair.

*Functions*
By breaking up the components of set phrases poets created parallel word-pairs. This must have been a stand-by technique in improvising

165. Dt 21,8; Isa 59,7; Ps 106,38, etc.
166. Cited by Melamed: 1961, 148, who also notes the related phrase 'blood shed for no reason' in 1 Sm 25,31 and 1 Kgs 2,31.
167. Adduced by Dahood: 1969, 36; see there for additional examples and cf. Viganò: 1976.
168. For instance the phrase *arkûti u panûti*, 'lower and higher in rank', of line 77 in the 'Dialogue of Pessimism' seems to reappear in broken form as the final, climactic couplet (lines 85-86; text *BWL*, 148). Further examples may be *Ee* III 67, break-up of *alāku urḫu*, 'to travel', and likewise for *dullam zabālu*, 'to suffer work', in *Atr* I i 2.
169. Whitley, *UF* 7 (1975) 493-99.
170. See Avishur: 1971-72.
171. For an attempt in this direction see my 'Trends in the Development of Classical Hebrew Poetry: A Comparative Study', *UF* 14 (1982) 265-77.

verse. A secondary effect was that the produce tended to evoke the original phrase and its associations. A series of additional functions of this device can also be mentioned here, with some illustration. One rhetorical function was the *avoidance of repetition* as in Nb 24,4 (also 16) where אל שדי is broken up:

| | |
|---|---|
| נאם שמע אמרי אל | The oracle of one hearing EL's words, |
| אשר מחזה שדי יחזה | of one seeing SHADDAI's vision. |

The use of 'Shaddai' in the second colon obviates repeating 'El'. Taboo expressions can be avoided, too, as in Job 18,3 (see under WORKED EXAMPLES). More important from the aspect of technique is break-up functioning as *merismus*. The compound 'a flaming fire' of Isa 4,5; Hos 7,6 and Lam 2,3 is re-used in Joel 2,3:

| | |
|---|---|
| לפניו אכלה אש | FIRE devours before him, |
| ואחריו תלהט להבה | and behind him a FLAME burns. |

The effect is merismus.[172] Similarly, 'heaven and earth' in Isa 49,13; Ps 89,11 etc.[173] *Alliteration and assonance* are created in Ps 107,11 when the name 'El Elyon' is split up:

| | |
|---|---|
| כי המרו אמרי אל | For they had rebelled against EL's words, |
| ועצת עליון נאצו | and spurned ELYON's counsel.[174] |

### Reversal

It is evident from the examples set out above that very often, when the components of a phrase are split up over parallel lines, their sequence is inverted as well. There seems to be no overall reason for this practice which in any case is inconsistent. It seems to be related to the A-B sequence in word-pairs as well as to sets where a constant first (A) element is paired with differing B elements. See 12.3 on INVERSION. So, part of the patriarchal death-formula, 'Abraham breathed his last and died (ויגוע וימת) at a happy, ripe age, old and full of years and was gathered to his kin',[175] is split up and inverted in Job 3,11:

| | |
|---|---|
| למה לא מרחם אמות | Why did I not DIE from the womb, |
| מבטן יצאתי ואגוע | come from the uterus and BREATHE MY LAST? |

172. Melamed: 1961, 137-39.
173. Melamed: 1961, 140-42.
174. Melamed: 1961, 118.
175. Gen 25,8 as translated by Speiser, *Genesis*, 186; also Gen 28,17; 35,29 and 49,33.

This matches the overall mood of Job 3, where normal values are
stood on their head: death is preferred to life.

*Recognition of break-up*
Curiously, although the technique of splitting up formulae is not so
well attested in Ugaritic (apart from composite divine names), quite
often a phrase known from Ugaritic provides the material (as it were)
for break-up in Hebrew. This is, therefore, one area where familiarity
with the Ugaritic texts can contribute to a better understanding of
Hebrew poetic technique. Examples have been collected by Dahood
and others; to them can be added the following. The technical term
*nǵr krm*, 'vineyard keeper',[176] underlies the couplet in Isa 27,2-3

| | |
|---|---|
| כרם חמר ענו לה | Pleasant VINEYARD, sing to it; |
| אני יהוה נצרה | I, Yahweh, am its KEEPER. |

Again, *šbt dqn*, 'greyness of beard',[177] is broken up in Isa 46,4:

| | |
|---|---|
| ועד זקנה אני הוא | Until OLD AGE I am the one, |
| ועד שיבה אני אסבל | until GREYNESS will I be support. |

Further, Isa 41,18 breaks up *mdbr špm*, 'desert of dunes' (*CTA* 23:4)
and Isa 47,7 echoes part of the stock Ugaritic blessing formula: 'May
the gods protect you ... forever and always (*'d 'lm*)'.[178] Finally,
Prov 11,1

| | |
|---|---|
| מאזני מרמה תועבת יהוה | False SCALES are taboo to Yahweh, |
| ואבן שלמה רצונו | but a full WEIGHT is his pleasure, |

has split up the Ugaritic phrase *abn mznm*, 'weights of the scales'
(*CTA* 24:36-37) and the reversal emphasises the contrast between
the two lines.

*For study*
Obd 16-17; Prov 30,4 and 9; Mic 3,12 and 4,2; Lam 4,12 and 15; Jer
30,12 and Mic 1,9; Prov 6,21 and Job 38,31; Ps 92,4 (contrast
Pss 33,2; 144,9).

---

176. *PRU* V, 106:17-18.
177. *CTA* 4 v 66; 3E v 9-10.32-33.
178. See D.N. Freedman, '"A Mistress Forever". A Note on Isaiah 47,7', *Bib* 51
(1970) 538, who did not notice the Ugaritic parallel. On Isa 30,8 and Ug. *lḥt spr*, 'letter
tablets', see Watson, *Bib* 56 (1975) 275-76.

*Cross-references*
CHIASMUS, HENDIADYS, INVERSION, MERISMUS, WORD-PAIRS.

BIBLIOGRAPHY

Avishur, Y. 'Pairs of Synonymous Words in the Construct State (and in Appositional Hendiadys) in Biblical Hebrew', *Semitics* 2 (1971-72) 17-81.

Braulik, G.
'Aufbrechen von geprägten Wortverbindungen und Zusammenfassen von stereotypen Ausdrücken in der alttestamentlichen Kunstprosa', *Semitics* 1 (1970) 7-11.

Dahood, M.J. 'The Breakup of Stereotyped Phrases: Some New Examples', *JANES* 5 (1973) 83-89.

—'The Breakup of Two Composite Phrases in Isaiah 40,13', *Bib* 54 (1973) 537-38.

—'The Chiastic Breakup in Isaiah 58,7', *Bib* 57 (1976) 105.

—'Further Instances of the Breakup of Stereotyped Phrases in Hebrew', *Bagatti FS*, 9-19.

Irwin, W.H. 'The Smooth Stones of the Wady', *CBQ* 29 (1967) 31-40, esp. 33-34.

Kselman, J.S. 'A Note on Ps 51:6', *CBQ* 39 (1977) 251-53.

Melamed, E.Z. 'Break-Up of Stereotype Phrases as an Artistic Device in Biblical Poetry', *ScrH* 8 (1961) 115-53.

Talmon, S. 'Synonymous Readings in the Textual Tradition of the OT', *ScrH* 8 (1961) 335ff.

Viganò, L. 'Il fenomeno stilistico di Break-up di nomi divini nei testi di Ras Shamra-Ugarit', *RBI* 24 (1976) 225-42.

Also Haran, *VTS* 22 (1971) 238-67; O'Connor, *Structure*, 108-09.112ff; Whitley, *UF* 7 (1975) 493-99.

## 11.15 Enjambment

*End-stopping*

Before considering enjambment[179] the concept of end-stopping needs to be understood, and it will be discussed first.

Every poem consists of a set of sentences, divided up into strophes. And each strophe comprises a number of cola. Usually, the divisions into strophe and colon coincide with grammatical divisions in the sentence, so that, for example, a colon will end with a comma or a full-stop. This is referred to as *end-stopping*. Since end-stopping is the norm, almost any paragraph of Hebrew poetry will serve as illustration, e.g.

---

179. For this spelling cf. Peabody: 1975, 282 n. 15, following Kirk.

תעבוני רחקו מני     They detest me and stand aloof;
ומפני לא־חשכו רק     from my face they spare no spit. (Job 30,10[180])

In fact, end-stopping is almost inevitable in a poetic tradition (such as
Hebrew) which uses sequences of parallel lines.[181] One effect of end-
stopping is to restrict the natural patterns of speech: every line has to
be a unit and end at a grammatical juncture, the result therefore
tending to be a little artificial.

## Enjambment

Enjambment means 'straddling (e.g. of a horse)', and is present when
a sentence or clause does not end when the colon ends but runs over
into the next colon. Hence the alternative name 'run-over line' or
even 'overrunning'. So, for instance in Lam 1,7:

ראוה צרים שחקו     Saw her, did the enemies; mocked
על משבתה     at her sorry state,

the grammatical division comes at 'the enemies', which ends the first
clause ('saw her did the enemies'). However, the metre (3 + 2) shows
the poetic line to end at 'they mocked', although the clause continues
into the next colon. The two lines of poetry are straddled by a single
grammatical line. Enjambment, therefore, is the exact opposite to
end-stopping.

## Effects of enjambment

With respect to metre enjambment is a deviation from the metrical
norm. It is 'the placing of a line boundary where a deliberate pause,
according to grammatical and phonological considerations, would be
abnormal'.[182] By going counter to the metrical flow of the poem,
enjambment provides an element of variety. The chief effect of
enjambment, though—related to the effect just mentioned—is to
bring verse closer to everyday speech. 'The poet's control lies chiefly
in his skill in so adjusting the natural speech movement that it does
not cloud but enhances or enriches the verse movement.'[183]

Finally, though Hebrew poetry is in the main composed of lines in
parallel this is by no means the absolute rule. Enjambment explains

180. Translation of Pope, *Job*, 191.
181. Gray, *Forms*, 127: 'Parallelism is, broadly speaking, incompatible with anything
but "stopped-line" poetry.'
182. Leech, *Guide*, 125.
183. Chatman: 1960, 168.

how some bicola are neither in synonymous nor antithetic parallelism
but 'structurally' parallel: a single sentence has been divided into two
simply to agree with the prevailing metrical pattern.

### Types of enjambment

Enjambment is a matter of degree, dependent on how closely the end
of one line is linked to the next. The array of types discussed here,
accordingly, is meant to illustrate this fact and is by no means
intended as a set of hard and fast definitions. The types range from
the strongest type of over-run line to the closest approximation to
end-stopping.

1. *Violent* enjambment occurs where a verse-end interrupts a
sequence drastically, for example, in mid-word. This extreme is
unknown in Hebrew.

2. In *integral* enjambment the two halves of a bicolon (for instance)
form a single sentence:

כאשר ראיתי חרשי און    As I have seen, those who plough iniquity
וזרעי עמל יקצרהו    and sow trouble, reap the same. (Job 4,8)

3. Where only weak puncuation is the separative factor, the
enjambment is termed *periodic* (cf. 'period' in the sense of full-stop),
e.g.

ראה אויבי כי רבו    See how numerous are my foes,
ושנאת חמס שנאוני    my treacherous enemies who hate me. (Ps 25,19)

4. Lastly, the weakest type is *progressive*, where the sentence could
have ended with the line, but instead has carried on into the next
line by the addition of further material. This is typical of oral
adding style and is very common in the parallel couplets of Hebrew
poetry:

הלאל תדברו עולה    Will you speak falsely for God/
ולו תדברו רמיה    And speak deceitfully for him?/. (Job 13,7)

Here, the first line could have ended at 'God' to form a complete
sentence; the second line, which continues the sentence to form a
bicolon, is an optional addition.[184]

### Enjambment in Semitic poetry

Some examples for Hebrew have already been given as illustration of

184. See Kirk: 1966 for the above terminology and for the distinctions made here.

various points (see below, too, under *functions* and *for study*). Gordis ventured the suggestion that enjambment, which occurs often enough in Lamentations, is perhaps characteristic of qinah metre.[185] Since the poetry of both Ugaritic and Akkadian is largely end-stopped, only relatively few examples of enjambment occur. An example in Ugaritic is

| | |
|---|---|
| *apnk 'ṭtr 'rẓ* | Then Athtar, the High-brow, |
| *y'l bṣrrt ṣpn* | ascended the heights of Zaphon. |
| | (*CTA* 6 i 56-57) |

Others are also to be found;[186] examples for Akkadian verse have been collected by Hecker.[187]

*Functions*
Enjambment serves to break the monotony of end-stopped lines, to assist the forward movement of a poem by creating tension between metre and grammar, and thirdly, to bring verse closer to normal speech rhythms. See above on the effects of enjambment.

*For study*
Pss 32,5; 59,8; 69,13; 32,2a; 5,8; 34,8; 35,27ab; 40,5a; 55,18b-19a; 69,2; 101,7b; 119,6.57.88.117.20.18.144; 129,4; 107,2; 111,4.6a; Ez 26,3; Job 9,4; 31,13; Jer 23,25. Note especially Ps 116 (five examples) and 132.

*Cross-references*
METRE, ORAL POETRY, PIVOT PATTERN, STICHOMETRY.

*BIBLIOGRAPHY*

(a) *General*
Chatman, S. 'Comparing Metrical Styles', Sebeok, *Style*, 165-69.
Heller, J.R. 'Enjambment as a metrical form in romantic conversation poems', *Poetics* 6 (1977) 15-26.
Kirk, G.S. 'Formular Language and Oral Quality', *YCS* 20 (1966) 153-74.

185. R. Gordis, *The Song of Songs and Lamentations. A Study, Modern Translation and Commentary* (New York, 1954. 1968. 1974) 120-21.
186. See Ginsberg, *Or* 8 (1936) 71.
187. Hecker, *Epik*, 79-80.121. Additional examples may be *Atr* I iv 225-226, 'With his flesh and his blood / Nintu covered the clay' (as translated by von Soden, *ZA* 68 [1978] 67); *Ee* I 4; Ludlul III 25-26 (text: *BWL*, 48) and *BWL* 74:63-64 (Theodicy).

Lord, A.B. 'Homer and Huso III: Enjambment in Greek and Southslavic Heroic Song', *TAPA* 79 (1948) 113-24.

Parry, M. *The Making of Homeric Verse: The Collected Papers of Milman Parry*. Edited by A. Parry (Oxford, 1971) 251-65 (= reprint of 1929 paper 'The Distinctive Character of Enjambement in Homeric Verse').

Peabody, B. *The winged word: a study in the technique of ancient Greek oral composition as seen principally through Hesiod's Works and Days* (Albany, 1975) 125-43.

(b) *Semitic*

No work has appeared on this topic. See Dahood, *Psalms* I, II and III.

## 11.16 *Delayed Identification*

*The Device*

Delayed identification (or delayed explicitation) is simply leaving the name of a subject to some time after his or her actions are described. In other words, instead of stating the subject of a verb as soon as grammatically possible, the verb (or verbs) is (are) set out first, no definite identity being provided till the second or even third line of verse. If we look at three different texts (from the three verse traditions represented in this book) a clearer picture will emerge.

(a) *īterbū ana bīt šīmti*     They entered the house of destiny
    *niššiku Ea erištu Mama*     (did) prince EA and the wise MAMI.
                                                                    (*Atr* I v 249-50)

(b) *tn ilm dtqh*     Give up, O gods, your protégé,
    *dtqyn hmlt*     your protégé, O crowd,
    *tn b'l [w'nnh]*     give up BAAL [and his attendants],
    *bn dgn artm pdh*     Dagan's son, so I may possess his
                                                gold. (*CTA* 2 i 18-19[188])

(c) צעקו ויהוה שמע     When they cry, Yahweh hears them,
    ומכל צרותם הצילם     and from all their anguish rescues them.
    קרוב יהוה לנשברי לב     Close is Yahweh to THE BROKEN-
                                                HEARTED,
    ואת דכאי רוח יושיע     and those crushed in spirit he saves.
                                                                    (Ps 34,18-19)

---

188. For translation cf. *CML*, 41, where 'your protégé' is given more literally as 'him whom you protect'.

In these examples it is not at once obvious who the person (or persons) in question is (are); their identity is delayed. In (a) the subject of 'they entered' comes in the second colon: the two deities Ea and Mami. In the quatrain (b) the gods are being asked to give up the person they are holding; that this person (or rather, god) is Baal himself is not specified till the third colon. Finally, the identity of 'them' in (c) is left vague till line 3.[189]

### Functions
The main function of delayed identification, evidently, is *to achieve suspense*. The listener (or reader) is left waiting to find out who the subject (or, at times, object) of the verb is. A secondary function is, perhaps, the avoidance of repetition. The device is akin to staircase parallelism, where the first colon is left incomplete until the second colon [see example (b) above]. It has been argued that it is psycho-linguistically absurd to imagine that a listener could withhold analysis of a sentence until it was complete[190] but the device just described suggests the contrary. It is also interesting that when the subject is eventually named identity is often made doubly clear by a parallel couplet, as in Jer 5,30-31:[191]

| | |
|---|---|
| שמה ושערורה נהיתה בארץ | An appalling and shocking thing has occurred in the land: |
| הנביאים נבאו בשקר | The prophets prophesy falsely, |
| והכהנים ירדו על ידיהם | and the priests lord it beside them. |

### For study
Since very little research has been carried out on this topic the list of texts will be longer than usual.
Isa 13,5; 23,11; 28,26; 30,6-7; 33,8.17.22.[192] Jer 2,26.28; 5,30-31; cf. 9,22-25. Mic 6,5.8; Pss 9,13; 18,19; 105,3.5-6.17.19; 110,2; 112,6; 121,4; 129,5; 135,6. Prov 22,12; Job 27,3; 29,18; 31,6; Ez 14,6.

### Cross-references
REPETITION, STAIRCASE PARALLELISM.

189. Other examples in Akk.: *Atr* I iv 192-93; ii 57-58; vi 15-18; *Erra* I 1-5. Boadt: 1980 cites *Ee* IV 3-6; *Atr* I i 93-96, as well as examples from Egyptian, Sumerian and Ugaritic poetry.
190. Greenstein, *JANES* 6 (1974) 87-105. See Kugel, *Idea*, 55, n. 133.
191. Following the translation by Bright, *Jeremiah*, 39.
192. For all except the first text cf. Irwin, *Isaiah 28-33*, 172.

BIBLIOGRAPHY

Airoldi, N. 'Esodo 22,28a: Esplicitazione ritardata', *Bib* 54 (1973) 63-64.
Boadt, L. *Ezekiel's Oracles against Egypt. A Literary and Philological Study of Ezekiel 29-32* (Rome, 1980), 60-61.

## 11.17 *Rhetorical Questions*

*Definition*

A rhetorical question is basically the posing of a question which requires no answer since either the speaker or the listener (or even both of them) already knows the answer. In practice, a reply is often given in poetic texts. The prophecy of Joel begins (Joel 1,2):

| | |
|---|---|
| שמעו זאת הזקנים | Listen, you elders, |
| והאזינו כל יושבי הארץ | hear me all you living in the land: |
| ההיתה זאת בימיכב | Has the like of this happened in your days? |
| ואם בימי אבתיכם | Or in your fathers' days? |

The answer is self-evidently 'No', so that here the rhetorical question is tantamount to emphatic denial. This is often the case, but by no means always. The device is common to literature in most languages.

*Rhetorical questions in Ugaritic and Akkadian*

While some attention has been paid to this type of question as a poetic device in Ugaritic literature,[193] none has been devoted to Akkadian material which also has its fair share. Occupying his newly-built palace, Baal 'asks':

| | |
|---|---|
| *u mlk u blmlk* | Should either king or non-king |
| *arṣ drkt yštkn* | establish a territory of dominion for himself? (*CTA* 4 vii 43-44) |

Similarly, Athtar makes a comparable claim:

| | |
|---|---|
| *mlkt an hm lmlkt an* | Am I king or am I not king? (*CTA* 2 iii 22) |

though in fact the answer comes that he is not since he has no wife (lines 22-23).

From the Babylonian Atrahasis Epic comes:

| | |
|---|---|
| *mannu annītam ša lā Enki ippuš* | Who but Enki could do this? (*Atr* III vi 13-14) |

193. Held: 1969.

namely, allowing the hero to escape the Flood. Appalled at the cosmic disaster, the goddess Mami moans:

| | |
|---|---|
| *ētellima ana šamê* | Shall I go up to heaven |
| *tuša wašbāku ina bīt nakkamti* | as if I were to live in a treasure-house? (*Atr* III iii 48-49[194]) |

*Rhetorical questions as couplets*

Since Hebrew poetry is largely composed of parallel couplets, it is not surprising that rhetorical questions tend to come in pairs:

| | |
|---|---|
| היש בלשוני עולה | Is there iniquity on my tongue? |
| אם חכי לא יבין הוות | Can my palate not discriminate words? (Job 6,30) |

Also: Isa 10,9.15; 27,7; 49,24; 66,9; Jer 5,9.22.29 (= 9.8); 3,5; Joel 1,2; 4,4; Am 6,2; Pss 78,20; 94,9; Prov 6,27-28; Job 8,3; 10,4; 11,2.7; 13,8.9; 22,3; 34,17; 38,33; 40,27; also 4,17; 6,12.

*Rhetorical questions in series*

There is a tendency for such questions to occur in clusters or series, from three (tricola) to as many as 16 in a row. Some sets are unrepresented. Many are sets of couplets.

*three*
Jer 2,14.31; 8,19.22; 14,19 (cf. 8,4-5; 49,1).

*four*
Mic 2,7; Job 6,5-6; 10,4-5; 11,2-3.7-8; 13,24-25; 17,15-16; 18,2-4; 35,6-7; 37,15-18; 39,1-2.19-20; 40,8-9; 4,6-8.

*six*
Ez 15,2-5; Ps 88,10-12; Job 13,7-9; 26,2-4; 6,11-13.

*seven*
Am 3,3-6; Mic 6,6-7; Ps 77,7-10.

*eight*
Isa 66,7-9; Job 39,9-12; 22,2-5.

*nine*
Job 41,1-6.

*eleven*
Job 7,17-21.

*sixteen*
Job 40,24-31.

*Extended rhetorical questions*

Like the simile, rhetorical questions can be expanded beyond the single line or couplet. For example: Job 10,10-11:

---

194. Other texts are cited in *CAD* M/1, 215.

| הלא כחלב תתיכני | Did you not pour me out as milk, |
| וכגבנה תקפיאני | curdle me as cheese, |
| עור ובשר תלבישני | clothe me with skin and flesh, |
| ובעצמות וגידים תסככני | knit me with bones and sinews? |

Also, 4,19-20; 20,4-5a; Am 8,8; Mic 3,1; 6,10-11. The same form of lengthy question is found in the Ugaritic texts.[195]

### Origin of the device

The indications are that the use of rhetorical questions (notably by wise men and the preaching prophets) has its origins in oral techniques of composing poetry. Only in late texts such as Isa 66,7-8 does the form become more literary and is reduced to a component of written style. Wisdom tradition certainly plays a strong role in the development of rhetorical questions, witness the intensive use in Job. Clues to origins of the form are provided by texts such as Isa 49,24:

| היקח מגבור מלקוח | Is a prisoner taken from the warrior |
| ואם שבי צדיק ימלט | or a captive from a victor rescued? |
| כי כה אמר יהוה | For so declares Yahweh: |
| גם שבי גבור יקח | Even a captive is taken from a warrior, |
| ומלקוח עריץ ימלט | a prisoner rescued from a tyrant.[196] |

### Rhetorical questions and style

Most books of the OT include rhetorical questions, but two works in particular show peculiarities of style in this regard. One is the book of Job, the other is the prophecy of Jeremiah.

*Job.* The most striking aspect about 'Job' with regard to rhetorical questions is their *frequency*. Chapter after chapter uses this device to a degree unparalleled by other books. It is highly likely that this is a component of *wisdom* tradition.[197]

Job is also notable for the sets of rhetorical questions *in series*—as is evident from the table set out above. Outstanding, though, is Job 38 which is almost entirely made up of this device.

*Jeremiah.* Almost exclusive to Jeremiah is the *triple* rhetorical question of the following type:

---

195. *CTA* 14 i 52-56; regrettably, the translation is uncertain.

196. Also Isa 50,2; Ez 15,2-5; Isa 66,7-9; etc. The answering element is a feature of Akkadian material: Gilg VI 180-85; X iii 1; *Ee* I 45 and 49-50; Gilg VI 32-33, etc.

197. Since most of the book of Job is cast in the form of speeches the high density of rhetorical questions offsets its literary style and provides an oral component.

הצרי אין בגלעד     Is there no balm in Gilead?
אם־רפא אין שם     Or no physician there?
(כי) מדוע לא עלתה     Why then is there no healing for my people?
ארכת בת־עמי

Jer 8,22 (similarly: 2,14.31; 8,19; 14,19.22).[198] The pattern comprises two consecutive lines beginning with ה and אם respectively, followed by a third (and final) line which opens with the word מדוע. The only other clear occurrence of this pattern is Mal 2,10 which is evidently later than Jeremiah,[199] so that it seems as if the format was developed by him as part of his oral delivery.

*Functions*
In general, the rhetorical question is used *for dramatic effect*: it involves the audience directly, if they are addressed, or it creates tension which then requires resolution. The following specific functions can also be distinguished:

    1. *To command the audience's attention*:

האמור בית יעקב     Can one ask, O House of Jacob:
הקצר רוח יהוה     Is the Lord's patience truly at an end?
אם אלה מעלליו     Are these his deeds?
הלוא דברי ייטיבו     Does not good come of the Lord's words?
                                        (Mic 2,7)

See also Joel 2,1.

    2. *As emphatic negation (or assertion)*:

היש בהבלי הגוים מגשמים     Can any of the false gods of the nations give rain?
ואם השמים יתנו רבבים     Or do the heavens send showers of themselves?
                                        (Jer 14,22)

Also Isa 50,1 (cited below); 50,2.

    3. *To open a stanza* (see function 1):

אי זה ספר כריתות     Is there anywhere a deed of divorce by which I
אמכם אשר שלחתיה     have put your mother away? (Isa 50,1)

And Job 11,2-3; 39 (each new animal introduced by a rhetorical question).

---

198. See also Jer 8,4-5 and 49,1; for details: Brueggemann: 1973.
199. Note, too, Jgs 11,25-26 and Job 21,4 though these do not follow Jeremiah's 'model' at all strictly.

4. *To close a stanza*:

| | |
|---|---|
| בעיניו יקחנו | Who is he that with his eyes can take him? |
| במוקשים ינקב אף | Can you pierce his nose with barbs? (Job 40,24) |

5. *As motivation*. A rhetorical question sometimes provides the form in which motivation is cast after an exhortation to good conduct, as in

| | |
|---|---|
| אשר ראו עיניך | What your eyes have seen, |
| אל תצא לרב מהר | do not hastily bring into court. |
| פן מה תעשה באחריתה | What will you do in the end |
| בהכלים אתך רעך | when your neighbour puts you to shame? |
| | (Prov 25,7b-8) |

Other examples: Prov 5,17-23; 22,26-27; Job 8,8-10; 12,7-9; Qoh 7,16-17; Sir 10,28-29. The same practice is attested in Akkadian texts found at Ras Shamra.[200]

6. *For irony*. Ironic intent is evident in Ps 114,5-6

| | |
|---|---|
| מה לך הים כי תנום | What is the matter, sea, that you should run away |
| הירדן תסב לאחור | or that you should turn backwards, Jordan, |
| ההרים תרקדו כאילים | or that you should skip like rams, Mountains, |
| גבעות כבני צאן | like lambkins, you Hills?[201] |

*For study*

Isa 40,28; Jer 14,22; Ps 94,9; Job 37,20; Ps 88,11; Mic 4,6-8; Qoh 5,5.

*Cross-references*

CHIASMUS, IRONY, SECONDARY TECHNIQUES: EXTENSION, STANZA.

BIBLIOGRAPHY

Brueggemann, W. 'Jeremiah's Use of Rhetorical Questions', *JBL* 92 (1973) 358-74.
Gordis, R. 'A Rhetorical Use of Interrogative Questions in Biblical Hebrew', *AJSL* 49 (1932-33) 212-17.
Held, M. 'Rhetorical Questions in Ugaritic and Biblical Hebrew', *ErIs* 9 (1969) 71-79.
Long, B.O. 'The Stylistic Components of Jeremiah 3 1-5', *ZAW* 88 (1976) 386-90.
Also Hobbs, *ZAW* 86 (1974) 23-29; O'Connor, *Structure*, 12.

---

200. Recognised by Smith in *RSP* II, 224-27 and 227 n. 2 (all texts cited by him).
201. Cf. *CTA* 4 vii 38-39 and Gibson, *CML*, 65 n. 9.

## 11.18 *Ballast Variant*

*The isocolic principle* (notes on theory)

The feature of parallelism now known as 'ballast variant'[202] is a corollary of the theory of balance[203] as expressed in the isocolic principle. In essence it is as follows: the two cola of a couplet in parallelism must balance. If some component of the first colon is missing from the second, then at least one of the components in this second colon must be longer.[204] For example:

| | |
|---|---|
| באר חפרוה שרים | The well which the princes dug, |
| כרוה נדיבי העם | the nobles of the people delved. (Nb 21,18.) |

Here lengthier $n^e d\hat{\imath} b\hat{e}\ h\bar{a}'\bar{a}m$ (// $\acute{s}\bar{a}r\hat{\imath}m$) makes up for the lack of $b^e'\bar{e}r$ in the second colon. Schematically it can be represented as follows:

| *standard (balanced) couplet* | *couplet with ball. var.* |
|---|---|
| a b c | a b c |
| a'b'c' | ø b'c'+d |
| | (where c'+d // c) |

Subordinate to the isocolic principle is the 'law of increasing members', according to which elements of the second colon (or the second colon itself) are generally longer than those of the first. Of course, the second colon is quite often longer than the first (e.g. Ps 38,22), but generally speaking the isocolic principle is primary. This is shown by cases where the isocolic principle is operative even where components of the *first* colon happen to be longer (which flouts the law of increasing members).

For instance:

| | |
|---|---|
| על ראשי ההרים יזבחו | Upon the mountain-peaks they sacrifice |
| ועל הגבעות יקטרי | and upon the hills burn incense. (Hos 4,13) |

The isocolic principle is also shown to be more powerful than the law of increasing members by many examples of 'double ballast variant'. In such examples there is compensation (so to speak) in *both* halves of the couplet, e.g.

202. A term coined by Gordon; see below for further discussion.
203. As proposed by Holladay, *JBL* 85 (1966) 407-08.
204. 'If a major word in the first stichos is not paralleled in the second, then one or more of the words in the second stichos tend to be longer than their counterparts in the first stichos': Gordon, *UT*, 135. This corresponds to 'incomplete parallelism with compensation' in Gray, *Forms*, 76-83.94 (with examples).

כי רב מאד מחנהו        For very great is his army,
כי עצום עשה דברו        powerful, who carries out his command.

(Joel 2,11)

Here *'ōśê d*ᵉ*bārô* in line two = *maḥnēhû* in line one; and *rab m*ᵉ*'od* of
line one corresponds to *'āṣûm* of the second colon. (Schematically: x
a+b c // x a' c'+d.) The result is a perfectly balanced couplet.
(Reversals of this kind are discussed below.)

### The ballast variant

It is now clear that a ballast variant is simply a *filler*, its function
being to fill out a line of poetry that would otherwise be too short.
This explains the name 'expletive' used by Austerlitz. A poet who
needed to make his second colon as long as the first but wished to
avoid repetition, could omit an item from the first colon and then
employ a ballast variant. Although a whole range of ballast variants
of differing types was available, they had a common function (see
below). Accordingly the varieties to be set out must be considered as
differing in description only.

1. *Simple ballast variant.* The ballast variant is parallel to its
counterpart, the respective lengths usually being two words and one
only. For instance,

מדוע בשש רכבו לבוא        Why is his chariot so slow in coming?
מדוע אחרו פעמי מרכבותיו        Why does the clatter of his war-wagons tarry so?

(Jgs 5,28)

Since *lābô'* (or its equivalent in meaning) does not reappear in the
second colon, the longer expression *pa*ᵃ*mê mark*ᵉ*bôtâyw* is used
instead of simply one word (e.g. *mark*ᵉ*bôtâyw // rikbô*).

Quite frequently such pairs are in fact word-pairs of the type *'aḥ //
bnê 'ēm*, 'brother // mother's son', used as ballast variants (Ps 69,9).
(See section on parallel pairs for other examples.) The poet could
draw on his stock of word-pairs of this kind which provided ready-
made ballast variants. Particularly useful were epithetic word-pairs.

2. *Expanded repetition.* The ballast variant in pairs of this kind is
formed by repeating the first component and then adding to it, as in

הנצל כצבי מיד        Save yourself, like a gazelle from the *hand*,
וכצפור מיד יקוש        or like a bird from the *hand of the fowler*.

(Prov 6,5)

the lengthier *yad yāqûš // yād*. This type of repetition was termed 'expanded repetition' by Freedman—Hyland[205] and can be symbolised as *a // ab*. Other examples: Isa 28,16; Ps 29,3.5.8.

3. *Ballast prepositions.* Akin to expanded repetition is the widespread use of a longer or compound preposition in the second colon, balancing the same preposition in simple form used in the first. For example:

| | |
|---|---|
| והיה שארית יעקב בגוים | And the remnant of Jacob shall be *among* the nations, |
| בקרב עמים רבים | *in the midst of* (the) many peoples. |

(Mic 5,7[206])

Also: Ps 47,4 (*tḥt // tḥt rglynw*); Prov 8,20 (*b // btwk*); Job 16,4 (*b // bᵉmô*); Isa 65,4; Ps 104,10; Job 30,6f; Prov 26,13; Lam 1,3 (*b // bên*); (*b // bᵉ'ad* in Isa 26,20; Prov 7,6 etc.)

4. *Ballast prepositions reversed.* Instead of the 'heavier' form coming in the second colon, there are times when it comes in the first. Such inversion may be due to these combinations being considered word-pairs. For example, *bᵉqereb // bᵉ* in Isa 6,12-13; Hab 3,2. Another instance is Isa 5,2:

| | |
|---|---|
| ויבן מגדל בתוכו | He built a tower *within* it. |
| וגם יקב חצב בו | A wine-vat, too, he dug *in* it. |

(similarly Ez 32,25 and note *bᵉtôk // bᵉ // bᵉ* in Ps 135,9). Other examples: *taḥat // bᵉ* Job 34,26 ('among, in'); Ez 17,23; Job 40,21 ('under, in'); *bᵉmô // bᵉ* Isa 43,2; Job 37,8; *kᵉmô // kᵉ* Isa 33,4; Ps 78,69; Job 41,16; Song 6,10; *'immôn // 'im* Ps 83,8.[207]

5. *Reversed ballast variant.* Here again the expected order is inverted

| | |
|---|---|
| על ראשי ההרים יזבחו | On the *hill-tops* they sacrificed |
| ועל הגבעות יקטרו | and on the *hills* burn incense. (Hos 4,13) |

6. *Double ballast variant.* Strictly speaking, parallel couplets of this kind do not use the ballast variant, but for convenience they will be listed here. Examples are Isa 31,2; 33,20; Prov 10,2. Joel 2,11 has been set out above.

7. *Ballast variants and gender.* Finally, it can be noted that quite frequently gender parallelism is operative, a masculine noun in the

---

205. Freedman—Hyland, *HTR* 66 (1973) 248.
206. Similarly, *CTA* 4 v 75-76.
207. As explained by Dahood, *Psalms II*, 275, who identifies MT *'mn* as 'the preposition *'m* with the afformative ending *-n*' and translates 'and with it'.

first colon being balanced by a feminine counterpart in the second.
Since the feminine noun is generally lengthier than its masculine
equivalent, the result is a ballast variant word-pair involving gender.
For instance:

אמרים לעץ אבי אתה      Those saying to the tree (m):
                                        'You're my father';
ולאבן את ילדתני        and to the stone (f):
                                        'You're "my mother"'. (Jer 2,27[208])

And, with the same word-pair: Isa 60,17; Hab 2,19.[209]

8. *Ballast variant and other devices.* The ballast variant does not
occur in isolation, whether within the couplet or considered in the
larger context of a poem. As has been seen it overlaps with gender
parallelism and the word-pair. It can also be termed a form of
repetition (see section on 'expanded repetition'). More specifically, it
can be used in combination with chiasmus, as in

ונטשתיך בארץ      I will cast you on the *ground*.
על פני השדה אטילך      On the *open field* I will fling you. (Ez 32,4)

And: Isa 14,25; Ez 17,23 (reversed); Pss 22,3; 132,4; 145,2; Job 28,16;
30,31; Prov 5,16 and Jgs 5,19 (reversed). Especially interesting is the
combination of ballast variant (*sok*, 'covert' // *mᵉᶜônâ*, 'lair'), chiasmus
and possibly gender parallelism in Ps 76,3

ויהי בשלם סכו      Sited was his covert (m.) in Salem (m.?),
ומעונתו בציון      in Zion (f.)    his lair (f.).

*Functions*
Within the couplet, and in terms of parallelism, the main function of
the ballast variant is to maintain the balance of colon-length.

In the larger context of stanzas and poems, its function is
occasionally climactic[210] as in

ימלך יהוה לעולם      Reign, shall Yahweh, for ever,
אלהיך ציון לדר ודר      your God, O Zion, for generations. (Ps 146,10)

---

208. Lit. 'You are "she-who-bore-me"'. For the noun-verb parallelism here cf. Isa
51,2.
209. Other examples can be culled from *RSP* I and II.
210. An example from Ugaritic is *CTA* 4 vi 29-31:

    *tikl išt bbhtm*          the fire consumed *in* the mansion,
    *nblat bqrb hklm*        the flames *in the midst of* the palace

where on the sixth and final day of burning, *b* // *bqrb* replaces *b* // *b* of the previous
lines.

A secondary function is to open a stanza, poem or book; examples are Am 1,2; Joel 1,2.

*Ugaritic and Akkadian poetry*

As already seen, it was Gordon's recognition of the ballast variant in Ugaritic poetry which led to its identification in Hebrew. Gordon provides a good range of examples.[211] These include the simple ballast variant:

| | |
|---|---|
| *trḥṣ ydh btlt 'nt* | The Virgin Anat washed her *hands*, |
| *uṣb'th ybmt limm* | her *fingers*, the progenitress of peoples; |
| | (*CTA* 3B ii 32-33) |

the expanded repetition: *šd // šd ddh* ('field, field of her love?', *CTA* 24:22-23); ballast prepositional pair: *b // bqrb* ('in, within', *CTA* 17 i 26-27; etc.) and epithetic parallelism: *b'l // rkb 'rpt* ('Baal, Cloud-rider', *CTA* 19 i 42-44).

Young commented: 'The use of ballast variants, or the 'deliberate' use of longer synonyms, does not demonstrate that these poets were attempting to abide by a metrical pattern. It simply shows that they did not like to balance very unequal stichs. The proof lies in the fact that ballasted stichs do not necessarily produce metrically exactly equal stichs, only those of approximate equality.'[212]

Akkadian poetry, too, exhibits the use of this device also (though no formal study has yet been published). Hecker notes the use of redundant personal pronouns as expletives, but this is also attested in both Ugaritic and Hebrew.[213] A particularly striking instance is

| | |
|---|---|
| *igisê šulmāni ušābilū* | Gifts, presents, sent |
| *šunu ana šâšu* | they to him. (*Ee* IV 134) |

211. Gordon, *UT* §13.116.
212. Young, *JNES* 9 (1950) 132, n. 26.
213. For Akkadian poetry cf. Hecker, *Epik*, 128, n. 1; also Lambert, *BWL*, 320. Note that Kugel, *Idea*, 45-48 and 71, is opposed to the notion of ballast variant. He writes: 'It must be noted that in this whole question of compensation and "ballast variants" there is a rather misleading assumption about intention. Behind these phrases lurks a prejudgement of purpose: the *extra* element in B *compensates* for something that is missing, and what is added is merely ballast. Were the need not there, the compensatory phrase would not have been written ... The whole notion of "ballast" or "compensation" asks us to decide about the Psalmist's intention in these lines [Pss 47,4; 66,10; 79,4 and 71,5]—it is an impossible question to answer in most cases, and a foolish one to ask.'

where the second (part of the) colon is artificially made up of pronouns.

*For study*
Ps 35,10; Ez 22,30; Prov 1,3; Job 6,15; 9,20; Pss 103,7; 122,7 and 146,10.

*Cross-references*
PARALLELISM; also ELLIPSIS, ORAL POETRY, WORD-PAIRS.

### BIBLIOGRAPHY

(a) *General*
Austerlitz, R. *Ob-Ugric Metrics* (*FFC* 174.8; Helsinki, 1958) 64-65.101.
O'Connor, *Structure*, 98-101.

(b) *Semitic*
Dahood, *Psalms I, II, III*; Gordon, *UT*, 135-37; Kugel, *Idea*, 45-48.71.

# 12

## SECONDARY TECHNIQUES

The selection of techniques discussed in this chapter derives from the primary techniques of poetry treated so far. They are therefore termed secondary. In certain cases, however, it is not crystal clear which technique (or device) came first, a good example being the list or catalogue. For convenience of presentation it seems preferable to consider them here as part of a mixed group. The two main categories into which such techniques fall are those of expansion and of inversion; the list can be classed as a form of expansion.

### 12.1 *Expansion*

*Expansion in general*
As has already been noted throughout the book certain devices can be extended in one (or both) of two ways: by *serial addition*, when a particular component is repeated in various ways (e.g. a sequence of five similes); and by *extension*, as when a simile fills not just one line of poetry but several, with the basic point of comparison remaining the same. Both types can be explained as part of the poet's way of lengthening a poem.[1] Since 'expansion' has already been mentioned in connection with many of the different topics discussed so far only two headings have been selected, both new. They are *tours* and the *list*.

*Tours*
A tour is 'a series of one or more verses where the poet lists pairs of from three to ten words all meaning roughly the same thing, or having something to do with the same subject, or being in some way

---

1. See now J.C. de Moor, 'The Art of Versification in Ugarit and Israel. III: Further Illustrations of the Principle of Expansion', *UF* 12 (1980) 311-16.

related'.[2] More succinctly, the tour is an *extension of the word-pair*. For example, in Job 4,10-11

| | |
|---|---|
| שאגת אריה | The *lion's* roar, |
| וקול שחל | the *fierce beast's* cry, |
| ושני כפירים נתעו | —but the *whelps'* teeth are shattered; |
| ליש אבד מבלי טרף | the *big-cat* wanders with no prey, |
| ובני לביא יתפרדו | the *lioness's* cubs are scattered; |

five parallel terms for a *lion* are used in five consecutive lines, any two of which could form a word-pair. Note that there is some degree of overlap with the next section—lists or catalogues—though strictly speaking they are distinct forms.[3]

An example in Ugaritic poetry is *CTA* 6 ii 31-35:

| | |
|---|---|
| bḥrb tbq'nn | With a sword she split him; |
| bḫtr tdrynn | with a sieve she winnowed him; |
| bišt tšrpnn | with fire she burnt him; |
| brḥm tṭḥnn | with mill-stones she ground him |
| bšd tdr'nn | —in a field she scattered him. |

Not only does the tour express completeness here (i.e. complete destruction), it also serves as a cohesive device, linking a series of lines within a poem. See, as well, *CTA* 6 v 11ff. Tours occur too in Akkadian poetry.[4]

Further passages in Hebrew include: Isa 35,5-6

| | |
|---|---|
| אז תפקחנה עיני עורים | Then, the eyes of the blind shall be opened, |
| ואזני חרשים תפתחנה | and the ears of the deaf unstopped, |
| אז ידלג כאיל פסח | then the lame shall leap like a deer, |
| ותרן לשון אלם | and the tongue of the dumb shout aloud. |

Also Isa 1,11.16-17; 3,2-3; Job 18,8-10 (see WORKED EXAMPLES, 12.4); 19,13-15; 28,1-2.15-19;[5] 41,18-22.[6]

---

2. Watters, *Formula Criticism*, 96; see also 95-98 and W. Whallon, *Formula, Character, and Context* (Cambridge, Mass., 1969) 152.

3. The *list* is a catalogue of nouns set out consecutively; the *tour* is a series of parallel lines each containing a noun or verb which is the focus of interest: an extended word-pair.

4. For example, *BWL* 72:28-29; 76:76-77; 84:245-250; 119:3ff; 136:176-177; 202(f):2-3. Also lines 58-61 and 118-121 of a Hymn to Gula (edition by Lambert, *Or* 36 [1967] 105-32).

5. Note ten consecutive lines in vv. 15-19.

6. For a list cf. Watters, *Formula Criticism*, 97-98; also, R. Gordis, *The Book of God and Man* (Chicago, 1965) 160 and 342.

## 12.2 *Lists*

*The list*

In a manner of speaking, most of the serial expansions discussed so far could be subsumed under the heading of 'list'. The catalogues collected here differ from those treated in *not* having a common poetic device; for instance, the list of professions in Isa 3,2-3 is simply that and nothing more (it could almost belong to an economic text). As usual, examples will be provided from Akkadian and Ugaritic.

Lists can be classified into three groups: simple lists; lists with a final total; lists with an initial total. Occasionally the total repeats all the items in the list—it is then termed a gather-line.[7]

1. *Simple lists.* Such lists can be long or short; what distinguishes them from similar lists in prose texts is their rhythm and metre, though at times these are hard to detect. Akkadian epic is fond of catalogues, perhaps because the scribes received their training by endlessly copying out encyclopaedic lists and bilingual vocabularies. Lists occur particularly often in *Erra*;[8] also:

| | |
|---|---|
| *pisannātika šēka kasapka bušēka* | Bring your chests, your barley, your silver, |
| *makkūrka ana āl dannūtika šūrib* | your goods, your valuables into your fort. (*CuthLeg* 160-161) |

Simple lists are rare in Ugaritic; note

| | |
|---|---|
| *ṭbḫ alpm* | He slaughtered oxen, |
| *ap ṣin* | also sheep, |
| *šql ṯrm* | felled bulls, |
| *wmri ilm* | and fattened rams, |
| *'glm dt šnt* | calves, one year old, |
| *imr qmṣ wllim* | skipping lambs and kids. |
| | (*CTA* 4 vi 40-43[9]) |

In Hebrew:

| | |
|---|---|
| כי אין אמת | For there is no truth, |
| ואין חסד | and there is no piety, |
| ואין דעת אלהים בארץ | and there is no knowledge of God in the land. |
| | (Hos 4,1) |

7. So Thiering, *JSS* 8 (1963) 191.198-99; see above under MERISMUS.
8. *Erra* I 31-38.62-70; IV 6-11.57; etc.; Hymn to Gula (see note 4) 65.
9. And parallels. However, Dahood, *Psalms I*, 51-52, may be correct in translating the first two lines 'He slaughtered large and small cattle', considered by him to be 'a generic expression which includes the animals that are later specified in the verse'—in other words, as merismus. Note, too, *CTA* 4 i 30-42; 6 ii 31-35; v 11-19; 17 i 27-34.

Also: Gen 12,6; Isa 2,12-16;[10] 10,28; 11,2.6-8; 13,21; 19,2.3.8-9; 60,17f; 65,13-14; Sir 11,14; 37,11; 40,9; 41,14-24; 42,1-5; etc.; Zech 10,4.

Note the *numerical lists*: Erra I 31-38 and *CTA* 14 i 14-21 (both enumerate seven things), with which can be compared the numerical sayings of Proverbs: 6,16-19; 30,7-9.15.15b-16.18-19.21-23.24-28.29-31.

2. *Lists with final total.* As indicated, some lists provide a kind of total or summative line at the end, much in the manner of totals in non-literary texts. In Akkadian:

> šēdū namtarū [utuk]kû rābiṣū lemnūte
> šipir Enlil šunu

> Demons, destiny-devils, spectres, ghosts, fiends:
> they are creatures of Enlil. (*CuthLeg* 67-68[11])

From Ugaritic:

| | |
|---|---|
| adr ṯqbm blbnn | The finest ash-trees from Lebanon, |
| adr gdm brumm | the finest sinews from wild-oxen, |
| adr qrnt byʻlm | the finest horns from goats, |
| mtnm bʻqbt ṯr | tendons from a bull's hocks, |
| adr bġl il qnm | the finest stems from vast beds of reed, |
| tn lkṯr wḫss | give to Kathiru-wa-Hasis: |
| ybʻl qšt lʻnt | so he may make a BOW for Anath, |
| qṣʻt lybmt limm | ARROWS for the sister-in-law of nations. |

(*CTA* 17 vi 20-25[12])

In the last text no total is specifically mentioned; it is implied in the end-product, the bow and arrows. Hebrew texts already mentioned in this category (cf. MERISMUS) include Isa 41,19; Ps 76,4.8; Sir 39,26-27.[13]

| | |
|---|---|
| [ראש כל צר]ך לחיי אדם | The chief of all things necessary for the life of man: |
| מים ואש וברזל ומלח | are water and fire and iron and salt, |
| [חלב חטה] חלב ודבש | and flour of wheat, and milk and honey, |
| דם ענב יצהר ובגד | the blood of the grape and oil and clothes. |
| | *total* |
| כל א[לה] ל[ט]ובים ייטיבו | All these things are for good to the goodly. |

Also Song 4,14; Zech 12,12-14.

---

10. On this text cf. Cathcart, *Herm* 125 (1978) 51-53.
11. Also lines 94-96.
12. And *CTA* 14 i 14-21 (total: 21-23); 14 i 52-56 (and par.).
13. Strictly speaking Sir 39,26-27 has both an initial and a final total.

3. *Lists with initial total.* Examples in Akkadian and Ugaritic are neither numerous nor clear; note

> *sinništu būrtu būrtu šuttatu ḫirītum*
> Woman is a pit, a pit, a hole, a ditch.[14]

Hebrew texts: Isa 3,18-23; Hos 4,3; Pss 146,6-9; 148,7-12. Also, the numerical sayings listed above and Ps 83,6-9:

|  | *total* |
|---|---|
| כי נועצו לב יחדו | Truly they conspire *with one mind* |
| עליך ברית יכרתו | against you they make a pact: |
|  | *list* |
| אהלי אדום וישמעאלים | The tents of Edom and the Ishmaelites, |
| מואב והגרים | Moab and the Hagarites, |
| גבל ועמונו עמלק | Byblos together with Amalek,[15] |
| פלשת עם ישבי צור | Philistia with the Tyrians, |
| גם אשור נלוה עמם | even Assyria has joined them, |
| היו זרוע לבני לוט | they are the 'arm' of Lot's children. |

### Lists of body-parts

Certain poems are evidently based on a catalogue of parts of the human body, and in origin were descriptions of divine statues. Later, such descriptions were used as love-poems, chiefly with reference to women, but occasionally to men. Examples are known in Sumerian, Akkadian, possibly in Ugaritic[16] and, of course in Hebrew, notably in the Song of Songs.

A description of the god Ninurta[17] uses the set: 'head, face, cheek, hair, hands (both right and left), chest, body, right foot, left foot'. Other examples are known.[18] The Ugaritic text mentioned is apparently a description of Baal, and refers to his head, forehead, feet, horns, head, feet, mouth and heart.

Full-length descriptions of this type are used in Song 5,11-16 (of the man); 7,2-10 (of the woman); note also the full sequence in Ps 115,5-7.

More often, though, such descriptions are *partial*: there is the extremely brief portrait of Keret's wife-to-be, Huray:

---

14. Text: *BWL* 146:51; contrast line 52.
15. Translation: Dahood, *Psalms II*, 275.
16. See L.R. Fisher and F.B. Knutson, 'An Enthronement Ritual at Ugarit', *JNES* 28 (1969) 157-69 (esp. 162-64); M.H. Pope and J.H. Tigay, 'A Description of Baal', *UF* 3 (1971) 117-30.
17. Cited *UF* 3 (1971) 119-20; cf. Köcher, *MIO* 1 (1953) 57-107.
18. See Köcher and *ANET*. Cf. Lambert, *BWL*, 23.

*Classical Hebrew Poetry*

| | |
|---|---|
| *dkn'm 'nt n'mh* | Whose loveliness is like the loveliness of Anath, |
| *km tsm 'ttrt tsmh* | whose beauty is like the beauty of Athtart, |
| *d'qh ib iqni* | whose eyeballs are lapis-lazuli gems, |
| *'p'ph sp trml* | whose eyelids are bowls of onyx. |

(*CTA* 14 iii 145-48[19])

See, for Hebrew, Song 4,1-5 (description of woman's head and torso); 6,4-7 (again, the woman's head); Dan 2,32-33 and Ez 1,26-28; 1,5-13.

Of particular interest here is the penchant of Near Eastern poets for clustering together names of parts of the body. Sometimes these form units, although the reason for particular sequences is sometimes obscure. Note, in Akkadian:

| | |
|---|---|
| *ana ummânī šunūti* | To those craftsmen |
| *libba rapša iddinšunūtima* | a vast HEART he gave them, |
| *išdišunu [ukīn]* | their FOUNDATIONS he made firm, |
| *uznī išrukšunūtim* | UNDERSTANDING he bestowed on them, |
| *qātēšunu ulalli* | their HANDS he made perfect; |

(*Erra* IIB 19-20)

where the literal meaning of 'foundations' and 'understanding' is 'lower part of the body' and 'ear' respectively.[20] In Ugaritic there is a stereotyped passage which occurs three times:[21]

| | |
|---|---|
| *hlm 'nt tph ilm* | Suddenly, Anath spied the gods, |
| *bh p'nm ttt* | at that her FEET stamped, |
| *b'dn ksl ttbr* | round about her LOINS she burst, |
| *'ln pnh td'* | above, her FACE did sweat, |
| *tġṣ pnt kslh* | she contracted the JOINTS of her LOINS, |
| *anš dt ẓrh* | the MUSCLES of her BACK. |
| *tšu gh wtṣḥ* | She raised her VOICE and screamed. |

In Hebrew there are many examples; there is the description of the wicked man in Prov 6,12-15 which includes the sequence:

19. Note that, exactly as in Song 4,1 there is a generic description of the woman as beautiful, before the detailed description. Another Ugaritic text is *CTA* 4 ii 10-12 (of eyes).
20. See also *Atr* II iv 12-18.
21. *CTA* 3D iii 29-33 // 4 ii 16-21 // 19 ii 93-97; the last passage is preceded by the sequence *npš, brlt, ap*, 'life, breath, nose'. On this passage cf. de Moor, *UF* 12 (1980) 427-28; Pardee, *BO* 37 (1980) 277.

| | |
|---|---|
| קרץ בעינו | Winking with his EYE, |
| מלל ברגלו | stamping[22] with his FOOT, |
| מרה באצבעתיו | pointing with his FINGERS, |
| תהפכות בלבו | subversion in his HEART.[23] |

Also: Isa 30,27-28a (nostrils, liver, lips, tongue, breath, neck, jaws);[24] 32,3-6 (eyes, ears, heart, tongue; kidneys, heart, throat);[25] Pss 115,5-7 (mouths, eyes, ears, noses, hands, feet, throat); 135,16-17 (mouths, eyes, ears, mouths); Prov 6,17 (eyes, tongue, hands, heart, feet).

Peculiar to Ugaritic, it seems, is the use of such lists within a poem in order to *link its components* more strongly. Sequences can be quite short as in *CTA* 23:61-62 (teats of breasts; lip, lip, mouth)[26] or extraordinarily long, with up to eleven consecutive items as in *CTA* 19 iii 113-119 (mouth, lips, wing, pinions, feet, gizzard, fat, bone, voice, wings, pinions).[27] These long lists straddle strophic segments and serve to link them together.

The *sequence* of items is significant, and can vary. Normally such descriptions (and derivative lists) run *downwards*, from top to toe. E.g. the description of Ninurta; Prov 6,17; Dan 2,32-33.

Occasionally the top-to-toe sequence reverts once more to the top: 'Description of Baal'; Ez 1,5-13; Song 5,11-16; Pss 115,5-7; 135,16-17. The order in the Ugaritic text cited above[28] is rather more strictly chiastic. *Upward* sequences are unusual; note Song 7,2-10.

Lists of all these types were clearly a great help to the composing poet; they presumably circulated as separate units[29] and may have been modelled on roll-calls for conscription and the like. This would explain the superficial similarity between lists of combatants in the

22. It must be a non-verbal gesture of some kind. The expression *tmll išdh* occurs in the Ugaritic description of Baal.

23. The list of body-parts is argument, perhaps, that the last line belongs to the quatrain, not to the lines which come after.

24. Irwin, *Isaiah 28-33*, 97-98.

25. *Ibid.* 121-122. On Ps 110 cf. Dahood, *Psalms III*, 113.

26. Also *CTA* 2 iv 17-18 (joints, frame); 13-15 (hand, fingers; shoulders, between arms; hand, fingers; crown, between eyes); 4 vii 29-32 (voice, lips, voice, lips); 4 iv 25-30 (feet; forehead, feet, fingers; voice); 19 i 7-10 (hand, fingers; 'stones of her mouth', teeth).

27. And *CTA* 19 iii 107-111 (six items); 18 iv 22-26 (// 33-37: crown, ear, blood, knees, breath, life, nose, noses); also, 5 vi 14-22 (head, crown; skin; sideburns and beard, collar-bone, chest, torso, voice); cf. *CTA* 6 i 2-5.

28. *CTA* 3D iii 29-33; etc.

29. Cf. H.M. Chadwick—N.K. Chadwick, *The Growth of Literature I* (Cambridge, 1932) 283.

Erra Epic,[30] the Keret Tale[31] and the trio Gen 49, Dt 33 and Jgs 5.[32] It is also evident that the audience delighted in catalogues, presumably because they combined entertainment with instruction. Certainly, if they had not been popular, long lists would not have survived constant transmission.[33]

## 12.3 *Inversion*

### *Inversion as technique*

Inversion of an accepted or established poetic device is itself a powerful way of producing further poetic devices of various types. The traditional A-B sequence of a parallel word-pair, for example, can be inverted (as B-A) to express reversal of state or to produce a chiastic pattern. Here, some of the more common types of inversion .will be listed with comments on their functions within a poem. It must be understood, though, that only a representative selection can be given and that the full range is much more extended. Inversion of the following poetic devices will be looked at (the sequence follows the order of presentation in the main part of this book): gender-matched parallelism; parallel word-pairs; number parallelism; three-synonym monocola; and staircase parallelism. Other possible topics include chiasmus, the terrace pattern, imagery, the inverted construct chain and role reversal.[34]

### *Gender-matched parallelism*

Inverted forms of this device have already been considered, but some illustration here will not go amiss. In Prov 3,22 for example, the standard m + m // f + f pattern has been inverted to m + f // m + f:

---

30. *Erra* IV 7-11 (note the total in line 6).

31. *CTA* 14 i 96-103 (again with total preceding).

32. See particularly Coogan, *CBQ* 40 (1978) 162-65. For further discussion of enumerations cf. Alonso Schökel, *Estudios*, 111-112.221. For lists in later Hebrew cf. W.S. Towner, 'Form-Criticism of Rabbinic Literature', *JJS* 24 (1973) 101-18, esp. 117-18.

33. The persistence of this ancient tradition is attested by later Hebrew poetry. The following random sample from T. Carmi (ed.), *The Penguin Book of Hebrew Verse* (London, 1981) gives some idea: 'Wine' (297); 'The Fear of Death' (299-301, esp. stanzas II, III and VI); 'The Ideal Woman' (360-61); 'The Conditions of Beauty' (456-57) and one of the most recent, dating to 1970: 'The Portrait' (575-76).

34. On inversion cf. G.M. Green, 'Some Wherefores of English Inversions', *Lang* 56 (1980) 582-601. The functions of inversion she mentions include buying of time in oral delivery, inner-discourse cohesion, introduction and emphasis.

ויהיו חיים לנפשך   They will be life (m) to your soul (f),
וחן לגרגרתיך   and adornment (m) for your neck (f).

In Job 5,9 the inversion is even more striking as the pattern has become f + m // f + m:

עשה גדלות ואין חקר   Doer of marvels (f) but scrutiny (m) there is none,
נפלאות עד אין מספר   of wonders (f) without number (m).

## Parallel word-pairs

It has been argued that while Ugaritic poets always used word-pairs in a fixed (A//B) sequence, Hebrew poets had the inventiveness and freedom to invert.[35] However, reversed word-pairs are to be found in Ugaritic—proportionately fewer than in Hebrew, however—which reduces the debate to a matter of degree.[36] How much more free were the Hebrew bards to invert word-pairs? The answer lies in the lists compiled in *RSP* I-III. Here it will be enough to look at the different functions of such inversion.

The most obvious function is the *portrayal of abnormal events*. In Ps 44,26 for example, the standard sequence עפר // ארץ ('earth // dust') found many times elsewhere[37] as well as in Ugaritic (as *arṣ //ʿpr*) becomes:

כי שחה לעפר נפשנו   For our neck is bowed down to the DUST,
דבקה לארץ בטננו   our body adheres to the EARTH.

Also Isa 34,9; 47,1; Mic 7,17. Exactly the same function can be discerned in the texts from Ras Shamra. Compare *CTA* 17 v 8

*ydn dn almnt*   He judged the WIDOW'S cause,
*ytpṭ ṭpṭ ytm*   he tried the ORPHAN'S case;

with *CTA* 16 vi 49-50:

*lpnk ltšlḥm ytm*   You do not feed the ORPHAN in front of you
*bʿd kslk almnt*   or the WIDOW behind your back;

35. For the debate see Dahood, *RSP I*, 77-78 and the bibliography under PARALLEL WORD-PAIRS.
36. See now W.G.E. Watson, 'Reversed Word-pairs in Ugaritic Poetry', *UF* 13 (1981) 189-92.
37. Isa 26,5; 29,4; 34,7; 49,23; Ez 24,7; Pss 7,6; 22,30; Prov 8,26; Job 14,8; 39,14; see Gevirtz, *JNES* 20 (1961) 41-46.

where the stock sequence *almnt // ytm* has deliberately been inverted, portraying how the king is acting unjustly.

Word-pairs can also be inverted *to produce chiasmus*. An example in Hebrew is Prov 18,6-7 where the sequence 'lips // mouth' of the first couplet has been reversed in the second to produce an ABBA quatrain:

| | |
|---|---|
| שפתי כסיל יבאו בריב | A fool's LIPS bring strife, |
| ופיו למהלמות יקרא | and his MOUTH invites a flogging; |
| פי כסיל מחתה לו | a fool's MOUTH is his ruin, |
| ושפתיו מוקש נפשו | and his LIPS are a snare to himself. |

Similarly Joel 1,19-20. For other examples, see CHIASMUS.

The word-pair can be inverted for *emphasis* (e.g. Isa 41,8), to fit into an *acrostic* pattern (Pss 25; 145,21) or for special reasons (e.g. in Am 6,1).[38]

It is noteworthy that the /lower/ parallel to /higher/ sequence in number parallelism is never inverted.[39]

*Three-synonym monocolon*
The only example of inversion in Hebrew poetry is Hos 9,11 where the natural sequence of events is reversed—depicting utter negation:

| | |
|---|---|
| | Ephraim's glory shall fly away like a bird: |
| מלדה ומבטן ומהריון | no birth, no pregnancy, no conception. |

*Staircase parallelism*
Normally, the vocative comes after an opening imperative (or its equivalent), as in Jer 31,21

| | |
|---|---|
| שובי בתולת ישראל | Return, O Virgin Israel, |
| שובי אל עריך אלה | return to these your cities. |

In what appears to be an inverted form of this structure, the vocative appears in the second line—for instance, Ps 96,1:

| | |
|---|---|
| שירו ליהוה שיר חדש | Sing to Yahweh a new song, |
| שירו ליהוה כל הארץ | sing to Yahweh *all the earth*. |

This may resolve the difficulty in Ps 135,1 which follows the same pattern:

38.  The standard sequence 'Samaria // Zion' is reversed 'possibly for the purpose of ending with Samaria, to which alone the prophecy is directed' (Haran, *VTS* 22 [1972] 245).

39.  The nearest to reversal is Isa 7,8 if one is to read 'within sixty or fifty' or 'within six or five'—but this is conjectural.

הללו את שם יהוה   Praise the name of Yahweh,
הללו עבדי יהוה   praise, *O servants of Yahweh.*[40]

## Closing remarks

As noted in the introduction, inversion could be studied in a whole range of poetic devices but unfortunately there is neither the time nor the space here. Research on this aspect of poetic technique is still in its initial stages[41] which makes it an interesting and challenging field of inquiry. The same applies to much that has been touched on throughout the book. Even that old die-hard, metre, promises to yield up its secrets with the correct application of modern linguistic theory and, who knows, future discoveries in the Near East may yet provide more clues.

40. Contrast Dahood, *Psalms III*, 257-59, who prefers 'Praise the name of Yahweh! Praise the works of Yahweh!'. As he himself notes, 11QPs$^a$ *inverts* these two lines— this suggests that inverted staircase parallelism was rare and therefore misunderstood.
41. See, for example, M. De Roche, 'The reversal of creation in Hosea', *VT* 31 (1981) 400-409. Also, P.C. Beentjes, 'Inverted Quotations in the Bible. A Neglected Stylistic Pattern', *Bib* 63 (1982) 506-23.

# 13

## APPENDIX: WORKED EXAMPLES

### 13.1 *Introduction*

A textbook such as this would not be complete without at least a selection of longer poetic passages, to complement the illustrative texts cited in the body of the book, most of which are very short.[1] Making and presenting a selection of worked examples, it is clear, does involve certain problems. The difficulty of choosing the actual poems is double-edged: a representative sample will include texts of extreme difficulty, while easier texts may not cover the same range. Some sort of middle course has to be followed. Discussion of philological and textual points, in any case, has been kept to a minimum, since a clutter of footnotes would only distract from the main issues in hand: poetic form, poetic technique, style and the like. Only a restricted number of longer poems is included, for reasons of space, leaving the reader to perform his or her own analysis of the remaining material. To complete the picture, a sample of Ugaritic poetry has been provided, and this is set out first.

### 13.2 *An Ugaritic Poem*

Most of the intelligible literary texts in Ugaritic are conveniently available with both text and translation,[2] so that there is little need to set out any here. Instead, a recently discovered prayer will be discussed, partly because the genre is rare in Ugaritic and partly because its social setting is known.[3] It is not easily to hand in English

---

1. Following the best traditions of Ley and Alonso Schökel, to mention only two scholars, widely separated in time. In literary studies, too, complete poems are analysed as part of main content of handbooks, e.g. Culler, *Poetics*, 1975.
2. Gibson, *CML*.
3. For another example of a prayer cf. de Moor, *UF* 11 (1979) 648-49.

translation. The prayer, *KTU* 1.119, is well understood in spite of some uncertainty in line 14[4] and has been transmitted within the framework of a ritual. The ritual need not concern us, but the prayer itself (rev. 11-17a) is prescribed for a particular occasion (lines 9-10):

| *kgr 'z tġrkm* | If a stalwart attacks your gate, |
| *qrd ḥmytkm* | or a warrior your walls, |

namely, when the city is under enemy attack. Furthermore, the words were to be recited in a particular posture:

| *'nkm lb'l tšun* | You should raise your eyes to Baal.[5] |

The prayer then follows:

| I | *yb'lm* | O Baal, |
| | *al tdy 'z ltġrny* | drive off the stalwart from our gate, |
| | *qrd lḥmytny* | the warrior from our walls. |

| II | *ibr yb'l nšqdš* | A bull-calf, O Baal, we will set aside,[6] |
| | *mdr b'l nmlu* | the vow,[7] Baal, we will fulfil; |
| | *d(?)kr b'l nšqdš* | a male,[8] Baal, we will set aside, |
| | *ḥtp b'l nmlu* | the crush-sacrifice,[9] Baal, we will fulfil. |
| | *'šrt b'l n'šr* | Libations, Baal, we will libate. |

| III | *qdš b'l n'l* | To the sanctuary, Baal, we will go up,[10] |
| | *ntbt bt b'l ntlk* | the temple-paths, Baal, we will tread. |

The effect of the prayer is then stated in lines 18-19 (repeating the phrases previously used): 'He (= Baal) will drive the stalwart from your gate / the warrior from your walls'.[11]

In general it can be said that the standard of poetry is not very high: *repetition* is its hallmark. Not only are the same words repeated

---

4. Studies: A. Herdner, 'Une prière à Baal des Ugaritains en danger', *CRAIBL* 1972 (1973) 693-703; B. Margalit, [A Ugaritic Prayer in Time of Siege (RS 24.266)], *Proceedings of the 7th World Congress of Jewish Studies 1977* (Jerusalem 1981) 63-83 (in Hebrew); P. Xella, 'Un testo ugaritico recente (*RS* 24.266, *Verso*, 9-19) e il 'sacrificio dei primi nati'', *RSF* 6 (1978) 127-36.

5. See Ps 121.

6. Lit. 'we will consecrate'.

7. Or 'offering'.

8. Herdner's reading *bkr*, 'first-born', seems improbable (so, too, Xella).

9. Like the Akkadian *ḥitpu*-sacrifice this apparently involved destruction of the victim by repeated blows with a stick; cf. P. Xella, '*ḥtp* = 'uccidere, annientare' in Giobbe 9,12', *Henoch* 1 (1977) 337-41 [unseen].

10. See Isa 2,3; Mic 4,2.

11. For a parallel see Ps 127,5b as translated by Dahood, *TS* 14 (1953) 87 and *Psalms III*, 221.225: 'But (he) shall drive back his foes from the gate'.

throughout (*b'l* eight times in the space of only 10 lines; *qdš*, three times), but the sentence structure remains identical for stanzas II and III. *Alliteration* is at its strongest in the last couplet (*b, l, ', n, t*) in combination with *wordplay* (*b'l—n'l* and perhaps *ntbt—bt*) of a rather elementary kind. The first couplet has both lines ending in *-ny*, forming simple end-*rhyme*; the alternation of line-endings in stanza II produces a similar effect. Other points to be noted are the *anacrusis* at the beginning of the prayer (extra-metrical *yb'lm*) and the abc/b'c' pattern of the initial strophe. Stanzas II and III may in fact form one unit: *b'l* is repeated throughout, and only in line 12-13 is it preceded by vocative *y-* as in the opening stanza. The word-pairs *'z // qrd*, and *tǵr // ḥmyt* (which occur in the same couplet) have counterparts in Akkadian[12] and Hebrew[13] respectively.

### 13.3 *Babylonian Poetry*

Partial studies of Babylonian and Akkadian poems are available in Hecker, *Epik*. A more detailed study of the Agušaya Hymn has been provided by Groneberg in her recent (unpublished) dissertation.[14] More conveniently a complete study of a hymn is readily accessible (in English) where attention is paid to poetic technique.[15]

### 13.4 *Hebrew Examples*

To avoid monotony of presentation the analytical procedure for the examples chosen will not be uniform. Instead, each text will be treated as an individual poem meriting its own approach. Only for Jer 46, Job 18 and Song 2 has the layout been modelled on the method outlined in the body of this book. As to the choice of passages, variety has been the main consideration. The rather hackneyed examples, such as Jgs 5, have been left out because in any

---

12. *qarrādū da[nnūtu] // bēl em[ūqi]*, 'strong warriors // mighty men' in *BWL* 265 obv. 8-9 (restored from Sumerian in bilingual proverb).

13. Prov 1,21. For further details, especially with regard to alliterative patterning and probable metre cf. Margalit: 1981 (note his table, 80-81). If the last two lines are considered as integral to the prayer, then they form an envelope figure with the opening couplet.

14. B. Groneberg, Untersuchungen zum hymnish-epischen Dialekt der altbabylonischen literarischen Texte (Münster, 1971). See now her 'Philologische Bearbeitung des Agušayahymnus', *RA* 75 (1981) 1-18.

15. W.G. Lambert, 'The Gula Hymn of Bulluṭsa-rabi', *Or* 36 (1967) 105-32, pls. VIII-XXIII. See, too, the additional comments by Barré, *Or* 50 (1981) 241-45.

case studies of them are easily obtainable. Generally speaking, the
first few examples are the shortest and the longest ones come at the
end. Note, too, that complete poems are also set out in the main part
of the book (e.g. Ps 95, under CHIASMUS).

### 2 Sm 19,1: David's Lament for Absalom (EVV 18,33)

In spite of being extremely brief, the first example exhibits some
interesting features. Set in a prose context (2 Sm 18,19–19,5), this
four-line lament is evidently verse:

| | | | |
|---|---|---|---|
| בני אבשלום בני | 1a | My son, Absalom, my son, | aba |
| בני אבשלום | b | my son, Absalom! | ab |
| מי־יתן מותי אני תחתיך | c | If only I had died in your stead! | cdef |
| אבשלום בני בני | d | Absalom, my son, my son! | baa |

*1a* is an 'aba monocolon', often used to open a poem. It is used as the
first line of the couplet *1ab* which combines qinah-metre (3 + 2
stresses) with the pivot pattern (the expected final stress: בני is not
present). The core of the lament, short as it is, is the rhetorical wish
expressed in *1c*. The final line simply varies the word-order of 1a.

An extremely abbreviated form of the dirge occurs in 2 Sm 19,5:

| | |
|---|---|
| בני אבשלום | My son, Absalom, |
| אבשלום בני בני | Absalom, my son, my son! |

This couplet is, in fact, identical to 1b and 1d of the longer lament.
Either the poet who composed the quatrain used the couplet (v. 5) in
the form of distant parallelism, or the couplet simply condenses the
content of the quatrain. It is difficult to decide which came first, but
the creator of the longer poem was able to exploit *repetition* so
skilfully that there is no monotony. Note the alliterative elements in
1c (perhaps based on the verb מות, 'to die').

### Isa 19,1-4: Oracle against Egypt

Part of a larger oracle or collection of oracles directed against the
Land of the Nile, Isa 19,1-4 has a very clear structure and is rich in
allusion to extra-biblical literature. The poem comprises *two stanzas*,
I, of 10 lines (tricolon, couplet, monocolon, quatrain) and II, of 7 lines
(monocolon, monocolon + couplet, tricolon). Two short *lists*, one in
each stanza, help fill out the poem.

I 1       הנה יהוה
רכב על עב קל
ובא מצרים

ונעו אלילי מצרים מפניו
ולבב מצרים ימס בקרבו

2       וסכסכתי מצרים במצרים
ונלחמו איש באחיו
ואיש ברעהו

עיר בעיר
ממלכה בממלכה

II 3     ונבקה רוח מצרים בקרבו
ועצתו אבלע

ודרשו אל האלילים ואל האטים
ואל האבות ואל הידענים

4       וסכרתי את מצרים
ביד ארנים קשה
ומלך עז ימשל בם

נאם האדון יהוה צבאות

I 1 A    See Yahweh,
          riding on a swift cloud,
          and coming to EGYPT.

     B    Do quail, the idols of EGYPT before him,
          and the heart of EGYPT melts within him.

   2 C    I shall smash EGYPTIAN with EGYPTIAN:
          Fight shall they, each against his brothers,
                   and each against his neighbour,
                   city against city,
                   and kingdom against kingdom.

II 3 B′    And emptied out shall be the courage of EGYPT from in him,

     C′    and his counsel will I confuse,
          though they consult idols and spectres, ghosts and spirits.

> 4  D   I shall confine EGYPT
>        in the hand of a harsh Master,
>        and a powerful King shall rule them,
>
> Oracle of the Master, Yahweh of Armies.

In spite of one or two difficulties,[16] the translation is unequivocal. Curiously, the gender of מצרים is masculine throughout, though normally names of countries are feminine.[17] *Gender-patterns* obtain in the list incorporated into C:

| Fight shall they: | | m.—m. |
| a man (m.) | against his brothers (m.) | |
| and a man (m.) | against his neighbour (m.) | m.—m. |
| a city (f.) | against a city (f.) | f.—f. |
| a kingdom (f.) | against a kingdom (f.) | f.—f. |

where they fulfil the double function of merismus (everybody is at war) and the expression of civil war (like fighting with like).

Note the parallel passage in Babylonian poetry:[18]

| *ālu itti āli* | City with city, |
| *bītu itti bīti inakkir* | house with house will be hostile, |
| *abu itti abi* | father with father, |
| *aḫu itti aḫi* | brother with brother. |

Gender-matching is used also in the couplet ('idols // heart', both m.) and in the two monocola at the beginning of stanza II ('spirit // counsel', both f.)—both times in order to link them.

The term מצרים occurs six times (I: 4×; II: 2×) as a *keyword*, driving home the fact that this oracle is against Egypt (see title in v. 1). This corresponds to the last line 'Oracle of the Master . . . ' which repeats the word 'Master' used in the final tricolon. Similarly,

16. The verb סכסכתי in v. 2 is usually derived from סוך, (pilpel), 'to goad'; it may be cognate with Akk. *sâku* (*zâku* or *suâku*), 'to pulverise (drugs)' (cf. *AHw*, 1013)—a meaning which also fits Isa 9,10. The verb סכר (v. 4) is discussed below. Note the simplifying textual variant ומסרתי, 'I delivered up', attested in the Geniza Fragments —cf. Goshen-Gottstein, *Bib* 48 (1967) 282.

17. The reason is that 'Egypt' (for example) is an elliptical form of 'the land of Egypt' and the gender of 'land' determines the gender of the whole expression even if not actually written; cf. M.H. Ibrahim, *Grammatical Gender, its origin and development* (The Hague, 1973) 96.

18. *CuthLeg* 136-37; cf. Watson, 'Pivot Pattern', 247 and note that the gender throughout is m.

choice of the two rare verbs סכסכתי and סכרתי seems to have been dictated by their quasi-keyword function. The derogatory expression אלילים also occurs once in each stanza.

The closing strophe is a direct *allusion* to Death, portrayed as a tyrant in charge of a prison (= Sheol)[19] the confines of which are sharply contrasted with Yahweh's freedom to travel freely and at speed (v. 1).[20]

Further items to be noticed are the use of a *tricolon* to both open and close the poem; the presence of a *stanza-opening monocolon* (v. 3a); the *word-pair* אדון // מלך (v. 4) equivalent to Ugaritic[21] and the *distant parallelism* linking B with B' by the split word-pair לבב // רוח.[22]

## Ps 123: A Plea

Though by no means a poetic gem, this psalm exhibits several devices and techniques within a very short compass and presents no textual or philological difficulties.[23]

| | | |
|---|---|---|
| אליך נשאתי את עיני הישבי בשמים | I | 1 |
| חנה | | 2a |
| כעיני עברים אל יד אדוניהם | | b |
| כעיני שפחה אל יד גברתה | | c |
| כן עינינו אל יהוה אלהינו עד שיחננו | | d |
| חננו יהוה חננו | II | 3a |
| כי רב שבענו בוז | | b |
| רבת שבעה לה נפשנו | | 4a |
| הלעג השאננים | | b |
| הבוז לגאיונים | | c |

19. Dahood, *Bib* 52 (1971) 350-51, identifies the monarch here as Death in view of Song 8,6 and considers the verb סכר to be a byform of סגר, 'to imprison'. Greenfield, *Albright FS* 1971, 263-65, understands the verb as 'the technical form for "handing over" slaves, prisoners, escapees, and for forced deportation'. Dahood's interpretation seems borne out by the parallel text from the Phoenician inscription of Eshmunazor (lines 21-22).

20. Yahweh's title evokes Baal's epithet *rkb 'rpt*, 'Cloud-rider', on which Moran, *Bib* 43 (1962) 324 notes, 'the description of the cloud as swift hardly makes sense unless the cloud is a vehicle'.

21. *CTA* 6 vi 56-57 *mlk* // *adn*. Also 16 i 56-57.59-60 (cf. *RSP* I 262-63).

22. Also Isa 57,15; 65,14 (cf. Watters, *Formula-Criticism*, 82).

23. 'O my enthroned one': the plethora of pronominal suffixes suggests ־י here may mean 'my'; Dahood prefers: 'who art enthroned', the final -*i* being an archaic genitive. The difficulty is the presence of both the definite article (either as a vocative or a relative pronoun) and the suffix. On the centripetal ל in 4a, here expressing dissatisfaction, see T. Muraoka, 'On the So-called Dativus-Ethicus in Hebrew', *JTS* 29 (1978) 495-98 (esp. 497). In 4a נפש may mean 'throat' (so Dahood), in which case, congruity of metaphor is operative (Dahood).

1  I     To you do I raise my eyes, O my enthroned one in the
        heavens.
        See:
2       Like the eyes of servants on their masters' hand,
        like the eyes of a maid on her mistress' hand,
        so are our eyes on Yahweh our god, till he pities us.

3  II    Pity us, Yahweh, pity us!

        For over-sated are we with contempt,
4       too long has our soul been sated
        with the scorn of the carefree,
        the contempt of the haughty.

The following points are illustrated: the *aba-monocolon* (3a) יהוה חננו
חננו; *anacrusis* (2a) הנה (and perhaps 3b: כי); the כן ... כ ... כ -*tricolon*
with its double simile (2bcd). There is also *repetition*: 'eyes' (4×); 'on'
(אל also 4×); 'to have pity' (3×); 'hand, to be sated, contempt', רב and
כ (each 2×). The pronominal suffix occurs 15[24] times in the space of
only 39 words. The repetition of the root חנן in שיחננו and חננו links
the two stanzas.

Turning to more complex forms, there is first the combination of
*gender-matching parallelism* with the alternation of singular with
plural nouns in 2bc:

> Like the eyes of servants     on their masters' hand,
>       *m. plur.*        *m. plur.*
> Like the eyes of a maid     on her mistress' hand,
>        *f. sing.*      *f. sing.*

Genders alternate also in 3b (m.) and 4a (f.), functioning as *merismus*.

The *structure of the poem* is not completely resolved; as set out
above, it comprises two stanzas, I made up of monocolon plus
tricolon, II consisting of monocolon plus quatrain. However, both 1
and 2d seem excessively long lines; no natural division which also
respects parallelism appears to break them into smaller units.

There is a degree of end-assonance which almost amounts to
rhyme: 1, 4b and 4c all end in *-îm*; both 3a and 4a end in *-nû*, and the
same suffix (*-ênû*) breaks up the lengthy final line of the first stanza
into three:

> *kēn 'ênênû*
> *'el yahweh  ᵉlohênû*
> *'ad šeyyᵉḥonnênû.*

24. See note 23.

Also present may be a combination of allusion and wordplay.[25] Note that the *delaying function* of the tricolon in 2bcd was deliberately chosen to express the feeling of waiting and suspense it portrays.

### Song 2,10-13: Love in Spring

Short though it is, this snatch of verse lends itself particularly well to stage-by-stage analysis and at the same time illustrates the use of exotic vocabulary.

| | | |
|---|---|---|
| ענה דודי | 10a | My love answered, |
| ואמר לי | b | to me he said: |
| קומי לך | c | 'Up now |
| רעיתי יפתי | d | my pretty darling, |
| ולכי לך | e | come on! |
| כי | 11a | For |
| הנה הסתו עבר | | the winter is past, |
| הגשם חלף הלך לו | b | the rain is gone and done with. |
| הנצנים נראו בארץ | 12a | The blooms can be seen in the land, |
| עת הזמיר הגיע | b | 'scale' time is near, |
| וקול התור נשמע | c | and the turtle-dove's voice can be heard. |
| בארצנו התאנה חנטה פגיה | 13a | In our land the fig ripens her fruit, |
| והגפנים סמדר נתנו ריח | b | and the vines in blossom give off scent. |
| קומי לך | c | Up now |
| רעיתי יפתי | d | my pretty darling, |
| ולכי לך | e | come on!' |

1. *Delimitation.* The stanza or poem is marked off from its context by the envelope figure or repetition of the same words in 10cde and 13cde. In addition, there is the introductory couplet 10ab ('In answer my love said to me') showing 10c to 13e to be reported speech. Whatever its relation to the rest of Song[26] there can be no doubt that 10-13 comprise a self-contained unit.

2. *Segmentation.* Aside from the introduction (10ab), the poem comprises two unequal parts: 11ab describing the negative side: winter has gone—and 12-13b portraying the positive aspect: spring is here. Considered as a whole, the poem (again ignoring 10ab) consists

---

25. For details cf. Dahood, *Psalms III*, 209 (on 3b-4a).

26. See especially J.C. Exum, 'A Literary and Structural Analysis of the Song of Songs', *ZAW* 85 (1973) 47-79; she considers our stanza to be part of the longer poem 2,7–3,5. Shea, *ZAW* 92 (1980) 386-87, considers the unit to comprise 2,10-15.

of a couplet, a tricolon and another couplet, bounded by initial and final tricola. It is, therefore, *structurally chiastic* as the table indicates:

| | |
|---|---|
| tricolon | (10cde) |
| couplet | (11ab) |
| tricolon | (12abc) |
| couplet | (13ab) |
| tricolon | (13cde) |

3. *Inner-strophic analysis.* As noted, *10cde* together with 13cde forms a frame for the poem. Rather than an ABA′ tricolon, as set out in the translation, the strophic pattern may be a chiastic bicolon:[27]

| | |
|---|---|
| קומי לך רעיתי | Up now, my darling, |
| יפתי ולכי לך | my beauty, come on! |

If it is a tricolon, then the expression רעיתי יפתי would be hendiadys: 'my beautiful companion' or the like.

After anacrusis (of כי), *11ab* is a parallel couplet in 3-beat metre. The letter ה occurs five times in initial position (alliteration) serving to bind the strophe together (cohesive function).

The central tricolon introduces the topic of spring growth in *12a* with alliteration (based on ארצנו, cf. last word of 12), the rhythm changing to two beats in 12b and 12c. There is wordplay in *12b* (זמיר = 'pruning' or 'song')[28] and assonance in *12c* (qôl—tôr) which verges on onomatopoeia. The strophic pattern seems to be ABA . It is difficult to decide whether the last word of 12, בארצנו, really belongs to the beginning of the following strophe. If it does, then the metre of that strophe (*13ab*) is exactly balanced with 4 + 4 stresses.[29]

Link-alliteration between פגיה - הגפנים in 13ab functions (as in 11ab) to bind the couplet together.

4. *Poetic devices.* The poetic devices used include alliteration, assonance and wordplay; anacrusis, chiasmus (strophic) and hendiadys. The *dominant device*, though, appears to be structural, namely, balance, resulting in the overall chiastic pattern of tricolon-couplet-tricolon-couplet-tricolon. Note, too, the structural function of the idiom 'הלך followed by ל + pronominal suffix'. It is used in the

---

27. If this is the case then the poem (minus 10ab) would number eleven lines.

28. In my translation 'scale' is an attempt at covering both these meanings. For the wordplay cf. Pope, *Song*, 395-96. For possible wordplay on the fruit of the fig-tree see 397-98.

29. It could also be argued that this word belongs to the end of 12c balancing בארץ at the end of 12a.

opening and closing strophes, and significantly at 11b where the topic changes from winter to spring.

5. *Tabulation.* As mentioned, recherché vocabulary is a peculiar form of the poem. Of the 26 lexical items used most are common enough, but seven, i.e. approximately a quarter, are either extremely rare or unique.

### Table of Common Lexical Items

| verbs | | nouns | | particles | |
|---|---|---|---|---|---|
| הלך | to go | ארץ | land (f.) | הנה | see! |
| חלף | to vanish | גפן | vine (f.) | כי | for |
| נגע | (Hiph.) to arrive | גשם | rain (m.) | | |
| נתן | to give | קול | voice (m.) | | |
| עבר | to pass on | ריח | scent (m.) | | |
| קום | to rise | תאנה | fig-tree (f.) | | *adjectives* |
| ראה | to see | תור | turtle-dove | יפה | beautiful |
| שמע | to hear | | (f. and m.) | | (here f.) |

### Table of Rare and Unique Lexical Items

| very rare | | unique poem | |
|---|---|---|---|
| חנט | to be ripe (?)[30] [also Gen 50,2.26] | זמיר | song, or pruning (m.) |
| סמדר | blossom[31] (m.) [also Song 2,15; 7,13] | סתו | winter (m.)[32] |
| | | פגה | unripe fig (f.) |
| רעיה | companion (f.) [also Song 1,9.15; 2,2; 4,1.7; 5,2; 6,4; and Jgs 11,37 (Kethib)] | נצן | blossom (m.)—the normal form is wither נץ or נצה[33] |
| | | עת | time (m.)—normally f. |

The second table shows clearly that the vocabulary used, practically speaking, is peculiar to the Song of Songs. Furthermore, many of the

---

30. For convenient discussion of these words see Pope, *Song*, 394-99.

31. With cognates in Jewish-Aramaic, Syriac, Mandaean, and neo-Assyrian—suggesting it to be an 'East Semitic' word. For a possible reflex in the Ebla Tablets cf. Dahood in G. Pettinato, *The Archives of Ebla* (Garden City, 1981), 312-13.

32. Note the Qere form סתיו; again an East Semitic item (Old Aramaic, Jewish-Aramaic and Syriac).

33. Note in Hebrew, as in Ugaritic, an -*n* afformative can be added to a noun without changing its meaning.

items are ancient and/or not native Hebrew. The poet therefore is both archaising (as shown by the m. gender of עת, a late form) and showing his erudition. A measure of his skill is the fact that the central word to the whole poem, זמיר, is an ancient Hebrew word, used in the Gezer calendar,[34] which both epitomises the theme of the song and refers to the larger context in which the poem is set (since the word can mean both 'pruning' and 'song').[35]

6. *Synthesis*. The poem is crafted in a combination of learned choice of vocabulary, skilful exploitation of technical devices and neatly balanced structure.

*Ps 47*

| | | | |
|---|---|---|---|
| I | כל העמים תקעו כף | All you peoples, clap hands, | 2 |
| | הריעו לאלהים בקול רנה | shout to God with joyful voice, | |
| | כי יהוה עליון נורא | For Yahweh is awesome Elyon, | 3 |
| | מלך גדול על כל הארץ | a great king over all the earth. | |
| II | ידבר עמים תחתינו | He made peoples prostrate under us, | 4 |
| | ולאמים תחת רגלינו | and folk under our feet; | |
| | יבחר לנו את נחלתנו | He chose for himself | 5 |
| | את גאון יעקב אשר אהב | majestic Jacob whom he loved. | |
| III | עלה אלהים בתרועה | On high went God to a shout, | 6 |
| | יהוה בקול שופר | Yahweh to a trumpet call. | |
| IV | זמרו אלהים זמרו | Sing, gods, sing! | 7 |
| | זמרו למלכנו זמרו | Sing to our king, sing, | |
| | כי מלך כל הארץ | For he is king of all the earth | 8 |
| | אלהים זמרו משכיל | Gods: sing a master song. | |
| V | מלך אלהים על גוים | God is king over nations, | 9 |
| | אלהים ישב על כסא קדשו | God is sitting on his holy throne. | |
| | נדיבי עמים נאספו עם אלהי אברהם | The peoples' gifts are collected for Abraham's god, | 10 |
| | כי לאלהים מגני ארץ מאד נעלה | for to God belong earth's presents, as a huge offering. | |

34. Approximately 10th century BC; a cognate to זמיר occurs together with *gpn*, 'vine', in the Ugaritic poem-ritual *CTA* 23:9 *yzbrnn zbrm gpn*, 'the vine-pruners pruned him (= Death)'. Possibly, therefore, in our poem there is an allusion to Death, in the guise of harsh winter, disappearing.

35. As noted by Schramm, *Cameron FS*, 179; see above under 'Janus parallelism'.

*Imagery*. The basic clue to correctly understanding this poem is provided by the *imagery*: God is depicted as a great king who has subjugated the world and to whom tribute (in the form of offerings as well as praise) is due. The main source of this imagery is v. 10, which is not without difficulties.[36]

*Strophe and stanza-patterns*. The first impression is that all nine couplets are in synonymous parallelism. Closer inspection reveals that four consecutive couplets (vv. 3-6) have the pattern

a b c
b′ c′

where c′ is an expanded form of c (see below on expletives). For example, v. 4:

ידבר עמים תחתינו
ולאמים תחת רגלינו

The rest exhibit varying strophic forms: v. 2 abc/b′dc′; 7-8 aba/aca/ de/ba′; 9 abc/ba′c′ (= partial chiasmus); while v. 10 is more complex.

The stanza formation (indicated in the translation) is as follows: I = vv. 2-3; II = 4-5; III = 6; IV = 7-8; V = 9-10, the poem being constructed *symmetrically*. Four 4-line stanzas (quatrains) are arranged around a central 2-line stanza. Stanza I is very similar to IV, both beginning with an invitation to praise followed by the explanatory כי, 'because':

| I | IV |
|---|---|
| כל העמים תקעו כף | זמרו אלהים זמרו |
| הריעו לאלהים בקול רנה | זמרו למלכנו זמרו |
| כי | כי |
| יהוה עליון ונרא | מלך כל הארץ |
| מלך גדול על כל הארץ | אלהים זמרו משכיל |

36. For a recent study of the Ps., with good bibliography, cf. J.J.M. Roberts, 'The Religio-political Setting of Psalm 47', *BASOR* 221 (1976) 129-131. The following philological points deserve mention: v. 4 'he made prostrate' follows Dahood; v. 5 'for himself', also follows Dahood—Roberts rejects this (preferring to emend) arguing that 'the direct object normally precedes the indirect in this construction with *bhr*' (130 n. 9) but it is attested in Gen 13,11; 1 Sm 13,2; 2 Sm 24,12; etc. V. 10 עם = 'toward' as in Ug. (so Hillers apud Roberts, 131 n. 12); although normally fem. נדיב is here the equivalent of נדיבה, 'free-will offering', Akk. *nidbû* (from Sum. nindabu), 'special offering' (*AHw*, 790), parallel to מנן, which corresponds to Ug. *mgn*, 'present'. In such a context, therefore, נעלה derives from עלה in its meaning 'be offered' (cf. *BDB*, 748, meaning 6), here as a verbal noun. Contrast (NEB for v. 10): 'The princes of the nations assemble with the families of Abraham's line; for the mighty ones of earth belong to God, and he is raised above them all'.

In content, stanza II corresponds to the final stanza, so that the overall pattern of the poem is A(I)-B(II)-C(III)-A'(IV)-B'(V). Note that סלה, which probably marks a major division, occurs just before the central bicolon (III).

*Poetic devices.* The most frequent word is אלהים (8×); next comes זמר (5×, plus 4 synonymous expressions: תקע כף, הריע, בקול רנה/שופר, תרועה). Of more significance are the *keywords* מלך (4×; cf. קדשו ישב על כסא), עם (4×, also לאם) and ארץ (3×). However, the less frequent words are of most importance, their main function being to link sections of the poem together. For example, stanza II has only one repeated word (עם cf. לאם) but it acts as a connector with עמים which occurs at both the beginning and end of the poem. Note, too, יעקב acting as a tie with the last verse where אברהם is mentioned. The pair תחת and תחת רגל also lend cohesion to stanza II. *Repetition* of קול increases the value of כל (3×).[37] The twin repetition of עלה (middle and end of poem) reinforces the divine title עליון and is echoed by the preposition על (3×).

The *ballast variant* (or expletive) is most evident in v. 4 תחת רגל // תחת. The same principle is operative also in vv. 3, 5 and 6 (as mentioned above, on strophic patterns). Note further ישב על כסא קדשו as a parallel to the single word מלך; the expansion in v. 5 אהב גאון יעקב as a parallel to the single word מלך; the expression זמרו משכיל which is paired with זמרו. Stanza-chiasmus in the form of an ABB'A-pattern obtains in vv. 7-8:[38]

| | |
|---|---|
| (pagan) gods | אלהים |
| our King | מלכנו |
| King | מלך |
| (pagan) gods | אלהים |

while vv. 2b-3a and 6 exhibit strophic chiasmus.

## *Job 18,2-21*

Since this passage contains a high proportion of synonymous parallelism it has been chosen as exemplifying the norm for Hebrew poetry.

---

37. Note, too, ־רגל in רגלינו and ־כל in משכיל.

38. Recognised by Roberts as an envelope construction (131). Other studies of this poem include A. Caquot, 'Le Psaume 47 et la Royauté de Yahwé', *RHPR* 39 (1959) 311-14.330-37, and W.A.M. Beuken, 'Psalm XLVII: Structure and Drama', *OTS* 21 (1981) 38-54. Beuken's translation differs from mine (notably in vv. 7 and 10) and the structure he proposes is as follows: Summons I (v. 2)—Execution I (vv. 3-6)—Summons II (v. 7)—Execution II (vv. 8-10a)—Execution III (v. 10b). Van der Lugt, *Strofische Structuren*, 262-65 proposes three stanzas (vv. 2-5; 6-9; 10).

It is also one of the shorter sections in Job and so suitable for inclusion here, in spite of some philological obscurities. The date is approximately the sixth century BC.[39] The methodical analysis which follows is more or less modelled on the procedure set out in METHOD.

1. *Delimitation*. There is no problem concerning the beginning and end of the segment of poetry. In 1, Bildad is speaking ('Bildad the Shuhite spoke up in answer') while the next chapter begins with the words of Job (19,1). Stanza-division by content seems to be:

| | | |
|---|---|---|
| I | 2-4: | introduction |
| II | 5-7: | extinction of light |
| III | 8-10: | traps |
| IV | 11-14: | disease |
| V | 15-19: | family destroyed |
| VI | 20-21: | conclusion. |

For further discussion, see below.

2. *Segmentation*. Almost all the strophes are couplets. Exceptions are 18 and 19, which are tricola and 5-6, a quatrain. Problems are presented by 4a which may be a monocolon, but could belong to either 3 or 4bc—and by 11.

3. *Inner-strophic analysis*

stanza I (2-4)

| | | |
|---|---|---|
| עד אנה תשימון קנצי למלין | 2a | How long will you set traps[40] for words? |
| תבינו ואחר נדבר | b | Consider, and after we'll speak. |
| מדוע נחשבנו כבהמה | 3a | Why are we reckoned as cattle? |
| נטמינו בעיניכם | b | (Why) are we unclean[41] in your eyes? |
| טרף נפשו באפו | 4a | Cutting his throat in his anger[42] |
| הלמענך תעזב ארץ | b | Would the earth be abandoned for you? |
| ויעתק צור ממקומו | c | Or a rock be moved from its place? |

*2a* opens with the formula עד אנה (also 19,2; etc.) in anacrusis. *2ab* is poor quality poetry: there is no parallelism; but ו occurs six times. In *3ab* the word-pair טמא // בהמה breaks up the legal expression בהמה טמאה, 'unclean beast'[43]—and *4a* probably belongs to this strophe. Good synonymous parallelism first occurs in *4bc* in combi-

---

39. For discussion of the date see the commentaries.
40. Akk. *qinṣu*, 'trap' (so Pope).
41. Taking טמא = טמה.
42. Meaning obscure, perhaps a reference to the expiatory sacrifice, Lev 5,6.
43. Occurring in Lev 5,2; 20,25; Nb 18,15; etc.—as suggested by Watters, *Formula-Criticism*, 198.

nation with alliteration (ר ק ץ ע). The word מקום recurs in 21 to form an envelope figure marking the limits of the poem.

*stanza II (5-7)*

| | | |
|---|---|---|
| גם אור רשעים ידעך | 5a | Even the light of the wicked is put out, |
| ולא יגה שביב אשו | b | his fire-flame will not shine; |
| אור חשך באהלו | 6a | light is darkness in his tent, |
| ונרו עליו ידעך | b | and his lamp over him is put out. |
| יצרו צעדי אונו | 7a | His powerful strides are shortened, |
| ותשליכהו עצתו | b | his schemes cast him down. |

*5-6* forms a quatrain linked by repetition of ידעך (5a, 6b), repeated use of words for *light* (נר אש שביב אור) and the sounds ש ר (ר) ג. *7* is a connective couplet, linking stanzas II and III. It is difficult to decide whether it does not form part of the next stanza, in fact, since it interlocks with 8a and 11-12 by the chiastic sequence: אונו אונו רגליו רגליו. There is alliteration between יצרו צעדיa and עצתוb.

*stanza III (8-10)*

| | | |
|---|---|---|
| כי | 8a | For |
| שלח ברשת ברגליו | | he is cast into a net at his feet,[44] |
| ועל שבכה יתהלך | b | and over a pitfall he walks, |
| יאחז בעקב פח | 9a | is seized on his ankle by a trap, |
| יחזק עליו צמים | b | a snare grabs him. |
| טמון בארץ חבלו | 10a | Hidden in the ground is a rope for him, |
| ומלכדתו עלי נתיב | b | and a gin upon the path. |

*8ab*: Anacrusis of כי is followed by two 3-beat lines. A tour of six successive synonyms for *trap* (מלכדת חבל צמים פח שבכה רשת) links 8-10 as a single stanza.[44a] Alliteration in *9* is based on the word חזק 'to grasp'. Use of gender-matched synonyms, reversed, in *10* creates a surprise effect which adroitly depicts a hidden and unexpected trap:

> Hidden in the *ground* (f.) is a *rope* (m.) for him,
> and a *gin* (f.) upon the *path* (m.).

Chiasmus (place-trap—trap-place) reinforces this effect.

*stanza IV (11-14)*

| | | |
|---|---|---|
| סביב בעתתו בלהות | 11a | Around do frighten him Terrors, |
| והפיצהו לרגליו | b | at his feet a-chase. |

---

44. Unless ברגליו means 'on the spot; instantly' as in Jgs 5,15—cf. Gerleman, *JSS* 4 (1958) 252-54.

44a. For a closely similar tour in *Maqlu* III 160-64 cf. Lichtenstein, *JANES* 5 (1973) 257-58.

| | | |
|---|---|---|
| יהי רעבבאנו | 12a | Despite his wealth he's famished,[45] |
| ואיד נכון לצלעו | b | calamity ready for his stumbling. |
| יאכל בדי עורו | 13a | Consumed by Sickness is his skin, |
| יאכל בדיו בכור מות | b | does consume his limbs Death's Eldest. |
| ינתק מאהלו מבטחו | 14a | Ripped from his snug tent, |
| ותצעדהו למלך בלהות | b | brought before the King of Terrors. |

*11ab* is a 'pivot-patterned' couplet (with silent stress) functioning as stanza-opener. In *12* the word-pair און // איד occurs. Wordplay is exploited in *13*, in the guise of repetition: בדיו // בדי. In *14b* בלהות forms an envelope figure with the same word in 11a, marking off the opening and close of the stanza. The letter ל occurs 4 times in *14*.

*stanza V (15-19)*

| | | |
|---|---|---|
| תשכון באהלו מבל | 15a | In his tent, fire is set, |
| ליזרה על נוהו גפרית | b | on his abode, sulphur scattered.[46] |
| מתחת שרשיו יבשו | 16a | Below, his roots dry up, |
| וממעל ימל קצירו | b | above do perish his branches.[47] |
| זכרו אבד מני ארץ | 17a | His memory perished from the earth, |
| ולא שם לו על פני חוץ | b | he has no name in the street. |
| יהדפהו מאור | 18a | He is thrust from light |
| אל חשך | b | into darkness, |
| ומתבל ינדהו | c | driven out of the world. |
| לא נין לו | 19a | He has no offspring, |
| ולא נכד בעמו | b | no descendant among his people, |
| ואין שריד במגוריו | c | no survivor where he used to live. |

*15ab*: the imagery of destruction is underlined by use of gender-matched synonyms (see on 10):

'tent' (m.)—'fire' (f.)[48]
'abode' (m.)—'sulphur' (f.)

again with mismatch of genders. In *16* the poet has rejuvenated an old saying[49] by imaginative use of alliteration: שרשיו יבשו and ממעל ימל. The word-pair 'above // below' constitutes merismus. In context the word-pair שרש // קציר is intended metaphorically. Yet another word-pair serves to link the two cola of *17*: זכר // שם. *18abc* is a chiastic tricolon with an ABA′ pattern, the central colon relating to

---

45. Reading רעב באנו (shared consonant or haplography).
46. So Dahood, *Bib* 38 (1957) 312-15; the final ל of the first colon is transposed to the second as emphatic *lamedh* in ליזרה; MT מבלי לו is repointed to \**mabbel* (from נבל), meaning 'fire'.
47. Here קציר (lit. 'branches') has the pregnant meaning 'harvest, fruit'.
48. The gender of this noun is indicated by the verb.
49. Used not only in Isa 37,31; 2 Kgs 19,30; Am 2,9—but also in Phoenician.

the two outer ones. The stanza closes with another tricolon (19) its lines gradually increasing in length. It opens with the alliterative word-pair נין // נכר also found as a unit elsewhere.[50]

*stanza VI* (20-21)

| | | |
|---|---|---|
| על יומו נשמו אחרנים | 20a | Appalled at his day[51] are Westerners, |
| וקדמנים אחזו שער | b | Easterners, horror seizes. |
| אך אלה משכנות עול | 21a | Surely such are the dwellings of the impious, |
| וזה מקום לא ידע אל | b | this is the place of 'he-knew-not-God'. |

*20* is a couplet marked by both chiasmus and the polar word-pair קדמנים // אחרנים which combine to depict merismus. שמם // שער is a further word-pair.

*21* brings the poem to a close with a bicolon, the dominant strophic form.[52] It may be accidental that the poem comprises $2 \times 22$ lines. Note the (feeble) wordplay: אלה-אל.

4. *Synthesis.* The stanza-division adopted here is based on a combination of content (see above) and structural indicators. These indicators are the chiastic use of אור-נר in II (5a, 6b), the opening pivot-pattern in IV (11), the final tricolon in V (19), the tour or list in III (8-10) and the envelope figure marking off IV (11 and 14). Apart from the frequent word-pairs (mentioned already), the poem is strongly characterised by certain *keywords* which can be tabulated as follows:

| | | PLACE | TRAPS | LIGHT/DARK | CALAMITY | OTHER |
|---|---|---|---|---|---|---|
| I | 2a | | קנץ | | | |
| | b | | | | | |
| | 3a | | | | | |
| | b | | | | | |
| | 4a | | טרף | | | |
| | b | | | | | |
| | c | מקום | | | | |
| II | 5a | | | אור | | דעך |
| | b | | | שביב אש | | |
| | 6a | אהל | | אור חשך | | |
| | b | | | נר | | דעך |
| | 7a | | | | | צער און |
| | b | | | | | |

50. Gen 21,23; Isa 14,22; Sir 41,5; 47,22.

51. Cf. Stuart, *BASOR* 221 (1976) 159-64.

52. Noteworthy is the noun-verb parallelism here, of the form construct + genitive // construct + finite verb; see Grossberg, *JBL* 99 (1980) 483-84, and section 6.6, above.

| | | PLACE | TRAPS | LIGHT/DARK | CALAMITY | OTHER |
|---|---|---|---|---|---|---|
| III | 8a | | רשת | | | רגל |
| | b | | שבכה | | | |
| | 9a | | פח | | | אחז |
| | b | | צמים | | | |
| | 10a | ארץ | חבל | | | |
| | b | | מלכרת | | | |
| IV | 11a | | | | בלהות | רגל |
| | b | | | | | |
| | 12a | | | | רעב | און |
| | b | | | | איד | |
| | 13a | | | | די | |
| | b | | | | בכור מות | |
| | 14a | אהל | | | | |
| | b | | | | | צער |
| V | 15a | שכן אהל | | מבל | | |
| | b | נוה | | גפרית | | |
| | 16a | | | | | |
| | b | | | | | |
| | 17a | ארץ | | | | |
| | b | חוץ | | | | |
| | 18a | | | אור חשך | | |
| | b | תבל | | | | |
| | c | | | | | |
| | 19a | | | | | |
| | b | | | | | |
| | c | | | | | |
| VI | 20a | | | | | |
| | b | | | | | אחז |
| | 21a | משכן | | | | |
| | b | מקום | | | | |

Synonyms for PLACE (or dwelling-place) are distributed throughout all six stanzas, giving the poem its basic unity. The word מקום (4c, 21b) serves as overall envelope figure. Of the seven words for TRAP, none is repeated, and apart from the metaphorical use in 2a, they only occur in stanza III, making it a structural unit. Terms for LIGHT/DARKNESS are exclusive to stanzas II and V, just as terms for CALAMITY are only found in stanza IV.

The mythical allusion in 13, in spite of its obscurity, lends some colour to the poem and also explains the real meaning of the expression 'King of Terrors'. It is noteworthy, on the other hand, that assonance is hardly present, and rhyme only occurs in 12 and 19a, perhaps unintentionally.

*Jer 46,3-12*

This oracle was chosen because it is not too hackneyed an example, is not over-long, exhibits certain interesting poetic features[53] and contains some unresolved difficulties which present a challenge to the advanced student. Furthermore, it can be precisely dated; the information provided in vv. 1-2 points to the date 605BC. Analysis of the poem will follow the procedure and sequence outlined above in the section on METHOD.[54]

1. *Delimitation.* The two prose sections vv. 1-2 and v. 13 which occur at the opening and close of the chosen text form the exterior limits of the poem. Vv. 1-2 introduce this oracle, while v. 13 introduces the following one. Whether the text itself is to be further subdivided into sections—whether as a set of poems or of stanzas of the same poem—remains to be determined (see paragraph 5, below).

2. *Segmentation.* By applying the basic criterion of *parallelism*, the following segmentation seems to hold:

| | | | |
|---|---|---|---|
| *quatrain*: | 7ab8ab[55] | *bicola*: | 3ab |
| | | | 4ab |
| *tricola*: | 4cde | | 5bc |
| | 5def | | 6ab |
| | 9abc | | 6cd |
| | 11abc | | 8cd |
| | | | 10ab |
| *monocola*: | 5a | | 10cd |
| | 5g | | 11de |
| | (5h) | | 12ab |
| | | | 12cd |

3. *Inner-strophic analysis.* For convenience of presentation the stanza division will be anticipated, and the poem set out stanza by stanza.

*stanza I* (vv. 3-4)

| | | |
|---|---|---|
| ערכו מגן וצנה | 3a | Prepare buckler and shield |
| וגשו למלחמה | b | and advance to battle; |

---

53. Including alliteration, vertical and gender parallelism, personification, simile, assonance, wordplay and certain structural patterns. For the text cf. J.G. Janzen, *Studies in the Text of Jeremiah* (Cambridge, Mass., 1973).

54. See conveniently J. Bright, *Jeremiah* (*AB* 21; Garden City, 1965). Note also R. Bach, *Die Aufforderungen zur Flucht und zum Kampf im vorexilischen Propheten-spruch* (*WMANT* 9; Neukirchen, 1962).

55. Unless two couplets; see below.

| | | |
|---|---|---|
| אסרו הסוסים | 4a | Harness the horses, |
| ועלו הפרשים | b | mount the stallions;[56] |
| והתיצבו בכובעים | c | In position, with helmets, |
| מרקו הרמחים | d | polish the spears, |
| לבשו הסרינת | e | put on armour. |

*3ab* is a structural bicolon, with no real parallelism; the repeated final -*a* sound creates end-rhyme. The word מגן recurs in 9d, perhaps as envelope figure.

*4ab* is good synonymous parallelism. The staccato, two-beat verse continues to the end of 6, evoking the rhythm of war, the main theme here. There is a degree of alliterative assonance (סר־סס־רש), but not marked. *4cde* is a clear strophic unit in triple parallelism. Note assonantic מרקו הרמחים. The ־ת ending of the last word (הסרינת) breaks the succession of ־ים terminations, providing a surprise effect, perhaps to mark a minor structural division.

*stanza II* (v. 5)

| | | |
|---|---|---|
| מדוע ראיתי | 5a | What did I see? |
| המה חתים | b | They are daunted, |
| נסגים אחור | c | turning back. |
| וגבוריהם יכתו | d | Their warriors hammered, |
| ומנוס נסו | e | in full flight.[57] |
| ולא הפנו | f | not even turning. |
| מגור מסביב | g | Ambush all round.[58] |
| נאם יהוה | h | Oracle of Yahweh. |

*5a* is a monocolon introducing a change of topic. Strictly speaking *5bc* is a single line in parallel with *5de*:

They are dismayed and have turned backwards.
Their warriors are beaten down and have fled hastily.

However, the dominant two-beat rhythm argues for the strophic arrangement adopted. In fact the four cola describe a sequence of events: fear—retreat—defeat—flight. It is difficult to determine whether *5f* belongs to the foregoing or forms a (structural) bicolon

56. Not 'Mount, O horsemen' or 'Prance, horses' in view of parallelism and v. 9.
57. For this reading, with enclitic *mem*, followed by inf. abs. and finite verb, cf. Freedman apud Bright: 1965, 301.
58. 'Ambush': Bach: 1962, 51 n. 3; or simply 'terror'.

with 5g. *5g* is a frequent formula (Jer 6,25; 20,3.10; 40,29; Ps 31,4) perhaps used here for assonance (גבר־מגור מסביב). *5h* is also a stock formula, here probably indicating a minor poetic division.

*stanza III* (v. 6)

| | | |
|---|---|---|
| אל ינום הקל | 6a | The swift cannot flee, |
| ואל ימלט הגבור | b | the warrior cannot escape. |
| צפונה על יד נהר פרת | c | Up North, by Euphrates River, |
| כשלו ונפלו | d | they have stumbled and fallen. |

*6ab* is a couplet in perfect parallelism; the rhythm is now three-beat. In *6cd*, on the contrary, there is vertical parallelism (as also in stanza VI) over two 2-beat lines.

*stanza IV* (vv. 7-8)

| | | |
|---|---|---|
| מי זה כיאר יעלה | 7a | Who is this, rising like the Nile, |
| כנהרות יתגעשו מימיו | b | like rivers, their water a-surge? |
| מצרים כיאר יעלה | 8a | Egypt is rising like the Nile, |
| וכנהרות יתגעשו מים | b | like rivers, its waters a-surge.[59] |
| ויאמר אעלה אכסה ארץ | c | He said: I will rise, covering land; |
| אבידה עיר וישבי בה | d | I will destroy the city and its dwellers. |

*7a* As sometimes happens, a new stanza begins with a simile. Together with 7ab, 8ab forms a quatrain (or double bicolon) which follows 'Sumerian' models exactly, as in:

> My city's increase is fish,
> its surplus fowl;

> Ur's increase is fish,
> its surplus fowl.[60]

*stanza V* (v. 9)

| | | |
|---|---|---|
| עלו הסוסים | 9a | Attack, horses! |
| והתהללו הרכב | b | Rage, chariotry! |
| ויצאו הגבורים | c | Away, warriors! |
| כוש ופוט תפשי מגן | d | Ethiops and Puntians: shield-wielders, |
| ולודים דרכי קשת | e | Lydians: bow-benders.[61] |

---

59. Note the plurals of amplification.

60. Text—from *JCS* 20 (1966) 139:25-26—cited conveniently in Lambert–Millard, *Atr* 159.

61. Lit. 'treaders of the bow', i.e. archers. The second תפשי is probably a scribal error and has been deleted.

*9ab* The two-beat 'battle' rhythm has returned; the word-pair רכב //
סום appears. As in 4, the pattern is VP—NP for the first three lines.
*9de* The structure here is unclear (and there may be textual
corruption); is it a tricolon? The repeated *-u*-sound (eight times in 5
lines) is intentional assonance. The overall stanza-pattern seems to
be AA'-B-CC'.

*stanza VI* (v. 10)

| | | |
|---|---|---|
| והיום ההוא לאדני יהוה צבאות | 10a | That day belongs to Lord Yahweh of the Armies, |
| יום נקמה להנקם מצריו | b | a day of vengeance, to avenge himself on his foes. |
| ואכלה חרב ושבעה | c | Devour, will the sword and be sated |
| ורותה מדמם | d | and drink its fill of their blood. |
| כי | e | For, (it's) |
| זבח לאדני יהוה צבאות | | a sacrifice of the Lord Yahweh of the Armies |
| בארץ צפון | f | in the Northland, |
| אל נהר פרת | g | by River Euphrates. |

It is difficult to tell whether *10ab* constitute prose or poetry. In מצריו
both wordplay and allusion are combined. the reference, of course,
being to Egypt (מצרים; cf. 11). The division of *10cd* is uncertain, and
the imagery (dependent on Isa 34,5-6) is graphic. Note the succession
of *-a*-sounds (eight in all). *10e* opens with an extra-metrical כי as
anacrusis.

*stanza VII* (vv. 11-12)

| | | |
|---|---|---|
| עלי גלעד | 11a | Climb Gilead, |
| וקחי צרי | b | and get storax, |
| בתולת בת מצרים | c | virgin daughter of Egypt. |
| לשוא הרבית רפאות | d | You have multiplied medicines uselessly; |
| תעלה אין לך | e | no healing for you. |
| שמעו גוים קלונך | 12a | Your renown, the nations have heard, |
| וצוחתך מלאה הארץ | b | the earth is full of your cry.[62] |
| כי | c | For, |
| גבור בגבור כשלו | | warrior stumbled over warrior, |
| יחדיו נפלו שניהם | d | together the two of them fell. |

*11abc* is a structural tricolon (perhaps forming a strophic unit with
11de). The rootplay between עלה and גלעד (etymologically unrelated)

---

62. קלון may either be the late Hebrew word for 'a shouter, crier', or simply the
standard Hebrew for 'voice' (קול) with the afformative -(ă)n common in Ugaritic
nouns. See Freedman, apud Bright: 1965, 302, who cites LXX 'your voice'.

is followed by a pun: צרי, 'balsam, storax'—מצרים, 'Egypt'—both times in mockery. *11c* is a common formula. In *11de* the (ironic) imagery of healing is continued, reinforced by the assonance between הרבית and רפאות, as well as by the play on the root עלה (11a) in תעלה 'scar'. *11e* is yet another formula which recurs in Jer 30,13. Matching of genders is used in *12ab* to achieve the effect of merismus:

'nations' (m.) + 'renown' (also m.)[63]

in parallelism with    'cry' (f.)    + 'earth' (also f.)    in a partially chiastic arrangement.

After anacrusis (first word of 12c), the phrase כשלו ונפלו of 6d is broken up to form the word-pair 'to stumble // to fall (in battle)', used with גבור, 'warrior' to evoke similar phraseology in the lament 2 Sm 1.

4. *Synthesis*. The stanza-division, largely based on content, is reinforced by several features. Both II and IV open with a question (and IV also with a simile); V and VII begin with an imperative of the keyword (עלה, see presently). There is evidently a break at v. 10, between V and VI, and the formula at v. 5h indicates stanza-closure. The ending of VI (v. 10fg) evokes the ending of III; the same applies to the closing lines of the poem.[64] The envelope figure—with repetition of מגן—marks off vv. 3-9 (stanzas I-V) as a separate unit, perhaps a complete poem, with prose elements appearing at v. 10.

Throughout, certain repeated words (keywords) occur. The most frequent is based on the root עלה, 'to go up': 'mount' (4b), 'rising' (7a, 8a), 'I will rise' (8c), 'attack!' (9a), 'climb' (11a), 'healing' (11e, literally 'overlay') and cf. גלעד (also 11a). Although not found in II, III and VI, this keyword does lend unity to the whole poem. The others are גבור (five times: 5d, 6b, 9c, 12c, 12c), and ארץ (three times: 8c, 10f, 12b).

As to literary form, the poem seems to be a doom oracle containing elements of the 'call to war'.[65]

---

63. Whether the word means 'voice' or 'crier' (see preceding note), the gender is m.
64. The total number of cola (ignoring 5h as intrusive) is 45 (44 + 1) which may relate to poems in multiples of 22 lines.
65. So Bach: 1962. J.R. Lundbom, *Jeremiah: A Study in Ancient Hebrew Rhetoric* (SBL Dissertation Series 18; Missoula, 1975) does not discuss these verses.

# CLOSING COMMENTS

Having reached the end of a comparatively long survey, certain observations, or rather doubts, come to the fore regarding method and conclusions. Perhaps taxonomy has been overstressed in the foregoing pages, resulting in a degree of disregard for content. It can also be argued that poetry does not fit the neat categories outlined here, nor are the categories even complete. Since this is principally a workbook guiding the scholar to his or her own conclusions I have no worries on that score. If every possible aspect had been covered this book would have been too long and correspondingly boring.

I have rather more diffidence now concerning the inclusion of Assyro-Babylonian poetic material than when I started, seven years ago. Partly this is due to the divergence between 'Canaanite' (Hebrew, Ugaritic, etc.) and Mesopotamian traditions.[1] If anything, though, the present study points to this divergence so often ignored since similarities are more obvious to see. In particular, the three-line strophe (tricolon), staircase parallelism and the graded numerical sequence appear to be rare in Akkadian poetry[2] whereas they are standard components of West Semitic verse. On balance, though, the

---

1. It is premature, of course, to bring the Ebla discoveries into the picture, but they indicate such divergences to be less extreme, perhaps. Comments such as 'What can be asserted without hesitation is that the contacts between the Mesopotamian and Syrian areas were certainly intensive even in the specific fields which could be called cultural' (P. Matthiae, *Ebla. An Empire Rediscovered* [London, 1980; translated by C. Holme from 1977 edition] 159) certainly point that way.

2. A particularly clear and perhaps unique example of the last-mentioned device comes from the incantation series *Šurpu* (IV 60-66); it uses an extended form of the graded numerical sequence in combination with matching the number of deities mentioned in each line with the 'number' of that line, as follows.

| | |
|---|---|
| 1 *lipṭur Šamaš qurādu* | First, may Shamash the warrior release; |
| 2 *lipṭurū Sin u Nergal* | second, may Sin and Nergal release; |
| 3 *lipṭurū Ištar Ba'u Anunītum* | third, may Ishtar, Ba'u and Anunitum release; |
| 4 *lipṭurū Anum Enlil Ea Nintu* | fourth, may Anum, Enlil, Ea and Nintu release; |
| 5 *lipṭurū Adad Ninurta Zababa* | fifth, may Adad, Ninurta, |
| *Tišpak Ningirsu* | Zababa, Tishpak and Ningirsu release; |
| 6 *lipṭurū Uraš Marduk Asari* | sixth, may Urash, Marduk, |
| *Asalluḫi* <sup>d</sup>*GAL Tutu* | Asari, Asalluḫi, GAL and Tutu release; |
| 7 *lipṭurū Sibitti ilāni rabūti* | seventh, may 'The Seven', the great gods release . . . the bond . . . etc. |

(Text and translation as in Reiner, *Šurpu*, 26-27; some recensions read *lipšur / lipšurū* for *lipṭur / lipṭurū*; the equivalent of <sup>d</sup>GAL is *Ai* or *Ḫumban*, but some texts have <sup>d</sup>PA: *Išum* or *Nabû*).

Assyro-Babylonian poetic texts have not been excised if only because so many recent studies fail to take them into account. It is true to say that many aspects of poetry in any tradition (Canaanite, Mesopotamian, even Egyptian and Arabic) have not been comprehensively examined—where, for instance, is there a detailed and full account of word-pairs in Akkadian verse?—so the last word has by no means been written or spoken on ancient Semitic verse.

As I write these final remarks I am aware that the upsurge of interest in Hebrew poetry continues unchecked. Carmi's recent anthology of Hebrew verse is one example.[3] The topic of metre is another; it has aroused interest and debate resulting in at least four papers in less than two years.[4] Much remains for further research and deeper analysis; much that has long been accepted must face new challenge. The study of classical Hebrew poetry and of ancient Semitic poetry in general will long be a lively, absorbing and expanding discipline.

3. T. Carmi, ed., *The Penguin Book of Hebrew Verse* (Harmondsworth, 1981).

4. D. Pardee, 'Ugaritic and Hebrew Metrics', *Wisconsin Symposium*, 113-30; T. Longman, 'A Critique of Two Recent Metrical Systems', *Bib* 63 (1982) 230-54; M. Halle—J.J. McCarthy, 'The Metrical Structure of Psalm 137', *JBL* 100 (1981) 161-67 and J. Wansbrough, 'Hebrew verse: scansion and parallax', *BSOAS* 45 (1982) 5-13. In addition, see B.P. Kittel, *The Hymns of Qumran. Translation and Commentary* (Chico, 1981).

# INDEXES

## 1

### INDEX OF SUBJECTS

a a′ a‴ '3-synonym' monocolon, 172
a // ab pattern, 345
a—bc // a—cb, 203
a—bc // b′c′—a′ , 203
ab // b′a′, 203
ab—c // b′a′—c, 203, 204
ab—c // c′—a′b′, 203
ab—cd // c′d′—a′b′, 203
aba′ chiastic line, 142
aba′ chiastic monocolon, 172
aba—monocolon, 150, 215, 216, 363, 367
abc 'standard' monocolon, 172
abc // a′b′c′, 119n.13
abc // b′c′ couplet, 174, 372
abc / b′c′ pattern, 362
abc // c′b′, 203
abc // c′b′ couplet, 176
a,b,c, // c,b,a, 201
abc // c′b′a′, 203
abc // c′b′a′ pattern, 43
A colon/cola, 136
A-word, 129, 134, 136
A // A, 132, 133
A // AB, 132
A/A′/B, 178, *180-181*
A/A′/A″, 178, *179-180*
AA′-B-CC′ pattern, 382
AABCC sequence, 187-188
A // B, 135
A // B sequence, 357
A // $B_1, B_2, B_3$, etc., 134
A-B pair (*see* word-pair), 128
A-B sequence, 330, 356
A-B terms, 136
A-B (word-pairs), 144
AB // A, 135
A/B/A, 178

ABA′, 181, 181n.61, 181n.62
ABA hexacolon, 188
ABA pattern, 369
ABA strophe, 204
ABA′ strophe, 204
ABA tricolon, 215, 215n.38
ABA′ tricolon, 187, 215, 369, 376
ABAB sequence, 186
ABAC sequence, 187
A/B/B′, 178
ABBA quatrain, 185, 358
ABBA quatrains, 194n.102
ABB′A′ quatrain, 205
A/B/C, 178
*ABC* tricolon, *182-183*
ABCB pattern, 207
ABCB quatrain, *186*
ABCBA pattern, 142
ABCB′A′ pattern, 187
ABCCBA strophe, 188
ABCC′B′A′, 206
ABCC′B′A′ pattern, 248n.104
ABCCBD strophe, 188
ABCDC′B′A′ strophe, 188
ABCDED′C′B′A′, 206
'a donkey's funeral', 313
'above // below', 376
absence of prose clements, 57
abstract // concrete , 133
abstract for concrete, *314-316*
accent, 11n.1, 89
acrostic(s), 8, 14, 25, 32, *33-34*, 64, 135, 189, *190-200*, 358
acrostic (as stanza marker), 163-164
'action and result' formula, 280
action-result sequence, 282
active/passive, 280
Adapa Legend, 280n.30

2

## INDEX OF NUMERICAL REFERENCES

3

## INDEX OF BIBLICAL REFERENCES

4

# INDEX OF HEBREW WORDS
## a. *In Hebrew characters*

### b. *In transliteration*

---

## 5

## INDEX OF HEBREW WORD-PAIRS

### a. *In Hebrew characters*

## b. *In transliteration*

6

INDEX OF UGARITIC TEXTS

---

## 7

## INDEX OF UGARITIC WORDS

## 8

## INDEX OF UGARITIC WORD-PAIRS

## 9

## INDEX OF AKKADIAN TEXTS

---

## 10

## INDEX OF AKKADIAN WORDS

## 11

## INDEX OF OTHER TEXTS

12

# INDEX OF AUTHORS CITED

# JOURNAL FOR THE STUDY OF THE OLD TESTAMENT
Supplement Series